Traders and Diplomats

ERNEST H. PREEG

Traders and Diplomats

*An analysis of the Kennedy Round of negotiations
under the General Agreement on Tariffs and Trade*

THE BROOKINGS INSTITUTION
Washington, D.C.

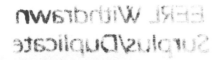

THE BROOKINGS INSTITUTION is an independent organization devoted to nonpartisan research, education, and publication in economics, government, foreign policy, and the social sciences generally. Its principal purposes are to aid in the development of sound public policies and to promote public understanding of issues of national importance.

The Institution was founded on December 8, 1927, to merge the activities of the Institute for Government Research, founded in 1916, the Institute of Economics, founded in 1922, and the Robert Brookings Graduate School of Economics and Government, founded in 1924.

The general administration of the Institution is the responsibility of a self-perpetuating Board of Trustees. The trustees are likewise charged with maintaining the independence of the staff and fostering the most favorable conditions for creative research and education. The immediate direction of the policies, program, and staff of the Institution is vested in the President, assisted by an advisory council chosen from the staff of the Institution.

In publishing a study, the Institution presents it as a competent treatment of a subject worthy of public consideration. The interpretations and conclusions in such publications are those of the author or authors and do not purport to represent the views of the other staff members, officers, or trustees of the Brookings Institution.

Foreword

THE KENNEDY ROUND, as it is generally known, was in fact an international conference, held under the auspices of the General Agreement on Tariffs and Trade (GATT), for the purpose of lowering trade barriers. Over four years elapsed between the ministerial agreement of May 1963 on the objectives of the negotiation and the signing of the final agreement on June 30, 1967. The specific accomplishments of the Kennedy Round include the reduction of tariffs on industrial products by slightly more than 35 percent on the average, a joint undertaking to supply 4.5 million tons of wheat per year as food aid, and the drafting of an international code to help standardize antidumping practices. In addition, a number of new issues likely to play a role in future trade negotiations were discussed. The negotiation, in short, was an event of major importance in post-World War II efforts to lower barriers to trade and promote closer economic cooperation among nations.

This study presents a history of the negotiations, an analysis of the results, and a brief evaluation of the significance of the Kennedy Round for future trade policy. The prologue gives a detailed account of the stormy ministerial meeting in May 1963. The first three chapters provide background, particularly concerning the impact of European integration on commercial relations and the passage by the United States of the Trade Expansion Act of 1962. Chapters 4 through 12 pick up from the prologue and carry the negotiation through to the signing of the final agreement. The next three chapters analyze the results: Chapter 13 presents calculations of nonagricultural tariff levels in the major industrial countries before and after the Kennedy Round. It also contains an analysis of the impact of the Kennedy Round on tariff dispersion and on products of special interest to developing countries, and it discusses the post-Kennedy Round common external tariff of the European Economic Community in relation to the tariffs of selected member states a decade ago. Chapter 14 provides a discussion and a rough estimate of the trade expansion likely to result from the tariff reductions, while Chapter 15 appraises the results in the agricultural sector. The final chapter of the study contains an evaluation of the Kennedy Round —first its accomplishments, and second its possible influence on future trade policy.

The author of this study, Ernest H. Preeg, was an active participant in the negotiation from the summer of 1963 to its conclusion in June 1967. He served in the Office of International Trade at the U.S. Department of State, in the office of Christian Herter (Special Representative for Trade Negotiations), and for the final two and a half years as a member of the U.S. delegation at Geneva. Mr. Preeg holds the Ph.D. in economics from the New School for Social Research and taught briefly at Brooklyn College before entering the Foreign Service. From August 1967 to July 1968, as an International Affairs Fellow of the Council on Foreign Relations, he was a Guest Scholar at the Brookings Institution. At Brookings, Mr. Preeg was associated with the Foreign Policy Studies Program.

The Institution is particularly grateful to Robert E. Asher, Robert E. Baldwin, William Diebold, Jr., and Walter S. Salant for their careful reading of the manuscript and their helpful comments. It also wishes to acknowledge with thanks the conscientious and competent editing done by Alice M. Carroll and the indexing by Helen B. Eisenhart. The author's Preface contains additional acknowledgments.

The views expressed in this book are, of course, those of the author and do not necessarily represent the views of those consulted during its preparation. Neither should they be construed as reflecting the views of the trustees, the officers, or other staff members of the Brookings Institution.

KERMIT GORDON
President

October 1969
Washington, D.C.

Preface

A<small>LTHOUGH THE</small> final agreement of the Kennedy Round was not an "open covenant openly arrived at," most of the significant facts about the negotiations have been publicly aired. The sources are widely scattered, however, and they often lack the perspective and balance essential to an understanding of the events that shaped the final agreement. The interrelations among substantive issues, the timing of critical decisions, and the influence of external factors are all fundamental to such an understanding. It is in this broader frame of reference that I have attempted to explain the experience at Geneva during the four years from May 1963 to June 1967.

The historical narrative basically follows a chronological course. Two topics, however—industrial sector groups and agriculture—are treated in separate chapters apart from the general sequence. Other issues are covered extensively at the most appropriate point. Finally, a glossary of technical terms and a chronology are included for reference.

I have tried to be objective in presenting the various points of view on the substantive issues. That the coverage of events on the American side is in some instances more detailed is attributable partly to my greater familiarity with these facts and partly to the habit of the American government of providing more thorough public discussion and reporting. The study was carried out while I was on leave of absence from government service, and the opinions expressed in it are not necessarily the official views of the United States government or the views of those whose assistance I acknowledge. Any errors of fact or interpretation are, of course, my responsibility.

Three sources of support were especially important to the writing of this account. First, it was largely through the encouragement of Hal Vaughan, press officer of the U.S. mission at Geneva for the five years through 1967, that I undertook this work. I wish to thank him for his partnership in the critical planning phase of the study, as well as for the use of his valuable file of European press comment on the Kennedy Round. Second, I wish to express my gratitude to the Council on Foreign Relations for granting me an International Affairs Fellowship, and to the Rockefeller Brothers Fund which financed the fellowship; to the program director John T. Swing and staff members Miriam Camps, David MacEachron, and Helena Stalson; and especially to William Diebold, Jr., for his assistance and encouragement throughout. Third, I would like to acknowledge the helpful support of the Brookings Institution and include my thanks to the persons mentioned in Kermit Gordon's Foreword. As a Guest Scholar, I benefited greatly from discussion and comment by other members of the Brookings staff.

The discussions I have had with members of country delegations and the secretariat of the General Agreement on Tariffs and Trade have all contributed to this study. I owe a particular debt of thanks to W. Michael Blumenthal, Helen Brewster, Joseph A. Greenwald, Bernard Norwood, Gardner Patterson, and Thomas W. Simons, Jr., for reading and commenting in detail on the entire manuscript. For the analytical chapters I likewise wish to thank Bela Balassa, Harry Bell, Theodore Gates, Lawrence Krause, John Pincus, Ladislav Till, and Mary Jane Wignot. My thanks also go to Nellie Heath for typing and retyping the manuscript to meet consistently unreasonable deadlines. Finally, I am grateful beyond words to Sally, who, in addition to the normal wifely forebearance, contributed greatly to the preparation of statistical material and the editing of manuscript.

ERNEST H. PREEG

Contents

Tables

Prologue: May 1963

When a man knows he is to be hanged in a fortnight,
it concentrates his mind wonderfully.
SAMUEL JOHNSON

CHRISTIAN HERTER, President Kennedy's special representative for trade negotiations, quoted a journalist in early 1963: "It is almost as dreary to read about tariffs as it is to write about them. Yet tariffs may well be the most vital diplomatic subject now facing the Western World." But "a subject that becomes vital tends to shake off its dreariness," Herter told his U.S. Chamber of Commerce audience in Washington on May 1.

Indeed, tariffs and trade had become the center of national and international discussion. The Common Market and the European Free Trade Association were gathering momentum toward regional free trade and economic cooperation. Their dynamism presented a challenge to outsiders, a challenge that did not go long unheeded. In October of the previous year, President Kennedy had signed the unprecedented Trade Expansion Act providing broad U.S. authority for reductions in tariffs and other barriers to trade. The American objective was to negotiate a multilateral lowering of trade barriers to offset the effects of the trade diversion created by formation of the European blocs and to form a harmonious trade partnership between the two centers of noncommunist industrial power.

Continued harmony in world trade, however, was gravely uncertain. General de Gaulle's January veto of Britain's bid for entry into the European Economic Community was a painful setback for proponents of a more liberal world trading system. In contrast to American enthusiasm, the initial reaction of the EEC to the Trade Expansion Act had been a highly qualified approval, and preliminary discussion of a new multilateral trade conference had confirmed the misgivings of some

1

critics that the Common Market would not be willing to negotiate a major reduction of trade barriers. In March and April a working party for the sixth round of negotiations under the General Agreement on Tariffs and Trade (GATT)—already being called the Kennedy Round—attempted to agree on the basic objectives for the negotiations and ended in deadlock. The exasperated American representative commented, "If a key country would say that they can only negotiate on a basis which is not possible under the Trade Expansion Act then it is tantamount to their saying that they do not want to negotiate."[1] On May 6, Representative Henry Reuss of Wisconsin warned in a speech before Congress, "If the Common Market is intransigent, if the Six says 'stop the world, we want to get off' we are apparently about to punish ourselves and the rest of the free world by calling off the negotiations for expanding trade. . . . Our present strategy merely rewards the Common Market for being intransigent. . . . Right now, before we get off to a false start, is a good time to change strategies."

In this mood of bleak disaccord, delegates of ministerial rank arrived at Geneva for a high level meeting scheduled for May 16–21, 1963, to attempt to establish the ground rules for an unprecedented lowering of barriers to world trade. The outlook was not promising.

The Issues in Contention

What were the irreconcilable issues? They were the product of a complicated set of economic and political factors. Differences were particularly apparent in two questions that had to be resolved before negotiation could really begin: the rules for tariff reduction on industrial products, and the position of agricultural trade in the overall negotiations.

The United States had proposed a very simple approach to tariff reduction. All tariffs, with a minimum of exceptions, should be cut in half, the cuts phased over five annual instalments. This procedure would make maximum use of the American negotiating authority. It would assure that all product groups were subject to substantial tariff reduction. And it would provide a reasonable basis for reciprocal tariff cuts by all participants.

The American proposal was widely supported during the early work-

1. *Guardian* (Manchester), May 7, 1963.

ing party meetings. Equal percentage, or linear, tariff cuts had been a favored approach for some time. It was the basis for internal tariff reduction by the EEC and the EFTA; it had been the EEC's initial offer position during the previous, Dillon Round of tariff negotiations; and it was specifically referred to in a GATT ministerial resolution of November 1961. The lack of sufficient negotiating authority by the United States, in fact, was the principal reason why this across-the-board approach to tariff cutting had not been adopted in the past.

But the EEC in particular had strong reservations about linear tariff cuts. Whereas Common Market tariffs were almost all in the medium 10–20 percent range, U.S. tariffs were widely dispersed, many very low and a good number at high levels ranging from 30 percent to 50 percent, and even a few over 100 percent. The United Kingdom also had numerous tariff rates above 30 percent. Unless something extra were done about these peaks, the Common Market tariff after a 50 percent cut would be uniformly low and relatively inconsequential, while high tariffs in other countries, especially the United States, would continue to afford substantial protection for certain industries.

In April 1963 the EEC Commission had proposed as an alternate plan tariff harmonization, or écrêtement.[2] Tariffs would be lowered halfway from their present levels to target levels, tentatively put at 10 percent for manufactures, 5 percent for semimanufactures, and zero for raw materials. The Council of Ministers of the six Common Market countries endorsed this approach of the executive body in Brussels on May 9.

Superficially, the two plans were similar: the U.S. plan would cut halfway to zero, the EEC plan halfway to target levels of 10 percent, 5 percent, and zero. The difference might be described as a matter of agreeing on an ultimate or "optimum" tariff level to shoot for.

In substance, however, the two approaches were quite different. Whereas the American plan would provide for a general 50 percent reduction in the level of tariffs, the EEC plan would at most result in an average reduction of only 10–12 percent. Moreover, moderate tariffs would be subject to little or no reduction under the EEC plan, and high tariffs—often applying to the domestically most sensitive industries— to disproportionately large cuts. Most suspect, the EEC, under its plan, would end up doing less tariff cutting than the other major countries.

2. Literally, the cutting off of the peaks.

The Americans interpreted the *écrêtement* proposal as an attempt, pressed by the French within the EEC, to undermine the basis for a major trade negotiation. A deadlock at this May meeting could result in referral of the whole matter to further technical discussion and a lingering death similar to the recent fate of the EEC-United Kingdom negotiations. Consequently, Christian Herter, head of the American delegation, was under instructions from President Kennedy to remain firm in reaching a decision for tariff reductions based on the linear approach. Primary attention would be given to impressing on other members of the Community—which had a strong commercial interest in a successful negotiation—and especially on Germany, that agreement was imperative at this meeting.

The impasse in agriculture was in some ways even more formidable. The GATT working party had agreed that agricultural products should be included in the negotiation. It had also agreed that certain product groups, such as cereals, meats, and perhaps dairy products, required a more comprehensive approach, directed to the negotiation of a global commodity arrangement. But no precise rules on how to handle the products in the commodity groups or other agricultural products were agreed to. Nor had the U.S. proposal for an interim arrangement to prevent any increase of agricultural protection during the course of the negotiations been accepted.

Agriculture was a critical issue in the Kennedy Round primarily because of the uncertain nature of the Common Market's emerging agricultural policy. A system of high support prices, variable import levies, and export subsidies threatened to insulate Community production from outside competition and substantially reduce the existing level of imports. A number of key decisions, such as the level of internal support prices, had not yet been agreed, but to most outsiders the handwriting was clearly on the wall. The Dillon Round had put the question of the common agricultural policy in abeyance through a standstill agreement for certain key products; the Kennedy Round negotiators were now faced with the task of reconciling the trade impact of the Common Market farm policy with the existing GATT rights of nonmember suppliers. The United States, in fact, had made clear that it would not engage in negotiations on industrial products without some assurance of the maintenance and expansion of markets for its agricultural exports.

These were the central controversial issues facing the ministers as they assembled at Geneva in mid-May 1963. There were, of course, other important questions—from the status of major trading countries like Japan and Canada to the participation of the many less developed countries. But the initial confrontation would in all likelihood center on the positions of the two largest participants, the United States and the Common Market. If they could agree, the negotiations would move forward; if they should fail to reach an accord, a serious and perhaps fatal crisis would undoubtedly follow.

On the surface the issues might appear as matters of varying trade interest. The eloquence with which the American administration had linked passage of the Trade Expansion Act with an improved balance of payments fostered a common European view of U.S. intentions: "The objective . . . is perfectly clear, it is a matter of increasing American sales abroad. And when they speak of 'foreign countries,' they mean above all the Common Market." [3]

The significance of this meeting was far greater, however, than narrow commercial interests. The Common Market would emerge either as a unifying force for the community of Western nations or perhaps as a new form of inward-looking Europe, regionally rather than nationally oriented. President Kennedy's bold new program, the centerpiece of the 1962 session of Congress, could become a successful diplomatic effort or an embarrassing miscalculation. Most important, the carefully built postwar trading system, a pillar of solidarity among noncommunist countries, would be seriously shaken if a breakdown should occur between its most powerful members. The *New York Times* on the eve of the meeting warned that "behind the tedious tariff schedules dealing with such prosaic subjects as frozen chicken, lie far deeper problems. For this conference will involve such basic Franco-American issues as nationalism versus internationalism, freer trade versus protectionism, and rival blocs versus partnerships." [4]

Proposals and Counterproposals

The meeting convened at Geneva on Thursday, May 16. Over six hundred delegates from eighty-two countries were present as participants and observers. The Palais des Nations, enduring symbol of the

3. *Journal de Genève*, May 15, 1963.
4. May 16, 1963.

League of Nations, was the setting for this new undertaking in international cooperation.

Three items were on the agenda. Rules for tariff cutting and agriculture were items two and three. The first order of business was the question of expanding trade for developing countries, and the first day's discussion centered on an eight-point action program prepared and sponsored by a group of less developed countries. The program called for such measures as a standstill against increases in trade barriers against imports from less developed countries, elimination of quota restrictions, and early tariff reduction on products of special trade interest to these countries. Herter, in his opening statement, endorsed the program with "certain minor qualifications," stating that "no task this meeting faces is more important than that of finding ways to improve the export opportunities of less developed countries." [5] The British and others followed suit, but the EEC, committed to its associated African countries, was not prepared to adopt such a program. The proposals, in its view, "referred only to measures for the elimination of barriers to trade, whereas, . . . more positive measures were required to achieve the marked and rapid increase in the export earnings of the developing countries as a whole, which was the fundamental objective." [6]

The issue of less developed countries was not expected, however, to develop into a serious confrontation at this meeting. The *Guardian* speculated that "if the Kennedy-Round of GATT negotiations cannot meet the interests of the underdeveloped nations they may turn instead to the 'Khrushchev-round' of United Nations economic and trade talks." [7] But most reporters, and delegates, were girding themselves for the U.S.-EEC clash on agenda items two and three, scheduled to begin on the second day.

On Friday morning, positions were quickly taken along expected lines. Herter's statement urged the ministers to "reach agreement that the maximum liberalization of trade can best be achieved by a negotiation which begins with across-the-board, equal percentage linear cuts, with limited and narrowly defined exceptions." He suggested 50 percent cuts as a good working hypothesis, and warned that "any formula based on unequal linear cuts imposes a serious limitation on the amount

5. Press release no. 748, General Agreement on Tariffs and Trade (GATT), May 16, 1963.
6. Press release no. 794, GATT, May 29, 1963, App. B, par. 6.
7. *Guardian* (Manchester), May 15, 1963.

by which the average tariff will be reduced . . . [and] it is almost sure to create inequalities which will increase the difficulties of the final negotiations." [8]

Turning to agriculture, Herter maintained the firm position that the U.S. government would not be prepared to conclude the negotiations until "equitable tariff and trade arrangements have been developed for agricultural products." He considered equitable arrangements "a degree of liberalization of trade in agricultural products comparable with that achieved . . . for other products." While supporting the possibility of broad commodity arrangements for such products as cereals and meats, he stressed the most effective way to reach the overall goal was "to include agricultural products to the maximum extent possible in the automatic linear reduction formula which is adopted." [9]

The chairman of the EEC Council of Ministers, Luxembourg's Foreign Minister Eugene Schaus, refused to accept the American idea of equal linear tariff cuts, and while denying dogmatic adherence to the EEC harmonization proposal, insisted on some formula for reducing disparities where the tariff rate for a particular product was much higher in one country than in another. He further suggested that the whole question of tariff cutting rules be referred to a GATT working group for additional study. As for agriculture, it would be included in the negotiations, but the details should be left for later. [10] Sicco Mansholt, the EEC commissioner primarily responsible for farm policy, warned at a press conference that the entire range of farm policy measures would have to be examined. He ruled out interim arrangements as undesirable temporary housing.

Other opening statements, mainly echoes of the American approach or appeals for conciliation, ran on through Saturday. At that point real negotiations began. During the next three hectic days a series of proposals and counterproposals was taken up, often more rapidly than newsmen or even some delegates could follow. The large U.S. delegation [11] and the EEC Commission and member-state hierarchy [12] both proved unwieldy for negotiations at this pace. A complicated dossier of

8. Press release no. 751, GATT, May 17, 1963.
9. *Ibid.*
10. See *Agence Europe Presse*, May 17, 1963.
11. Besides Herter and his deputy, William Gossett, there were seven assistant and deputy assistant secretaries plus ten other senior advisers.
12. The EEC Commission, described in Chap. 2, is responsible for conducting trade negotiations although negotiating authority is delegated by the member state Council of Ministers. At this meeting Jean Rey was the chief Commission representative and Eugene Schaus was spokesman for the Council of Ministers.

technical issues is always a hazardous thing to place before a crowded, high-level meeting with a tight deadline. The harrowing experience in May 1963 was well remembered four years later in the final days of the Kennedy Round.

On Sunday evening an EEC-U.S. bilateral meeting was scheduled at Des Bergues Hotel. The United States had put forward a proposal that contained some elements of compromise, but remained firm on equal linear cuts, and rejected any specific harmonization or disparity formula. The EEC turned it down flatly. Although at press conferences "some progress" was claimed, the continued deadlock was evident. Monday papers resounded with "full-scale crisis," "possible breakdown of talks," and "brink of failure."

On Monday morning, while newsmen stalked the corridors of the Palais in anticipation of an EEC internal meeting, two key figures slipped away for one of the few unnoticed events of the conference. In one of several meetings between the two, German Economics Minister Ludwig Erhard showed Herter a new proposal, subsequently labeled the "Erhard compromise." It accepted the linear approach as a general rule for tariff cuts but superimposed an automatic formula for reducing tariff disparities. The form of the disparity rule was left for later discussion. Erhard had worked hard to gain his colleagues' acceptance of this proposal. It went a long way toward the linear concept in the American proposal. Herter, however, found the formulation unacceptable because it left completely open the definition and scope of possible disparities. The two men parted, agreeing to keep their meeting secret and await formal transmission of the proposal.

By noon, however, EEC spokesmen were releasing the Erhard compromise to the press before it was officially transmitted to the Americans. The U.S. delegation was pressed to give its reaction, and in this peculiar situation the American spokesman emphasized that the proposal had not been received by the U.S. delegation, but that "the proposal reported in the press would not be acceptable to the United States." The U.S. position remained that the negotiation should be based on a plan of substantial and equal linear tariff cuts. The Common Market's proposal, while only accepting linear cuts where disparities did not exist, was seen as requiring deeper reductions by the United States than by the Common Market where disparities did exist. "This is a requirement the United States is plainly unwilling to accept." Furthermore, the United States rejected the suggestion that the whole matter be referred to a technical group for continued study. The American statement contained general language about certain high tariffs possibly preventing a balance of advantages, but this was a far cry from an automatic disparity formula.[13]

By late Monday hope was fading rapidly. Herter announced his firm intention of leaving soon after the closing session on Tuesday. French Finance Minister Giscard d'Estaing, essential for any further concession by France, had already departed. Another evening bilateral discussion between the EEC and the United States was suddenly called off. Speculation rose that the United States might put forward a resolution for a vote the next day to isolate the Community. But this was just a more glaring way of announcing failure. The Tuesday morning edition of the *New York Times*, under the headline "U.S.-Trade Bloc Meeting on Tariffs Near Collapse," began: "The six nations of the European Common Market rejected early this morning [Tuesday, May 21] a last-minute United States compromise proposal on how to reduce tariffs and create freer world trade."

Was the unprecedented authority of President Kennedy's Trade Expansion Act to be frustrated before it had a chance to see the light of day? Were the critics of the EEC right when they predicted the Community's intention to torpedo the Kennedy Round and turn increasingly inward in its commercial policy? Were the Americans unrealistic in insisting on maximum tariff cuts and unfair in objecting to any concrete concession on tariff disparities? Would the broad community of interest between countries on both sides of the Atlantic be soured by the inability to find a mutually acceptable rule for cutting tariffs?

The Adoption of Objectives

Actually, the *Times* story was overly pessimistic. Fervid diplomatic activity continued; delegates were on the phone to their capitals. The political consequences of failure loomed large as a breakdown became imminent. The EEC delegation began deliberations Monday evening, and with the return of Giscard d'Estaing continued on until two o'clock Tuesday morning. They considered still another American counterproposal, and finally agreed to it with only small changes, which were,

13. Press release, U.S. Information Agency, Information Service, May 21, 1963.

in turn, accepted by the Americans. The *Baltimore Sun* announced on Tuesday morning: "Officials of the six Market nations met until 2 a.m. today considering the Herter proposal, rejected part of its wording and countered with an offer of their own. . . . There were indications last night that other members of the Common Market had put heavy pressure on French representatives because of the possible political effects of failure."

With this decisive breakthrough, events moved to a successful conclusion on Tuesday. A last minute dispute arose over the commitment of countries that depended largely on exports of agricultural and primary products, especially Canada. Canadian Trade Minister Mitchell Sharp contended that equal linear tariff cuts would not provide reciprocal trade benefits for Canada. The United States had conceded that a problem might arise for Canada, but the EEC, informed of this after having reached the basic compromise with the United States, resisted the Canadian demand for special treatment for seven long hours in a meeting held in a basement conference room of the Palais. The Canadian view was finally accepted by the EEC, but with deep resentment over the way it had been pressed upon them.

In general, however, the final compromise resolution on tariff cutting was received with satisfaction and relief by virtually all delegates.[14] The agricultural objectives were agreed in broad principle and a work group was established to elaborate "the rules to govern, and the methods to be employed in, the creation of acceptable conditions of access to world markets for agricultural products in furtherance of a significant development and expansion of world trade in such products."

The agenda item on trade expansion for developing countries was not resolved on a harmonious note (in spite of the fact that eleven pages of the thirteen-and-a-half-page final resolution were devoted to it). The EEC could not endorse the proposals of the action program and suggested instead an "effort to organize international trade in products of interest to the less-developed countries." [15] Other industrial countries accepted the basic points of the program but hedged considerably on the requested timing and product coverage. The ministers of the developing countries "expressed disappointment with the understandings and positions as set out by some industrialized countries and found

14. Excerpts from the final resolutions are contained in Appendix C.
15. Press release no. 794, GATT, May 29, 1963, par. 6.

them unhelpful." [16] A Latin American delegate commented: "Conferences such as this have been a monotonous repetition of unsatisfied requests and frustrated hopes." [17] Unfortunately, this meeting proved to be only the first of a series of north-south frustrations in the Kennedy Round.

As for the impasse on tariff cutting rules, the final text was not very different from the original Erhard compromise. It stated that "the tariff negotiations . . . shall be based upon a plan of substantial linear tariff reductions with a bare minimum of exceptions. . . . The linear reductions shall be equal. In those cases where there are significant disparities in tariff levels, the tariff reductions will be based upon special rules of general and automatic application." The final concession to the Americans was qualification of "significant" as "meaningful in trade terms." This interpretation was presented by the conference chairman and then adopted unanimously—a fancy turn of diplomatic footwork. Precise criteria for meaningful disparities, however, were left for follow-up discussions. The depth of the linear cut was also left open. In summing up at a midnight press conference, Herter expressed satisfaction that the issues had been successfully resolved "in a manner of compromise." [18] Regarding tariff disparities, he stated optimistically, "The question . . . is no longer an issue. It has disappeared." Ludwig Erhard was more cautious and more correct: "We have agreed on the shell of an egg. What will be in the egg we do not know." [19]

And so the Kennedy Round cleared the first hurdle. The foundation was laid for what could become the most far-reaching reduction of trade barriers ever undertaken. The contention generated at this initial meeting had a sobering effect on those who had envisaged a quick, easy negotiation. The negative reactions, in fact, overshadowed the importance of the resolution adopted on May 21, 1963. For the objectives established during these six days in May 1963 would largely endure the four years of discussion, delay, and maneuver, and the substance of the final agreement would be essentially in accord with them.

16. *Ibid.*, par. 9.
17. *New York Times*, May 17, 1963.
18. Press release, U.S. Information Agency, Information Service, May 22, 1963.
19. *New York Times*, May 22, 1963.

CHAPTER ONE

Converging Trends

THE KENNEDY ROUND was the sixth in a series of postwar multilateral conferences to lower trade barriers under the auspices of the General Agreement on Tariffs and Trade (GATT). It lasted longer and accomplished more than any previous GATT negotiation. Over four years elapsed between the initial ministerial agreement on objectives in May 1963 and the signing of the final agreement on June 30, 1967. And this termination date was only met under the pressure of the five-year U.S. negotiating authority which expired on June 30. Under the agreement, more than $40 billion of trade was subject to some form of concession by participating countries—eight times that included in the previous, Dillon Round of negotiations.[1] Tariffs on industrial products were reduced on the average by over 35 percent [2] and substantial reductions were made on agricultural products as well.

Moreover, a current of change pervaded the negotiations. A vastly more ambitious program was undertaken and new techniques of negotiation introduced. By 1963 the prevailing method of bargaining reciprocal tariff reductions on an item-by-item basis had become clearly inadequate. It limited the outcome and resulted in an uneven distribution of benefits among participants. The Kennedy Round, in response, adopted the procedure of across-the-board, or linear, tariff cuts. The wide range of so-called nontariff barriers to trade had become more important as tariffs were progressively lowered and a first serious attempt was made in the Kennedy Round to deal with some of these

1. See press release no. 1008, General Agreement on Tariffs and Trade (GATT), Nov. 8, 1967, p. 19.
2. See Chap. 13.

12

problems. During the 1950s, trade in agricultural products had been largely reserved from GATT negotiations even though levels of domestic support and technological change resulted in large differences in national cost levels. The Kennedy Round included agriculture as an integral part of the overall negotiation.

The negotiation was also a response to recent challenges to the principles of the GATT system. Past negotiations had been based on the concepts of reciprocity and nondiscrimination. Many developing countries, however, claimed that reciprocal tariff cuts were inimical to their economic development and that they were in fact discriminated against under the existing form of nondiscrimination. Even more momentous was the dramatic success of regional free trade in Europe which threatened a fragmentation of the global trade structure into a polycentric system of competing trade blocs. A major objective of the Kennedy Round was to respond in a positive way to these challenges while maintaining the framework of a multilateral trading system.

Finally, the Kennedy Round was a testing ground for a new orientation of economic forces. The first GATT conference in 1947 was dominated by a willful and paternalistic United States with strong United Kingdom support. Succeeding rounds continued, to some extent, in the shadow of this initial arrangement. By 1961, however, the Dillon Round exposed a new focus of powers that bloomed during the Kennedy Round. The developing countries' chorus of dissent became an impatient leitmotiv of the negotiation. Other countries, notably Japan, assumed a larger role. But the greatest impact was the emergence of the Common Market as a unified and coequal bargaining force with the United States. This situation required adjustment on both sides. The United States, for example, came to realize that third countries, such as those in the European Free Trade Association (EFTA), were at least as concerned with what the European Economic Community did as with what the United States did. The EEC, on the other hand, now bore equal responsibility for success—or failure—and would consequently share fully the credit or blame for the outcome. The Kennedy Round was the first major negotiation and agreement between two equal poles of economic power across the Atlantic.

A full understanding of what was accomplished—and what was not accomplished—during the Kennedy Round requires a perspective of time and events. It requires an appreciation of the constraints imposed by external forces and the linking of diverse individual interests which is fundamental to a bargaining process. The issues themselves were so complex that one observer commented "the arguments . . . would make Byzantine lawyers dizzy." [3] There is also a tendency to exaggerate the significance of immediate events, the drama of the final confrontation, and to forget the longer strands of effort that led eventually to agreement. And there is the often subtle distinction between substance and tactics. A distinguished Harvard economist concluded, "The only economic decision made in the Kennedy Round was that a reciprocal reduction of trade barriers is desirable. Everything else is tactics." His overstatement illustrates one extreme. Striking an even balance here as among the many factors requires a far more detailed account.

This study traces the course of the negotiation from its early roots, through the four years of discussions, and on to the final agreement. Several longer trends that bore on the course of events at Geneva are outlined in this chapter. Chapters 2 and 3 cover the more immediate influence of European economic integration and the Trade Expansion Act. The negotiations from the May 1963 ministerial meeting through the signing of the final agreement are traced in Chapters 4–12. The results are analyzed in Chapters 13–15 and briefly evaluated in Chapter 16.

Three Decades of Liberal Trade

The year 1934 was marked by worldwide economic depression. It was a year when average duties paid on U.S. imports reached one of the highest points in history and when world trade, crippled by the depression and the autarkic response of trading nations, was stagnant. It was also the year of the original U.S. Reciprocal Trade Agreements Act, a personal victory for Secretary of State Cordell Hull. The new Hull program was not a radical change in the principles underlying U.S. trade policy. The most-favored-nation principle,[4] for example, had been adopted a decade earlier. But the trade act of 1934 reversed the trend toward higher levels of protection by providing the President with authority to negotiate, within carefully defined limits, a reciprocal reduction of tariffs between the United States and its trading partners. Until that time Congress had determined tariff rates, which often re-

3. Edwin L. Dale, Jr., *New Republic*, Feb. 11, 1967.
4. The application of duties on the same, most-favorable basis to all countries afforded such treatment.

sulted in a log-rolling of higher rates for the geographically dispersed special interests.[5] Nor was there prior to that time congressional authorization to reduce tariffs on U.S. imports in return for reductions abroad on American exports.

The Hull program for reciprocal reductions of trade barriers has made steady progress. From 1934 through 1946, bilateral trade agreements were concluded with twenty-nine countries. Starting in 1947 the series of multilateral conferences held under the auspices of GATT facilitated the process of combining bilateral reciprocity with the multilateral benefits accorded under the most-favored-nation application of duties. The average tariff paid on dutiable U.S. imports dropped from 54 percent in 1933 to 12 percent in 1963. It has been estimated that about half of this reduction resulted from negotiated tariff reductions [6] while the other half was due to the impact of inflation on specific duties.[7]

The steady progress in implementing this liberal trade policy obscures, however, its tenuous existence during most of this period. The original act was defended before Congress as a temporary antidepression measure. Secretary Hull testified in early 1934: "There should, I repeat, be no misunderstanding as to the nature or the purpose of this measure. It is not an extraordinary plan to deal with ordinary or normal conditions, nor an ordinary plan to deal with extraordinary conditions. Its support is only urged as an emergency measure to deal with a dangerous and threatening emergency situation. . . ."[8] It was not until

5. Senator Arthur Vandenberg referred to his experience in congressional tariff-making as lacking "any element of economic science or validity," and suspected that his nine Senate colleagues who wrote the last tariff "would join me in resigning before they would be willing to tackle another general Congressional tariff revision." Quoted in William B. Kelly, Jr. (ed.), *Studies in United States Commercial Policy* (University of North Carolina Press, 1963), p. 78.

6. See Paul H. Douglas, *America in the Market Place* (Holt, Rinehart & Winston, 1966), p. 102.

7. A specific duty is a fixed money charge per physical unit (for example, 10 cents per pound). An ad valorem duty is levied as a percent of the value of the commodity. An increase in the price of traded goods reduces the protective effect of specific but not ad valorem duties. U.S. dutiable imports are about half specific, half ad valorem. Specific duties are primarily on unprocessed bulk imports like petroleum, sugar, lumber, and tobacco, while ad valorem rates are mostly on finished manufactures. The ad valorem share of total imports has been rising because imports in the latter category have been growing at a faster rate. Other countries tend to favor ad valorem duties. The EEC has almost all ad valorem rates. Switzerland is an exception, with virtually all specific rates.

8. *Reciprocal Trade Agreements*, Hearings before the Senate Committee on Finance, 73 Cong. 2 sess. (1934), p. 5.

1949, after a number of extensions of the act, that the phrase "present emergency" was finally dropped.

The trade agreements program was also alien to much of the New Deal philosophy of active intervention in the marketplace. It was in direct conflict with the Agricultural Adjustments Act provisions for domestic support, import quotas, and export subsidies, which ultimately led the United States in 1955 to request a waiver of GATT obligations on certain actions it was required to take under the agricultural act.

The most striking experiences of the long struggle for a liberal trade policy were the series of congressional debates over extension and revision of the trade act. Between 1934 and 1958 the act was renewed eleven times. The legislative history is marked by sharp differences in view, restrictive amendments, and narrow votes. In 1955 a motion in the House to recommit the bill, which would have killed it, was voted down by only 206 to 199. Although a substantial number of Republican votes has since developed in support of a liberal trade program, this shift has been partially offset by increasing opposition from Southern Democrats, largely from textile districts.[9]

The transformation of a highly protectionist United States in the early 1930s to a strong advocate of liberal trade in the early 1960s was gradual and at times uncertain. The growing role of the United States in world affairs undoubtedly supported this development. It was not until 1962, however, that the Congress took an unequivocal initiative to open world markets and strengthen commercial ties between all noncommunist trading nations.

The Atlantic Community

A combination of political, economic, cultural, and family ties across the Atlantic has shaped a strong community of interest between Europe and North America. The troubled state of affairs in Western Europe following World War II converted these affinities into a more formal Atlantic community of cooperation and alliance. The problems of postwar recovery fomented a mutual effort in the economic sphere, starting with the Marshall Plan and continuing in today's prosperity under the Organization for Economic Cooperation and Development (OECD).

9. For a brief discussion of political developments in the United States related to tariffs and trade, see Douglas, *America in the Market Place*, pp. 97–101.

The Soviet military threat to Western Europe inspired the North Atlantic Treaty Organization (NATO). The need for effective leadership to maintain stability and growth throughout the world has prompted close consultation and cooperation among the Western industrial powers in other forums as well.

A new dimension in the relation between the two sides of the Atlantic was added with the move toward economic integration among European states. The grouping of European nations into a bloc comparable in size and potential stature with the two colossi of East and West has had a profound effect on the attitudes and hopes of many Europeans. Rather than continue as several secondary powers, Western Europe can now aspire to equal world power status.

The bonds of international trade have provided a solid base for other ties across the Atlantic. The exchange of goods has been a vehicle for the exchange of ideas and of technological advance. U.S. trade with Western Europe has increased rapidly in the postwar period: exports and imports combined totaled $5.6 billion in 1950, $11.4 billion in 1960, $14.3 billion in 1964, and $18.2 billion in 1967.

A rebuilt and fully competitive Europe, and the Common Market in particular, however, entailed a challenge for transatlantic trade. A resurgent inward-directed Europeanism, so divisive in the past, could easily manifest itself in the field of trade. The trade diversion inherent in the European Community structure could weaken cohesion across the Atlantic just as it was strengthening it among its members. Growing strains in the military alliance and world monetary problems meanwhile might forestall the necessary momentum to deal effectively with commercial interests. The new Europe of the 1960s demanded a constructive and forward-looking approach in trade policy.

Temperate Agricultural Revolution

Just as the industrial revolution transformed the structure of European society in the early nineteenth century, a revolution in agricultural production is having a similar impact, on a wider geographic scale, in the mid-twentieth century. North America is in the vanguard of this new wave of technological advance. In the United States one farmworker feeds thirty-five people today compared with eight in 1920. During the 1950s, output per man-hour of the American farmworker increased 5.1 percent per year, compared to an annual increase of only 2.2 percent in nonfarm industry. Yield per acre, farm size, and capital investment have all moved steadily upward. The result of these gains was summed up by Secretary of Agriculture Freeman: "The United States, with scarcely 6 percent of its people still on the farm, is feeding 200 million Americans, 60 million Indians and the equivalent of at least another 100 million people in other parts of the world." [10]

Impressive gains have been made in other temperate areas as well, and even Western Europe, whose arable land resources are limited, may significantly increase its self-sufficiency in food through the incentives of domestic support programs. The revolutionary advances in food production by temperate countries have been on the whole uneven, however; coupled with deep-rooted protectionist policies for domestic farmers,[11] this uneven progress has led to a substantial widening of national differences in cost and price levels. In the early 1960s, barley, a principal European feedgrain, was marketed for roughly 90 cents per bushel in Canada compared with over $2 per bushel in West Germany; poultry meat, selling at 25–30 cents per pound in the United States, was about double that price in the Common Market.[12] A GATT study of Swiss agricultural protection stated, "The maintenance of high internal prices . . . required the Swiss consumer to pay more than double the price for butter, cheese, beef and lamb than the consumer in the United Kingdom." [13]

In contrast to the rapid though uneven gains in temperate industrial countries, developing countries, until recently, were unsuccessful in their efforts to increase food production. Moreover, total food consumption in these countries has been rising steadily as a result of population growth and higher per capita income. Trends in agriculture in developing countries are shown in Table 1–1. In nine of the countries, which include 90 percent of the population of the twelve countries

10. Orville L. Freeman, "Malthus, Marx and the North American Breadbasket," *Foreign Affairs*, Vol. 45 (July 1967), p. 587.

11. According to John O. Coppock, "agricultural policies in the industrial countries are essentially isolationist, and international relations—trade—are little more than a patchwork of import restrictions and export subsidies, both essentially opportunistic in origin." (*Atlantic Agricultural Unity: Is It Possible?* [McGraw-Hill for Council on Foreign Relations, 1966], p. 19.)

12. Quoted in a speech by W. Michael Blumenthal before the National Council of American Importers, New York, Sept. 16, 1965.

13. *Trade in Agricultural Products: Reports of Committee II on Country Consultations* (1962), p. 416.

Table 1–1. Growth in Food Production and Consumption in Twelve Developing Countries, Recent Years

Country	Population, 1960 (in millions)	Annual increase in food demand, 1950–60 (in percent)	Annual increase in crop output, 1948–63 (in percent)
India	429	3.4	3.1
Pakistan	93	2.4	1.8
Japan	93	5.6	2.8
Brazil	71	4.4	4.2
Nigeria	35	4.9	2.6
Mexico	35	4.2	6.3
Spain	30	3.0	2.7
Poland	30	5.1	3.0
Turkey	28	4.5	4.5
Philippines	27	4.5	5.2
Thailand	26	4.9	4.4
United Arab Republic	26	4.0	2.0

Source: U.S. Department of Agriculture, *Changes in Agriculture in 26 Developing Nations* (1965), pp. 4, 6, 62. The 12 countries in the table are the largest of the 26, and cover over 87 percent of the population in the 26 countries.

listed, food demand rose faster than crop output over the periods given. Only Mexico and the Philippines show a faster rate of growth for crop output (and Turkey broke even). Belated attention is now being given to farm production in developing countries, in some cases with great success, but in many countries, the ability of domestic supply to keep up with demand is still uncertain.

The combination of these contrasting developments in world food production and consumption over the past decades is reflected in radically changed patterns of world trade. The evolution of grain trade, shown in Table 1–2, is most striking. Between the 1934–38 period and 1966, Latin America shifted from the largest net exporter of grain to a barely self-sufficient status; Africa, Eastern Europe, and Asia changed from net exporters to net importers; Western Europe maintained a steady level of net imports; and the North American breadbasket emerged as the dominant supplier to food deficit areas. The share of imports held by the commercial markets of Western Europe declined steadily, and the import requirements of developing countries, largely in the form of food aid, rose.

In contrast with its success in liberalizing industrial trade, GATT was conspicuously ineffective in coping with developments in agricul-

Table 1–2. World Grain Trade by Major Geographic Regions, Selected Years [a]

Region	Net exports (in millions of metric tons)		
	1934–38	1960	1966 (estimated)
North America	+5	+39	+60
Latin America	+9	0	+2
Western Europe	−24	−25	−23
Eastern Europe (including USSR)	+5	0	−14
Africa	+1	−2	−3
Asia	+2	−16	−30
Australia and New Zealand	+3	+6	+8

Source: Orville L. Freeman, "Malthus, Marx and the North American Breadbasket," *Foreign Affairs*, Vol. 45 (July 1967), p. 580.
a. Minor imbalances between world imports and exports in a given year are due to rounding or variations in reporting methods used by various countries.

tural trade during the 1950s.[14] The comprehensiveness of farm support programs made the normal GATT procedures of tariff reduction and relaxation of import quotas inappropriate. It was recognized that broader commodity arrangements might be a means for coming to grips with agriculture, but resistance to commodity arrangements, particularly by the United States, stifled moves in this direction. The appeal of a comprehensive approach strengthened, however, as the growing imbalance between surplus production in exporting countries and food deficits in developing countries, and the ineffectiveness of GATT procedures became more apparent. The Haberler Report in 1958 [15] and subsequent GATT studies of agricultural policies in individual countries helped clarify the situation. By 1960 a major concerted effort to adopt practical measures for improving the conditions of trade in farm products seemed a reasonable possibility.

The Third World

Arnold Toynbee prophesied that our century "will be remembered chiefly neither for its horrifying crimes nor for its astonishing inventions, but for its having been the first age since the dawn of civilization . . . in which people dared to think it practicable to make the benefits of

14. See Gerard Curzon, *Multilateral Commercial Diplomacy* (London: Michael Joseph Ltd., 1965), Chap. 7.
15. Gottfried Haberler, *Trends in International Trade* (GATT, 1958).

civilization available for the whole human race." [16] Perhaps he should have narrowed his statement to the second half of the century, but there is no question that the challenge of material progress for the economically less advanced parts of the world is a central issue today, and may yet come to overshadow the political differences between nations.

Economic development is closely related to the problem of food production. In 1961, 92 percent of the Pakistani population was engaged in agriculture, as was 70 percent of the Indian population. The comparable figure for the United States was 8 percent (and this figure had dropped to 5.5 percent by 1967). Rural as a share of total population dropped from 63 percent to 37 percent in Japan during the 1950s while the ratios for India and Pakistan remained almost stationary, above 80 percent. Economic development depends upon modern production techniques, which in turn require an accumulation of physical tools and technical skills; but as long as a country's energies are heavily employed merely to meet current subsistence requirements, the cumulative process of growth cannot be rapid.

Economic development is also closely tied to trade; [17] the appropriate role of trade has been a matter of debate in recent years, however. The struggle for growth during the first postwar years often centered on the manufacture of products that had theretofore been imported—a development strategy of "import substitution." This approach at times sacrificed economic efficiency for national self-sufficiency and became increasingly costly for nations with small internal markets and scarce resources of capital and technical skills. Mounting imports of capital equipment were also required as development programs proceeded, and the foreign exchange provided by aid and international private investment was not sufficient to meet these growing requirements. The need for a new development policy crystallized with the United Nations proclamation of the 1960s as the development decade. Its goal of 5 percent annual economic growth for developing countries would require accelerated imports of investment goods and would lead to a predicted trade gap of $10–$20 billion per year by 1970.

These stark calculations emphasized the fact that 80–90 percent of

16. "Not the Age of Atoms But of Welfare for All," *New York Times*, Oct. 21, 1951.

17. See Harry G. Johnson, *Economic Policies Toward Less Developed Countries* (Brookings Institution, 1967), and John Pincus, *Trade, Aid and Development* (McGraw-Hill for Council on Foreign Relations, 1967).

imports by developing countries were paid for with export revenues. Perhaps trade, not aid, was the primary vehicle to successful economic growth. To this question Raúl Prebisch, secretary-general of the United Nations Conference on Trade and Development (UNCTAD), directed his report, *Towards a New Trade Policy for Development*.[18] Prebisch called for a positive program to encourage exports of developing countries to replace the passive and nondiscriminatory approach of GATT toward trade liberalization. In order to offset the "persistent trend towards external imbalance" and the limited possibilities for import substitution, a program of commodity agreements to assure "equitable" prices for primary products, compensatory finance for shortfalls in export revenues, and temporary tariff preferences by industrial countries to developing countries for manufactured products was put forward. Preferential tariff reductions to widen markets among developing countries were also encouraged.

Prebisch's report was the catalyst of the first conference on trade and development, held in Geneva from March 23 to June 16, 1964. The meeting culminated two years of laborious preparation, especially by the "group of seventy-seven" developing countries. Although the conference ended without any substantive accomplishments and many industrial countries cast negative votes or abstained on the final resolutions, UNCTAD established a concrete challenge for the rich nations. The elements of a "new trade policy" would be confronted again at the second conference, scheduled for 1967. During the interim, a major GATT negotiation, the Kennedy Round, would run its course.

The General Agreement on Tariffs and Trade

The Kennedy Round capped twenty years of achievement through the General Agreement on Tariffs and Trade.[19] The multilateral agreement embodying reciprocal rights and obligations was instituted in 1948, pending entry into force of the Havana Charter and the creation of an international trade organization. But after hope for the latter organization was abandoned in 1950, GATT—"a slender reed on which to base progress toward a multilateral regime . . . permeated by an

18. Published by United Nations, 1964.
19. For a thorough study of GATT, see Curzon, *Multilateral Commercial Diplomacy*. For a shorter description, see press release no. 1008, GATT, Nov. 8, 1967.

atmosphere of impermanence . . ." [20]—gradually acquired resiliency as its achievements grew. The original membership of twenty-three countries grew to seventy-four full members and twelve provisional or other related members by the end of 1967.

Although the text of the agreement is highly technical, and covers many aspects of trade, the main GATT activities are based on the following four principles: (1) *Nondiscrimination*. Article one, the most-favored-nation obligation, is the cornerstone of the GATT trading system. A major exception to this principle is the provision for customs unions and free trade areas, such as the EEC and the EFTA. Preferential arrangements that predate GATT, such as the British Commonwealth, are permitted to continue, though they are subject to negotiation. (2) *Tariffs only*. Protection shall be afforded exclusively through tariffs, and specifically not by means of import quotas. Exception to the no quota provision is granted notably for temporary balance-of-payments difficulties and agricultural support programs that act to restrict domestic production. A more recent exception is contained in the GATT Long-Term Arrangement Regarding International Trade in Cotton Textiles which provides for quotas to prevent "market disruption." (3) *Consultation*. GATT provides the mechanism for consulting on potential trade problems and for settling trade disputes in a mutually satisfactory way. (4) *Negotiation*. Periodic negotiations are convened to reduce trade barriers on a reciprocal and multilateral basis.

The first decade of GATT activity was successful largely because the work program was practical and nonpolitical. The program's pragmatism is exemplified in the approach to negotiating tariff reductions on a reciprocal basis. A concession, in GATT parlance, is a reduction or other limitation of one's own trade barriers, while a benefit is a reduction or other limitation of barriers abroad that will expand one's export opportunity. Though advocates of liberal trade are quick to point out the potential benefits of unilateral tariff reduction, this enlightened view has seldom achieved a national consensus. Protectionist resistance to tariff reduction on particular products is difficult to offset by widely dispersed gains in efficiency or consumer welfare. Moreover, short-run factors such as balance-of-payments disequilibrium and unemployment are real policy constraints. The bargaining approach, on the other hand, through which gains for export industries are matched against

20. Richard N. Gardner, *Sterling-Dollar Diplomacy* (Oxford, 1956), pp. 349, 379–80.

increased imports, has greatly strengthened the appeal of trade liberalization.

A practical limitation on GATT's scope of action during its early years was its concentration on barriers to trade in industrial products. The immediate postwar years were characterized by high tariffs, import quotas, and currency restrictions. The nations that formed GATT sought, as their initial objective, to reduce these direct trade restraints and restore a stable trading system of expanded and equal access to markets. While currency restrictions were dealt with elsewhere, GATT succeeded in progressively eliminating quotas on almost all nonagricultural products and in reducing tariffs substantially. It succeeded also in binding the reduced tariffs—that is, securing a nation's obligation not to raise the tariffs again, or if that proved unavoidable, either to compensate exporting countries with other tariff reductions or to accept in retaliation higher tariffs against its own exports. GATT bindings have proven to be an effective deterrent to tariff increases.

Finally, GATT managed to avoid serious political frictions, which can stalemate the activity of an international organization, largely because its initial membership was limited to noncommunist countries. The bulk of obligations was in fact undertaken by the major industrial countries of the West, which as a group account for over 60 percent of global imports.[21] The recent accession to GATT of a growing number of developing countries and some communist countries [22] has not changed basically the nonpolitical tenor of GATT deliberations.

By the close of the 1950s, however, GATT's success in dealing with tariffs and quotas in industrial products underlined, by contrast, its failure to deal with other trade problems, such as restrictions on agricultural trade and the wide range of nontariff barriers. Changing patterns of trade also necessitated a reappraisal of GATT procedures: negotiated tariff reduction on matched individual products was becoming more difficult as larger volumes of imports entered under moderate tariffs; developing countries, whose participation in GATT was growing, were dissatisfied with their rather passive and unproductive role

21. In 1960, North America, the EEC, the EFTA, and Japan accounted for 61 percent of global imports, developing countries 23 percent, and communist countries 12 percent; the remainder went to Australia, New Zealand, South Africa, and nonspecified countries. See GATT, *International Trade, 1965*, Table D.

22. Czechoslovakia joined GATT before the communist takeover in 1948, and remained a largely dormant member of the organization; Yugoslavia and Poland acceded to GATT during the Kennedy Round.

in the organization; and the creation of the EEC and the EFTA raised a number of commercial policy questions.

The response of GATT to these challenges dates from 1958. The report of the Haberler panel of experts dealt not only with agriculture, but also with other areas of trade policy, especially as related to exports of developing countries.[23] Preparation for a new assault on trade barriers was continued in follow-up study groups and through the establishment of three standing committees to develop new techniques of negotiation for trade in manufactures, agriculture, and products of special interest to developing countries. A meeting of GATT ministers in November 1961 produced firm statements of intent for an ambitious new trade conference, the sixth round of negotiations at Geneva.

No discussion of GATT is complete without a note on its director general, Eric Wyndham White. Seldom has the work of one man so pervaded the character and development of an organization. He had served as head of the GATT secretariat since its inception in 1948, and his statements and initiatives, with the weight of unrivalled experience, acquired a growing suasive force through the years. On May 6, 1968, the Swiss diplomat Olivier Long succeeded Wyndham White as director general. But it is doubtful whether anyone could have fully replaced him.

23. *Trends in International Trade.*

CHAPTER TWO

European Economic Integration

The evolution of European economic integration, from the establishment of the European Coal and Steel Community in 1951 to the final consolidation of a customs union among the countries of the European Economic Community in July 1968, has profoundly altered the balance of economic forces both within Europe and between Europe and other parts of the world. A consolidated EEC market of 190 million people provides a production potential equal to that of the United States or the Soviet Union, creates pressures for further steps toward economic integration, and attracts participation by other European nations. European integration has had great political significance as well. The United States has strongly supported a unified Western Europe for the political stability and strength it would give to the noncommunist world. The United Kingdom, forced to choose between its traditional insular independence and an integrated European role, has gradually come to opt for the latter. Eastern European countries are attracted to a closer relationship with the dynamic prosperity of the West.

The greatest direct effect of European integration thus far, however, has been in the field of trade, and the initial adjustments have related mostly to commercial policy. The launching of the Common Market led to the formation of the European Free Trade Association (EFTA). In the United States it prompted (after some lesser efforts) the ambitious Trade Expansion Act of 1962. And these developments, in turn, were the principal motivating forces for the Kennedy Round of negotiations under the General Agreement on Tariffs and Trade.

Integration's Effect on GATT

The European Economic Community, for purposes of commercial policy, is a customs union: tariffs have been eliminated among its members and a "common external tariff" has been established for imports from nonmember countries.[1] Other steps toward economic integration, such as harmonization of national tax systems, are also part of the Community program. The EFTA, in contrast, is a free trade area: tariffs have been eliminated among member countries but separate national tariffs remain in effect for imports from nonmember countries; no significant additional movement toward economic integration is anticipated.[2]

Another distinction between the two groupings is that the EEC, unlike the EFTA, includes the agricultural sector in its program of economic integration. The "common agricultural policy" of the EEC is based on a system of uniform price levels throughout the Community. For such products as grains and olive oil, target prices are decided upon and the Community, through the European Agricultural Guidance and Guarantee Fund, is obliged to buy any domestic production, which cannot be sold otherwise, at an intervention price slightly below the target price. In order to prevent imports from underselling this guaranteed internal price, a variable import levy is applied that amounts to the difference between the target price and the import price. Imports are therefore prevented from disrupting internal prices, and become, in effect, residual supplies that may be tapped if demands cannot be met internally at the target price. An increase in domestic production automatically displaces an equal amount of imports. Finally, export subsidies are provided for selling surpluses on world markets.

For other farm products, such as poultry, pigmeat, beef and veal, and some fruits and vegetables, the form of domestic support or market intervention varies, but in each case a minimum import price and a

1. See Isaiah Frank, *The European Common Market, an Analysis of Commercial Policy* (Praeger, 1961). The designations EEC, Common Market, the Six, European Community, and the Community are used interchangeably in this study. The members of the EEC are Belgium, France, West Germany, Italy, Luxembourg, and the Netherlands.

2. The original members of the European Free Trade Association were Great Britain, Sweden, Norway, Denmark, Austria, Switzerland, and Portugal. Finland became an associated member in 1961.

variable levy prevent imports from competing below a certain price. Export subsidies are also available. For a large number of other farm products, no support price or variable levy is provided, and the normal customs duty remains the principal barrier to imports.

The Rome Treaty of 1957, which established the Common Market, did not specify the form of the future farm policy; the decisions that defined this policy were made between 1962 and 1966 and were closely related to progress in the Kennedy Round. The initial decisions, in January 1962, covered grains, pigmeat, eggs, and poultry, but did not include the precise level of unified internal grain prices. Since the ultimate prices would be within the "fork" between the high German prices and the low French prices, however, it was assumed from the outset that there would be a price increase and expanded production for the largest and most efficient Community producer, France. In view of the automatic application of the variable levy, the potential increase of internal production threatened a corresponding decline of imports and caused considerable alarm among outside suppliers.

Within GATT, preliminary discussions of the trade implications of the EEC started in April 1957, the month after the Rome Treaty had been signed. GATT Article XXIV provides for the establishment of a customs union—which by its nature conflicts with the most-favored-nation principle—under two major stipulations: (1) "duties and other restrictive regulations of commerce . . . are eliminated with respect to substantially all the trade between the constituent territories of the union . . ." and (2) "the duties and other regulations of commerce imposed at the institution of such union . . . shall not on the whole be higher or more restrictive than the general incidence of the duties and regulations of commerce applicable prior to the formation of such union. . . ."

GATT member countries entering into a customs union are to present the details of the proposed union to other GATT contracting parties who then examine the plan to see whether it conforms with the rather vague provisions of Article XXIV. Recommendations by non-members that take account of their trade interests can lead to modifications in the customs union proposal. Discussion on the Common Market during 1957 and 1958 centered on the averaging technique for deriving the common external tariff, the lack of a specified agricultural policy, the application of quota restrictions, and the status of associated French-African countries. Debate was most heated over the last point, and in the end GATT adopted a wait-and-see attitude on the impact of the EEC on nonmember trading partners.

The EFTA agreement, signed in November 1959, was examined by a GATT working party in the second half of 1960. Since the EFTA, as a free trade area, did not establish a common external tariff, only the GATT provision that "substantially all the trade" between the members be included was applicable. Although agricultural products were excluded, over 90 percent of total trade within the EFTA was included for duty elimination and this was proffered as "substantially all" trade. Again the GATT contracting parties reserved judgment and requested regular reports on the progress of the free trade area.

By early 1962 the preliminary GATT response to European integration had been made. Despite the official reservations, the de facto acceptance of the EEC and the EFTA was not questioned. By March 1962 both trading blocs had reduced internal tariffs to 60 percent of their most-favored-nation levels, the EEC countries had brought their external rates 30 percent of the way toward their common external tariff, and the EEC's common agricultural policy for the first group of products was scheduled to enter into effect in June. In the Dillon Round, basically concluded also in March 1962,[3] the common external tariff was accepted for almost all industrial products, but the trade provisions of the EEC farm policy, which had been agreed internally in initial form only two months before the close of the GATT conference, were deferred for later negotiation. Pending future talks, the EEC agreed to an interim, standstill arrangement to maintain national import systems on at least as favorable a basis to nonmember countries as then existing for such products as corn, wheat, rice, and poultry.

In addition to establishing the legal procedures for bringing the EEC and the EFTA into conformity with GATT, however, the contracting parties had to deal with the inevitable trade diversion caused by the preferential groupings. The second step in the GATT response to European economic integration therefore was to attempt to mitigate disruptive trade effects through a major multilateral reduction of trade barriers. This was the task of the Kennedy Round. The urgency of the objective depended, of course, on the anticipated trade impact of the

---

3. The United States concluded its negotiations with other participants in March, but because of delays in some other bilateral negotiations, the final protocol was not signed until July 1962.

European blocs. How would the exports of outsiders fare when tariffs were eliminated among members on industrial products? What were the expected trade implications of the common agricultural policy?

Bloc Imports of Manufactured Goods

The impact of the EEC and the EFTA on trade in manufactures can be broken down into two principal components. The first is the price effect on trade patterns resulting from changes in tariff levels. The elimination of tariffs among members of a free trade area is both trade creating—new trade is stimulated between members—and trade diverting—members gain part of the market formerly held by nonmembers. Moreover, for the EEC, a customs union, some tariffs are increased and others reduced as members align their national tariffs to the common external tariff. The second component is the effect of an enlarged free trade market on the level of imports. The incremental growth in national income induced by the incentives and economies of an enlarged free trade market should lead to a higher level of imports from all sources.

Quantitative estimates of these effects are difficult to make and require some rather shaky assumptions. A series of estimates by Lawrence Krause, however, does provide a rough indication of the expected impact of European integration on international trade in manufactures.[4] Krause gives an estimate of the price effect on trade patterns for the EEC and the EFTA based on 1958 trade. He also estimates the additional annual growth in national income as a result of economic integration to be 0.18–0.22 percent for EEC countries and 0.03–0.25 percent for EFTA countries, and converts this to an estimate of increased imports. Table 2–1 presents his estimates of the impact on nonmembers of the trade pattern and income effects. The change in the trade pattern is negative to nonmembers for both the EEC and the EFTA, but relatively larger for the EEC: the estimated loss amounts to 21.9 percent of EEC imports from nonmembers and 14.2 percent of EFTA imports. The rise in imports from the incremental growth of national income, which tends to offset the trade pattern loss, however, is larger for the EEC. The incremental income effect reduces the trade pattern loss by almost 50 percent for the EEC compared to about 30

4. *European Economic Integration and the United States* (Brookings Institution, 1968), Chap. 2.

percent for the EFTA. The net result is an estimated loss of $547 million of exports by nonmembers in the case of the EEC and $597 million in the case of the EFTA. The U.S. share of these losses is $162 million and $77 million, respectively, or 14.4 percent and 9.8 percent of total U.S. exports of manufactures to these groups of countries in 1958.

Table 2–1. Estimated Change in Nonmember Sales of Manufactured Products Due to Changes in Trade Patterns and Income Growth of EEC and EFTA during Transition Periods

In millions of dollars, 1958 prices

Item	Total	United States	EFTA countries	EEC countries	All other countries
Estimated net change in EEC imports	−547	−162	−279	. . .	−106
Due to changes in trade patterns	−975	−273	−485	. . .	−217
Due to increases in income growth	+428	+111	+206	. . .	+111
Estimated net change in EFTA imports	−597	−77	. . .	−378	−142
Due to changes in trade patterns	−828	−108	. . .	−523	−197
Due to increases in income growth	+231	+31	. . .	+145	+55

Source: Lawrence B. Krause, *European Economic Integration and the United States* (Brookings Institution, 1968), pp. 48, 53, 56.

Significantly, these figures indicate that the changes in intra-European trade—although the blocs' losses offset each other—are much greater than the changes in trade with the United States. The net combined effect of the EEC on the EFTA is 1.7 times that on the United States; the net combined effect of the EFTA on the EEC is 4.8 times that on the United States. These ratios reflect the relatively greater magnitudes of intra-European than of transatlantic trade, an important factor during the Kennedy Round negotiations.

The outlook for U.S. exports of manufactures, in sum, was an estimated loss of about 10 percent of its EFTA market and close to 15 percent of its EEC market. The estimated combined loss totaled $239 million. These figures must be viewed, however, in the perspective of rapidly expanding overall trade in the period following 1958. Intrabloc trade as a share of total trade, as expected, rose in both the EEC and the EFTA, but the absolute level of trade more than doubled for most product categories during the next seven years. EEC imports of manufactures from the United States rose by $1,718 million from 1958 to 1965, and EFTA imports from the United States by $1,165 million from 1959 to 1965. Although the determinants of these growth figures are difficult to ascertain, it can at least be said that the estimated trade loss from the formation of the EEC and the EFTA was in the order of 10 percent of the growth in trade over the next few years, and that adjustment was primarily in the rate of growth rather than in displacement of existing markets.

In 1962, however, these growth trends were not so apparent, and there was continuing concern that the rate of trade diversion from regional free trade would accelerate as the differences in internal and external tariffs increased, perhaps with a time lag. And the final changes in rates were not scheduled until 1967 for the EFTA and 1968 for the EEC.

The Common Market and Agricultural Trade

The impact of the Common Market farm policy on international trade was far more difficult to predict, which probably added to the apprehension of exporters. The brunt of the impact was concentrated in particular geographic regions. Denmark was highly dependent on meat and dairy exports to the EEC, but otherwise the EFTA countries had a relatively minor stake in the common agricultural policy, removing the mutual European interest that proved to be a constructive element for Kennedy Round negotiations on industrial trade. The Mediterranean countries were the main suppliers of fruits and vegetables, and the United States, Canada, Argentina, and Australia the principal grain exporters. The tropical developing countries in Africa and Latin America vied for the market in coffee, cocoa, sugar, and bananas.

The United States held the largest and most diversified export interest in farm products, although there was heavy concentration in a few major product groups. As shown in Table 2–2, about 40 percent of U.S. agricultural exports to the Common Market were in variable levy products, and of this over two-thirds was feed grains (in 1966 and 1967). In nonvariable levy commodities, two groups—oilcake and meal, and soybeans—have been growing rapidly, from a total of $70 million in 1958 to $291 million in 1964 and $451 million in 1967. The three large groups—feed grains, oilcake and meal, and soybeans—together increased from about 30 percent of total U.S. farm exports to the Community in 1958–60 to 57–58 percent of the total in 1966–67. Almost the entire growth in farm exports over the period 1958–67 can be attributed to these products.

Table 2–2. U.S. Agricultural Exports to the European Economic Community, Selected Years

In millions of dollars

Commodity	1958	1960	1962	1964	1966	1967
Variable levy						
Feed grains	158	198	317	326	476	374
Wheat grain and flour	79	65	56	61	108	97
Dairy products	13	5	4	54	1	1
Poultry	3	25	50	29	21	17
Other	n.a.	n.a.	56	63	57	59
Subtotal	n.a.	n.a.	483	533	663	548
Nonvariable levy						
Cotton	197	313	106	189	66	72
Fruits and vegetables	69	58	91	85	87	78
Oilcake and meal	8	19	46	77	144	157
Soybeans	62	123	162	214	279	294
Tallow	33	38	26	35	35	25
Tobacco, unmanufactured	90	82	106	106	120	149
Other	n.a.	n.a.	131	177	167	137
Subtotal	n.a.	n.a.	668	883	898	912
Total	822	1,099	1,151	1,416	1,561	1,460

Source: U.S. Department of Agriculture, *Foreign Agricultural Trade of the United States* (October 1964, April 1968); U.S. Bureau of the Census, *U.S. Exports: Commodity by Country*, F.T. 410 (1958, 1960).
n.a. = not available.

This shifting pattern of EEC imports toward concentration in the bulky, basic farm commodities and away from quality, processed products may represent a longer run transition in European agricultural production.[5] It certainly adds to the problem of predicting the effect of the common agricultural policy on future levels of production and

5. The initial decisions for the common agricultural policy do not indicate a conscious policy in this direction; the merits of the concept, however, have long drawn influential support. Curzon discusses it with reference to the work of Wilhelm Röpke (Gerard Curzon, *Multilateral Commercial Diplomacy* [London: Michael Joseph Ltd., 1965], pp. 206–07). The Italian economist Mario Bandini has urged that Europe put "the greatest stress on the development of production of quality products," and import "at the lowest possible price, products which can support the agricultural processing industries" ("Agricoltura Europea e Kennedy Round," *Progresso Agricolo*, May 1966, pp. 3–8).

trade. Projections in fact often center on grains, the bottom layer of the production pyramid, for their price relations with other agricultural products are the least complicated. The anticipated response of farmers to price change—the price elasticity of supply—nevertheless is highly conjectural. How much more (or less) will farmers produce as a result of price changes caused by the adoption of the common agricultural policy (which, among other things, requires deciding what price levels would have prevailed in the absence of the policy)? A number of volatile factors complicate the question of price motivation. Changes in technology—capital equipment, fertilizer, farm size—evolve to a large extent independently of prices. The steady exodus of farmers to urban life, competing uses for arable land,[6] and relative price levels among farm products and between agricultural and nonagricultural products are other factors that prevent simple projections of price related trends.

The target prices for grains adopted by the EEC in December 1964, shown in Table 2–3, result in generally higher French prices and lower

Table 2–3. EEC Basic Target Prices and Import Prices for Grains, 1964 and 1967

In dollars per metric ton, EEC standard quality

Grain	Target price effective July 1964			EEC target price effective July 1, 1967	Most favorable import price 1964 [a]
	Germany	France	Italy		
Soft wheat	118.87	100.22	113.60	106.25	60.86
Durum wheat	—	117.26	143.20	125.00	75.15
Rye	108.13	81.79	—	93.75	60.78
Barley	103.00	83.00	72.22	91.25	58.21
Maize	—	98.32	68.42	90.63	60.01

Source: Krause, European Economic Integration and the United States, p. 92.
a. C.i.f., Rotterdam.

German prices. Krause, discussing the impact of these unified grain prices on the future level of imports, estimates that the common agricultural policy will result in an increment of about three million tons in production, or roughly 30 percent of net imports, by 1970.[7] An im-

6. The price of arable land doubled in France from 1959 to 1965. Nonagricultural users were considered an essential and durable element in this trend. Expansion of urban areas, new industry, tourist facilities, highways, the influx of French *pieds noirs* from Algeria, and land speculation were all mentioned in a study by L'Institut de la statistique, summarized in *Les Echos* (Paris), Jan. 20, 1967. This trend is particularly relevant in light of the major role of land utilization in France for the expansion of EEC grain production.

7. *European Economic Integration and the United States*, pp. 102–07.

portant factor in this evaluation is an estimate by the U.S. Department of Agriculture that France could increase grain acreage by about 17 percent if prices to farmers were increased by over 20 percent.

Prorating the exporter shares of the three million tons requires a distinction between wheat and feed grains. EEC grain imports (see Table 2–4) show a gradually increasing self-sufficiency in wheat but a rising import trend in feed grains. Wheat imports, in fact, are primarily Canadian hard wheat, which is not effectively produced in the Community, while the EEC, and France in particular, has become a normal

Table 2–4. EEC Grain Production and Net Imports, Selected Years

In millions of tons

Grain	1957–60 (average)	1963–64	1964–65	1969–72 (estimated)
Wheat				
Production	24.9	24.3	29.2	30.2
Net imports [a]	1.3	0.6	2.1	0.0
Feed grains				
Production	25.5	24.7	30.3	33.2
Net imports	7.6	10.4	9.4	10.0
Total grains				
Production	50.4	49.0	59.4	63.4
Net imports	8.9	11.0	7.3	10.0
Percentage of needs self-supplied	85	84	87	86

Source: The Common Agricultural Policy (European Community Information Service, July 1967), p. 15.

a. Including flour in grain equivalents.

exporter of soft wheat. The large net import market for feed grains, on the other hand, is dominated by the United States. EEC consumption of wheat and feed grain is affected, however, by the conversion, or "denaturing," of surplus wheat for use as feed.[8] Krause estimates, on the basis of these differences in supplier interests, that the loss to U.S. exports of all grains to the Community by 1970 will be about $65 million per year.

8. The financial loss to the EEC in this transformation is an alternative to the loss incurred through export subsidization. The arithmetic, based on the target and import prices for soft wheat and corn given in Table 2–4, results in a $45.39 export subsidy per ton of soft wheat and a loss of $15.62 (the internal price differential) plus a loss of $30.62 in import levies for corn if the wheat is used for feed. This calculation does not take account of any differential in nutritional content, the distribution of the loss among EEC member states, or the presentational advantage of one form of loss relative to the other.

For commodities other than grains, prediction of the impact of the common agricultural policy is even more difficult. Krause attempts to estimate the loss in total U.S. farm exports for the period 1958 to 1963–64 caused by the Common Market, or more properly by anticipation of the Common Market farm policy. His analysis rests on two tenuous assumptions: money prices to farmers in the six member states, in the absence of the common policy, would have remained stationary (except for a moderate upward adjustment in France), and the price elasticity of supply for the farm sector as a whole is $+0.2$ (for example, a 5 percent increase in price would induce a 1 percent increase in output). From these assumptions Krause estimates a loss to U.S. exports by 1965 of $150–$200 million per year.

These figures are illustrative not only of the possible trade impact of the common agricultural policy but also of the extreme uncertainty inherent in the method of prediction. Krause assesses a total negative impact on U.S. exports of $215–$265 million per year, for example, but two-thirds of this figure is based on highly debatable assumptions about the period prior to 1965.

EEC Decision Making

One other aspect of European integration relevant to the Kennedy Round is the decision-making process in the Common Market.[9] Member governments, represented in the Council of Ministers, reserve the power to decide issues not specifically codified in the Rome Treaty. Under the treaty, decisions were to be based on unanimity until January 1966, at which time qualified majority voting would be instituted. France, however, challenged this transition during the Community crisis in the second half of 1965 and the status of ministerial voting has been unsettled since then. France maintains the right of veto when very important interests are at stake, while the other five members stand by the Rome Treaty. So far this disagreement has not been tested and the prevailing attitude is to avoid a confrontation.

The executive functions of the Community are carried out by the EEC Commission, which is not directly responsible to member governments. The Commission, among other things, has the power to make proposals

9. The EFTA countries negotiated individually in the Kennedy Round. The Nordics, at a later point, did function as a unified negotiating group, but not as an official EFTA organization.

for consideration by the Council and to represent the Community in negotiations with other countries. The European Parliament and the Court of Justice, also part of the institutional structure, had no significant role in the Kennedy Round. Since July of 1967 the European Coal and Steel Community (ECSC) and the European Atomic Energy Community (Euratom) have merged jurisdictions with the EEC.[10]

For the Kennedy Round, the Council first had to reach unanimous agreement on a mandate within which the Commission would negotiate on behalf of the Community at Geneva. The Council was assisted by the "111 committee" composed of lower level, member state representatives with special expertise in trade matters. This committee often handled technical matters and prepared the dossiers for use at ministerial meetings. The 111 committee worked closely with the Commission, and for short periods of time, especially toward the end of the negotiation, at Geneva. At formal Kennedy Round meetings, representatives of member states were usually present as observers although the negotiations were conducted by representatives of the Commission.

Commission responsibility for the Kennedy Round rested with Jean Rey, commissioner in charge of foreign affairs, although Commissioner Sicco Mansholt retained his primary role in the agricultural sector. Until the final six months of the negotiation, however, negotiations were conducted at Geneva by the Commission's chief trade negotiator, Theodorus Hijzen, supported by a technical staff of commodity and area specialists.

EEC decision making is an interplay between Council and Commission. The divergence of member state interests has led to grouping of Council decisions to form a balanced package of benefits and concessions. The Commission often acts as honest broker in developing these packages and has been particularly successful in balancing member state interests so as to make maximum progress toward consolidating the Community structure. On several occasions the Council, in its first confrontation with a problem, has merely agreed on a deadline for specific decisions, leaving the Commission to work out compromise proposals during the interim. Although this procedure has generally been effective, it was the route that led to the French boycott of the

10. The ECSC and the Euratom maintained separate jurisdictions for their respective industries during the Kennedy Round. Throughout this account, however, the term EEC is normally used to mean the appropriate representatives of the six countries.

Community from July 1965 to January 1966. Considering the subsequent confrontation over majority voting in the Council, however, the role of the Commission was only one factor, and probably not the major factor, in that crisis.

The basic decision facing the Council of Ministers in the Kennedy Round was how precise a mandate to give to the Commission negotiators. The desire of the French to keep the Commission closely in check dictated a preference for rigid, narrowly defined mandates. The difficulty with this approach, however, was that Council decisions—debated at length and taken at meetings attended by large numbers of people—quickly became public knowledge. It was virtually impossible to maintain security at Brussels (a consideration aggravated by the widely held belief that the Americans, in particular, had ready access to Community information). As a consequence of rigid, publicly known mandates, the Community spokesmen at Geneva could not effectively negotiate, and became primarily conveyors of messages to and from Brussels; moreover, the forehand knowledge of Community positions eliminated the leverage of uncertainty—the maximum offer, once known, immediately became the minimum offer. The problem for the Council of Ministers was to reconcile the need for secrecy of negotiating positions with a reasonable limitation on Commission powers.

CHAPTER THREE

A Bold New Program: The Trade Expansion Act

THE MOST URGENT economic problem facing President Kennedy when he took office was recession in the domestic economy. By February 1961 the rate of unemployment had reached 8 percent of the labor force. The need to get the nation moving again had been a central theme of the election campaign, including a campaign promise of a 5 percent annual growth in national income, and the President's first economic message to the Congress on February 2, 1961, was primarily directed to this end.[1] A second economic problem that weighed heavily on the President was the balance-of-payments deficit. The net outflow of dollars, welcomed during the early 1950s as an offset to dollar shortages abroad, had accelerated sharply from 1958 to 1960, reaching close to $4 billion in the latter year. President Kennedy was highly sensitive to the steady decline in U.S. gold reserves, partly out of concern for charges of fiscal irresponsibility by the heavy conservative ranks in Congress, partly because "it's a club that De Gaulle and all the others hang over my head."[2] In contrast, trade policy, though related to these pressing problems, was in a period of gestation during most of 1961.

Interim Period for Trade Policy

The principal trade issue in 1961 was the impact of the Common Market. The matter was discussed at Geneva in the Dillon Round of

1. See Arthur M. Schlesinger, Jr., *A Thousand Days* (Houghton Mifflin, 1965), Chap. 23, and Theodore C. Sorensen, *Kennedy* (Harper & Row, 1965), Chap. 16. According to Schlesinger, Kennedy's first question when he was introduced to Walter Heller during the election campaign was, "Do you really think we can make good on the promise . . . of a 5 per cent rate of growth?" (*A Thousand Days*, p. 626).
2. Sorensen, *Kennedy*, p. 408.

talks on the General Agreement on Tariffs and Trade (the round was named for the principal U.S. negotiator, Under Secretary of State Douglas Dillon). U.S. participation in the negotiation ran from September 1960 to March 1962, thus bridging the transition of administrations in the United States. The overriding concern with the Common Market was evident in the summary press release issued by the White House to announce the results of the negotiations: "The commercial importance of the negotiations was matched by their political significance, since they constituted the first test of whether the United States and the European Economic Community . . . would be able to find a mutual basis for the long-run development of economic relations critical to both areas." The entire summary was devoted to the European Economic Community (EEC) except for an alphabetical listing of other participants at the end. The term "less developed country" did not appear.[3]

The Dillon Round, however, was never destined for great accomplishment. The first phase of the talks, from September 1960 to May 1961, was essentially a negotiation of the balance of tariff commitments resulting from changes the EEC had made in forming its common external tariff. It had been scheduled to end four months earlier, but difficult haggling dragged on until the Common Market made concessions adequate to the other GATT parties. The second phase of the Dillon Round was a multilateral reduction of tariffs by all participants similar to previous GATT rounds. The Common Market initially offered a flat 20 percent cut in its common external tariff, subject to reciprocity. United States negotiating authority to reduce tariffs by 20 percent was severely limited, however, by the peril point procedure, under which the U.S. Tariff Commission recommended limits on duty reductions in order to prevent serious injury to domestic industry. The U.S. offer, because of this limitation, fell far short of the 20 percent across-the-board figure, and a massive pullback of offers by others was saved in the last minute when President Kennedy, "at his peril," authorized the American delegation to go beyond the peril points on $76 million of U.S. imports. Nevertheless, the average reduction in industrial tariffs was only about 10 percent for the EEC and slightly less for the United States. Less yet was achieved for agricultural products because the basic form of the Community agricultural policy was not

3. Press release, White House, March 7, 1962.

decided until shortly before the close of the Geneva negotiations. Though the Dillon Round's gains were only modest, it did establish the basis for a mutual reduction of trade barriers between the Common Market and the United States, and maintained a forward momentum for subsequent negotiations.

Another major event affecting trade during 1961 was the United Kingdom decision, announced on July 31, to apply for membership in the Common Market. This initiative was welcomed by the United States for its political significance, in contrast to the somewhat cool reception of the commercially motivated European Free Trade Association (EFTA) agreement two years earlier. The words of Prime Minister Macmillan, in his opening speech before parliament on August 2, could hardly have been more appropriate for the Washington audience: it was better to "play our role to the full and use the influence we have for the development of the life and thought of Europe . . . our right place is in the vanguard of the movement towards the greater unity of the free world, and that we can lead better from within than outside." [4] The prospect of the United Kingdom and other EFTA countries joining the preferential Common Market, however, increased the urgency for the United States to act to forestall adverse effects on its commerce from European integration.

A final important event in commercial diplomacy during 1961 was the GATT ministerial meeting at Geneva from November 27 to 30. This meeting culminated the program for the expansion of international trade inaugurated at a ministerial meeting in November 1958. Special reports and committee preparation had in the interim been completed and digested by the representatives of the contracting parties, and the Dillon Round, nearing its unspectacular conclusion, confirmed to the ministers the need for a fresh GATT program. The agreed conclusions of November 30, 1961, therefore, focused on three principal fields of action: [5] The ministers requested the contracting parties to work out negotiating procedures "for the creation of acceptable conditions of access to world markets for agricultural products," and established a special group to study the problems of trade in grains. The ministers also agreed that immediate steps should be taken to establish programs

---

4. Quoted in Miriam Camps, *Britain and the European Community, 1955–1963* (Princeton University Press, 1964), p. 359.

5. See press release, General Agreement on Tariffs and Trade (GATT), Nov. 30, 1961; it includes quotes in this and the following paragraph.

of action, and target terminal dates, "for progressive reduction and elimination of barriers to the exports of less-developed countries." Industrial countries, in addition, adopted "a sympathetic attitude on the question of reciprocity" for developing countries—later translated into the principle of nonreciprocity.

The most significant step taken by the ministers, however, pertained to the method of negotiating tariff reductions on industrial products. The item-by-item reductions used "both in the past and during the present [Dillon Round] tariff conference . . . were no longer adequate to meet the changing conditions of world trade." The ministers therefore agreed that consideration should be given "to the adoption of new techniques, in particular some form of linear tariff reduction." This approach was recommended for prompt examination with the recognition that "in working out new procedures, such as linear tariff reductions or specific programmes of phased reduction over a period of years, full account would have to be taken of the differing characteristics of the trade, tariff levels and economic structure of contracting parties which arose for countries exporting only a few commodities."

The desirability of automatic rules for reducing tariffs had long been recognized.[6] The prevailing method of picking individual items of trade interest to particular pairs of countries tended to result in a lowest common denominator of achievement. In particular, the major export products of countries with little bargaining leverage—such as small European countries with already low tariffs, or developing countries generally—were apt to be ignored. The first GATT attempt to lower tariffs in a comprehensive way was the so-called French plan of 1951, sponsored by French Minister of Commerce Pierre Pflimlin. This plan called for an *average* 30 percent reduction of tariffs in each industry grouping, but the lack of authority by the United States to proceed on this basis, plus some statistical complications in the plan's application, resulted in a quiet shelving of the proposal. Linear tariff reductions among members of the EEC and the EFTA revived interest in an automatic approach to tariff cuts and the EEC offer in the Dillon Round of

6. The U.S. Tariff Commission warned in 1933, "It must be remembered that tariffs are so complicated that multilateral bargaining on individual articles must be regarded as impossible; no multilateral bargaining can be envisaged unless the nations can agree on some simple formula applicable to all tariffs" (*Tariff Bargaining Under Most Favored Nation Treaties*, p. 3).

a flat 20 percent reduction on all products demonstrated that linear cuts could be a practical course in GATT if only other countries, and particularly the United States, were able to make comparable offers.

Of particular significance, in light of the later disagreement over harmonization and disparities, was the strong endorsement of linear tariff cuts given by representatives of the EEC at the November 1961 GATT meeting. German Secretary of State in the Ministry of Economics Ludgar Westrik, as spokesman for the Six, stated: "As the Community sees it, substantial progress towards the reduction of tariff barriers will in the future be achieved only by the method of linear reduction. The integration programmes now being operated [that is, the EEC and the EFTA] have, moreover, shown that by this method the very understandable resistance of those whose interests are affected can be overcome and the particularly high customs duties which, for various reasons, have so far not felt the effects of GATT action can also be reduced."[7] Tariff disparities were not specifically mentioned in the statement and, in fact, the comment about high tariffs was the substance of the later American position that linear reduction is the only practical way to include substantial cuts for sensitive high tariff industries.

The general caveat in the GATT resolution about "differing characteristics" in "tariff levels" certainly permitted the issue of tariff disparities to be raised, along with many other possible problems, at a later point. But the overwhelming endorsement of the linear approach by all major countries as the backbone of the next effort to reduce tariffs was unquestionable—at least to the members of the U.S. delegation headed by Under Secretary of State George Ball.

7. Press release no. 635, GATT, Nov. 27, 1961. Similar statements were made by other Community representatives. Jean Rey stated: "We have found that, if we are to achieve a really substantial reduction in tariffs, we must follow the linear method.... I think that this meeting should not adjourn without deciding that all the governments represented here should be urged to equip themselves at home with the political, legislative, and administrative weapons that will enable them to take part next time in negotiations for reducing tariffs not on a product-by-product but on a linear basis." French Minister of Finance and Economic Affairs Wilfred Baumgartner stated: "I agree with Mr. Ball ... that automatic linear reductions, jointly agreed upon, can give good results.... The experience recently gained in this matter by the EEC and the EFTA shows that linear reductions are practical and effective. I would, therefore, fully agree that, without entirely excluding tariff negotiations of the traditional type, we should embark on linear reductions made by stages and adapted to the structure of various tariffs." (Press releases nos. 644 and 633, GATT, Nov. 27, 1961.)

Kennedy's Trade Policy

Toward the close of 1961, President Kennedy was finally faced with a major decision on trade policy. In fact, there were two decisions, one of substance and the other of timing. The substantive question was whether the administration should seek an amended extension of the existing legislation or, in light of new circumstances, respond with a completely revised program. As for the timing, the existing trade agreements act would expire the following June, and the question was whether to submit trade legislation to the second session of Congress in 1962, or to let executive authority lapse until the new Congress convened in 1963, when the situation between the Common Market and the United Kingdom, in particular, would have become more definite.

These questions had been under discussion throughout the year. One group of advisers, loosely associated with the veterans of past negotiations, and representing the normal measure of inertia within the policy machine, advocated an extension of negotiating authority within the framework of the existing act. In contrast, a preinaugural task force under the direction of George Ball had recommended a bold new trade program keyed to the challenge of the Common Market, and Ball's subsequent appointment as under secretary of state for economic affairs strengthened the hand of the innovators. Special White House adviser Howard Petersen (after some initial wavering) and his deputy Myer Rashish—who had been secretary to the Ball task force—also pressed for a new approach.

A difference of view between the Petersen office and George Ball developed, however, over the issue of when to submit new legislation to Congress. The former preferred a prompt approach to Congress in 1962, with the convincing arguments that an early American initiative was desirable and that a considerable time lag would be incurred in any event to get legislation through Congress and to hold preliminary discussions for a major international conference. Ball, on the other hand, initially preferred postponing action until 1963, not only to avoid a controversial trade bill during election year, but in deference to the United Kingdom bid for membership in the Common Market. The Labor party was giving tentative support to Macmillan's effort, in good part because earlier negotiations for a broader free trade area had failed. If the United States now offered an attractive alternate to Common Market membership in the form of an ambitious GATT negotiation, it might undercut Macmillan's narrow margin of support.

President Kennedy was not a fundamentalist on liberal trade. His textile program, for example, not only reflected a sympathy for his former Massachusetts constituency, but a political sense of avoiding head-on collision with a powerful protectionist group. He was primarily concerned with the political importance of world trade, and a program oriented to a strengthening of the Atlantic community had great appeal for him. Kennedy also realized that a trade bill related to broad foreign policy objectives would be more palatable for Congress. It was not surprising, therefore, that he finally decided on the Ball approach for a bold new program. It was equally in character that the President chose to take an early initiative in 1962 rather than to risk allowing events to pass him by.

The critical point was reached on November 1, 1961. Two strong appeals were made that day for a far-reaching new trade program. The first was a statement to the foreign economic policy subcommittee of the Joint Economic Committee by former Secretary of State Christian Herter and William Clayton, an early administrator of the trade agreements program. They described the broad sweep of current events, including the increasing interdependence of nations, the role of technology, and the world population eruption, and concluded that "the Trade Agreements Act as it stands today is hopelessly inadequate. . . ." In its place they recommended that "the United States open negotiations, as soon as practicable, for a trade partnership with the European Common Market, at the same time stressing the absolute necessity of enlarging that area." The second statement was a speech by George Ball before the National Foreign Trade Convention at New York. Ball opened with the warning that "pervasive change will be the dominant characteristic of the years that lie ahead." He described the polarization of the American and European industrial markets: "What we may well see emerge is the concentration of nearly 90 percent of total Free World exports of industrial products in two great Common Markets—the Common Market of Europe consisting of over 300 million people and an as yet undetermined number of states, and the Common Market of the United States. . . . And each of these areas will be surrounded by a common external tariff." As for the road ahead, Ball did not outline specific proposals, but suggested "certain minimum specifications," including the recognition that "the process of tariff reduction involves the acceptance of some degree of structural adjustment by individual industries" for which "the Federal Government will provide assistance to speed the transfer . . ." and the fact that "we can no longer afford to limit our negotiators to trading on an item-by-item basis. . . . The Common Market countries cannot conduct their negotiations on any basis other than across-the-board cuts."

The Ball speech was a trial balloon to test public reaction to a new trade initiative and the results were dominantly favorable. President Kennedy joined the appeal at a November 8 press conference. He warned that the United States must be in a position to negotiate for its own interests in the face of the major challenge of the Common Market, and "the time to begin is now." On November 29 the President announced that a tentative decision had been made to seek wide tariff-cutting authority, and on December 6 and 7 he made strong presentations to the National Association of Manufacturers in New York and to the AFL-CIO convention at Bal Harbour, Florida. The manufacturers were surprisingly receptive to the President's appeal, although no firm commitment was made, while George Meany gave unqualified support from the labor group.

The final decision was made in mid-December. The British did not oppose an early American move in the trade field and, with no strong doubts from his congressional advisers over the prospects for passage, the President decided to put his new program before the Congress in January 1962.

The official announcement came in the State of the Union message: "We need a new law—a wholly new approach—a bold new instrument of American trade policy." The text of the Trade Expansion Act was submitted to Congress on January 25 accompanied by a cogent analysis of recent world developments.[8] The *Guardian* commented, "The challenge of the Common Market has never been explained to the British people with anything like the clarity and imagination of President Kennedy's recent statements."[9] Kennedy's message to Congress identified "five fundamentally new and sweeping developments [which] have made obsolete our traditional trade policy": (1) growth of the European Common Market, (2) growing pressure on the balance of payments, (3) need to accelerate growth, (4) communist aid and trade

8. See Appendix B.
9. *Guardian* (Manchester), Feb. 1, 1962.

offensive, and (5) need for new markets for Japan and the developing countries. These developments were then related to various objectives of U.S. domestic and foreign policy, and the message concluded with the ringing appeal: "At rare moments in the life of this nation an opportunity comes along to fashion out of the confusion of current events a clear and bold action to show the world what it is we stand for. Such an opportunity is before us now. This bill, by enabling us to strike a bargain with the Common Market, will 'strike a blow' for freedom."

Scope of the Act

The substance of the Trade Expansion Act can be conveniently divided into three parts: tariff-cutting authority, safeguards for domestic industries and labor, and the structure of executive authority for carrying out trade negotiations with other countries.[10]

The basic tariff cutting authority permitted up to 50 percent reductions across the board for all tariff positions except those on a small number of products previously subject to escape clause action and on products where tariff reduction would threaten to impair the national security. Low duties of 5 percent or less could be eliminated entirely. Reductions were to be made on a most-favored-nation basis and staged in five annual instalments (or over a period of four years and a day). Negotiating authority was granted to the President for a five-year period through June 30, 1967.

An additional set of tariff cutting provisions was directly linked to the European Economic Community. The most far-reaching, as it was originally conceived in the Petersen office, was the authority to eliminate tariffs completely on product groups where the United States and the EEC together accounted for at least 80 percent of world exports. In addition, duty elimination was permitted for agricultural commodities under certain conditions and for tropical products not produced in significant quantities in the United States. Action on tropical products required comparable action by the EEC.

All authority was, of course, permissive and dependent on reciprocal

10. See *Trade Expansion Act of 1962*, H. Rept. 11970, 87 Cong. 2 sess. (1962). For an analysis of the act, see Stanley D. Metzger, *Trade Agreements and the Kennedy Round* (Fairfax, Va.: Coiner Publications Ltd., 1964).

reductions in trade barriers affecting U.S. exports.[11] To give added bargaining leverage to U.S. negotiators, an amendment introduced by Senator Paul Douglas authorized the President to suspend or withdraw previous concessions. In order to gain the support of the American Farm Bureau Federation, the largest farm organization, the section on foreign import restrictions was amended to make obvious reference to the community agricultural policy: "Whenever a foreign country or instrumentality the products of which receive benefits of trade agreement concessions made by the United States . . . maintains non-tariff trade restrictions, including variable import fees, which substantially burden United States commerce . . . the President shall, to the extent that such action is consistent with the purposes of section 102 . . . suspend, withdraw, or prevent the application . . . or refrain from proclaiming benefits of trade agreement concessions to . . . such country or instrumentality." [12] The reference to the general purposes of the act in section 102 made this provision a stern warning rather than a compelling restriction on presidential authority.

A radical innovation of the Trade Expansion Act was the provision for adjustment assistance to domestic firms and workers that suffered or were threatened with serious injury as a result of increased imports caused by tariff reductions. This provision recognized that a lowering of trade barriers could upset the existing industry structure and accepted government responsibility for assistance in such cases. Prior to 1962, the United States maintained an escape clause to raise tariffs or impose quotas if domestic industry were injured, and although implemented sparingly, this procedure bred mistrust abroad of the American commitment to a liberal trade policy. The Trade Expansion Act retained the escape clause as an alternative, but in addition provided for adjustment assistance in the form of financial aid and low interest loans to help firms shift into new lines of production, and unemployment and retraining payments to the workers affected.

Another significant change in the procedure for safeguarding domestic interests was a revision in the Tariff Commission's advisory role. Instead of establishing a peril point for each commodity, the commis-

---

11. The wording of the act regarding reciprocity, "affording mutual trade benefits" (sec. 102), was quite vague, but the U.S. negotiators interpreted reciprocity in a very strict way in keeping with past practices, congressional expectations, and the general bargaining atmosphere at Geneva.

12. *Trade Expansion Act of 1962*, H.R. 11970, sec. 252. See also Metzger, *Trade Agreements and the Kennedy Round*, pp. 30–37.

sion would advise the President as to the probable economic effect of tariff reductions. This change was a recognition that precise peril points in the tariff, below which industry is threatened with substantial injury, are based in good part on subjective evaluation. The evaluation becomes even more complex in the context of across-the-board tariff reductions at home and abroad.

Finally, the structure of executive authority for conducting trade negotiations was substantially modified by the Trade Expansion Act. To alleviate concern that the State Department, which had primary responsibility for the trade agreements program, was unduly influenced by the foreign policy aspects of trade, the new act created the position of special representative for trade negotiations, responsible directly to the President. The special representative would seek advice and information from representatives of industry, agriculture, labor, and appropriate government agencies, and would supervise preparation of negotiating positions. For the first time, members of Congress were to be accredited as members of the U.S. delegation. Two members (not of the same political party) of both the House Ways and Means Committee and the Senate Finance Committee were to be selected for this purpose.

Response to the New Program

President Kennedy's imaginative new trade program, stressing America's role in world affairs, was in many respects a stroke of politi cal genius. It mobilized widespread support and relegated much of the traditional hassle between protectionists and free traders to secondary position. The Kennedy initiative was a belated articulation of the fact that foreign economic policy is a potent element of American free world leadership. And the assertion of strong leadership in this area struck a highly responsive chord throughout the nation.

The campaign for passage of the act was energetic and well organized. The administration anticipated a tough fight. Howard Petersen of the White House staff, with massive help from the Commerce and State departments in particular, conducted a saturation campaign, using flashy trade promotion literature that included separate brochures for each state. Strong support was received from the independent Committee for a National Trade Policy headed by Carl J. Gilbert. Exhaustive Cabinet level testimony before the House Ways and Means Committee and the Senate Finance Committee was led by Secretary of Commerce

Luther Hodges, backed up by Under Secretary of State George Ball, Secretary of Labor Arthur Goldberg, Secretary of the Treasury Douglas Dillon, and Secretary of Agriculture Orville Freeman. In May, President Kennedy and four Cabinet members participated in a one-day conference of twelve hundred people from one hundred organizations sponsoring the Trade Expansion Act. On May 4 in New Orleans President Kennedy first uttered his "trade or fade" warning. The beleaguered opposition came back with "prevent ghost job conditions."

The Trade Expansion Act became the centerpiece of the 1962 legislative program. There was feeling in some parts of the administration that it was oversold, not only to the detriment of domestic programs, but relative to the expectations of what would eventually be accomplished from international negotiation.[13] Voices outside the administration were also raised to protest the hard sell. Oscar Gass in the *New Republic,* under the title "The Crusade for Trade," lamented "the dish is being wildly over-advertised." The statement that really provoked Gass came from a George Ball speech: "In the long run, unity among free nations cannot be assured by force, by psychological strategy, or even by diplomacy. Unity will ultimately depend upon the development of a real community of interests—involving all of the varied activities and aspirations of man. Trade is the warp and woof of such a community."[14]

One aspect of the trade act that was imprudently oversold was its relation to the U.S. balance-of-payments deficit. A reciprocal reduction of trade barriers would provide the opportunity for the United States to strengthen its balance-of-payments position, especially in view of its consistently substantial trade surplus. But it was not possible to forecast an immediate gain in the trade balance from an anticipated GATT negotiation based on reciprocity, no matter how that term might be defined. Luther Hodges was careful to maintain this distinction during his congressional testimony: "The Trade Expansion Act will open the doors of opportunity for us to achieve a higher export surplus . . . but neither it, nor any other legislation or tariff negotiating authority can offer immediate short-run solutions to this issue."[15]

13. See Schlesinger, *A Thousand Days,* p. 847.

14. Because of a last minute change, the speech was actually delivered by Under Secretary of State for Political Affairs George McGhee before the Associated Business Publications Forum on Jan. 31, 1962. See *New Republic,* March 19 and 26, 1962.

15. *Trade Expansion Act of 1962,* Hearings before the House Committee on Ways and Means, 87 Cong. 2 sess. (1962), pp. 63–64.

Secretary of the Treasury Dillon, however, went considerably further: "Thus we have a favorable basis for enlargement of our trade surplus through reciprocal reductions of tariffs. . . . If tariffs on our exports and imports are reduced to a comparable extent, the neutral assumption would be that exports and imports would rise by the same percentage. As a result, the American trade surplus would become larger. . . . Conditions now evident, and likely to persist for a number of years, make it more likely, however, that American exports to Western Europe would rise by a greater percentage than the exports of Western European countries to the United States. . . ." [16]

The difficulty that these assertions, largely subjective in any event, might later create for the U.S. negotiators at Geneva was clear to many. At the end of the Dillon testimony, Representative Eugene J. Keogh of New York asked, "Is it not difficult, if not impossible, and also is it not unwise, for us to give advance notice of the strategy or the techniques of negotiation, that we might have even with friendly allies?" [17] Persistently troubled with the dollar outflow, however, President Kennedy became one of the most insistent advocates of hooking the Trade Expansion Act to the balance of payments. When he was warned of the substantive and tactical reasons for avoiding a direct connection, he would answer, "Yes, I get it, I get it." But on the next occasion he was apt to bring the subject up again in much the same way.

The most controversial issue of the Trade Expansion Act, as it turned out, was the special authority to eliminate tariffs when the United States and the Common Market accounted for 80 percent of world exports. The purpose of this provision, in addition to helping to bring together the "two great Common Markets" across the Atlantic, was to give the United States maximum flexibility in responding to developments in Europe and it was not necessarily anticipated that the authority would be fully implemented or even offered. The provision also added to the image of the act as a bold response to the Common Market.[18] But while the form of the authority was appealing in some ways, it was open to criticism on several counts. Many European supporters of the

16. *Ibid.*, p. 818.
17. *Ibid.*, p. 821.
18. Metzger comments: "The special authority's principal function was always, in the view of many, more optical in terms of the political presentation of a 'new program' than real in terms of being used to bring discrimination down to the point where it would be of minor significance as a deterrent to American exports." (*Trade Agreements and the Kennedy Round*, p. 27; see also p. 101.)

Common Market viewed it as a mortal threat to the cohesion of the common external tariff, a Trojan horse for attempting the free trade area approach that had earlier been refused to the British. The strong net export position of the United States in products covered by this authority increased the suspicion of U.S. motives.[19] The provision also faced some U.S. industries with the prospect of complete loss of protection, strengthening the pockets of opposition. And the process of singling out trade sectors of primary importance to the industrial countries supported the contention of developing countries that the GATT nondiscrimination approach to the reduction of trade barriers contained de facto discrimination against products that were of major export interest to the developing countries.

The major public debate over the 80 percent authority was, however, on the geographic composition for calculating the 80 percent. The administration proposal, strongly defended by George Ball, was that the 80 percent be restricted to the United States plus the EEC. Under these circumstances, only two unpropitious categories of products, aircraft and margarine, would have qualified unless the United Kingdom became a member of the Common Market. While this procedure prevented the Labor party from using the 80 percent authority as an alternative to Common Market membership, it was also a form of pressure by the United States on the course of the negotiation between the United Kingdom and the EEC. An amendment sponsored by Representative Henry Reuss and Senator Paul Douglas, in contrast, included EFTA trade in the calculation of the 80 percent minimum. The amendment, despite administration opposition, was passed by the Senate but later dropped in conference between the two houses of Congress. The De Gaulle veto of British entry in January 1963, perhaps in a minor way aggravated by this form of United States pressure for British membership, therefore nullified the substance of the novel 80 percent authority as well.

The campaign for passage of the act was on the whole more successful than had been anticipated. Industry generally supported the bill, with notable exceptions in the textile and chemical industries. Opposi-

19. Secretary Hodges testified that U.S. exports of products that would qualify under the 80 percent authority totaled $8.8 billion versus $1.8 billion of U.S. imports. United States trade with Western Europe was $2.1 billion in exports, $1.2 billion in imports. His figures included the United Kingdom and several other EFTA countries. *Trade Expansion Act of 1962*, House hearings, p. 97.

tion had been softened through earlier actions by the President. The GATT Long-Term Arrangement Regarding International Trade in Cotton Textiles, negotiated during 1961 as part of the President's textile program, effectively curtailed imports of these products, particularly from Japan and Hong Kong, and on March 17, 1962, President Kennedy announced substantial escape clause tariff increases on Wilton carpets and flat glass.[20] The adjustment assistance provision came closest to being lost. It was opposed by those against federal assistance to firms and workers and by those who considered it a vehicle for greater tariff reduction. The president of Du Pont, Crawford H. Greenewalt, stated quite plainly that it would "provide an undesirable cushion for unskillful negotiations." [21] The adjustment assistance provision squeaked by the House Ways and Means Committee by a vote of 13 to 12. In the final vote, however, the act received broad bipartisan support. It passed the House by 298–125 on June 28, and the Senate by 78–8 on September 19, and was signed into law by President Kennedy on October 11, 1962.

Foreign Reaction to the Act

The signing of the act was generally well received abroad, especially because of the linear tariff-cutting authority and the adjustment assistance alternative to the unpopular escape clause. But the support was qualified. The 80 percent authority continued to be suspect, and its uneven trade coverage had been quickly picked up in the European press.[22] A more comprehensive wariness of the American initiative appeared in the French press during the fall of 1962. Pierre Drouin in *Le Monde* on September 26 described the success of the "new deal" in American commercial policy, but then, citing President Kennedy on the U.S. export surplus and the anticipated trade advantages to the

20. The action on carpets and glass, while easing domestic opposition to the proposed act, caused a sharp reaction in Europe, especially by Belgium, the principal exporter of these products. Coming only ten days after the completion of the Dillon Round negotiations, it was called by Belgian Trade Minister Maurice Brasseur a political blunder that risked compromising past and future trade agreements (*New York Times*, March 31, 1962). The EEC quickly retaliated by raising tariffs on roughly comparable amounts of U.S. exports of five other products.

21. *Trade Expansion Act of 1962*, Hearings before the Senate Committee on Finance, 87 Cong. 2 sess. (1962), Pt. 3, p. 1273.

22. See *Economist*, March 24, 1962, p. 1094, which cites the figures from Secretary Hodges' testimony.

United States, concluded, "It will be necessary now to be extremely vigilant." A detailed discussion of tariff structure and disparities was included. On October 31, French Minister of Industry Maurice Bokanowski, around whom protectionist interests rallied, went a step further: "The Trade Expansion Act, which was just passed by Congress, means in the immediate future for France, and undoubtedly for certain other European countries, sacrifices and risks that it would be well to limit. If not there will be grave peril of diluting in a generalized free trade world the preference accorded to each other by members of the EEC." [23]

The United States, for its part, was quick to follow up passage of the act with a recommendation to GATT, submitted jointly with Canada, that a ministerial meeting be convened in early 1963. President Kennedy emphasized the priority he was giving to trade matters with the nomination, in November, of Christian A. Herter as his choice for special trade representative. Governor Herter was highly respected at home and abroad and, because he was a prominent Republican, his appointment underlined the bipartisan support for the new trade negotiation.

A GATT working party was established in December 1962 to prepare for the requested ministerial meeting, with the decisions of the November 1961 GATT meeting, including the linear approach to tariff cuts, as the terms of reference. It was about this time that the EEC, in direct conversations with the United States, made clear that linear cuts related to the Trade Expansion Act would involve difficult problems, especially in regard to some very high U.S. tariff rates. In view of the EEC's strong earlier endorsement of linear reductions, this warning was at first considered of minor importance by the Americans. In preceding months, however, a mutual misunderstanding had developed, in part because of insufficient consultation. Once the American administration had decided to submit the Trade Expansion Act to Congress in late 1961, all energies had turned to the domestic campaign and little attention was given to reactions abroad. The 80 percent authority, for example, came as an unexpected surprise to the Europeans. The Common Market in the meantime was developing its position on tariff disparities, and in August 1962 completed a rather detailed elaboration of the problem that concluded, "It is clear that a simple linear reduction

23. *Le Monde* (Paris), Oct. 31, 1962.

will lead to concessions of unequal value." [24] This evolution of the EEC position from the general endorsement of some form of linear reduction at the November 1961 GATT meeting to a strong reservation on linear cuts because of tariff disparities did not become clear until late 1962, after the passage of the Trade Expansion Act and the Kennedy administration's deep commitment to multilateral tariff cuts based on a simple linear reduction.

The GATT working party nevertheless got off to an apparently good start in January 1963. Discussion centered on the means for adapting linear tariff cuts to the diversity of national trade structures, although the EEC Commission wished to study further the problem of "peaks and lows" in the tariff structure. In late February, Eric Wyndham White announced agreement for a ministerial level meeting in May, and added that there is "good prospect that ministers would be able to set sights on a target of 50 percent across-the-board reductions on a wide variety of goods." [25] The British, especially after the De Gaulle rebuff on January 14, solidly supported, along with other EFTA countries,[26] a 50 percent linear reduction. Japan also accepted this approach conditioned upon action to end discrimination against Japanese exports.

By March, however, the position of the Community had stiffened considerably over the disparity issue. There was some basis for complaint,[27] and the Community intended to press its point. But it now appeared that the French had picked up this issue as a means of limiting the scope of the May conference or even undermining it completely. Another working party meeting in March again deliberated on a linear approach although differences over the disparity issue remained unresolved. Then, in mid-April, the EEC informed its trading partners that instead of the linear approach to tariff cuts it would put forward a

---

24. *Premières Etudes sur le "Trade Expansion Act"* (Communauté Economique Européenne, Directions Générales, Aug. 31, 1962), p. 29.

25. At a press conference quoted in the *Washington Post*, Feb. 22, 1963.

26. EFTA, as used in the context of the Kennedy Round negotiations, excludes Portugal, which participated under different rules as a nonindustrialized country.

27. As another example of how the need to sell Congress and the public on the merits of the Trade Expansion Act could later haunt U.S. negotiators at Geneva, the disparity issue also found its place in the congressional hearings. George Ball pointed out, while describing how well U.S. negotiators had defended American interests in the past, "There are about 900 items on which we levy a duty of 30% or more. Products covered by such high rates are largely excluded from the American market.... Whereas, over one-sixth of the rates in the U.S. tariff are above 30%, less than one-fiftieth of Europe's rates run over 30%" (*Trade Expansion Act of 1962*, House Hearings, pp. 639–40).

plan of tariff harmonization, or *écrêtement*, at the ministerial meeting in May.

The stage was thus set for a full-dress confrontation. The United States, through the Trade Expansion Act, had armed itself well for the subsequent bargaining of commercial interests although events in the winter and spring of 1963 had cast a shadow over earlier optimism. George Ball told the American Society of Newspaper Editors in mid-April: "While these last few weeks have been periods when it has been useful . . . for all of us to take a look at problems confronting us . . . we still have the same compelling reasons for trying to work out effective institutional arrangements under which the industrialized powers on the two sides of the Atlantic can work in a common effort toward the protection of the free world and to assure the survival of the common ideals which we share." On a less idealistic plane, the London *Times*, shortly before the ministerial meeting, observed, "Nothing shows the perversity of human affairs more clearly than tariff negotiations." [28]

28. May 1, 1963.

CHAPTER FOUR

Establishing the Rules

May 1963–May 1964

THE CONFLICTS OF THE May 1963 ministerial meeting of the General Agreement on Tariffs and Trade were settled in compromise on May 21. The resolution setting the objectives of the Kennedy Round was, in Ludwig Erhard's words, only the shell of an egg. The general press reaction, especially in Europe, was far less gentle. According to *Le Monde*, the arrangement had been concluded in a blind clarity (*"clarté aveuglante"*); the *Journal de Genève* characterized it as "the accord of equivocations"; the *Guardian* referred to a "form of words";[1] other reactions included, "France has only moved her roadblock down the road," "the conference was a success because it wasn't a failure," and in regard to the interests of the developing countries, "masterpiece of prevarication." A more sympathetic American press still stressed the problems ahead.

The significance of the May 1963 meeting was underestimated at the time, however, by the participants as well as by the press, an understandable reaction considering the stormy course of that initial encounter. The major achievement had been agreement on the basic approach to tariff reduction for industrial products:

> The tariff negotiations ... shall be based upon a plan of substantial linear tariff reductions with a bare minimum of exceptions which shall be subject to confrontation and justification. The linear reductions shall be equal. In those cases where there are significant [that is, meaningful in trade terms] disparities in tariff levels, the tariff reductions will be based upon special rules of general and automatic application.[2]

1. *Le Monde* (Paris), May 23, 1963; *Journal de Genève*, May 24, 1963; *Guardian* (Manchester), May 22, 1963.
2. See Appendix C for the text of the agreed resolution of May 21, 1963.

The form and dimensions of the disparity rule remained open but it was hoped the issue could be settled during the months ahead; and although the anticipated schedule was not kept, the eventual outcome was in keeping with these expectations. The participants' continuing commitment to concluding the negotiation successfully was of course essential, but the rule of across-the-board tariff cuts except in special circumstances provided a solid foundation upon which to build a substantial final agreement.

Another positive aspect of the May 1963 meeting was the unity of the members of the European Economic Community (EEC) at a major international conference. There were internal differences, but the differences were resolved. Negotiating on an equal footing with the United States gave the Community a boost in prestige, and the fact that an accord, however tenuous, had been reached lifted Community spirits from the doldrums brought on by De Gaulle's veto of United Kingdom membership four months earlier.

But while the initial Kennedy Round confrontation produced important positive results, it also left a measure of bitterness and mistrust. Many Americans and others felt that the Common Market had unfairly switched from the linear to the *écrêtement* approach just prior to May 1963 as a tactic either to water down the entire negotiation or to seek additional concessions as a price for mere participation. The Community, on the other hand, resented the strong pressure put on it at the ministerial level to reach agreement. The Community's subsequent reluctance to accept firm deadlines or to escalate major issues to ministerial decision was at least partly a result of the experience of May 1963.

Preparations for Discussions

The immediate business for the participants was to establish the procedures for carrying out the ambitious program contained in the ministerial resolution. The formal opening of the negotiation was set almost a year ahead, for May 4, 1964. The details for tariff cutting rules, including the elusive disparity formula, however, were scheduled for agreement by August 1, and all other matters, such as agriculture, trade problems of developing countries, and nontariff barriers, were to be settled by the beginning of 1964. That would leave the early months of 1964 for preparing detailed lists of initial offers. The Trade Negotiations Committee was set up as the senior working group to elaborate the rules and supervise the conduct of the negotiations. In addition, there were a committee on agriculture and subcommittees on the tariff negotiating plan, nontariff barriers and other special problems, and participation of less developed countries.

The U.S. administration was preparing itself at home for the difficult negotiations ahead. Upon the resignation in June of William Gossett, Christian Herter's deputy, it was decided to appoint two deputies in his place. One position subsequently filled by William M. Roth, a liberal Democratic businessman from California, would back up Herter on the Washington side. The other deputy would be stationed in Geneva to take charge of the day-to-day bargaining sessions with other delegations. The administration chose for this post W. Michael Blumenthal, who had served as U.S. negotiator of the International Coffee Agreement and the GATT Long-Term Arrangement Regarding International Trade in Cotton Textiles. He had, moreover, been U.S. representative at the earlier Kennedy Round working parties and had participated in the May ministerial meeting.

Herter attempted to maintain the momentum of the May meeting with a trip through European capitals in mid-July. He conferred with senior government officials, stressing the political importance of the Kennedy Round: "It is clear to us all that the negotiations far surpass the bounds of commercial interest. . . ." He appealed to the mutual interest in commerce and spoke of the "important step towards achieving the Atlantic partnership which we all are seeking. . . ." [3] His mood was generally optimistic. Support also came from the top. At a news conference President Kennedy approved the satisfactory settlement at Geneva which "indicates both sides realize that the West can't possibly afford to have a breakdown in trade relations." [4] During his talks with Konrad Adenauer in June he again pushed the GATT negotiations. With good judgment he urged that the talks be carried on at a high level. He was concerned, however, over the use of his name for this risky venture, and wondered why it wasn't called the Adenauer round or the De Gaulle round.

The opening buoyancy soon faded, however, as talks bogged down over the quest for agreed general and automatic rules. A number of unanswered questions would spell the difference between a good or

3. Press release, U.S. Information Agency, Information Service, July 18, 1963.
4. *New York Times*, May 23, 1963.

bad overall deal for any particular country. What would be the "bare minimum" of exceptions to the linear rule? What were disparities "meaningful in trade terms"? What new export opportunities would emerge from the agricultural negotiations? Where would a nontariff restriction nullify the benefits of a concession granted under the tariff-cutting rules? Technical problems were also formidable. Each country's tariff had literally thousands of different product categories. The categories did not match from country to country and were subject to frequent change—the United States, in fact, implemented a new and substantially revised tariff nomenclature in September 1963. For some countries tariff classifications did not match available import data.

Under these uncertain circumstances, talks moved cautiously—and slowly. Center stage from May 1963 to May 1964 was occupied by the great debate over disparities.

The Disparities Problem

The May ministerial meeting was in one sense just an interlude in the technical discussion of tariff disparities dating back to the beginning of 1963. The working group that prepared for the ministerial meeting devoted itself primarily to the question of whether the EEC was justified in rejecting a simple linear rule as the basis for reciprocal tariff reduction; it also examined the merits of the *écrêtement* formula put forward by the Community. The ministerial resolution settled the question: there would be a special disparity rule where there was a significant spread in rates between countries for particular products. The two remaining questions consequently were: what constitutes a disparity "meaningful in trade terms," and what form of tariff cutting would apply to accepted disparities?

There were three distinct aspects, or levels, of the disparities discussion in the Kennedy Round. One involved the basically tactical question of the relative practicality of linear tariff cuts compared with some form of tariff harmonization and, in a related way, the motivations of the EEC for advocating the latter approach. The second level of discussion revolved around the concept of reciprocity in the narrow sense of immediate trade benefits that would result from the negotiation. And finally there was the broader question of the comparative tariff structure that would emerge in the post-Kennedy Round period, and the implications of this structure for trade and future trade negotiations.

Tactical considerations had dominated earlier GATT discussions, and the simplicity and automatic application of linear tariff cuts had been unanimously acknowledged at the November 1961 meeting of GATT representatives as a desirable way to achieve a major reduction in tariffs.[5] The change of attitude by the EEC in early 1963, apparently initiated by France, to a preference for some form of tariff harmonization was therefore viewed as at least in part an attempt to reduce the scope of the negotiation. Any doubt of this was dispelled when the Community put forward its *écrêtement* proposal, aimed at a maximum average reduction in tariffs of 10–12 percent compared with the 50 percent cuts proposed by the United States. The countries of the European Free Trade Association (EFTA), in particular—and they were certainly not sympathetic to the very high protection afforded some U.S. industries—realized that 50 percent cuts were a substantial gain and that the linear approach was the best practical means to obtain it. *Ecrêtement* or a complicated disparity formula, on the other hand, would reduce the scope of the final agreement and create a serious conflict between the two largest participants, perhaps even leading to the collapse of the across-the-board approach to tariff cuts and reversion to unproductive item-by-item negotiation.

The relation of linear tariff cuts and disparities to reciprocity in terms of immediate trade benefits [6] was the main focus both in the early discussion at Geneva of whether linear tariff cuts constituted a reasonable basis for negotiation and in the later efforts to define a disparity meaningful in trade terms. The Common Market arguments to demonstrate that equal linear cuts would not provide a balance of trade advantages for the Community, however, were generally unconvincing.[7] The most straightforward one, that a 50 percent cut in a very high rate is less meaningful to trade than a 50 percent cut in a moderate rate because the former will still be high after the cut while the latter will have been stripped of all its protective effect, is based on the assumption that the high rate contains excess protection at the outset. If both tariffs fully reflected cost differentials between domestic and imported products, however, the cut in the high rate would result in a larger reduction in import price and, other things being equal, a correspondingly larger

5. See Chap. 3, pp. 42–43, including the strong EEC endorsement.

6. A "trade benefit" in this context can be read as "increased export opportunity" (see Chap. 1, p. 23).

7. See Robert E. Baldwin, "Tariff-Cutting Techniques in the Kennedy Round," *Trade, Growth, and the Balance of Payments* (Rand McNally, 1965), pp. 68–81.

increase in imports. In fact, many U.S. industries protected by high tariffs—textiles, watches, hats, gloves—face a relatively high degree of import penetration, a prima facie case that these high tariffs do not contain "excess protection."

A closely related argument was that high tariffs induce exporters in third countries to divert their shipments to low tariff areas, and that this situation would be aggravated by 50 percent cuts in both high and low tariffs. Again, if tariffs were fully effective at the start, a 50 percent cut in the high rate should reduce rather than aggravate such trade diversion. For example, when the United States raised its watch duties in 1954, Swiss exporters diverted part of their sales to the European market, though they continued to supply a large share of the American market. A 50 percent cut on both sides in these circumstances (the United States from about 60 percent to 30 percent, the EEC from 15 percent to 7.5 percent) would undoubtedly have caused some shift of exports back toward the United States.

Some additional aspects of tariff dispersion related to reciprocity that could have been raised were not, perhaps because they were too technical or numerically insignificant. For example, a 50 percent tariff cut results in a slightly smaller reduction of the average rate the more a country's rates are dispersed around a given average.[8] Another aspect, demonstrated by Richard Cooper, is that since high tariffs are related to smaller import values, a 50 percent cut in a more dispersed tariff will result in a smaller increase in imports than a less dispersed tariff, for a given *unweighted* average tariff.[9]

The third level of the disparity discussion was related to the widely held opinion in Europe that a moderate, harmonious tariff, such as the EEC tariff, was in principle a less objectionable form of protection than a widely dispersed tariff. Reduction of the dispersion among the national tariffs to form the common external tariff could be viewed, in

8. Assume country A has two rates at 10 percent and 30 percent, while country B has only one rate at 20 percent. Cut them all in half and the reduction in import price is 8 percent in country A, 8.3 percent in country B. The reason for this is that the duty is part of the final import price while the tariff *rate* applies to the value of the good before the duty is paid (a 50 percent cut in the 20 percent duty, c.i.f., is therefore $0.10/[1 + 0.20] = 0.083$).

9. See Richard N. Cooper, "Tariff Dispersion and Trade Negotiations," *Journal of Political Economy*, Vol. 72 (December 1964), pp. 597–603. Actually, since the U.S. tariff was slightly higher than the EEC's common external tariff even when weighted by imports, this effect would be offset by the difference in average levels. The argument also assumes a similar linear demand elasticity for imports at all tariff levels.

this respect, as a move in the direction of a more liberal trading system. This point of view was not pursued in a rigorous, analytical way at Geneva. For example, there was no discussion of the relative distortion in the allocation of resources between a dispersed and a uniform tariff,[10] or of the possible increase in effective tariff protection that dispersion might imply.[11] It was argued, however, that if all tariffs were cut in half during the Kennedy Round, the EEC would end up with uniformly low or modest rates, virtually all in the 5–11 percent range, while the United States would retain a number of pockets of high protection, and the Community would thus be put at a disadvantage in any future bargaining situation. In other words, three post-Kennedy Round tariff rates at 8 percent would not have the bargaining leverage of one 24 percent rate. While this was to a certain extent valid, several reasons why such a problem should not necessarily lead to a rejection of linear cuts were put forward. Although the EEC might come out of the Kennedy Round with many low rates on industrial products, other possibilities—in agriculture, for example—could make future negotiations attractive to its trade partners, and even industrial tariffs in the 5–11 percent bracket were by no means negligible. Moreover, future bargaining leverage vis-à-vis the United States was unlikely to be gained through a disparity rule that, in effect, withheld full concessions by the EEC on products where the United States maintained high tariffs. A country usually does not have an export interest for highly protected industries. Finally, as a practical matter, a negotiation based on reciprocity of trade benefits could not be expected simultaneously to achieve balance for some hypothetical future negotiation.

One other significant factor in the disparity debate was that accounts, especially in the press, confused the real issue of *disparities* in rates on individual products with *average* tariff levels. If tariffs were reasonably adjusted to provide comparability, there was only a small difference in

10. There is often little communication between economic theorists and policy officials on such matters. For instance, J. Vanek published an article at the height of the disparity discussion, which went unnoticed at Geneva, demonstrating that if world protection is to be reduced so that welfare increases at every step, tariffs should be reduced from the top downward, cutting the highest to the level of the second highest, then both to the next highest, etc. ("Unilateral Trade Liberalization and Global World Income," *Quarterly Journal of Economics*, Vol. 78 [February 1964], pp. 139–47.)

11. Effective protection relates the nominal tariffs on goods at various stages of production to the value added in the production process (see Chap. 13, pp. 232–36, especially p. 233).

average levels between the United States and the EEC and certainly not enough to call into question the linear principle. But identification of the limited share of U.S. rates that were very high with the overall level of U.S. tariffs caused misunderstanding, particularly in Europe, that added one extra layer of unnecessary contention to the disparity question.

These were the major pros and cons for rejecting or altering the linear rule because of disparities. The EEC insisted that a form of tariff harmonization, beyond that contained in linear cuts per se, be a substantial if not the dominant factor in the negotiation. The United States, supported by the EFTA countries and Japan, recognized that in certain individual cases a rate disparity might cause a problem, but that such problems, like all other problems, could be handled item by item, and that the linear rule should prevail as the basis for negotiation. And so the ministers compromised with a special rule of "general and automatic application" where "disparities in tariff levels" were "meaningful in trade terms."

Developing a Disparities Rule

A workable automatic rule for disparities, however, presented major problems, both of technique and of substance. The simplest approach undoubtedly would be to cut the peaks in the tariff schedule by something greater than the general linear amount. Instead of 50 percent, for example, cut the peaks by 75 percent—or on a sliding scale from 50 percent to 75 percent. But this was unacceptable to the United States for two reasons: First, maximum tariff cutting authority in the Trade Expansion Act was 50 percent for virtually all high rates.[12] Therefore, if high rates were cut the full 50 percent, the general linear cut would have to be much lower—perhaps 25 percent or 30 percent. This would greatly reduce the scope of the negotiations and, in addition, would result in the politically awkward situation whereby the United States and the United Kingdom would cut a number of rates by 50 percent while the EEC would not cut any by the full amount. Second, highly protected industries would not only be subject to a greater absolute tariff cut (as they would under the linear rule) but to a larger percentage cut as well. It would not generally be possible, either economically or

12. Authority to reduce duties by 100 percent was limited almost entirely to low tariffs and, under certain conditions, agricultural products.

politically, to single out high tariff American industries—many with a long record of pressure from import competition—for greater percentage cuts than other industries.

The first condition on a disparity rule, therefore, was that instead of the high rate country cutting more than the linear amount, the low rate country would have to cut less. And this, in turn, created a complicated trade effect generally referred to as the "third country" problem. The high tariff country is normally an importer and not an exporter of the product in question. It therefore has little export interest in what the low tariff country does. When the low tariff country cuts less than the linear amount, it is generally some third country that is affected. For example, if the EEC cut 25 percent instead of 50 percent on watches, Swiss exports rather than U.S. exports would suffer. If the EEC cut 25 percent instead of 50 percent on dyestuffs or certain cotton textiles, Switzerland again would bear the principal loss. Switzerland, in fact, would more often than any other country be caught in the middle of this triangular squeeze.[13]

There were also technical problems in identifying disparities. Tariff nomenclatures are not the same from one country to another. A single high U.S. tariff item might match parts of ten or twenty EEC items. The chemical and textile sectors, the most important areas of possible disparity claims, also happened to be the most disparate in tariff nomenclatures. In 1963 there was neither an agreed concordance available nor a reasonable working concordance.[14] Nor were comparable tariff rates readily available. "Specific" rates (for example, 10 cents per pound) had to be converted to an ad valorem basis, which changes from year to year, or from shipment to shipment for that matter. Rates also had to be adjusted for differences in value base.[15] Finally, import data did not always coincide with tariff nomenclature, which complicated attempts to match parts of one country's tariff items with parts of another country's.

13. This may be due to the fact that the American tariff evolved largely in response to imports from traditional European industries, and that Swiss exports still follow the earlier pattern.

14. It was late 1966 before the American and Community customs experts were finally able to produce a fairly complete, agreed concordance.

15. For example, the United States and Canada generally assess ad valorem duties on an export value or f.o.b. basis, while the EEC, the EFTA countries, and Japan use a c.i.f. value base which includes insurance and freight charges to the port of destination. The United States also employs the American selling price for certain chemicals and a few other products (see Chap. 10, pp. 169–70).

Once particular arithmetic criteria for a disparity rule were suggested, therefore, a herculean task of analysis was required to estimate the trade impact. Which rates were affected? How much trade? Between which countries? There was even the exotic question of "shadow disparities." Suppose, to take a simple case, a rate ratio of two to one constituted a bona fide disparity and in such instances the low duty country would cut only 25 percent instead of 50 percent. If country A has a duty of 40 percent, country B 22 percent, and country C 20 percent, country C would have a valid claim against A and thus cut only from 20 percent to 15 percent. But country B has to go all the way from 22 percent to 11 percent, and ends up considerably lower than C even though it started out higher. That seems unfair. Therefore, the in-between country B perhaps should have the right to stop at 15 percent when it reaches the level of country C. Expand this three-country–three-rate case to twelve major countries, each with three thousand to six thousand items, few of them matching, and estimate the possible trade impact of a "shadow disparities" rule. And contrary to some reports, the Americans had no computers running at that time.

Disparities Issue Shelved

As was widely predicted, the August 1 deadline for agreeing on a disparity rule passed almost without notice. The initial discussion over a possible rule was based on a minimum cutoff of 30 percent or 40 percent for the high rate and a spread of 10 or more points between the high and the low rates. In other words, if the tariff on a product were 30 percent or more in one country and at least 10 points less in another, a 30/10 prima facie disparity relationship existed, and the country with the lower rate would presumably cut by less than the linear amount. The summer of 1963 and part of the autumn were spent trying to figure out what this would mean in trade terms. The EEC produced an illustrative preliminary list of 557 of its tariff items (roughly a fifth of its non-agricultural items) whose low rates, in whole or in part, would be in disparity with high U.S. rates under the 30/10 hypothesis. The list was incomplete against the United States and contained none of the substantial claims the EEC might make against high U.K. rates. About 35 percent of the list was chemicals and another 20 percent textiles.

The severity of the third country problem stood out in this list. Switzerland was the main supplier to the EEC for 106 items, the United

Kingdom for 143, and other EFTA countries for more than 50 additional. The United States was first supplier for only 162 of the 557 listed, of which half were chemicals. Over 10 percent of Swiss global exports were in the selected EEC import categories, whereas only about 1 percent of U.S. and U.K. exports were included. The *Neue Zürcher Zeitung* commented, "The examination of the EEC proposals regarding disparities leads . . . to the conclusion that a European rather than an Atlantic problem has been created . . . it leads to the unpleasant conclusion . . . that Switzerland actually becomes the main sufferer and whipping-boy of the EEC." [16]

Discussion during the fall of 1963 centered on attempts to find a way of qualifying a basic rule to distinguish those disparities that were meaningful in trade terms. Major emphasis was given to the third country effect. By November, the United States, the EFTA countries, and Japan had agreed on an approach that was incorporated in a report by the subcommittee on the tariff negotiating plan. They recommended a cutoff and point spread as the preferable approach, but with some important qualitative criteria, and in particular the following: (1) The high duty country should be a substantial or principal supplier to the low duty country. This alleviated the third country problem and helped maintain future bargaining power by the low country against the high country. (2) Disparities are *not* meaningful if there are substantial imports over the high duty, reflecting import competitiveness at the present duty level. (3) Disparities could only be invoked against three key participants: the United States, the United Kingdom, and the EEC.

The EEC, however, which had discussed the 30/10 approach on a hypothetical basis, and had recognized the problem areas that the principal supplier and substantial imports criteria dealt with, was not willing to accept the whole package outlined in the subcommittee report. Among other things there would not be many disparities left to invoke under those conditions. Consequently, in December the EEC Commission developed an entirely new formula that was adopted by the EEC Council of Ministers later in the month and presented to the Trade Negotiations Committee on January 27, 1964. It had the appropriately distinguished French name of *"double écart."* Maurice Couve de Murville described it at a press conference as not perfect but "the most just and the least inequitable." [17]

16. Dec. 17, 1963. The article includes the figures on EEC imports.
17. *New York Times*, Jan. 25, 1964.

The basic formula required the high rate to be at least twice the low rate and a minimum of 10 points above it; for semimanufactures no point spread was required; [18] the low duty country would cut about 25 percent instead of 50 percent but on a sliding scale so that very low duties would be cut less than 25 percent and others more. As for the qualitative criteria, the EEC would consult the appropriate countries on an item-by-item basis when there was a problem of European trade; they would consider individual cases where the EEC already exported substantial amounts to the high tariff country; and they would drop a number of insignificant trade items.

The numbers game resumed. Even dropping insignificant trade items, the new EEC formula was more comprehensive than the earlier 30/10 approach: over 700 items or some 30 percent of EEC dutiable industrial imports were involved (although the 30 percent overstated the case because only a part of many tariff positions was properly included; a very rough estimate would bring the 30 percent down to 20 percent of EEC imports actually in disparity). The "European clause," as the reference to European trade was called, was left open pending subsequent bilateral discussion, and therefore could not be quantified at the time.

The United States came back quickly with a counterproposal on February 26. While still preferring a cutoff approach, the United States was willing to accept the *double écart* formula if the qualitative rules governing principal suppliers and substantial imports became automatic. This would reduce the number of disparities to less than 300 and trade coverage to 10 percent (or less taking account of the "part" items). Ironically, while the EEC had pressed for an automatic rule in May 1963, it was now the United States who proposed automatic criteria while the Community wanted to proceed item by item.

The United States also indicated items on which·it could invoke disparities under the *double écart* formula. But like the EEC, the United States would end up doing major harm to third countries. The largest single item where the American rate was on the low end, automobiles, would hit West Germany hardest, but would have substantial impact on Britain, Sweden, and Japan as well. The basic position of the United

18. For example, a high rate of 18 percent and a low rate of 9 percent would not qualify as a disparity on a manufactured product even though the rates were in a ratio of two to one because the point spread between them is only 9; but the same situation would qualify as a disparity for a semimanufacture. The extreme case for a meaningful disparity on a semimanufacture under the EEC proposal would be a "high" rate of 2 percent and a low rate of 1 percent.

States, the EFTA countries, and Japan was therefore to renounce the intention of invoking disparities but reserve the right to adjust their level of offers if disparity claims upset the overall balance of trade benefits.

A high level bilateral meeting was held in Washington on March 5 and 6. Jean Rey and Robert Marjolin presented the EEC Commission's position on disparities. Herter and Blumenthal were the principal protagonists on the U.S. side. Two full days of discussion covered virtually all aspects of each side's proposal and the many permutations possible for compromise.

And then . . . nothing happened. Both sides went home with ringing press statements of hope and goodwill. But although no one realized it at the time, the great disparity debate had ended.

Probably the main reason that disparities were quietly shelved for what turned out to be about three years was the realization that the May 4 grand opening was just around the corner, and nobody wanted another ministerial confrontation over disparities. A second crisis would almost certainly be fatal. Another reason was that the gap in positions was still very wide despite a common approach along the *double écart* lines. The EEC interpretation of the European clause might bring the two sides closer together, but it would be months before item-by-item talks with the Swiss, the Swedes, and others could be completed. Finally, the utility of discussion on abstract rules had just about ended. The main disparity areas were chemicals and textiles and in both of these sectors perhaps greater problems than disparities lay ahead. The practical move at this point was to wait until specific offers were tabled before proceeding any further. And so all parties agreed that there was no agreement on disparities. No commitments of any kind were made and all participants remained free to adjust their offers at a later date in the light of subsequent events.

It might appear that the ten months of discussion were completely futile. No agreement was reached and the only apparent beneficiaries were the airlines that were transporting delegates back and forth to Geneva. But "no commitment" is in fact the normal cover when compromise cannot breach a difference in views. The EEC, which would have to take the initiative in invoking disparities, had clearly defined its basic approach. Other countries had remained united in their opposition to certain provisions of the EEC rule and had indicated where the greatest problems would be. Even the maximum number of EEC disparities, meaning a cut of about 25 percent on 20 percent of dutiable nonagricultural imports, would only lower the average overall cut from 50 percent to 45 percent, and this difference could conceivably be offset elsewhere if necessary. The problem was reasonably contained. Much depended on how liberal the EEC would be in dealing with the Swiss and other Europeans. Much depended on the negotiations in chemicals and textiles. Meanwhile the problem of disparities was left to smolder.

Other Negotiating Issues

The ministerial resolution of May 1963, in addition to tariff cutting rules, outlined objectives in three other areas: (1) "In the trade negotiations every effort shall be made to reduce barriers to exports of less developed countries. . . ." (2) "The trade negotiations shall deal not only with tariffs but also with non-tariff barriers." (3) "The trade negotiations shall provide for acceptable conditions of access to world markets for agricultural products."

The resolution spelled out in some detail the question of export expansion for developing countries, but not much was accomplished from May 1963 to May 1964. The subcommittee on the participation of less developed countries met for the first time in November. The position of developing countries was more favorable in the Kennedy Round than in past GATT negotiation for two reasons. First, the linear approach to tariff cutting would apply equally to the export interests of all participating countries. In the past, bilateral request and offer lists tended to concentrate cuts on products of interest to the major industrial countries. Second, the Kennedy Round explicitly absolved developing countries from the obligation of reciprocity. This change in GATT principles was to be codified later in the new GATT chapter pertaining to developing countries, but the May 1963 ministerial resolution had already affirmed that "the developed countries cannot expect to receive reciprocity from the less-developed countries." Despite the fact that full reciprocity was not required, some countries, and particularly the United States, insisted that some positive contribution be made by each participant. Discussion at the initial meeting of the subcommittee on less developed countries, among other things, elaborated the kind of contribution by developing countries as that which would be possible in light of their development needs.

The GATT special group on trade in tropical products held a meeting in February 1964. Possibilities for action during the Kennedy Round in this group were limited. Attention focused on the six major commodities: coffee, cocoa, bananas, tea, tropical oilseeds, and hardwoods. The United States, however, already provided duty-free entry for the first four and part of the others; and the EEC would not yield its preferential protection to its associated African states except for tea and tropical hardwoods. Progress had been made in the latter case when the EEC and the United Kingdom announced on January 1, 1964, that duties on most tropical hardwoods were suspended pending permanent duty elimination as part of the final Kennedy Round agreement. The United States followed suit by seeking the necessary legislation which was finally signed by President Johnson on April 13, 1966.

The widest attention for trade expansion of developing countries came with the opening of the United Nations Conference on Trade and Development (UNCTAD) on March 23, 1964. The preparatory report by the conference's secretary general, Raúl Prebisch, criticized the GATT approach of lowering trade barriers to the free play of economic forces; what was needed was a "conscious and deliberate effort to influence the course of economic events," to redress the inequities between the rich and poor nations.[19] This veiled attack on GATT had special significance in view of the uncertain outcome of the Kennedy Round talks, for if GATT were unable to produce meaningful results for the trade interests of developing countries in this negotiation, it might lose the support of many of these countries. Eric Wyndham White, speaking before the conference, gave a slightly veiled prediction of his own in reply to UNCTAD enthusiasts. The solution to the problem of less developed countries "lies really in the will of governments to act."[20]

The nontariff barrier talks, like the less developed country discussion, remained in the preparatory stage while attention was focused on the major question of basic tariff cutting rules. Participants submitted lists of nontariff barriers they would want to have on the agenda. The lists were broad and general, including such categories as government procurement, border taxes, antidumping regulations, and customs valuation. But although delegates were not yet specific in their requests, a statement in April by the International Chamber of Commerce noted that an "outstanding example of a non-tariff barrier in the field of cus-

19. *Towards a New Trade Policy for Development* (United Nations, 1964).
20. *New York Times*, April 9, 1964.

toms valuation is the American Selling Price (ASP) system . . . the International Chamber of Commerce hopes it will be possible from the outset for the U.S. Government to enter into . . . a commitment to eliminate ASP. . . ." This comment, on one of many nontariff barriers, was not given special attention by the U.S. government at the time. The American selling price was a longstanding nontariff irritant to trade, however, and was destined to play a critical role in the final Kennedy Round bargaining.

Agriculture was of far more vital concern in the months preceding May 1964.[21] Although the resolution of the previous May had specified that the negotiations "shall provide for acceptable conditions of access to world markets for agricultural products . . . in furtherance of a significant development and expansion of world trade," the rules and methods for achieving these objectives were left to the Trade Negotiations Committee. For grains, meats, and dairy products it was agreed that a broader commodity arrangement might be required, and special groups were established to pursue this possibility.

The major new development between May 1963 and May 1964 was the EEC Commission proposals—the Mansholt proposals—that came before the EEC Council in December 1963. These proposals constituted a bold move by the Commission to force decisions on the internal farm policy, in part by linking it with progress in the agricultural sector of the Kennedy Round.[22] In the changed mood of the Community following the French veto of United Kingdom membership, the Germans had become reluctant to make further commitments on agriculture of principal benefit to France. For grains, a gradual adjustment toward unified prices by 1970 had been agreed to in January 1962, but in April 1963, when prices for the 1963 crop came before the Council, Germany, which would have to make the most difficult downward price adjustments, refused to make any change in its domestic price levels. General de Gaulle, in turn, warned in July that the Community would "disappear" if deadlines were not met for agriculture. This struggle became linked to the Kennedy Round because Community farm policy decisions were to a certain degree prerequisite to Kennedy Round offers in agriculture, and because the Germans wanted a successful Kennedy

21. The agricultural sector of the negotiations is discussed in Chap. 9.
22. For a fuller account of this situation, see Miriam Camps, *What Kind of Europe? The Community since De Gaulle's Veto* (London: Oxford University Press, 1965), pp. 20–34.

Round but were concerned that the French would undermine the nego-tiations, especially in late 1963, with an overly rigid position on tariff disparities.

Consequently, the Commission in November 1963 made several proposals as the basis for a balanced package of member state commit-ments. One proposal (Mansholt I) provided for a single move to uni-fied grain prices, with compensatory payments through 1970 for farmers in Germany, Italy, and Luxembourg. A second proposal (Mansholt II) contained the basis for EEC agricultural offers in the Kennedy Round. The level of internal support (*montant de soutien*)—the unified prices in the case of grains—would be bound for three years, on the basis of reciprocity. A third proposal contained the Com-munity position in the Kennedy Round on disparities for industrial products (the *double écart* approach). Additional proposals pertained to other aspects of the internal farm program. A marathon meeting of the EEC Council in December reached agreement on most of these proposals, including Mansholt II for agricultural offers and the dis-parity formula for industrial goods; but on unified grain prices, Ger-many held out for higher price levels than those suggested by the Com-mission, and this decision was left for further discussion.

When the Community presented at Geneva, as its contribution for agriculture in the Kennedy Round, an offer to bind the level of internal support, however, the reaction of agricultural exporters was extremely negative. A binding of the support level did not appear to improve market conditions for imports, and the proposed grain prices, which were about halfway between the French and German prices, in fact constituted a price increase for France, the largest internal producer. The proposals contained no commitment on access to EEC markets, and allowed the variable import levy to continue to operate unimpeded. Exporters considered that the unified grain prices were too high and that additional guarantees of acceptable access were required. They also requested action on the products that would remain subject to a simple customs duty, and that were not included in the initial Com-munity offer. But the discussion in the spring of 1964 did not progress beyond an elaboration of the many subtleties of the calculation and application of the level of internal support.

In sum, as the conference approached its official opening, there was no agreement on basic rules and procedures for agriculture. One other event during this preparatory year, however, did have a substantial influence on the farm talks. It was not part of the Kennedy Round, but it became to many a symbol of the iniquities the Common Market farm policy might hold in store. It was commonly referred to as the "chicken war."

The Chicken War

In 1589, when Henri IV stated in his coronation speech, "I hope to make France so prosperous that every peasant will have a chicken in his pot on Sunday," it had the ring of an exaggerated campaign promise, and certainly did not appear as a circumstance that might lead to war. Yet almost four hundred years later, in 1962, as a result of American technology and aggressive marketing, Europeans were being bombarded with frozen chickens from abroad at a rapidly accelerating rate, and the situation eventually led to a highly emotional, if limited, trade war.

Between 1948 and 1962 production of broiler chickens in the United States increased from 1.2 billion pounds to 6.8 billion pounds. This rapid expansion was largely due to advances in technology and management. Feed requirements per pound of meat were reduced from 4 pounds to 2.4 pounds; initial chick costs were cut almost in half; mass production techniques cut costs in many other ways. As a result, the average price received by producers dropped from 32 cents per pound in 1948 to 15 cents in 1962.

Success at home encouraged the industry to develop markets abroad. West Germany seemed to offer especially good prospects. European producers maintained it couldn't be done. Consumers in Germany ate fresh stewing chickens and would never buy frozen broilers. But the experts were wrong. U.S. exports of broilers to West Germany increased from 3.5 million pounds in 1956 to 122 million pounds in the year ending June 1962. Although exports increased to other countries as well, West Germany accounted for 56 percent of total U.S. poultry exports in the year ending June 1962 (and about 85 percent of exports to the EEC). Nor was this phenomenal increase at the expense of Common Market producers. Poultry production rose in each Common Market country in each of the years from 1956 to 1962. The fact was that consumption was skyrocketing for the attractively priced broilers. Whereas EEC poultry production increased by 65 percent from 1956 to 1962, consumption increased by over 80 percent. Annual per capita consumption in West Germany rose from 4.6 pounds to 12.3 pounds during this period (the U.S. figure in the latter year was 37 pounds).

On July 30, 1962, the EEC initiated its variable levy system, imposing levies on a group of products that included poultry. The immediate impact on U.S. exports of broilers to Germany was a doubling of the previously GATT-bound duty of roughly 15 percent. In the three subsequent years it was to rise to over 70 percent. After the first nine months of the new system, West German imports from the United States had dropped to about 40 percent of the previous year's level while imports from Belgium, France, and the Netherlands had increased sharply. Higher internal prices encouraged a rapid growth of domestic production in the Common Market and dampened consumption. By 1965, U.S. broilers had been virtually wiped out of the German market.

The initial reaction of the United States in July 1962 was to try to obtain a rollback of the higher tariff levies. But after almost a year of consultation, no progress had been made, and on May 31, 1963, ten days after the Kennedy Round ministerial meeting ended, the United States invoked its GATT rights either to receive compensation through tariff cuts by the EEC on other products or to retaliate against EEC exports. The EEC was not prepared to offer compensation during talks in June and July, so the United States announced on August 6 its intention of raising duties on $46 million of EEC trade.

Although the right of retaliation was not contested, the EEC did dispute the $46 million figure, claiming a reasonable figure to be only $19 million. The wide difference reflected difficult problems of analysis. Which base period was representative? What adjustment was necessary for German quantitative restrictions in earlier years? The rapid growth of U.S. exports made any single value to some extent arbitrary. But in November an impartial GATT panel of experts arrived at a "reasonable" figure of $26 million, which both sides accepted, and on December 4, 1963, President Johnson proclaimed tariff increases on light panel trucks, potato starch, dextrine, and certain brandy, all of export interest principally to the Common Market.

Officially the poultry war had ended. It was a step backward for liberal trade, even though a relatively small one in trade volume. The *New York Times* termed it "an ironic, not to say ludicrous, overture" to the Kennedy Round. "The ultimate stakes are far too high for a game of tit-for-tat." [23]

23. Dec. 9, 1963.

In fact, the impact of the Common Market's agricultural policy on poultry trade did not end in December 1963. The Danes, also shut out of the German market, adopted a two-price system which, in effect, subsidized exports. Danish exports still could not compete on the German market so they were diverted into other markets such as Austria and Switzerland, again displacing U.S. exports. The French and Dutch also began exporting outside of the EEC with the benefit of subsidies. The U.S. share of Swiss imports of broilers dropped from 65 percent in 1961 to almost zero in 1965. The United States, which had no price support program for poultry and had never engaged in subsidizing exports, was temporarily forced to subsidize exports to Austria and Switzerland in order to remain competitive with subsidized exports of other foreign suppliers. This, in turn, elicited a vehement reaction from the Danes about a possible new chicken war.[24] Within the Common Market, surpluses continued to build up and prices sagged. Three thousand French poultry farmers in Brittany stormed the town hall at Morlaix in protest on December 19, 1966.[25] It seemed that the Germans were increasing poultry production so fast they were cutting back imports from France. And so the snowball continued to roll.

The poultry affair, as a case study in commercial policy, illustrates the far-reaching and disruptive impact a new and rigid system of regulations can have on international trade. It was particularly relevant to the Kennedy Round, however, because developments in poultry trade were so clear and startling to everyone concerned during 1963 and 1964. In some ways poultry production is not a good example of the workings of the common agricultural policy; it is more a manufacturing than a farming process, and manufactured products such as chickens are more susceptible to a runaway surge of new production than farm products that are limited to some extent by restraints of acreage and weather. But poultry was the first concrete test of the new European farm policy, an experience that frightened and embittered many people toward future trade with the Community in agricultural products. It also made clear how seriously the Americans could be expected to treat farm products in the Kennedy Round and underlined the possibility that if adequate benefits were not accorded to U.S. agri-

24. See *Information* (Danish press), Sept. 29, 1965.
25. See *Les Echos* (Paris), Dec. 20, 1966.

cultural exports, the industrial exports of America's trading partners would suffer.

Preparing Negotiating Lists

While discussions at Geneva dragged on with generally disappointing results, proponents and opponents of the Kennedy Round in the various countries strove to influence events. Governments, of course, tried to bolster support with firm statements. The EFTA countries consistently urged maximum tariff cuts, and in a communiqué in December called the Kennedy Round the "most important immediate target." [26] Ambassador Blumenthal, visiting Tokyo in January, elicited the strongest response to date from the Japanese for linear tariff cuts. Canadian Prime Minister Lester Pearson stressed the need for reduction in trade barriers on a trip to Paris in early 1964. The EEC continued full public support, although doubts about how far it really wanted to go were reinforced by statements like that of French Minister of Industries Bokanowski in March: it is wiser to "progressively develop limited competition inside Europe of the Six rather than to face in shoreless Europe the shock waves of disorderly (outside) competition." [27]

The focal point of domestic activity in the United States was the public list of tariff items to be considered for possible reduction, and the subsequent public hearings on the expected consequences of such reductions. The Trade Expansion Act, in keeping with previous legislation, required the President to announce such a public list. In the past the list had been carefully screened of sensitive items, which limited negotiating possibilities at the outset. The linear approach to tariff reduction, however, removed the burden of proof from those items that could be offered for reduction and placed it on those exceptional cases that could not be offered for reduction. The availability of adjustment assistance, moreover, provided a means of offering tariff reduction even where some injury to the domestic market might result. Consequently, Herter announced in September at a blue ribbon White House conference on export expansion, attended by the President, five Cabinet members, and two hundred business executives, that the entire U.S. tariff would be placed on the public list except for a handful of items

26. Dec. 31, 1963.
27. Quoted in *New York Times*, March 5, 1964.

that were mandatorily excluded from any tariff cut. November 20, 1963, was set as the deadline for filing requests to testify on the tariff list before the Trade Information Committee (a part of Herter's organization) or the Tariff Commission.

Although the blanket list was compared with waving a red flag before the bull of American protectionism, the hearings proceeded with little fanfare. Fifteen hundred witnesses appeared before or submitted statements to the Tariff Commission, which was to study and advise on the economic impact of tariff cuts, and a thousand gave testimony to the Trade Information Committee, which was primarily interested in expanded export opportunities. Testimony was mostly protectionist, but importers and export-oriented firms also spoke up. After four months of hearings, from December 1963 to March 1964, a fairly com plete documentation of U.S. industry fears and aspirations was available to the U.S. negotiating team.

The next step was for the Tariff Commission, drawing on testimony and its own expertise, to advise the President on the probable impact of tariff cuts. Their advice remained secret, except on fifteen escape clause cases where they had found injury caused by imports but the President had decided not to increase tariffs or take other remedial action. In these cases, where no recent improvement was found, the Trade Expansion Act mandatorily excluded any tariff cut in the Kennedy Round. However, most of the clearcut escape clause cases pertained to industries of small national significance. For example, of the fifteen cases, the Tariff Commission found no recent improvement for umbrella frames, baseball gloves, briar pipes, and straight pins, and improved conditions for garlic and bicycles; the commissioners split evenly over the question of spring-type clothespins.

The Negotiating Terms

As the May 4 date approached, the many threads and strands, in Geneva and in national capitals, slowly began to be woven into the fabric of the most comprehensive negotiation of trade barriers ever attempted. A year of preparatory talks had been devoted more to the exposition of problems than to their solution. There would be general rules for tariff cutting, but important exceptions to these rules. There would be negotiations on farm products that might have to include discussion of the whole spectrum of government intervention in farm markets. There would be a mutual effort to reduce or eliminate non-tariff barriers, especially where they tended to nullify the value of a tariff concession. And beneath this superstructure of general guidelines were the thousands of individual products, each susceptible to greater import competition, new export potential, or both. Participants were pledged to achieve "a balance of advantages," or in a word "reciprocity." But who could tell in the spring of 1964 whether the final mix of offers would in fact contain such a balance?

It was no wonder, then, that delegates to the ministerial meeting of May 1964 were reluctant to make concessions or take firm commitments in one area when the outcome in other vital sectors was still so uncertain. The Americans were most concerned over the impasse in agriculture. The Community had received no commitment from others on a disparity rule. EFTA countries were apprehensive about the "bare minimum" of exceptions to the linear rule that the two largest participants would eventually put forward. Many old hands in tariff negotiations had discounted from the start the fanfare about automatic rules. They favored having each country table a list of specific offers and letting the haggling begin. By April 1964 the general feeling was that the time had come to set aside theory and abstraction, and to deal with specific offers. The press played up EEC reluctance to confront the major substantive issues at the May meeting, and the scheduled departure of the French minister, Giscard d'Estaing, after the opening day ceremonies, made this intention clear. Other delegations, however, were also prepared to keep the ministerial meeting harmonious and therefore primarily ceremonial.

Could it have been otherwise? John Diebold, evaluating the potential of computers in foreign affairs, commented: "Both in the negotiation of trade agreements and in their execution, an agreed-upon data base can make almost automatic the evaluation of the impact of concessions and the responses to the withdrawal or tampering with concessions. Perhaps the principal function of the future trade negotiator will be, first, to arrive at an agreed-upon data base and, second, to negotiate on the basis of this evaluation of the national interest involved in facts known to all." [28]

The linear approach undoubtedly goes a long way toward committing the bulk of tariff cutting to an automatic formula. If the EEC

28. "Computers, Program Management and Foreign Affairs," *Foreign Affairs*, Vol. 45 (October 1966), p. 133.

had agreed to this rule, much of the initial year's fencing could have been avoided. There was also a conspicuous lack of organized preparation of the voluminous statistical data required for the negotiation. But ad hoc statistical support, except perhaps during the first months of the disparity discussion, resulted primarily in a more hectic pace of events rather than a delay in the progress of the negotiations.[29]

Rarely, however, can general rules be derived that are not subject to exceptions and interpretation. Seldom are conditions reasonably comparable from country to country. If debate often appears to be over the appropriate numbers, a look below the surface is more apt to uncover a difference in subjective evaluation. The Kennedy Round was perhaps inordinately burdened with contentious issues. But it is doubtful whether trade negotiations will ever reach the "almost automatic" stage—or put in a more hopeful way, if they should appear to become automatic it will probably be the result of a more enlightened statesmanship rather than of a more powerful computer.

29. During the final two years of the negotiation, the American delegation did have available detailed machine tabulations of basic trade and tariff data. Perhaps in the future the benefits, and the cost, of such a program might be shared by all participants.

CHAPTER FIVE

Specific Offers

May 1964–June 1965

THE KENNEDY ROUND of negotiations under the General Agreement on Tariffs and Trade officially opened on May 4, 1964. Sessions of the three-day ministerial meeting were held in the large, square assembly hall of the Bâtiment Electoral in the old-city section of Geneva. The mood was relaxed since there was tacit agreement not to have a confrontation over any major issue. Attention during the previous weeks at Geneva had in fact been directed to the stormy sessions of the United Nations Conference on Trade and Development, which opened on March 23 and overlapped the GATT meeting. For the Kennedy Round, May 1964 was a complete contrast with the tense and trying days of the ministerial meeting one year earlier.

May 1964 Agreements

Two important points were unanimously agreed upon at the meeting. The first was adoption of 50 percent as a working hypothesis for the linear cut. The depth of cut had been left open in the 1963 resolution, although the United States and the countries of the European Free Trade Association (EFTA) had pressed for 50 percent from the beginning. The European Economic Community (EEC) had considered this decision part of a complete set of commitments, including disparities, and the qualification "as a working hypothesis" was made at its insistence.

The other agreement was to set September 10 as the date for linear countries—those that had accepted the linear cut obligation—to exchange their exceptions lists. An exception, in this sense, was an item that was not being offered for the 50 percent cut. Any item not specified on the exceptions list was automatically offered for the full cut. Both the linear cut and the exceptions list applied only to nonagricultural products.

A third commitment in the declaration agreed to on May 6, 1964, was the acceptance of Canada as a country with "a special economic or trade structure," and Australia, New Zealand, and South Africa as countries with "a very large dependence on exports of agricultural and other primary products." In keeping with the May 1963 understanding, "equal linear tariff reductions may not provide an adequate balance of advantages" for such countries, and therefore the objective should be "the negotiation of a balance of advantages based on trade concessions . . . of equivalent value." The real confrontation on special status for these countries had occurred at the earlier meeting, however, and the language in the May 1964 declaration was merely an elaboration of that earlier accord. The most important trade involved was between the United States and Canada, and the difficulties of agreeing on "equivalent value" would fall primarily on the two North American participants.

Christian Herter, in a statement on May 4, made a brief appeal to the delegates to get on with the job. He opened with a message from President Johnson: "Your meetings . . . exemplify the hope and commitment of our late President to bring together the nations of the world in peaceful pursuits. I believe, as he did, in the necessity of success in your work." [1] In a second statement, at the close of the meeting, Herter was more to the point. "I must again express the disappointment . . . at the progress that has been made over the past year." Turning to key problems, he stated: "I place agriculture at the top of this list . . . unless progress can be made in establishing the basis for successful agricultural negotiations it would be impossible for my Government to foresee a successful overall negotiation." [2]

EEC Commissioner Jean Rey took a more optimistic view. Pushing aside memories of écrêtement, he recalled that "it was the Community

1. Press release, U.S. Office of Special Representative for Trade Negotiations, May 4, 1964.
2. Ibid., May 6, 1964.

... which, drawing on its experience of the Treaty of Rome, suggested the procedure on which the present conference is based—linear reduction of tariffs—as long ago as 1960." For agriculture, "we hope to convince our partners that our proposals are realistic and effective." His optimism extended to the projected schedule for completing the negotiations: "The Commission thinks . . . that the whole of 1964 should be devoted to a parallel exploration of all the factors in the negotiations: tariffs, exceptions, agriculture, non-tariff obstacles, aid to the developing countries. . . . We could then devote the first half of next year to working out comprehensive solutions and technical and political compromises so that the negotiations can be brought to a close in about the summer of 1965." [3]

The only footnote to the ministerial meeting was extension of the September 10 date for tabling exceptions to November 16, safely past the national elections in the United States and the United Kingdom, thereby avoiding an election issue over Kennedy Round offers on domestically sensitive products.[4] Although exceptions lists were to remain secret, their wide circulation among delegations would make leaks inevitable. The postponement was agreed to at a meeting in Geneva on May 29.

The period from May to November 16 was primarily occupied by two subjects. One was preparation within governments of the exceptions lists. The other was a continued effort to make progress in the agricultural sector; ultimately the question became whether industry and agriculture had to move ahead in strict parallel, or whether the latter could be permitted to lag behind temporarily.

3. Press release, European Economic Community (EEC), May 4, 1964.
4. The Kennedy Round did arise briefly in the United States during the campaign. Republican vice presidential candidate William E. Miller declared to an Indiana audience: "Of course Senator Goldwater and I have sympathy for the oppressed abroad, but we also have sympathy for you. We want to see you working . . . and now the Administration wants a 50% reduction in tariffs so more foreign made goods can flood our markets. . . . This makes less than little sense. This reduction is wrong in theory and in practice. We have seen how many industries have been affected adversely; how many jobs have been lost; how many plants have been closed—from foreign competition. Do we have to make the same mistakes over and over again?" *New York Times* (Sept. 8, 1964). The *New York Times* (Sept. 11) commented dryly, "If Mr. Miller keeps up his archeological field work, he may dig himself right into the Harding era." Dean Rusk replied that the negotiations, if successful, would result in "more jobs for Americans and more jobs for people in other countries" (*New York Times*, Sept. 15). This brief domestic debate had no significant effect, however, on the Geneva deliberations.

Preparation of Exceptions Lists

The ministerial meetings at Geneva had remained vague on the criteria for excepting items from the linear cut, stipulating a "bare minimum" for cases of "overriding national interest." An alternative approach could have been to limit exceptions to a certain percentage of imports; but aside from the reluctance of participating countries to commit themselves far in advance and some statistical problems with an import share measurement, it was not legally possible for the United States to agree to a limitation on exceptions until a thorough internal examination of the probable impact of tariff reduction was completed. This examination and the selection of the U.S. exceptions list, directed and coordinated by Herter's office, included the four months of public hearings before Herter's Trade Information Committee and the Tariff Commission. The Tariff Commission, in addition to its appraisal of the impact of tariff cuts, produced fifty-five volumes of digests with pertinent background facts and figures for each commodity. A large volume of correspondence was received from the Congress, mostly on behalf of local constituents. Agencies in the executive branch—Commerce, Labor, Interior, Agriculture, State—submitted voluminous material prepared by their commodity specialists. And there was considerable additional help from many of the three hundred technical specialists who were designated by industries and trade associations to advise Herter's office on technical matters.

Collation and evaluation of this mass of information was a mammoth undertaking. Herter's staff, with the help of executive agencies and several outside consultants, spent the summer and early fall of 1964 on this task. Every effort was made to uncover and take account of significant economic problems. The continued buoyancy of the American economy and the relatively small price impact in many instances of tariff cuts phased over five annual instalments limited the number of potential problem areas, but in those cases where tariff reduction was likely to cause real hardship, a decision was made to offer less than a 50 percent cut, or perhaps to make no offer. Recommendations were made by interagency committees chaired by the Herter office, initially through the technical level Trade Staff Committee. Any agency could appeal this committee's decision to the policy level Trade Executive Committee, thence to the Cabinet subcommittee chaired by

Herter, and finally to the President. Appeal to the ultimate authority was used sparingly, however, probably because of the consistent support given by both Presidents Kennedy and Johnson to their special trade representatives.

While other countries had a less rigid procedure to follow, each faced the same problem of priorities in drawing up its exceptions list, and each responded differently. The EFTA countries kept matters simple at this initial stage: Austria, Denmark, Norway, Sweden, and Switzerland declared no exceptions whatsoever, and the United Kingdom and Finland submitted very short lists. Japan, whose support for the linear approach was tempered by concern over nontariff restrictions on its exports, confirmed its more cautious approach with a lengthy list.

The EEC, with six separate governments involved, had the greatest difficulty in reaching agreement on an exceptions list. The process was complicated by French insistence that decisions for the Kennedy Round be linked to German acceptance of unified grain prices. The Commission had recommended a modest list; the French initially pressed for a very long list but relented somewhat in the last minute; the Italians and Belgians, in particular, negotiated for additional products to be put on the list. Last-minute internal bargaining, including a twenty-hour ministerial marathon, resulted in compromise. The final list was considerably longer than the original Commission recommendation but shorter than the combined demands of the member states.

While preparation of exceptions lists occupied industry specialists, agricultural talks continued at Geneva. The danger from the American point of view was that negotiations on farm products would never reach the stage of concrete offers. Debate over the Community farm policy could continue indefinitely without any tangible result. Previous negotiations had been disappointing, and experience thus far in the Kennedy Round, despite lofty words, was hardly encouraging. The agreed November 16 date for tabling industrial exceptions lists brought the matter to a head. If negotiations on industry moved ahead of agriculture then, agriculture might be left behind permanently. The U.S. Department of Agriculture in particular, never sanguine over Kennedy Round prospects, rested much of its hope on a firm link between the two sectors, holding attractive U.S. offers on industrial products conditional on a European response in the agricultural sector. The United States, therefore, warned its trading partners throughout the summer of 1964 that the November 16 date for industry presupposed parallel

progress in agriculture. Herter stated on July 6 that "unless the capabilities of the EEC to negotiate on industrial and on agricultural products including grains are restored in one way or another, the timetable
and even the final results of the Kennedy Round could be put in serious
jeopardy." [5]

The EEC was stalemated, however, over agreement on unified grain
prices. At the Council of Ministers meetings in December 1963 Germany had refused to accept the Commission proposals on price levels.
In further discussions in the spring of 1964 no progress was made and
the Germans indicated they would be unwilling to agree on the level of
unified grain prices until after the federal elections in the second half
of 1965. Strains between France and Germany were developing in
several other areas, particularly over French resistance to German-
American efforts to establish a multilateral nuclear force, and by the
fall of 1964 France was stepping up pressure on Germany in regard to
both unified grain prices and the nuclear force.

The Commission, with strong French support, had also linked agreement on grain prices to EEC agricultural offers in the Kennedy Round.
Commission President Walter Hallstein stated that "lack of decision
[on grain prices] will cause a slowdown and possibly the collapse of
the whole [Kennedy Round] negotiations." [6] But a decision was not in
fact essential. The Community could have gone on with negotiations,
leaving the internal price level open, or using hypothetical price levels, a
possibility referred to in the joint communiqué at the close of Chancellor Ludwig Erhard's visit to President Johnson in June 1964. Playing
down the importance of agreement on unified grain prices reflected the
American view that the level of internal EEC prices was not the key
element in a Kennedy Round grains agreement in any event, and that
other commitments on access for imports would be necessary. By
October 1964, however, the French and the Commission were clearly
making agreement on unified grain prices prerequisite to Kennedy
Round offers in the agricultural sector. This pressure on the Germans,
moreover, was reinforced by American insistence that the November
16 date for industrial exceptions lists be accompanied by similar progress in agriculture.

As November approached, it was highly doubtful the Americans
would be willing to keep the November 16 date, a fact the French seized

5. *New York Times*, July 7, 1964.
6. *Ibid.*, June 28, 1964.

upon to question continued preparation of the EEC industrial exceptions list. The United States did not want to get in the middle of the
internal EEC debate over grain prices, however, or to give the French
the occasion to postpone agreement on an exceptions list. Consequently,
the Americans softened their position and accepted a delayed link
between the two sectors. The EEC and the United States agreed on
November 3 to proceed on schedule and table exceptions lists on
November 16, while the American statement added, "It is expected
that the substantive negotiations on both industrial and agricultural
products will begin at an early date in 1965." [7] At about the same time
the Germans put forward new proposals for unified grain prices,[8] and
the EEC Council on December 15 agreed to unified grain prices at
approximately the level of the original Mansholt proposal.

Submission of Exceptions Lists

On November 16, 1964, sixteen countries—the United States, Japan,
the six EEC members, seven EFTA members (including Finland but not
Portugal), and Czechoslovakia [9]—submitted their exceptions to an
otherwise across-the-board cut in industrial tariffs. It was an unprecedented accomplishment following eighteen months of difficult nego
tiation. Once exceptions lists were tabled, however, there was some
question about what to do next. The linear approach, especially the procedure of listing exceptions rather than offers, was successful in getting
maximum offers on the table at the outset. But unless there were common agreement that the trade significance of these initial exceptions lists
was roughly comparable, how could differences be adjusted? The threat
of withdrawal of offers by countries with short exceptions lists could
start a dangerous unravelling of offers by all. A procedure of multilateral confrontation and justification had been agreed to earlier; each
participant would take its turn in the dock to explain, for each exception, why it could not offer a full 50 percent reduction, and to submit to
cross-examination. These sessions, lasting from January 19 through
February 12, 1965, were an education in the detailed rationale, facts,
and figures, valid and spurious, for maintaining tariff protection. It was

7. *Ibid.*, Nov. 4, 1964.
8. *Ibid.*; Foreign Minister Gerhard Schröder confirmed the reports a week later
(*ibid.*, Nov. 15, 1964).
9. The role of East European countries in GATT is discussed in Chap. 8.

especially exhausting for those delegates with long lists to defend. But the content of the lists did not change since they were now a subject of negotiation rather than debate.

As expected, the sizes of the lists were not comparable, nor was there agreement on how differences in size should be treated in measuring reciprocal concessions. Most EFTA countries claimed no exceptions. Of total dutiable nonagricultural imports, the U.K. list included less than 10 percent while those of the EEC and Japan included roughly 20–25 percent. These were only approximations since many exceptions covered only part of the tariff positions, and trade allocations within tariff positions, especially at the outset, were not available. Moreover, most EEC exceptions were marked for partial cuts (less than 50 percent) but the precise figure was generally not specified. The terms for reaching a balance of concessions also depended upon supplier grouping: should the general approach be bilateral, linear countries together, GATT countries, most-favored-nation countries, global imports?

The United States exceptions list was quite short—less than 10 percent of dutiable nonagricultural imports—except for one large item, petroleum, which comprised almost a quarter of these imports. The U.S. duty on petroleum was very low (about 4 percent), however, and the principal barrier to imports from overseas suppliers was a quota control declared for reasons of national security. Thus a tariff cut would be of little trade significance. In addition, petroleum imports were supplied principally by countries neither members of GATT nor participants in the Kennedy Round.[10] The Americans, on the basis of previous GATT procedure, claimed that items primarily supplied by nonparticipants need not be considered in the reciprocity debate. The issue was never settled, but in the final bargaining, negotiations did center almost entirely on direct trade interests, and the petroleum question gradually faded away. In the first months after November 1964, however, this issue complicated the balancing of linear offers by the share of total imports on the exceptions list and increased the uncertainty as to the basis for an eventual agreement.

10. Canada had a large interest in petroleum exports to the United States ($266 million in 1964), but as an *overland* supplier was exempt from the quota restriction. Also, as a nonlinear country in the Kennedy Round, Canada was not involved in the initial discussion of the relative sizes of exceptions lists. The Netherlands Antilles, an overseas territory of the Netherlands, supplied $286 million of U.S. petroleum imports. Total U.S. petroleum imports in 1964 were $1,873 million (based on Standard International Trade Classification 33, "petroleum and petroleum products").

Among the many questions concerning the measurement of overall reciprocity [11] was how to combine industrial and agricultural offers; that problem alone was sufficient to restrain the Americans from any balancing of industry before the agricultural sector caught up. Moreover, the mood in the winter of 1964–65 was to avoid any new quest for complicated, automatic rules. There was also a particular reluctance to abandon a completely multilateral approach for the hazards of bilateral balancing between pairs of countries.

Another major area of uncertainty led to an interim phase for industrial products in the negotiation. In several key industry sectors, offers by one country were linked to action by others. In some instances the conditions were explicit in the exceptions lists, in others they emerged during early discussions. The outcome in these sectors, moreover, would probably set the pace for the overall industrial settlement. Not only were the industries large in terms of trade, but they were of strategic political importance domestically. The question was how to negotiate these sectoral problems most effectively.

The logical procedure, to establish a separate negotiating subgroup of the countries involved for each problem sector, entailed two distinct dangers. In the first place, negotiation within industry sectors might induce delegates to seek a balance of export benefits within each sector. This, however, would elicit a low level of offers, since a particular sector normally has dominantly exporting and importing countries, and the former would stand to expand exports more in a mutual lowering of trade barriers. Multilateral negotiation of all trade is in fact designed to balance out bilateral and industry sector imbalances. The second danger of sector negotiations was their effect on the basic linear rule. In the spring of 1965 the survival of the 50 percent linear cut was uncertain: the 50 percent figure remained only a working hypothesis, exceptions lists for some key countries were longer than had been expected, and disparities would eventually dilute the linear offer further. Perhaps the whole concept would disintegrate if several major industries were now withdrawn and negotiated under special rules.

On the other hand, offers that were conditioned on reciprocal offers from a number of participants would probably degenerate to a minimum of final offers unless some positive and constructive action were initiated. Delegates therefore agreed, despite the pitfalls, to a proposal

11. See Chap. 8, pp. 130–34.

of Eric Wyndham White to establish sector working groups for five industries: chemicals, cotton textiles, iron and steel, nonferrous metals (principally aluminum), and pulp and paper. Membership in each group was limited to the countries with a major trade interest in that industry. Each group would examine conditions that might prevent a normal linear negotiation, and seek, where necessary, a solution that would facilitate an eventual settlement in keeping with the general rules of the negotiation. Factors other than straightforward tariff cuts could be considered where relevant. An even balance of trade benefits within each industry would not be an objective of the sector groups. Sector group meetings, in fact, would usually open with the chairman, Wyndham White, asking what specific factors prevented negotiations from proceeding on a normal linear basis. The burden of proof rested with those who were not making a linear offer.

Sector group discussions began in the spring of 1965 and in most cases continued intermittently to the final weeks of the negotiation in early 1967. Concessions were generally held back until the final stages of overall bargaining, but the basis for the final settlement was developed during the course of the sector group talks.[12]

Country Delegations at Geneva

In the first months of 1965 the country delegations arrived at Geneva and began to establish day-to-day working contacts with each other. Prior to the exchange of exceptions lists in November 1964, only a few permanent delegates had been in Geneva; the major preparation was carried out in capitals and appropriate people were flown to Geneva for periodic meetings. Once specific offers (or nonoffers in the case of exceptions lists) were tabled, however, it became necessary to accumulate a complete file of facts on individual tariff positions and to develop priorities for adjustments in these offers. This entailed a continuing series of bilateral meetings between country delegations in addition to the multilateral meetings on broader topics. For example, during the course of the negotiations there were eighty-eight official bilateral meetings between the United States and Canada, and fifty-eight between the United States and Japan. The minutes of these meetings contained a detailed account of virtually every product of trade interest to the countries involved.

12. A brief discussion of each of the sector groups is contained in Chap. 6.

The Canadian delegation was the first of the major delegations to arrive in the fall of 1964 and had to wait some time for its interlocutors. The first head of the delegation, former Under Secretary of State for External Affairs Norman Robertson, was later succeeded by career diplomat Ambassador Sidney Pierce. There were roughly a dozen members of the Canadian delegation,[13] about half of whom were from the Department of Trade and Commerce. Its organization was structured heavily toward negotiations with the United States, since almost two-thirds of Canadian trade is with its southern neighbor.

The Japanese delegation, headed by Ambassador Morio Aoki, one of the senior members of the Japanese diplomatic service, was relatively large, consisting of about twenty resident delegates. A large number of other Japanese usually appeared at meetings as well, reflecting in good part representation of the various ministries that vied energetically for influence over decisions on commercial policy.

The composition of European delegations was influenced by their proximity to Geneva. The small EFTA countries had an ambassador and perhaps two lower level officers resident at Geneva for the negotiation, but carried out most technical support work at home, flying in specialists when necessary. The United Kingdom, on the other hand, maintained a fairly large staff at Geneva of about twenty-five delegates. Headed by Ambassador Eugene Melville, ably seconded by Roy Denman of the Board of Trade, the British delegation was sometimes compared to an iceberg: only a handful of people ever appeared at meetings with other delegations while the remainder worked in seclusion at the United Kingdom mission.

The EEC was the only major participant that never established a resident delegation at Geneva. The reasons given for not doing so were the shortage of manpower and the need for key Commission officials to be in constant touch with Brussels. But the lack of a day-to-day contact at Geneva often hampered effective communication, and the presence of a Community delegation was frequently though unsuccessfully urged by other countries. Theodorus Hijzen, the Community counterpart to the resident ambassadors of other delegations, and his staff were consequently frequent travelers on Geneva-Brussels shuttle flights.

13. Although there was some turnover in personnel in all delegations during the course of the negotiations, the overall sizes remained about the same; the figures used here are based on GATT lists of delegates circulated in October 1966. The numbers do not include clerical workers and secretaries.

While the EEC Commission did the actual negotiating for the Community, member state representatives residing at the permanent country missions to the United Nations at Geneva were usually observers at official Kennedy Round meetings.

More important than the EEC's lack of a permanent delegation at Geneva, however, was its representatives' lack of negotiating flexibility. During the disparity debate, the agricultural talks, and the follow-up discussion of industrial exceptions and sector groups, it was often apparent that the Commission representative, acting within expressly limited Council mandates, was not able to go beyond these limits, even in making recommendations. This slowed down the negotiating procedure and discouraged other delegates from indicating what they might be willing to do or recommend.

The United States, with the broadest geographic trade interests, established the largest delegation of almost forty members. Under the direction of Ambassador Michael Blumenthal and his deputy James Lewis, a foreign service officer whose career in the commercial policy field stretched back to the Cordell Hull era, the bulk of the U.S. delegation was divided into five country negotiating teams, responsible for: the EEC, the EFTA, Canada (and other Commonwealth countries), Japan, and the developing countries. Each team had a chairman, a technical secretary (in all but one case both positions were filled by foreign service officers), and several commodity or country specialists from other executive agencies and the Tariff Commission. Congressional members of the U.S. delegation made occasional visits to Geneva to observe and comment on the negotiations. By far the most active was Representative Thomas B. Curtis of Missouri, whose reports were a major means of communication between the delegation at Geneva and the Congress. Many of the appointed nongovernmental advisers also visited Geneva, bringing the delegation up to date on conditions within industries and, more importantly as the negotiations proceeded, helping to establish priorities on concessions by other countries that were of value for U.S. exports and concessions by the United States that were apt to cause difficulty for U.S. firms. Of course, if the domestic industry was basically opposed to trade liberalization, its adviser tended to be reluctant to admit that any concession abroad would be useful or any at home was more or less undesirable.

Developing countries mostly had small delegations with little technical support. Some delegates resided in other European capitals. The

American delegation made it a practice to analyze its offers from the point of view of each participating developing country and to transmit copies of the analysis to the other delegations. The shallow representation of these countries was to some extent due to the shortage of technically competent people, but it also reflected the fact that developing countries had little of trade value to offer as bargaining leverage and tended to be passive recipients of what other participants were willing to give.

The Geneva based delegates carried on the bulk of the discussion and negotiation during the ensuing two and a half years. In addition to official meetings, personal relationships and informal contacts came to be important in anticipating problems and developing new initiatives. Delegations were supplemented from time to time by personnel from capitals, particularly specialists in such fields as the agricultural commodity groups and cotton textiles, and as the final stages of decision approached, a number of senior officials accompanied their countries' chief negotiators for varying periods of time. But the mass of technical knowledge and an appreciation of the subtleties of interrelated problems accumulated by the Geneva delegations were an essential ingredient when all issues converged during the last hectic weeks of negotiation.

Negotiations Fully Engaged

Industrial negotiations were thus fully engaged by early 1965. There were substantial differences in the size of initial exceptions lists, but the lists were not beyond negotiation and compromise. Much depended on clarification of technical matters, such as offers on parts of tariff positions and specification of offers for reductions of less than 50 percent. The greatest uncertainty concerned the five sector groups, which constituted about 30 percent of manufactured imports by the major participants.[14] Machinery and transportation equipment, on the other hand, covered 36 percent of imports and presented no serious multilateral problem, although a number of important exceptions to the linear cut were listed. The remainder included a diverse range of products, often of special interest to one or a few particular exporters, and problems could be taken up in the appropriate bilateral context.

14. Based on imports of countries in the Organization for Economic Cooperation and Development.

The stalemate in agriculture appeared to be broken in mid-March 1965. After much prodding by the Americans, a proposal by Wyndham White to halt general discussion and set a timetable for specific offers was officially agreed to on March 18. Proposals for a world cereals arrangement would be tabled in April and negotiation based on these proposals would begin soon thereafter. Aside from grains, the period from May to September would be used for a detailed examination of the various elements of agricultural protection, and regardless of the outcome, specific offers on meat, dairy, and all other agricultural products would be made no later than September 16, 1965. The April date for grains did slip to May 17, but on that date proposals were tabled by all major participants. They were general proposals in many respects; some key elements were left blank in the EEC proposal and there was, of course, wide divergence between exporters and importers on the crucial points. But talks began in June, first to clarify the content of the proposals and second to start the long process of trying to bridge the differences.

A touch of optimism was in the air as summer approached. A hopeful appraisal in *U.S. News and World Report* noted, "Negotiators are quite cheerful at the prospects. . . . Europeans are predicting tariff slashes may average 25%." [15] André Naef of the *Tribune de Genève*, while describing the "complex and at times Byzantine aspects" and the "jungle of technicalities," recognized the substantial if uneven progress made thus far.[16] Christian Herter, before the Metropolitan Washington Board of Trade on May 20, scolded the European Community on its excessive exceptions list: "It is a fact that some of its negotiating partners, including the U.S., consider this list to be overly large. . . ." But considering the unprecedented offers of other countries, he hoped that "these offers will prompt the Common Market to reduce its own exceptions list in the course of the negotiations. . . ." Finally, to put the whole matter in a positive perspective, Herter emphasized that "what is already *on* the bargaining table . . . is much more important, much more meaningful, than what is not."

The first half of 1965 ended the first phase of the Kennedy Round, the effort to table initial offers. On the whole it was successful, especially in comparison with past negotiations. The question now was whether the relatively high level of initial offers could be negotiated to

15. March 8, 1965.
16. May 31, 1965.

a balanced agreement at an even higher level, or whether the final bargaining would whittle away the initial offers to a lower or lowest common denominator of agreement.

The first half of 1965 also brought to an end, or at least severely dampened, the high political hopes for the Kennedy Round. The political importance of a prosperous commerce had been a basic factor in the American initiative and the European response to the negotiation. A successful Kennedy Round would provide a needed boost to American attitudes toward the Common Market, and to the general unity of purpose within the Atlantic community. These goals had been stressed in the appeal for a successful negotiation. Herter, before a Dutch audience in February 1965, spoke of "the overriding, the inescapable fact that the important problems today are wider-than-national, and we must perforce seek greater-than-national means of dealing with them. . . . Those, whether in Europe or America, who urge us to declare independence from one another are at best ignorant and at worst malevolent. . . . Our goal is a genuine Atlantic partnership, adequately organized to meet the political, military, and economic challenges of this era." As for the Kennedy Round, "the significance of these negotiations transcends guilders and dollars, pounds, francs, or deutschmarks." [17]

The political consequences of the negotiations remained an important element in major policy appraisals. But they ceased to be set forth in quite such lofty terms after June 1965. Partly this was because the bargaining became more specific and the raw commercial interests sharper. Partly it marked the general tension in the Atlantic community over the crisis within the North Atlantic Treaty Organization. Partly the Kennedy Round became a lower key commercial operation when the French delegate walked out of the EEC Council of Ministers meeting at two o'clock on the morning of July 1, 1965.

17. Feb. 4, 1965, at Amsterdam, before the Dutch chapter of the European Movement.

CHAPTER SIX

Industry Sector Groups

BEFORE MOVING INTO the period of delay and dismay for the Kennedy Round caused by the crisis within the European Economic Community in the latter half of 1965, the negotiations within the industry sector groups are summarized. This chapter describes the discussions within the pulp and paper, aluminum, iron and steel, and cotton textile sectors, following through to their conclusion in the last phase of Kennedy Round bargaining. The chemical sector, which became intimately involved with the final package agreement, is only introduced at this point.

The sector discussions were in some respects the most interesting part of the industrial negotiations. Once initial exceptions lists were exchanged, negotiation on other industrial products was limited almost entirely to bargaining on individual tariff positions—the traditional haggling inherent in the bargaining situation. But in the sector groups an attempt was made to consider the broader trade impact or overall industry structure as well. Trends and prospects for consumption, production, and trade, the effect of policy measures—tariffs, quotas, tariff quotas, valuation procedures—and tariff rate relationships within an industry or between countries were all discussed where relevant. This is not to say that the facts uncovered were solely or even in major part responsible for the final outcome. But they did help.

The form of negotiation varied considerably among the sector groups. There was extensive multilateral negotiation in the chemical and steel sector groups while the cotton textile negotiations were mostly bilateral. The pulp and paper and aluminum sector talks, on the other hand, consisted mainly of technical discussion, and the final negotiation became merged with the general balancing of total concessions.

Pulp and Paper

For a number of reasons the already large world trade in pulp and paper is growing steadily. The raw material, pulpwood, is unevenly distributed, and rich forest regions in the Nordic countries [1] and North America supply most of the pulpwood deficit in Western Europe and Japan. (Pulpwood reserves in Russia and some developing countries are largely inaccessible or undeveloped.) The initial transformation from pulpwood to pulp and the production of cheap bulky paper like kraft linerboard (heavy cardboard boxes) are most efficiently carried out near the source of the pulpwood. Quality paper production, on the other hand, is often advantageously located near large consuming areas. Consumption of paper in a modern industrial economy has risen sharply in recent years and this trend is expected to continue in the future. The following comparison of per capita consumption, in kilograms per year, illustrates the growth in a ten-year period: [2]

	1955	1965
Italy	17.5	45.8
Japan	24.0	72.0
France	42.0	72.1
West Germany	54.5	101.4
United Kingdom	81.4	112.0
United States	172.7	216.0

All major countries have maintained a healthy rate of growth in production and trade of paper. From 1955 to 1965 paper production increased 38 percent in the United Kingdom, 45 percent in the United States, 89 percent in the Common Market, 119 percent in the Nordic countries, and 231 percent in Japan. As a result of this prosperity the supply of Nordic pulpwood is rapidly approaching full utilization.

1. In the pulp and paper sector the Nordic countries were Finland, Norway, and Sweden. Toward the end of the Kenndy Round, a Nordic bloc that included Denmark as well was formed to negotiate jointly on all matters (see Chap. 8, pp. 125–26).

2. Organization for Economic Cooperation and Development (OECD), *Paper and Pulp 1965/66*, p. 22.

European importers of pulp are increasingly relying on the readily available North American supply, especially in British Columbia. The British were among the first to make the shift, but Germany's largest paper firm, Feldmühle, and Sweden's Svenska both established joint ventures with North American pulp producers in the early 1960s. Norwegian Borregaard, moving in a slightly different direction, announced plans in May 1966 to import much of its future pulp from Brazil.

This structural shift in global production, however, threatened an adjustment problem for EEC paper mills. The tightening pulp supply in the Nordic countries, in conjunction with a trend by Nordic paper mills to absorb larger shares of domestic pulp, could limit the supply available to continental mills. In 1965 Nordic pulp producers attempted to maintain their established export price levels even though new low-cost American pulp had created a temporary excess of supply in world markets. Continental mills feared that their pulp costs would be higher than those of integrated Nordic mills, and that they would in consequence be caught in a cost squeeze for paper production.

The EEC position in the Kennedy Round reflected these recent developments, a traditionally protectionist attitude in the Community paper industry, and strong views in some Commission and French circles that the pulp and paper market should be better organized. If tariffs were to be reduced, at least something had to be provided to keep Nordic paper exporters from seriously undercutting the continental market. Perhaps tariff cuts could be tied to a pricing policy or a price relationship between pulp and paper. Countries such as the United States and Canada would never sign an agreement related to pricing, but in 1965 the Nordics supplied two-thirds of EEC pulp imports and over three-quarters of EEC paper imports. The major objective was clearly to keep the Nordics in check.

Exporting countries were strongly opposed to conditional tariff cuts by the Common Market. Growth prospects in the EEC appeared to assure expanded markets for both domestic and foreign producers. Ample pulp supplies, especially from North America, would remain available to continental mills. Moreover, a clear and adequate offer by the EEC in this sector was a dominant factor in the balance of offers between the EEC and the Nordic countries as well as Canada. For the United States, pulp and paper was also one of the fastest growing export categories to the EEC and elsewhere. As an added complication, the United States realized that if the EEC did not make an adequate offer, the United Kingdom, whose paper industry was already struggling against preferential imports from the Nordic members of the European Free Trade Association and Commonwealth Canada, would be reluctant to lower its most-favored-nation duty to the United States.

Thus the trade problem in the pulp and paper sector was basically between the EEC and the Nordic countries although important trade interests of other countries would be affected by the outcome.[3] The EEC was unable to specify offers in November 1964, pending bilateral discussion with the Nordics, particularly with regard to export pricing. The 6 percent EEC duty on pulp was largely suspended, and a substantial cut was anticipated. But any reduction in the duties on paper, mostly in the 15–20 percent range, was highly uncertain. The sector group was therefore established to bring those diverse interests into accord. It was mostly an informal arrangement with few official meetings. The EEC and the Nordics entered into a long series of technical bilateral discussions, keeping the other members of the group informed of the progress. In July 1966 the Community was finally able to specify offers. The duty on pulp was offered for the full cut from 6 percent to 3 percent; small unconditional cuts were initially offered for paper, and these offers were improved during the final bargaining between the EEC and the Nordics in early 1967, resulting in reductions of approximately 25 percent for most categories; newsprint, of primary export interest to Finland, was treated separately for several reasons, and a bound duty-free quota was established by the Community. Considering that this sector had been one of the difficult problem areas, the results were generally satisfactory. Significant tariff cuts were made, and they were made on an unconditional, most-favored-nation basis.

Aluminum

World aluminum trade has some parallels with pulp and paper trade, although the factors involved are more complex and less clear-cut. Primary, or ingot, aluminum production tends to be located near the raw material, bauxite, or cheap power. Low-cost hydropower, particularly in Canada and Norway, has attracted a relatively large pro-

3. Japan's initial offer in this sector was very meager, but the trade involved was small, and the problem involved mainly North America. It therefore was not necessary to deal with this situation in the multilateral sector group.

portion of world ingot production. In 1965 these two countries accounted for about 20 percent of noncommunist world production and well over half of exports.[4] Fabricated aluminum, on the other hand, can be advantageously located near consumer markets; there is, nevertheless, a substantial multilateral trade in fabricated aluminum, the largest exporters being the EEC, the United States, and the United Kingdom, in that order.

Aluminum is the wonder metal with a growth in consumption of 8–10 percent per year since 1960, and this rate of growth is expected to continue almost indefinitely. It is predicted that U.S. consumption alone will more than quadruple from 1966 to 1986; and European per capita consumption, which is only one-third the U.S. level now, could expand at an even faster rate.[5]

Ingot production is changing structurally, however, because of the approaching full utilization of available hydropower and the eventual use of atomic energy. These developments will undoubtedly influence the pattern of aluminum production and trade, although it is difficult to predict the magnitudes or timing of the change.

Finally, aluminum production is dominated by several large, capital-intensive, integrated international firms. Roughly three-quarters of noncommunist world ingot capacity is owned, in whole or in part, by three large U.S. producers—Alcoa, Reynolds, and Kaiser—Canada's Alcan, France's Pechiney-Ugine, Norway's Aardal, and Switzerland's Alusuisse.[6] Moreover, these large primary producers have been integrating their ingot production with fabricating operations, often through foreign subsidiaries, thus increasing the amount of intrafirm shipments in world trade. The most striking example is Canada's Alcan. Long an ingot supplier to other countries, Alcan invested $156 million in fabricating facilities between 1959 and 1963. Sales of fabricated products jumped by over 70 percent and by 1966 Alcan maintained full or partial ownership of some sixty fabricating plants in thirty countries.

4. The United States produces 50 percent of noncommunist world output of aluminum ingot, but is nevertheless the largest net importer.
5. See "A Look Ahead" and "Aluminum Overseas," *Modern Metals*, January 1966, pp. 33–42 and 54–94. Industry figures in succeeding paragraphs, not otherwise cited, are from these articles.
6. Sterling Brubaker, *Trends in the World Aluminum Industry* (Johns Hopkins Press, 1967), p. 101, estimates that 63.9 percent was owned directly and another 12.7 percent consisted of a share ownership in 1963. He cites a study by Hans Bachmann for the United Nations Conference on Trade and Development that attributes 85 percent of total noncommunist capacity to these firms.

Pechiney-Ugine controls the largest single aluminum plant in the United States, near Seattle, Washington, inaugurated with great fanfare and the participation of the French ambassador in September 1966.

All of these circumstances seem to augur a move for maximum reduction in tariffs. In fact, some interest in completely free trade was expressed during the Kennedy Round, especially by Canada. Although the United States is by far the largest importer of ingot and fabricated aluminum, domestic industry firmly supported reciprocal 50 percent cuts in tariffs by all major countries. This attitude was based not on a dollars and cents calculation, but on a longer view of tariffs as a hindrance to international firms in this dynamic industry. It was also realized that global tariff cuts would strengthen the aluminum industry's ability to compete with substitute products, particularly steel.

And yet aluminum became a problem in the Kennedy Round—a problem which in the end resulted in a very modest and disappointing amount of tariff cuts. Japan considered it difficult to make substantial tariff reductions on aluminum, partially because of its obligation to grant most-favored-nation treatment to imports from the Soviet Union; but as in the pulp and paper sector, this was primarily a bilateral problem between Japan and North America. The principal stumbling block was the EEC, and primarily the French, which resisted making a significant offer on primary aluminum. Higher power and capital costs were claimed to disadvantage Community producers, although preferential power rates to large users and the actual cost of capital are difficult to document precisely. On the other hand, Pechiney-Ugine is technologically in the forefront in an industry where innovation is important [7] and is firmly established in international operations. The firm's aluminum production, moreover, of which about 40 percent is exported, more than tripled from 1950 to 1965 and increased by another 17 percent in 1966.[8]

The economic reasons for the EEC's withholding aluminum from tariff reduction were technically complex and certainly open to question. The EEC did not specify an offer for aluminum in November 1965, and the sector group set to work to examine the economic prospects

7. For example, Pechiney receives almost twenty times as much in royalties as it pays out, and power consumption by its principal producer was stated to be below 14,000 kwh. per metric ton, or significantly less than the average in the industry. See *Entreprise*, Feb. 17, 1966, and *Aluminum*, January 1965.
8. See *Les Echos* (Paris), April 5, 1967.

for aluminum trade and the implications of this sector on the overall balance. Norway and Canada had the largest stake as exporters, although the United States was also a major supplier to the Community. Furthermore, the United States was unlikely to make a full offer unless the other major import market, the EEC, made a comparable effort. The U.S. tariff of about 6 percent on ingot was already lower than the 9 percent common external tariff, and U.S. industry vehemently opposed a widening of this spread. The U.S. offer, however, was of principal interest to Canada and Norway, not the EEC, which further complicated the problem.

The form of a possible EEC offer was also a matter of discussion. The rate for aluminum ingot was bound at 9 percent under the General Agreement on Tariffs and Trade, although large amounts were imported by Germany and Belgium at 5 percent on a year-to-year permissive basis. This was a continuation of these countries' pre-Common Market procedure of importing ingot at low duties for their domestic fabricators. The option under consideration by the EEC in the Kennedy Round was whether to reduce the 9 percent rate or to bind an annual quota at 5 percent. Exporters preferred a reduction in the 9 percent rate. The range of possible bound quotas at 5 percent appeared to be below current levels, and with the anticipated rise in consumption, the 9 percent rate would remain the determinant of export growth.[9]

After considerable discussion of all aspects of the negotiation on aluminum, the sector group requested the GATT secretariat to undertake a study of aluminum production and trade in order to provide a convenient focal point for technical clarification in the final phase of the negotiations.

The EEC's initial offer, in July 1966, consisted of about 25 percent average cuts for fabricated aluminum and a GATT binding at 5 percent of an annual quota for ingot aluminum. The exporters were particularly dissatisfied by the quota offer on ingot and pressed for a reduction in the 9 percent, most-favored-nation rate. The issue remained unsettled until the last weeks of the negotiation. At that stage a tentative reduction from 9 percent to 7 percent was discussed at Geneva by the Commission but it was subsequently rejected by the EEC Council of Minis-

9. There were some advantages to a bound quota at 5 percent. The quota would bind a revenue transfer of the difference between 5 percent and 9 percent. It would also provide bargaining leverage for exporters if the EEC should decide in the future to consolidate its tariff with a single rate.

ters, and the final EEC concession for aluminum ingot was a binding at 5 percent of 130,000 metric tons per year (compared to total EEC imports from nonmembers in 1966 of 287,000 tons, of which 166,000 tons was imported by Germany and Belgium). The United States, in its final offer, reduced the duty on ingot aluminum by 20 percent and on fabricated aluminum by an average of about 25 percent. Japan reduced the effective tariff on ingot aluminum from 13 percent to 9 percent but made little reduction on fabricated aluminum.

Iron and Steel

A number of factors has converged to cloud the outlook for world trade in steel. Rapid construction of modern plants in many parts of the world has posed a continued threat of excess capacity. Substitute products such as aluminum and plastics have challenged steel in a number of its traditional markets. Some governments, especially in developing countries, equating steel production with national prestige, have subsidized expansion of high cost output. The United States, once a leading exporter of steel products, is now a large net importer. Total U.S. imports in 1966 were about 11 percent of consumption, although the figure for *net* imports, including indirect steel imports and exports in the form of machinery and other finished manufactures, was a more modest 7 percent. European production has fallen far short of capacity in recent years. Steel production in the EEC countries, consistently above 90 percent of capacity up until 1962, slipped to about 80 percent in 1965–66. Japan, on the other hand, has increased production from less than 20 million tons annually before 1960 to over 50 million tons in 1966. U.S. imports from Japan have increased from about 600,000 tons in 1959–61 to 4.9 million tons in 1966.[10]

But the concern over steel imports that built up in the United States during the Kennedy Round did not center on the level of tariffs, or even a significant reduction in them. Industry was primarily disturbed by alleged inequities in such matters as export subsidy and tax policy, or more generally, "distressed world market prices." Existing tariffs were in fact moderate: unweighted tariff averages in November 1964 were

10. These figures are all from *The Steel Import Problem* (American Iron and Steel Institute, 1967), except the figure on indirect steel trade, which appears in *Congressional Record*, daily edition, May 1, 1967, p. H4899, as part of a statement by Representative Thomas Curtis.

about 9 percent in the United States and the EEC, 11 percent in the United Kingdom, and 15 percent in Japan. Moreover, there was a distinct advantage to be gained by the United States in the Kennedy Round through tariff bindings. Of the three large consuming markets—the United States, the EEC, and the United Kingdom—only the United States had steel tariffs that were generally bound in GATT prior to the Kennedy Round. Thus if market conditions worsened, the EEC and the United Kingdom could raise tariffs without obligation to their trading partners, whereas the United States, if it raised tariffs, would be obliged to give massive compensation or face the threat of retaliation, in accordance with GATT procedures. If all countries bound their rates, on the other hand, future difficulties could be met on even terms.

The steel sector negotiations were headed for trouble even before the November 1964 tabling of exceptions lists, however, over the question of the base rates from which the Common Market would make its cuts.[11] The Paris Treaty of 1951, which established the European Coal and Steel Community (ECSC), provided for some harmonization of member-state external tariffs by the end of the transition period in 1958. The average legal rate of all the member states combined was about 15 percent at the time the ECSC was formed, although the actual duties paid were substantially lower because of temporary reductions and suspensions. The average rate also varied by country from about 4 percent in the Benelux countries (Belgium, the Netherlands, and Luxembourg) to over 21 percent in Italy. In 1958, external rates were harmonized to a large degree. Benelux and Germany adopted roughly the former Benelux rates plus 2 percent (or 6 percent) and France and Italy adopted rates 1–4 percent above the Benelux-German rates. The resulting average was slightly below 7 percent.

The Paris treaty required a GATT waiver, primarily because it departed from most-favored-nation treatment; the waiver also stipulated that duties at the end of the transitional period would be "lower and less restrictive than the general incidence of duties and regulations of commerce [heretofore] applicable." This latter point was not formally examined in 1958 when the transitional period ended, although it was fairly obvious that the harmonized 7 percent rates were below the

---

11. For most products in the steel sector, the Common Market countries were represented by the High Authority of the European Coal and Steel Community. The term Common Market is used here to mean the EEC and the ECSC, individually or together, as appropriate.

average of the earlier rates. As a further complication, in 1957 the United Kingdom and the ECSC had reached a separate agreement, outside GATT, in which the ECSC agreed to maintain the 7 percent rates in return for substantial tariff reductions on the part of the United Kingdom. Either party, however, could unilaterally increase duties after consultation with the other.

In February 1964 the ECSC "temporarily" increased its duties from 7 percent to about 9 percent. For its November 1964 Kennedy Round offer, moreover, it proposed to cut 50 percent, but from a set of rates constructed at a level of roughly 14 percent. In a press statement of November 16, the ECSC explained the 14 percent level as "slightly lower than the average of tariffs in force in the countries of the Community before the establishment of the latter. . . ." It further explained that the final level would therefore "be close to 6–7 percent," or about the same as before the temporary increase of February 1964.

This legalistic rationale to cut 50 percent from a set of constructed rates and end up with the same effective protection as before the negotiation started was unacceptable to the other Kennedy Round participants as a basis for agreement in the steel sector. They contended that the ECSC tariff cuts should be from the 7 percent rates that were in effect before February 1964, and conditioned their offers on improvement in the initial ECSC offer. The most adamant opposition came from the British, who had already paid once in 1957 for maintenance of the 7 percent rates, and now were being asked to cut their rates a second time, by 50 percent, for the same 7 percent rates in return.

By the spring of 1965, discussion on steel was completely deadlocked. There was disagreement on the base rates from which tariffs would be cut. There were also some possible disparity problems. Of all the sectors, steel seemed least appropriate for the linear approach. Consequently, the steel sector group decided to terminate the base rate debate and make a clean start. One objective that had received wide support was a move toward harmonization of steel tariff rates in the major trading countries. Harmonization would put to rest the idea that tariff differentials caused a deflection of exports from high to low duty markets. Steel might also be a sector where a degree of harmonization, in response to the EEC desire to reduce rate disparities in the Kennedy Round, could be undertaken in a mutually acceptable way. With this possibility in mind, the sector group therefore began by establishing a detailed concordance of steel tariff nomenclatures in all the major countries, and examining the alternatives for obtaining a harmonious reduction in tariffs.

For about a year and a half the laborious process of matching rate relationships continued but no clear solution emerged. Attempts to establish target rates for selected products foundered on the choice of targets. It was not until early 1967, when the sector was on the verge of dropping out of the Kennedy Round negotiation altogether—with serious repercussions elsewhere in the negotiation (see Chapter 10, p. 168)—that the rationale for the eventual agreement began to take shape. The new proposal consisted of a form of tariff harmonization whereby the United States basically would cut to the extent necessary to match the final Community tariff level for each tariff position. Since it was fairly clear that the EEC would at most cut from its current "9 percent level" to slightly below the original "7 percent level," the United States would be required to make a small but significant average cut of roughly 10 percent. Other countries would make a comparable but not necessarily a matched rate offer. Actually, in the final agreement, the United Kingdom cut generally by a flat 20 percent and Japan by 50 percent.

In sum, the steel settlement was a form of tariff harmonization, which appealed to Common Market *écrêtement* adherents; it resulted in tariff cuts of 10–20 percent by major importing countries; and it obtained GATT bindings on the previously unbound European tariffs. The member states of the European Coal and Steel Community, as part of the final agreement, also aligned their external tariffs uniformly. The United Kingdom, as it turned out, found the steel proposal least attractive, especially in view of its earlier agreement with the Common Market. The steel settlement, in fact, was not reached until the last days of bargaining and constituted a major concession by the United Kingdom in the final package agreement.

Cotton Textiles

The sector problem for cotton textiles was to combine Kennedy Round tariff reductions with continued operation of the GATT Long-Term Arrangement Regarding International Trade in Cotton Textiles. The arrangement, undertaken at the request of the United States in accord with President Kennedy's seven point program of assistance to the textile industry, was signed in February 1962. It initially covered the five-year period ending September 30, 1967. While the arrangement recognized the need for constructive action to facilitate exports of developing countries, its operative provisions were designed to protect markets threatened with disruption by imports. Importers could unilaterally restrain imports or reach bilateral agreements with exporting countries to do so. Import quotas were generally based on the level of imports in the previous year plus about 5 percent per year to allow growth.

Two structural shifts have affected the pattern of trade in cotton textiles in recent years.[12] First, exports of cotton textiles have been losing ground relative to other textiles, especially man-made fibers. Whereas the increase in exports of all textiles during the period 1960–66 roughly equaled that in all trade, exports of cotton textiles increased only marginally while exports of other textiles grew by more than 60 percent. The development of fiber blends, however, helped strengthen the position of cotton textiles in 1965 and 1966. The second structural shift has been the gain in developing countries' share of cotton textile trade. From 1960 to 1965 the volume of exports of cotton yarn and woven fabrics by industrial countries participating in the long-term arrangement declined by 21 percent and 13 percent, respectively, while exports of the participating developing countries increased by 22 percent and 10 percent. This trend continued in 1966 for yarn and fabric and has carried over to clothing as well since 1965.

The prospects of the cotton textile industry, including the relative status of industrial and developing countries, are not only a complicated but a controversial question. A 1966 GATT study stressed the dynamic elements of the industry.[13] Representative Thomas Curtis, citing both optimistic and pessimistic prognoses, referred to the American textile industry as "a veritable Janus." [14]

In the Kennedy Round, however, there was no question that importers would insist on an extension of the long-term arrangement as a condition to any significant tariff reduction. The EEC had made that explicit in its initial offer while other industrial countries, including the United States, were equally firm in their discussions with exporting

12. The following facts are taken from General Agreement on Tariffs and Trade (GATT), *International Trade 1966*, pp. 127–37.
13. *A Study on Cotton Textiles.*
14. *Congressional Record*, daily edition, July 24, 1967, p. H9228. This remark is taken from a lengthy statement on the textile industry as related to trade policy, pp. H9222–37.

countries. Developing countries, on the other hand, emphasized that the results in the textile sector would weigh heavily in their overall assessment of the negotiations. Textiles were the one major manufacturing industry in which these countries had developed a highly competitive export sector in spite of generally high levels of protection by importing countries. Exports of cotton textile manufactures, including clothing, by developing countries as a group totaled $1.8 billion in 1965, or over 40 percent of total manufactured exports by these countries.[15] Moreover, many developing countries were dissatisfied with the more restrictive features of the long-term arrangement and pressed for revisions during the Kennedy Round to liberalize it.

The sector group therefore sought an agreement combining maximum tariff cuts, renewal of the arrangement, and greater flexibility in the arrangement to permit increases in imports. Negotiations were predominantly bilateral. The United States stressed the domestic pressures that made revision of the existing arrangement extremely difficult, although it was disposed to discuss more satisfactory quota levels in some cases. Talks were long and arduous, especially with India, and it was not until early 1967 that an unrevised extension of the long-term arrangement for another three years became fairly certain. At this point the EEC was finally able to offer a tariff reduction of about 20 percent. The United States, which had earlier indicated that deeper tariff cuts might be possible if all major importers acted together, made a corresponding final offer of cuts only slightly more than 20 percent. Then, in the final days, the EEC, followed by the United States, indicated that tariffs might even "snap back" to their former levels if the long-term arrangement were discontinued at some future date. The final outcome, in consequence, was very disappointing to the exporting countries.

Chemicals

The chemical sector was to become the cause célèbre of the Kennedy Round, although the gravity of its problems was not fully realized in the spring of 1965. Traditionally, U.S. industry was opposed to major tariff reductions, but there were a number of reasons why reciprocal tariff cuts with only minimum exceptions would be beneficial to the

15. See *International Trade 1966*, p. 58. The figure pertains to all textiles, although for developing countries the overwhelming share consists of cotton textiles.

chemical industry. The industry in the United States and abroad was dynamic, characterized by large, diverse, international firms. New products were constantly being developed, and growth of sales was consistently high. From 1958 to 1965 the average annual increase in production was 8 percent in the United States, 10.5 percent in Western Europe, and 16.5 percent in Japan. Although wages were higher in the United States, so was productivity: value added per worker in 1965 was $22,340 in the United States, $7,660 in Western Europe, and $5,770 in Japan. Similarly, investment per worker in the United States was 50 percent higher than in Europe or Japan.[16] U.S. exports, roughly three times imports, contributed a healthy $1.6 billion surplus to the trade balance.

The negotiations on chemicals, however, were beset with problems. In the first place, tariff disparities were most heavily concentrated in this sector. Both the United States and the United Kingdom had numerous high rates even though each was a strong net exporter of chemicals. The disparity problem was complicated by differences in nomenclature that prevented direct matching of rates. Most EEC tariff positions were related in part to high American or British rates, although it was difficult, and sometimes impossible, to determine how much so.

There were also many chemical items on the initial exceptions lists. The EEC had a number of sensitive items listed, and the United Kingdom had a special problem with plastics. Plastics are traded in large volume by the giants of the industry, and reportedly are often "unloaded offshore"—a euphemism for dumping. British tariffs on plastics, however, were only about 10 percent, while Community rates were 20–25 percent and American rates approximately 40 percent. On the other hand, British tariffs were not bound in GATT. As a consequence the United Kingdom was unwilling to cut or bind its tariff on plastics except as part of a major all-round reduction. There was even reason to believe that short of this result, the United Kingdom would raise its tariff to the EEC level after the Kennedy Round.

The real stumbling block in the negotiations, however, was the American selling price (ASP) system of duty valuation for certain benzenoid chemicals. Although the system applied to only a small share (about 10 percent) of the U.S. chemical market, it had long

16. The foregoing facts are taken from OECD, *The Chemical Industry 1965–1966.*

caused bitter resentment among European exporters. Basically, duty was assessed on the value of a comparable U.S. product, rather than the value of the imported product. The American selling price frequently required a much higher duty payment than would the value of the imported product; moreover, the uncertainty of the eventual duty assessment made costs difficult to project. The situation was aggravated by the widely held view in Europe that products highly protected by the American selling price in the United States were scoring the largest U.S. export gains on the European market.[17] In consequence, the EEC and the United Kingdom conditioned a major part of their chemical offer on U.S. action to abolish the American selling price system and substitute normal valuation procedures.

The combination of disparities, exceptions, and the American selling price system resulted in a very small initial chemical offer by the United Kingdom and the EEC, but this bleak fact did not immediately cause alarm for several reasons. In the spring of 1965 the general preoccupation was still agriculture, and the later negotiation of exceptions and disparities was considered largely an overall balancing problem rather than isolated problems within particular industries. The American selling price system, on the other hand, could appropriately become a matter for the nontariff barrier committee, but considering the reluctance of other participants to negotiate seriously in the nontariff barrier field, the United States did not feel the problem was especially pressing. Probably most important was the unprecedented U.S. offer in the chemical sector based on a 50 percent linear cut. No offer even remotely comparable had ever been made in the past. The trade significance of the American selling price system was small by comparison, and it appeared unlikely that the Europeans would risk losing the opportunity to obtain deep linear cuts in the American tariff. But the Americans did not realize the irrational and emotional response the system could provoke. The issue became exaggerated far out of proportion to its trade significance, and in the end the Europeans paid handsomely for their objective. Meanwhile, participants in the sector group slowly dug in their opposing positions for the long siege.

17. See Pierre Millet, "L'American Selling Price," *Communauté Européenne*, July-August 1965.

CHAPTER SEVEN

Anxious Interlude

July 1965–February 1966

THE REASONS FOR THE crisis in the European Economic Community (EEC) from July 1965 to January 1966 are complex.[1] The crisis brought into the open the underlying conflict between General de Gaulle's concept of a *Europe des Patries* and the evolving supranational aspects of the Common Market, although the issue did not become explicit until two months after the initial break. The ostensible cause of the crisis was an invitation by the Council of Ministers, in December 1964, to the Commission to submit proposals by March 31, 1965, on the financing of the common agricultural policy for the period 1965–70, and on the budgetary conditions once the farm policy was in full effect, or at the single market stage. The Commission developed a set of bold and interrelated proposals that went much further than the French, at least, had anticipated. It first proposed that the single market stage begin in July 1967, and it submitted prorated budgetary keys for the two-year period up to that time. After 1967 there would be, as suggested in article 201 of the Rome Treaty, a gradual transfer of revenues from the common external tariff on industrial products from the member states to the Community to finance the Community budget, the largest part of which was the cost of the farm policy. (It had already been agreed that levies on agricultural imports would be used for the farm program, but this source of revenue would cover only part of the total cost.) In addition, the Commission proposed revisions of articles 201 and 203 of the Rome Treaty to give the European Parliament a significant role in the budget making process. As one element in the

<hr>

1. See Miriam Camps, *European Unification in the Sixties: From the Veto to the Crisis* (McGraw-Hill for Council on Foreign Relations, 1966), Chap. 2.

explanation for this ambitious timetable, the introduction to the proposals mentioned "the need to be able to discuss all imporant agricultural products in the Kennedy Round negotiations on the basis of the Community's margin of support." [2]

EEC Negotiations in Brussels

As expected, France objected to a decision at this time on the use of revenues from the common tariff, adamantly opposed greater power for the European Parliament, and pressed for unconditional agreement on financing the cost of the farm program through 1970. The other five member states generally supported the Commission proposals but with some qualifications. Since France would benefit most from agreement on financial regulations, it was felt that some commitment by France on the related institutional questions might be extracted at this point.

As the June 30 deadline for the decision approached, there was great uncertainty about the outcome, but events prior to the final confrontation, and particularly bilateral talks beween the French and the Germans, indicated that some sort of negotiated compromise was in the offing. Perhaps an agreement on financing could be worked out in conjunction with a declaration of intent on the other issues. The final meeting, in keeping with Community practice, was a marathon ministerial session that ran from June 28 to June 30. Maurice Couve de Murville, the conference president, stressed the sanctity of the June 30 deadline for reaching agreement. But as the deadline approached, the deadlock continued. The apparent harmony between the Germans and the French changed to sharp disagreement on a number of points. A last minute attempt at conciliation by Belgian Foreign Minister Paul-Henri Spaak failed. A recourse could have been to stop the clock and try again in early July, but Couve de Murville adjourned the meeting at two in the morning on July 1 and announced to the press, "We have been compelled to record that agreement was impossible." [3]

Effect on the Geneva Negotiations

The breakdown at Brussels was immediately felt in Geneva. As a result of the "shock waves of President Charles de Gaulle's explosion under the European Common Market . . . the Kennedy Round . . . sud-

2. *European Community Bulletin*, supplement, No. 5, 1965, p. 5.
3. Agence Europe Presse, July 1, 1965.

denly has sagged to a point where it is all but impossible to find a pulse beat." [4] This zealous press account described more accurately the effect on delegates than on the negotiations proper, but as soon as it became evident that a major and probably lengthy crisis had set in, the crippling effect on the talks on the General Agreement on Tariffs and Trade was equally clear. The EEC Commission had been negotiating within narrowly defined mandates, unanimously agreed to by the Council of Ministers. Although some technical work could continue under the existing mandate, any significant steps forward would require a new Council decision, with French participation.

Even if the EEC crisis were eventually resolved, a prolonged suspension in decision making at Brussels raised two dangers in regard to the timing of the Kennedy Round. First was the loss, or further loss, of momentum to push the talks to a successful conclusion. The longer tariff offers lay exposed on the negotiating table, the greater would be the pressure to reduce their scope or to let the agreement slide by altogether. Protectionists were always ready to press their case for withdrawing offers on particular items, and there were other convenient reasons—balance of payments, technology gap, consolidation of the customs union—that might be effectively mobilized to urge that tariff cuts be postponed for another day. The second danger was the possibility, taken seriously for the first time, that time could run out on the U.S. negotiating authority. June 30, 1967, still a good way off, rolled steadily closer as the negotiators at Geneva waited out the Brussels discord.

The complexion of the negotiation was also bound to change, regardless of how and when the Community crisis was resolved. The unity of the Six had been badly shaken, and the Commission role was soon to be challenged by the French. The Geneva talks became, temporarily at least, more an ad hoc pursuit of a mutual commercial interest than a show of European solidarity.

One immediate mitigating circumstance was the approach of the August vacation period which in Europe amounts to a virtual halt of all but the most urgent official business. The Kennedy Round had been scheduled to recess during August. The principal activities during July were continuation of the technical agricultural discussions and a confrontation and justification procedure for industrial exceptions of par-

4. *Los Angeles Times*, July 11, 1965.

ticular trade interest to developing countries. Although the French delegate was conspicuously absent as an observer at these meetings, the Commission representatives were able to proceed under the existing mandate. The mood was tense but so far there were no overt signs in Geneva of the Brussels crisis. As one delegate commented, "It's like being at a dinner party where the hostess is absent. You politely pretend to believe your host's excuse that his wife is upstairs with a headache, when you know perfectly well that she has run away." [5] On July 23 the GATT negotiations were recessed for the summer holidays under an ominous storm cloud.

Dilemma of the Other Participants

The top level American officials both in Geneva and Washington, however, were unable to enjoy a leisurely European holiday in August 1965. The EEC crisis had provoked a major policy decision for the United States and other Kennedy Round participants. September 16 had been agreed as the date for tabling specific offers on all remaining agricultural products. It was now apparent that, short of a miraculous European reconciliation, the EEC would not be able to participate in that exercise. Would other countries therefore postpone their offers until the EEC was in a position to reciprocate, or should they proceed and make their offers on September 16 without the EEC?

The United States, which had stressed from the beginning the necessity of including agriculture in the final agreement, foresaw advantages—or more precisely, disadvantages—to either alternative. If September 16, after all the previous delay, were now postponed indefinitely, agriculture might drop out of the negotiation altogether. Pressure to settle for a hurried industrial package would be hard to resist in light of the EEC internal situation and the terminal date for U.S. negotiating authority. The members of the European Free Trade Association (with the exception of Denmark) and Japan had never been enthusiastic about agriculture in the Kennedy Round and they might prove more than willing to dispose of this thorny sector as a casualty of the EEC crisis.

Going ahead without the EEC, on the other hand, could reduce pressure on the Community to make significant offers at a later time. The

5. Quoted in the *Journal of Commerce* (New York), July 27, 1965.

principal leverage to date had been a parallel schedule for all countries, with an indirect link, at least, between progress in industry and agriculture. Another disadvantage to moving ahead was the possibility that offers, once tabled, might have to be withdrawn en masse at a later point (if the EEC did not eventually put forward offers). A number of U.S. farm products were sensitive to import competition and would not be offered without a comparable effort on the part of the Community. Withdrawal at a later point, however, could have a serious effect on third countries, and put the United States in the uncomfortable position of the initial unraveler.

A partial solution to the potential withdrawal problem was to separate items of primary interest to the EEC out of the September 16 offer. But this approach was limited by the overlap of trade interests. The best example was canned hams, one of the fastest growing U.S. import categories. The EEC share, mostly Dutch, was $25 million in 1964, or about 15 percent of U.S. dutiable agricultural imports from the EEC. Danish exports to the United States, however, were $45 million, or one-half of total U.S. dutiable imports from Denmark, both industrial and agricultural.[6]

After a careful weighing of the pros and cons, the United States favored moving ahead on schedule and tabling offers on September 16. Items of major interest to the EEC, however, would be held back from the initial offer and the official announcement by Christian Herter on August 19 explicitly warned that U.S. offers "are made in the expectation that the other major participants will make . . . offers of like degree. If this proves not to be the case, the United States will withdraw or modify its offers on both agricultural and industrial products to the extent it deems necessary to achieve reciprocity in the negotiations."[7]

The United States also took the initiative in Geneva to convince other participants to proceed with the September 16 date. With some misgivings the strategy of maintaining the schedule was accepted. As for the EEC, the Herter statement summed up the general view: "We under-

6. By 1966, U.S. imports of canned hams had increased to $47 million from the EEC and $83 million from Denmark. Actually, the U.S. duty was about 4 percent, but of far greater significance was the fact that it was one of the few important American tariffs not bound in the GATT. The final agreement resulted in a GATT binding of the 4 percent level, a good example of a valuable concession that does not appear in an analysis of depth of tariff cuts.

7. Press release, U.S. Office of Special Representative for Trade Negotiations, Aug. 19, 1965.

stand the difficulties confronting it at this time and hope they may be resolved. We anticipate that the EEC, which occupies a key role in the negotiations, will be able to table agricultural offers, if not on September 16 then at an early date."

The French Rebuff

Events took another gloomy turn with General de Gaulle's press conference on September 9. The EEC Commission was rebuked as an "embryonic technocracy, for the most part foreign." [8] More fundamental, for the first time qualified majority voting in the Council, scheduled for January 1, 1966, was specifically challenged. This thrust to the core of the Community structure confirmed the pessimists who had predicted far more than an agricultural problem in the June 30 breakdown. At the same press conference a correspondent asked, "Mister President, what do you feel are the prospects for the Kennedy Round at Geneva?" [9] But in the sweep of the general's replies, this question was left unanswered.

The September 16 tabling of agricultural offers gave a boost to the Geneva talks even though the Common Market demurred. Aside from that event and the technical follow-up discussions, however, the ensuing months were a discouraging time for Kennedy Round delegates. As Bernard Nossiter summed up, "Negotiators . . . are dutifully meeting each other nearly every day . . . but nobody has any illusions . . . because of the impasse in Brussels . . . the bargainers here are working on a host of marginal issues." [10] As a clear indication that the French government would not engage the Kennedy Round problems while the internal EEC crisis prevailed, a scheduled visit to Paris on September 20–21 by Eric Wyndham White to speak with French officials was abruptly canceled by the French government two days before. Although a GATT official explained to the press that "the mission would be more useful at a later stage," [11] this rebuff of the director general was interpreted at Geneva as renewed evidence of French negativism toward the Kennedy Round.

Another visitor to Paris, this time Ambassador Blumenthal, delivered

8. *Communauté Européenne*, October 1965.
9. *Tribune de Genève*, Sept. 15, 1965.
10. *New York Herald Tribune* (international edition), Oct. 23/24, 1965.
11. *Financial Times* (London), Sept. 21, 1965.

a measured warning of the gravity of the EEC stalemate to the Kennedy Round in a speech before the Anglo-American Press Association on October 28. The speech was widely quoted in Europe and the United States. He alluded to a common European view:

> There are people, though favoring the principle of trade liberalization, who feel the time is not right, that perhaps a date five years from now would be more suitable. Let me say plainly that we do not have the luxury of such a choice. The timing of the Kennedy Round is far more than a secondary or tactical matter. It is a unique opportunity, a coincidence of favorable circumstances that may not repeat itself in the future if it is not made to succeed today. . . . We are in fact reaching a critical point from which there may be no return. The coming months will be crucial ones, for if we approach another summer without the makings of a balanced final agreement, we may have missed the tide that will take us safely over the bar. If support wanes, if the time clock runs out, we could be left stranded with the remains of an "almost agreement." . . . It is also important to realize the consequences of an unsuccessful negotiation. A continuation of the status quo is not the likely outcome. . . . There is a tenuous balance in many countries between the supporters of more liberal trade and those advocating a return to increased tariffs and protection. Impotence to achieve results in Geneva could well swing the balance in the direction of higher protection. . . . The threat of regression in our trading relations is a real and constant danger which should not be borne lightly.

Kennedy Round activity reached its nadir in the last weeks of 1965 and expressions of apprehension were widespread: Professor Karl Winnacker, head of the Chemical Industry Association of Hannover, on the decreasing chances for success at Geneva: "Throughout the world a phase of disintegration threatens." The *National Zeitung* of Basel: "1965 was a year of stagnation." Dr. Marcus Wallenberg, president of the International Chamber of Commerce: If progress is not made, "it is feared that many countries will return to the restrictive policies that the ICC has always vigorously condemned." André Naef of the *Tribune de Genève:* "Since June, the Kennedy Round has been like a car that has run out of gasoline. As long as the road is downhill it keeps rolling. Then . . ." [12]

Alternatives to EEC Participation

Another reaction to the stall in the negotiations was a spate of speculation and serious thought about alternative courses of action if

12. Respectively, *Handelsblatt* (Hannover), Nov. 16, 1965; *National Zeitung,* Dec. 29, 1965; *Les Echos* (Paris), Dec. 29, 1965; *Tribune de Genève,* Nov. 5, 1965.

the EEC were to cease participation in the talks altogether. A provocative piece in the *New York Herald Tribune* by Don Cook,[13] claiming that the United States had been discussing with Britain, Sweden, Canada, and Japan the idea of eliminating the Common Market from the GATT talks, evoked a hasty and definitive denial from the State Department. A more searching question was raised in a series of suggestions for some kind of Atlantic free trade area without the initial participation of the Common Market.[14] Senator Jacob Javits, at a news conference in London on November 10, suggested an Atlantic common market of the United States, Canada, Britain, and any other EFTA or EEC countries who wanted to join. Tariffs might be gradually eliminated over a twenty-year period. Edward English, a prominent Canadian economist, argued persuasively for a wider group including Australia, New Zealand, and Japan. Representatives Henry Reuss and Robert Ellsworth advocated, if the EEC failed to negotiate satisfactorily, proceeding with the GATT talks but withholding most-favored-nation tariff reductions from the EEC until it could and would make comparable concessions.

These ambitious alternatives had an unrealistic ring in Europe toward the close of 1965. Except for the unlikely possibility of a complete disintegration of the Common Market, which would require a painful and probably lengthy stocktaking by all countries, the prevailing concern was bridge building rather than bridge burning between the two Western European blocs. Withholding most-favored-nation treatment from the EEC or even forming a broader economic bloc without initial Community participation would exacerbate the split and make reconciliation more difficult. The priority of European trade to Europeans was evident in the prevailing pattern of trade: two-thirds of Swiss industrial trade was with the EEC versus a tenth with the United States; for Sweden, the figures were a half versus a tenth; even the United Kingdom had about twice as much trade with the EEC as with the United States.

A related problem in any far-reaching effort to liberalize trade without the Community was where to draw the line on membership. Canada had long demurred on a broad arrangement limited to North America;

13. International edition, Oct. 11, 1965.
14. The concept of such a free trade area had been under discussion for some time. See Maxwell Stamp Associates, *The Free Trade Area Option: Opportunity for Britain* (Ditchling Press, November 1967), pp. 26–36.

free trade with Japan raised problems in both directions; should developing countries be invited, or would it be a restricted, rich man's club? These are important questions that will arise in any appraisal of new initiatives in world trade. They appeared especially overwhelming in late 1965 when one-half of Western Europe was steeped in internal crisis and the other half was watching nervously with crossed fingers.

A far more modest but perhaps more acceptable immediate response to the EEC paralysis would have been a Kennedy Round settlement on a most-favored-nation basis limited to tariff items in which the EEC had little or no export interest. This traditional GATT procedure for dealing with nonparticipants rests on the practical assumption, however, that all major trading partners actively participate. It is one thing to exclude a Thailand or even a Mexico, but quite another to minimize benefits to the single largest trading bloc. Again the situation of the EFTA countries illustrates the point: The EEC was the principal supplier in 90 percent of the dutiable nonagricultural tariff categories of Swiss imports in 1964, and those categories included about 70 percent of U.S. exports to Switzerland. Categories where the EEC was principal supplier accounted for 60 percent of U.S. exports to the United Kingdom, and 50 percent to Sweden. A much smaller share of U.S.-Canadian and U.S.-Japanese trade was so affected, but even in these cases, existing supplier shares may not reflect the scope of future trade benefits. Japan, for example, with a relatively small share of its imports from the Community in 1964, might anticipate a substantial increase after tariff cuts.

In short, there was no good alternative to EEC participation in the Kennedy Round. Bold new ventures appeared unrealistic for some time to come if the present negotiations ended in bitter disaccord. A limited most-favored-nation package without the EEC would do little more than save face for the long and disappointing effort. Even a drawn out or partial conciliation of the Six, resulting in a last minute Kennedy Round agreement based on existing offers, would be a preferable outcome. It would have more substance and keep the air clear for the future.

In the meantime, public speculation about exalted alternatives was distracting and tended to discredit the limited progress achieved thus far at Geneva. The frustrations of the past two and a half years had dissipated the original enthusiasm for the Kennedy Round and talk of brave new strategies only exaggerated, as Mark Twain would say, the reports of its death. Governments, in turn, took frequent occasion to stem the waning interest by reaffirming their intentions. A particularly significant statement was contained in the Johnson-Erhard joint communiqué, at the conclusion of the latter's visit to Washington on December 21: "The President and the Chancellor agreed that the successful conclusion of the Kennedy Round trade negotiations is of major importance . . . these historic negotiations must move forward as rapidly as possible with the active participation of the EEC."

End of the Deadlock

By November there were faint signs of a break in the Community deadlock. The "five" had maintained a unified front against French demands but at the same time were seeking a reasonable means to bring France back into the fold. At a Council meeting of the five on November 29–30 the Council president, Emilio Colombo of Italy, was designated spokesman to engage in discussions with Paris. The objective, based on an earlier proposal by Paul-Henri Spaak, was to arrange a meeting of the Six ministers within the Community framework, but without participation by the Commission, to discuss the political issues involved. A neutral location, Luxembourg, was chosen for the meeting.

The Commission also showed signs of rejuvenation. A technical but pressing problem concerning the minimum import price for oranges was effectively handled with the participation of the French representative to the management committee. As for the Kennedy Round, the Commission was instructed by the Council (of five) to draw up a detailed position report, outlining the need for additional Council decisions to complete the negotiations. The report was scheduled for completion in January, and served as a useful focal point of operations once the Community was fully back in operation.

A definitive answer from Paris awaited the French presidential elections in December. Strong electoral support for the Common Market, especially by farm groups, was partly responsible for De Gaulle's failure to win a majority vote in the first round of balloting on December 5. The French attitude became markedly more conciliatory during the election interim, and shortly after General de Gaulle's victory in the runoff election on December 19, France agreed to meet with its Common Market partners as proposed by the Council of five.

The first Luxembourg meetings took place on January 17–18, 1966.

A second set of meetings was scheduled for January 28, and it was apparent that agreement was in sight. Hopeful speculation about the Kennedy Round sprouted accordingly, and attention shifted to setting a new timetable for the negotiation, an exercise now of counting backwards from the June 1967 deadline.

The long anxious interlude had passed. Negotiations had remained engaged and intact, although the weight of the protracted marking of time hung heavy. All participants, weary of swearing allegiance to the Kennedy Round, were anxious to terminate the affair. Developing countries were more impatient than ever with the continuing delay. Stirrings for a new United Kingdom bid for entry into the Common Market and the second United Nations Conference on Trade and Development scheduled for mid-1967 were already competing for the attention of commercial policy officials. As 1966 began, it was widely proclaimed the final year of decision for the Kennedy Round.

CHAPTER EIGHT

Luxembourg Compromise: Negotiations Resume

February 1966–December 1966

THE MINISTERS OF THE European Economic Community, at a Council meeting in Luxembourg on January 30, 1966, agreed to disagree and the Common Market crisis ended. The overriding political question—whether qualified majority voting would determine Community actions as stipulated in the Rome Treaty—was left open. France claimed the right to a veto "when very important interests are at stake" while the other five stood by the Rome Treaty. Noting that "there is a divergence of views" on this issue, the countries unanimously agreed to get back to work on the backlog of Community business. The general mood was one of relief and there was a concerted effort to play down the significance of the political disagreement in the so-called Luxembourg compromise and to concentrate on the practical matters facing the Community in the months ahead.

The two principal areas of outstanding business for the Community were internal farm policy and the Kennedy Round. Apprehensions about French intentions in the Kennedy Round were dispelled to some degree by General de Gaulle in his first postelection press conference on February 21. In typically vague terms he spoke of the need to strengthen the French economy in order to meet the competition of a coming worldwide lowering of tariffs.[1] This course was dictated not only by commercial self-interest, but by the balance of commitments that had been worked out within the Community. German agreement on internal agricultural decisions was informally but strongly linked

1. "Ces mesures sont en concordance avec ce qu'exige de nous la concurrence internationale, telle que nous l'affrontons dès à présent dans le Marché Commun et telle que nous la rencontrerons plus tard dans un système d'abaissement mondial des tariffs." (Quoted in *Entreprise*, June 30, 1966.)

to French cooperation in Kennedy Round matters. The post-Luxembourg period was especially devoid of generosity that earlier may have been ascribed to Community spirit. Any concession by one member was now in response to or anticipation of a benefit derived from others. This package-deal approach was not new to intra-Community bargaining. The scales were merely adjusted with greater precision.

But package dealing can be time consuming, and a growing threat to the Kennedy Round was the expiration of the Trade Expansion Act, now only a little more than a year away. The real negotiating deadline was even closer, for a number of months would be required after basic agreement had been reached to settle the myriad of minor details and to prepare, translate, and check the lengthy tariff schedules of each participant. Eric Wyndham White had circulated a report in early January that surveyed the status of the negotiations and stressed the time pressure. It dealt in detail with industrial sector groups, agriculture, and trade interests of developing countries. In particular, the report clearly indicated the points on which a Community decision was required to get negotiations moving again.

The weeks following Luxembourg, however, were disappointing for those who anticipated a rapid resurgence of activity at Geneva. February and March slipped by mainly in preparation, within the Community, of the various dossiers; in general, priority was given to the internal agricultural policy. Discussion was resumed on the financial regulations of the farm policy that had precipitated the crisis, and at the end of March the Commission also proposed marketing regulations for most outstanding commodities, in particular beef and veal and dairy products. Kennedy Round matters were relegated to the lower level "111 committee" of member state representatives who were to study the hundred-page Commission report that had been in preparation since the past November. The major area of the Kennedy Round where the Community lagged behind, of course, was agriculture. Important elements of the EEC grain proposals were still lacking, and no offers had yet been made on the whole range of other farm products. For industry, specific offers in the aluminum and pulp and paper sectors, plus a number of scattered items elsewhere, were outstanding.

An EEC ministerial meeting on April 5–6 produced the first concrete movement for the Kennedy Round with agreement on two relatively minor matters—specified partial offers on several chemical products, and a decision to offer a tariff quota at 5 percent for aluminum ingot (although the size of the quota was not specified). Even though the latter decision was disheartening to exporters, the fact that there were decisions was a fresh breath of air after almost a year of inactivity. Hopes rose for a more comprehensive move during another meeting scheduled for early May.

Meanwhile, anxiety over continued slippage of time was being expressed, particularly by the Americans. Ambassador Blumenthal stressed the time factor in speeches at Rome and Bad Godesberg in March: [2] "Failure to make decisions will be a decision to fail." A stern warning came from Wyndham White in his report to the annual meeting of the contracting parties to the General Agreement on Tariffs and Trade: "Unless governments are able, in a very short time . . . to have delegations in a position to engage negotiations actively and continuously on all fronts, we must begin to yield to a certain pessimism as to the possibilities of carrying the negotiations forward to a successful conclusion. . . . I would therefore be failing in my duty to the contracting parties if I were not to express my deepest concern at the situation." [3] Christian Herter, in a statement before a Senate subcommittee, described as perhaps the most pessimistic since his appointment as special trade representative, linked the Kennedy Round with deteriorating circumstances elsewhere in the Atlantic community. But although the trade negotiations "are not going well and have suffered serious setbacks," he expressed hope for an improvement in the next few months.[4]

The stage, in fact, was being set for a completion of all outstanding offers by summer, leaving the fall and winter to negotiate a final agreement.

Problems To Be Settled

Events did begin moving again in May. The EEC Council of Ministers reached agreement on May 11 at five in the morning on the financial regulations that had precipitated the crisis a year earlier: a complicated burden-sharing procedure until 1970, noteworthy in that France would pay a slightly higher share than Germany; a unanimous

2. Before the Institute for International Relations, March 12, 1966, and the Carl Schurz Association, March 16, 1966.
3. Press release no. 957, General Agreement on Tariffs and Trade (GATT), April 22, 1966.
4. Press release, U.S. Information Agency, Information Service, May 6, 1966.

declaration of intent about the use of receipts from common external tariffs for the Community budget after 1970; and a declaration of intent by the five (but not France) to reinforce the authority of the European Parliament. The Germans, however, made the accord on farm finance conditional upon reaching the necessary decisions for the Kennedy Round.

A number of Kennedy Round decisions were taken at a Council meeting of June 13–14. Modest but unconditional most-favored-nation offers were adopted for paper and pulp; [5] the size of the ingot aluminum quota as well as offers for tariff reduction on fabricated aluminum products were specified; and the blanks were filled in on the cereals proposals. The rest of agriculture carried over into July, but after a five-day Council meeting, both internal regulations and Kennedy Round agricultural offers were finally agreed to on July 27 for all but a handful of especially difficult products. Three years and two months after the initial GATT ministerial meeting, a virtually complete set of offers was on the table.

Complete was not, of course, synonymous with adequate, and there were quick reactions of "only token offers" and "no offer at all," especially in regard to ingot aluminum and nongrain farm products. Herter characterized the Common Market's agricultural decisions as "at first glance very restrictive" and its poultry offer as "absurd." [6] But in addition to genuine anxiety, statements by all participants were taking on an increasingly hard line in anticipation of the bargaining ahead.

The approach of the final negotiating stage provoked activity on a number of other fronts as well. One interesting development was consolidation of the Nordic countries (Denmark, Finland, Norway, and Sweden) into a single negotiating unit. The final bargaining sessions were apt to be restricted to a limited number of participants, and the small countries in the European Free Trade Association (EFTA) consequently excluded. The four Nordic countries therefore announced that for the remainder of the Kennedy Round they would negotiate jointly under the unified command of Swedish Ambassador Nils Montan. The four-country market of 20 million people combined im-

5. See Chap. 6, p. 99.
6. *Foreign Policy Aspects of the Kennedy Round*, Hearings before the Subcommittee on Foreign Economic Policy of the House Committee on Foreign Affairs, 89 Cong. 2 sess. (1966).

ports of $3.8 billion annually from the Common Market, an amount comparable to U.S. imports from the Community and larger than that of the United Kingdom. The Nordic group, as well as the Swiss, played a key role in the closing phase of the negotiation. In particular, their offer of linear cuts without an exceptions list acted as a gadfly to the European Community. Whether the problem were a particular disparity claim, a sector group such as pulp and paper, or some other special interest, a concession could be made to a small European neighbor that would not be considered for the larger trading partners.

The United States was also faced with new decisions as the pace of the negotiations began to pick up. One question was whether the administration should seek an extension of the Trade Expansion Act beyond June 30, 1967. Unforeseen events, such as the EEC crisis, might justify extending the negotiating deadline in order that it could not be held responsible for any shortcomings. In particular, the United States had to guard against being coerced by its own negotiating time limit into making last minute concessions. On the other hand, the year remaining appeared sufficient time if participants had the political will to negotiate actively, and after all of the delays caused by the Common Market the United States could hardly be blamed if five years proved inadequate to bring the negotiations to completion. Moreover, considering the mood of frustration and even hostility in the United States to recent events in Europe and a growing surge of protectionist pressure, any attempt to extend the act ran a serious risk of having crippling amendments tacked on in process. There were several bills floating in Congress as good cases in point. Finally, there was a strong feeling that the difficult final decisions would only be made in the face of a firm deadline. Extension of the act for another year would invite another twelve months of foot-dragging.

The issue was open to speculation during the spring and summer of 1966. Representative Wayne Hays of Ohio, a member of the House Foreign Affairs Committee, assured Europeans at a meeting of the Council of Europe in May that if the President asked for it there would be an extension of the Trade Expansion Act. Herter, before a congressional committee in August, ducked the question of whether an extension of the act would be necessary. But by early fall it was made clear at Geneva that the die was cast for June 30, 1967; and other countries, relieved in a way to have a firm negotiating deadline, were generally careful not to press the Americans for an extension.

A more serious question for the United States was how to respond in the chemical sector to demands that the American selling price system be abolished. It was now apparent that the Europeans would not negotiate significant tariff reductions for chemicals unless something were done about the system. It was also apparent that if a major sector like chemicals were to be dropped out of the negotiations, prospects for a settlement in other difficult areas would be seriously reduced. Earlier signs that no one was prepared to negotiate nontariff barriers were proving overly pessimistic. There was hopeful movement in the talks for a uniform antidumping code and faint indications that the EEC might respond to the U.S. request to modify the de facto discrimination against American automobiles in European road taxes.

The whole complex of issues for chemicals—exceptions, disparities, American selling price—had led the British in February 1966 to make the first attempt at a big-package deal for the entire sector. The EEC should make a straight 50 percent cut without exception or disparity; the British would consider greater than 50 percent cuts for high rates; and the United States should abolish the American selling price system and cut 50 percent from the published rates.[7] But no response was forthcoming to the British proposal.

The United States had been awaiting, in particular, the results of a laborious study of the American selling price system by the Tariff Commission to establish a set of roughly comparable rates based on normal methods of valuation. When a preliminary set of these converted rates was made public in early May, the United States finally responded at Geneva by asking, strictly as a working hypothesis, what others would be willing to offer, both as tariff and nontariff concessions, if the United States converted to these rates and then cut by 50 percent.[8]

A further complication was growing opposition at home to any negotiation of the American selling price system. This was due partially to the attitude of those parts of the chemical industry protected by the system. But a more subtle factor was congressional prerogative. Abolition of the system would require additional congressional authority, and certain senators, in particular, were strongly opposed to negotiation of such ad referendum agreements in the Kennedy Round. There was

7. A 30 percent rate, as published in the tariff schedule, subject to American selling price, which had a comparable protective effect of 50 percent f.o.b. would be reduced to 15 percent f.o.b. This procedure would generally lead to reductions of more than 50 percent for U.S. tariffs subject to the American selling price.

8. The 50 percent f.o.b. converted rate would be cut to 25 percent f.o.b.

no legal reason why the President could not enter into an agreement of this kind. The concern was mostly that the ad referendum part of the Kennedy Round might be so closely tied to the overall agreement that Congress would be under strong pressure to approve a fait accompli. Reference was made to this kind of situation when the recently concluded U.S.-Canadian free trade arrangement for the automotive industry was submitted to Congress.

The matter came to a head over Blumenthal's two European speeches in March in which he stated that the United States was prepared to negotiate on American selling price in the Kennedy Round. The accompanying qualifications dispelled any undue optimism in Europe, but the reaction of some members of the United States Senate was vigorous. A resolution, sponsored by Senator Abraham Ribicoff and twelve of his colleagues, expressed the sense of the Senate that the American selling price system should not be negotiated without prior consent of Congress. Herter carefully explained that the Blumenthal statement "said no more than the United States has been saying since the Kennedy Round began. . . . In this context, the word 'negotiate' is in fact synonymous with the word 'discuss' . . . a comprehensive conversion of ASP rates, whether or not pursuant to a trade agreement, could be accomplished only by Congressional action. . . . Moreover, it is clearly understood that any such agreement will be separate and distinct from the overall Kennedy Round agreement. Therefore, in considering whether to enact the necessary implementing legislation, the Congress would be able to appraise any agreement on its individual merits, without getting enmeshed in the rest of the Kennedy Round." As for the Ribicoff resolution, Herter continued, "Senate Concurrent Resolution 83 is to be regretted, because it seeks to cast doubt on the President's clear Constitutional authority to negotiate and conclude an agreement subject to subsequent action by the Congress. Senate Concurrent Resolution 83 therefore raises a false issue and by doing so in no way assists the United States in the Kennedy Round but only serves to obscure an already complex problem." [9] Nevertheless, the Senate adopted the resolution on June 29 by a voice vote, although no more than ten senators were on the floor at the time.

After this bruising domestic encounter, and the positive decision to proceed with a working hypothesis, the unkindest cut came in the EEC

9. Letter to Senator Paul H. Douglas, inserted in *Congressional Record*, daily ed., June 6, 1966, pp. S11770–72.

ministerial meeting of June 13–14. Instead of giving some indication of what the EEC might be willing to offer in return, as requested, the Council's communiqué dismissed the U.S. proposal which "could not produce a satisfactory and balanced solution for all participants, unless it were substantially improved." [10] In the face of this unwillingness to discuss the elements of a possible compromise, the chemical talks, now clearly the "one especially dangerous bog in the swamp of issues surrounding the Kennedy Round," [11] were abandoned once again.

A schedule for the remaining months of the negotiations was outlined by Wyndham White at a meeting of the Trade Negotiations Committee on July 8. Although the official committee session was attended by the appropriate day-to-day negotiators, such as Blumenthal and his counterpart Theodorus Hijzen for the EEC, senior representatives from capitals, including Herter and Jean Rey, were also on hand for informal discussion of the status of the negotiations. The key passage in Wyndham White's proposal called for participating governments, by the middle of November, to "reach an assessment against which they can reconsider their initial negotiating position. The fruits of these assessments and reconsiderations would then be shared with the other negotiators so that by, say, the end of November governments would be in a position to consider against a comprehensive background the negotiating instructions with which to equip the negotiators for the final bargaining stage, which I envisage starting in mid-January and hopefully leading to an overall and positive settlement in the following weeks." [12]

As usual, the largest share of the text was devoted to developing countries, and five desiderata were enumerated, including accelerated tariff cuts and compensation for preferences lost as a result of cuts in the most-favored-nation tariffs. And as usual the developing countries expressed their disappointment with both the slow pace of the negotiations and the inadequate progress made in meeting their requests. It was at this meeting that the articulate Indian representative, K. B. Lall, commented that since India would have little of real value to industrial countries in the way of tariff cuts to withdraw if the situation did not improve, the only thing Lall could withdraw was himself. The threat was well taken.

10. Agence Europe Presse, June 15, 1966.
11. *New York Times*, July 3, 1966.
12. Press release no. 966, GATT, July 12, 1966.

While searching for means to accommodate the developing countries, however, the major participants also turned their energies to assessing the balance sheet for the November confrontation, and to the interpretation of that elusive term "reciprocity."

The Balance of Offers

The May 1963 ministerial resolution did not attempt to define a "balance of advantages" or "reciprocity." The negotiations on industrial products were to be based on equal linear tariff reductions plus a disparity rule, but there was also provision for a "bare minimum" of exceptions, unspecified exemption for countries with a special trade structure, and recognition that "a problem of reciprocity could arise in the case of countries the general incidence of whose tariffs is unquestionably lower than that of other participating countries." The relation of agriculture and nontariff barriers to the overall balance was left open. Developing countries were not expected to provide reciprocity. And as a final catchall safeguard, the resolution stated that "it shall be open to each country to request additional trade concessions or to modify its own offers where this is necessary to obtain a balance of advantages between it and the other participating countries." [13]

The lack of comparability among these factors made reaching a precise overall balance almost impossible. Many elements of an appraisal would not yield to automatic statistical accounting. The closest approach by the United States to a definition of "balance," contained in a footnote of the final report on the negotiations,[14] illustrates the problems:

> In order to simplify the presentation, the results of U.S. participation in the Kennedy Round tariff negotiations are presented in this report solely in terms of the value of trade covered by the concessions and the depth of the tariff reductions. However, in the course of the negotiations, numerous other factors were considered in evaluating the balance of concessions—the height of duties, the characteristics of individual products, demand and supply elasticities, and the size and nature of markets, including the reduction in the disadvantage to U.S. exports achieved through reductions in the tariffs applied to the exports of the United States and

13. See Appendix C.
14. U.S. Office of Special Representative for Trade Negotiations, *Report on United States Negotiations* (1967), Vol. 1, p. iii.

other non-member countries by the European Economic Community (EEC), the European Free Trade Area [sic] (EFTA), and those countries in the British Commonwealth preferential system.

Nevertheless, the November 1966 preliminary assessment required that participants make some measure of the existing balance or lack thereof. This assessment naturally would be oriented to quantifiable measures, but qualitative comment could be added. Despite the complete set of positive offers supposedly on the table, however, a number of critical uncertainties prevented a definitive assessment even at this late date: (1) All five industry sector groups remained largely unsettled. There were almost no firm commitments in the steel and chemical sectors. (2) A precise list of disparity claims by the EEC had not yet been put forward. The problem of disparities was related to settlements in the chemical and textile sectors and in bilateral negotiations between the EEC and small EFTA countries. It was hoped that if these other issues were settled, residual disparities would not substantially upset the overall balance of offers. (3) The status of the agricultural sector could not be quantified. Agreement had not been reached on any specifics in grains; and the initial EEC offers on other farm products were so inconsequential as to be unacceptable even as a basis of negotiation. (4) Response in bilateral negotiations to requests for improved offers was vague or conditional for most items. U.S. negotiations with Canada and Japan were particularly important in this respect.

A number of more technical adjustments added to the imprecision of the measure. Although 1964 import data with complete detail by tariff position were available during the last months of the negotiation, comparable data were not available in the fall of 1966: 1962 was the most recent year for EEC import data, 1963 was the earliest year for Japan, and 1964 was the only year for Canada. U.S. import values and tariff levels had to be adjusted, where appropriate, from f.o.b. and American selling price valuation to the c.i.f. basis used by other linear countries.[15] In some cases there was a question as to the appropriate base rate from which the tariff reduction should be calculated. The most important instance by far was the European Coal and Steel Community offer,[16] but other cases also existed, usually involving a difference

---

15. Generally 10 percent was used for converting f.o.b. to c.i.f. values, although a more precise calculation was applied for some products. The first estimate of the f.o.b.-c.i.f. differential for U.S. imports on a narrow commodity basis, *C.I.F. Value of U.S. Imports*, was published by the U.S. Tariff Commission on Feb. 7, 1967.

16. Described in Chap. 6, pp. 104–05.

between the rate legally bound in GATT and the temporarily lower rate or suspension actually in effect.

These many uncertainties and adjustments made the preliminary tally of positive offers little more than a rough estimate. Assumptions or alternative assumptions were made in some cases. Moreover, in view of the various factors that compose reciprocity, it was clear that no single measure, but a series of different or complementary measures would be required. The four principal measures considered were:

Average depth of cut. This was the most obvious means of measuring linear tariff reduction, and it received the widest public reference both during and after the Kennedy Round. It is relatively clear conceptually and simple to calculate: [17] 50 percent would be a perfect score, a smaller figure proportionately less. Such a measure might serve (with or without a disparity rule) as a practical approximation of reciprocity. But in the Kennedy Round—because of the problems of nonlinear countries, agriculture, and, especially, the qualitative differences once the *average* cut departed significantly from the 50 percent level—depth of cut was somewhat unsatisfactory and certainly not sufficient as the single measure of overall reciprocity.

Trade volume offered for concession. The balance of trade volume subject to tariff concession, adjusted to a common year and value base, is the traditional method of keeping accounts in a GATT negotiation. This measure would differ from average depth of cut to the extent that the initial balances of trade were uneven. The difference was especially prominent in the U.S.-Japanese and EFTA-EEC balances. In order to adjust for tariff cuts of less (or more) than 50 percent, trade figures were uniformly converted to "50 percent equivalents" (for example, $2 million of imports cut by 25 percent would equal $1 million of 50 percent equivalents).

Loss of duties collectible. This measure is calculated by multiplying import value by the *absolute* tariff reduction.[18] It takes account of the

17. Weighting the depth of cut by import values was commonly adopted. A more subtle distinction was whether to weight trade by the percent cut or calculate a weighted average tariff level before and after and then compute depth of cut from the difference between these averages. The former method was normally used because of its simplicity. The latter would be appropriate if high or low tariffs were consistently cut by a larger or smaller percent than the norm.

18. For example, if a 20 percent tariff is cut to 10 percent and the value of imports is $5 million, the loss of duties collectible would be calculated as follows: $(0.2)(\$5 \text{ million}) - (0.1)(\$5 \text{ million}) = \$0.5 \text{ million}$.

presumedly greater impact on import price of a given percent cut in a high duty, and was particularly relevant to U.S.-Canadian offers.

Projected trade impact. The impact of tariff and other concessions on future trade might be considered the main criterion of reciprocity. It is not possible, however, to calculate the effect precisely. Assumptions must be made as to supply and demand elasticities, which can vary from commodity to commodity and country to country. Differing interpretations of the value of tariff protection complicate the calculation further. These projections, when carried out during the Kennedy Round, were primarily for internal use, although statements about qualitative differences in the value of offers rested on some kind of assumption as to the expected trade-creating effect of the concessions.

One other significant factor in the balance sheet was bindings. A GATT binding on an existing low rate of duty can be a valuable safeguard against future tariff increase; a free binding on imports that already enter duty free is the maximum offer for such products. GATT recognizes these bindings as "equivalent in value to the reduction of high duties," in deference to low duty countries with little apparent bargaining leverage. In the Kennedy Round, countries generally claimed that bindings on free entry were equivalent to a full linear cut, although in many cases the bindings were on primary or semiprocessed products that were required for domestic industry and would probably enter duty free under any circumstances. In such cases the United States, a particularly large net recipient of offers to bind free entry, contested the qualitative equivalency of the offer.

This brief description of the problems of statistical accounting illustrates the impediments to reaching an agreed mechanical balancing of concessions. Fundamental differences in interpretation would require a settlement based, to some degree, on compromise rather than on statistics. This was certainly apparent to Geneva delegations as they prepared their initial assessments during the summer and autumn of 1966. These preparations, in fact, led to three general conclusions for the November confrontation: (1) The initial assessment was at best an approximation, and any reconsideration of existing offers put forward at this stage would be approximate as well. (2) No single measure could adequately account for all of the factors comprising reciprocity; a number of alternative, or complementary, measures would be necessary. (3) A multilateral balance was only a first step to the necessary bilateral accounts. A participant, after establishing, or proclaiming, a lack of overall balance, would request improvements or threaten reconsiderations of present offers, and this could most effectively be handled bilaterally.

Neglected Issues

During the period just prior to the final bargaining stage, an implicit set of priorities in negotiating objectives developed. While some issues would emerge as the key elements of a final settlement, others would be put aside for future negotiation or included in the agreement in a more modest and noncontentious way. The original agenda was comprehensive to allow the widest scope for developing an agreement, but no one expected every trade problem discussed to be settled in the negotiation. Even so, an initial exchange of views on a problem can have a salutary effect in preparing the ground for later serious negotiation. Or a strong warning might deter action that would otherwise aggravate an existing problem.

Three areas of trade interest that either did not play a prominent role in the final negotiations or were substantially reduced in scope were nontariff barriers, the meat and dairy groups, and East-West trade. Of these, the most comprehensive in scope was the nontariff barrier field. Nontariff barriers often involve deep-rooted domestic laws and regulations, and modification of these measures can affect nontrade as well as trade interests. There is also a wide variance in the applicability and hence the trade significance of nontariff barriers: some apply to a single product, others to all products. A national support policy for agriculture might be considered one big, complicated nontariff barrier, although agriculture was dealt with as a separate sector in the Kennedy Round rather than as a part of the nontariff barrier discussion. Similarly, quota restrictions were usually discussed in context with tariff reduction and not as an independent area of negotiation. Many temporary quotas were, according to GATT obligations, to be removed unilaterally at the earliest possible time and were not therefore matters for reciprocity in the Kennedy Round.

The first round of discussions on nontariff barriers was an articulate exposition by each participant of what others should do, including in every instance a conspicuous unwillingness to consider specific actions on its own part. Nevertheless, two important matters were eventually negotiated successfully: an international code on antidumping (described in Chapter 10) of mutual benefit to all participants, and a separate agreement related to the American selling price system of customs valuation that included nontariff action on a particular product by each major party.

Aside from these significant accomplishments, however, consideration of nontariff barrier problems did not advance beyond the discussion phase. Prominent among the barriers against individual products were the American wine gallon assessment on imported whiskey [19] and the various restrictions against U.S. exports of coal, especially the complete embargo on imports in the United Kingdom. The two most comprehensive issues in the nontariff barrier field that did not reach the stage of serious negotiation were government procurement and border taxes.[20] The preparatory technical work and the internal accord necessary to a discussion of these matters were not sufficiently advanced at the time to warrant a definitive move. Moreover, these subjects were too much additional weight for the already deeply laden Kennedy Round to absorb. Government procurement strikes to the heart of public spending prerogatives. Preference for domestic suppliers in government purchasing is commonplace; the Buy American Act, because it is precise and open, is well known, but the informal procedures of other countries can be equally inhibiting. Some governments fail to disclose either the price quoted by successful bidders on a government contract or even the name of the successful bidder.

The issue of border taxes rests on a GATT provision that permits full offset of internal indirect taxes at the border but does not permit offset of direct taxes. The theory underlying this provision is that the indirect taxes are included in the final price of the taxed goods while the direct taxes are not, and hence indirect taxes, unless offset, worsen the taxing country's competitive position but direct taxes do not. In practice the effect is not so clear. The price incidence of an indirect value-added tax, as commonly applied in Europe, and the American corporate profit tax, for example, may be more similar than dissimilar. The major discussion

19. See H. G. Grubel and H. G. Johnson, "Nominal Tariff Rates and United States Valuation Practices: Two Case Studies," *Review of Economics and Statistics*, Vol. 49 (May 1967), pp. 140–41.

20. For a full discussion on government procurement, see William B. Kelly, Jr., "Nontariff Barriers," in Bela Balassa (ed.), *Studies in Trade Liberalization* (Johns Hopkins Press, 1967), pp. 265–314; for a discussion on border taxes, see Helen B. Junz, "The Border Tax Issue Defined," in Subcommittee on Foreign Economic Policy of the Joint Economic Committee, *Issues and Objectives of U.S. Foreign Trade Policy*, 90 Cong. 1 sess. (1967), pp. 31–40.

of border taxes thus far has taken place in the Organization for Economic Cooperation and Development. The only action taken in the Kennedy Round was a note by the United States that it reserved the right to initiate action under the GATT to seek compensation if changes in border taxes impaired or nullified Kennedy Round trade benefits. The EEC, in response, refused to accept the implication that border taxes might impair Kennedy Round benefits.

Finally, a perennial topic in the nontariff field is uniform customs classification and valuation procedures. The American selling price system was originally part of this discussion that included other broader, if less burning, issues such as adherence to the standard Brussels Tariff Nomenclature. The United States and Canada are the two major countries that do not use the Brussels nomenclature although both have made recent steps in that direction.[21] Customs procedures, however, are generally not matters of great trade significance. Perhaps for this reason and because of their highly technical nature, revision of these procedures tends to evolve slowly. The only concrete steps on customs matters taken in the Kennedy Round were on the American selling price, but hopefully the discussion served to prepare the ground for serious consideration of useful action at a later date.

If the results of the nontariff barrier committee were mildly disappointing, the meat and dairy groups were destined to be the least productive area of discussion. Negotiation of global arrangements for trade in meat and dairy products was in some respects subsidiary to negotiation of a grains arrangement. In addition to the relative magnitudes of trade and the economic interrelationships, an important sequence in timing was involved. Serious negotiations were engaged (as described in Chapter 9) to attempt a comprehensive arrangement for world trade in grains. Success in grains may have led, in turn, to a concerted effort in the other two commodity groups. But as the grains talks dragged on, the hope for a detailed arrangement on meat or dairy products in the Kennedy Round faded.

Reasons other than the tandem relationship of the three groups, however, weighed against a negotiated settlement for meat or dairy products. It was highly doubtful, for example, that minimum international prices, which played a central role in the grains discussion, were at all

21. The revised tariff schedule of the United States, implemented in September 1963, moved much closer to the Brussels nomenclature. Canada revised its chemical tariffs on the basis of that nomenclature during the Kennedy Round.

feasible for trade in quality differentiated meat and dairy products. Nevertheless, between the fall of 1965 and the summer of 1966, a thorough examination was made in the meat and dairy groups of national policies, trends in production, consumption, and trade, and international prices for each major exporter and importer. In the dairy group, special attention was given to proposals by New Zealand to seek a standstill and limitation on export subsidies, encouragement of consumption, and a multilateral aid program for surplus production.

When EEC proposals, including the variable levy, international reference prices, and export subsidies, were finally presented in July 1966, however, it was clear that positions were irreconcilably far apart. The United States, seeing little or no improved access for imports in the EEC offer, was more unwilling than ever to consider relaxation of existing import quotas [22] or large tariff reductions for its market. Major exporters—Argentina, Australia, New Zealand, and Denmark—were thus faced with a stalemate between the two largest consumer markets, and final negotiation shifted from attempts to establish a global arrangement to bargaining limited concessions for tariff cuts or quota relaxation in individual products.

One other aspect of the Kennedy Round that was not headed for dramatic achievement was negotiation between the market economies of the West and the centrally planned economies of Eastern Europe. This was less a fault of the negotiation than of frequently exaggerated or at least fuzzy expectations. Substantial change in the basis and form of East-West trade was beyond the scope of these GATT negotiations. It was significant, in fact, that three communist countries—Czechoslovakia, Poland, and Yugoslavia—accepted, to the degree applicable, the objectives of the negotiation and entered as full participants. Their attitude was in sharp contrast, for example, to that expressed in an article in a Russian economic journal in 1965, entitled, "The Kennedy Round: A Maze of Contradictions": "The Governments of the leading capitalist countries, especially the United States, attach exceptional importance to these talks. They regard them as a means of stepping up foreign trade and overcoming the contradictions between the major powers of the capitalist West, as a step toward building the economic base for the political unity of the NATO countries . . . they seek to con-

---

22. The United States has a strict quota system for imports of most cheeses and a relatively liberal contingency quota, passed by Congress in 1964, for imports of beef.

ceal the fact that the cutting of customs duties will benefit primarily, and to the greatest extent, the biggest capitalist monopolies." [23]

Negotiations with Yugoslavia were the most profitable because the autonomy granted to Yugoslav producing units gives a measure of economic meaning to the customs duty. The comprehensive Yugoslav economic reforms of July 1965, which occurred during the Kennedy Round, lowered tariff levels from about 23 percent to 11 percent and eliminated an additional 3 percent import surcharge. The Yugoslav offer in the Kennedy Round consisted primarily of GATT bindings on many of these lower rates plus a few additional cuts.

Tariffs have little meaning at present in Poland and Czechoslovakia because government purchases, which cover all but a minuscule part of imports, are exempt from duty payment. Czechoslovakia neverthe-less cut its tariffs generally by 50 percent. Poland, instead, made its offer in the form of a purchase commitment: the value of imports from GATT countries as a group would increase by not less than 7 percent per year over the next five years. Phasing out of Polish bilateral trade agreements, especially with Western European countries, and adoption of an impartial multilateral trade relationship with GATT countries was discussed in the Kennedy Round, but no agreement was reached.

Poland and Yugoslavia also applied for full GATT membership during the course of the Kennedy Round. Yugoslavia became a full member in August 1966 and Poland in October 1967. Normally a new member is required to pay an initiation fee of tariff cuts or other trade concessions to compensate for the rights it acquires upon accession to membership. In the case of Yugoslavia, tariff concessions that were made as accession payment were distinguished from those that were part of the Kennedy Round offer. The form of the purchase commit-ment by Poland, however, necessitated a combined settlement for both accession and the Kennedy Round offer.

The more fundamental questions of state trading countries, however, were not resolved in the Kennedy Round. Article 17 of the GATT states that a state trading enterprise shall, "in its purchases or sales involving either imports or exports, act in a manner consistent with the general principles of non-discriminatory treatment," and shall "make any such purchases or sales solely in accordance with com-mercial considerations, including price, quality, availability, market-

23. V. Kur'erov, *Vneshniaia Torgovlia*, 1965, No. 4 (translated in *American Review of Soviet and Eastern European Foreign Trade, 1965*).

ability, transportation and other conditions of purchase or sale, and shall afford the enterprises of the other contracting parties adequate opportunity, in accordance with customary business practice, to compete for participation in such purchases or sales." The offer and acceptance of the Polish purchase commitment in the Kennedy Round illustrates the gap between these lofty principles and the hard facts of day-to-day trading. If purchases by state trading agencies in Eastern European countries were solely in accordance with commercial consideration, a purchase commitment would not only be unnecessary, but possibly undesirable. In practice, however, trading is largely related to needs determined by central planners and often based on bilateral accords regarding technical assistance or marketing arrangements.[24] Greater autonomy for producing units, such as presently practiced in Yugoslavia, and as may gradually be introduced elsewhere in Eastern Europe, tends to reconcile the difference between GATT theory and practice for state trading enterprises. But the Kennedy Round, in this regard, was ahead of its time.

Assessment of Offers

Negotiations resumed in earnest at the beginning of September. The most pressing sector, as usual, was agriculture. EEC offers, submitted at the end of July, were examined item by item. The grains group was in continuous session trying to reach some common ground between the divergent views of exporters and importers. The disappointment of the Americans over the Common Market agricultural offers, already apparent in August, was stated bluntly by Herter: "We are very disappointed in the initial offers of the Community and have said so in Geneva."[25] The U.S. Department of Agriculture, which had characterized the whole set of internal and external EEC farm policy decisions as likely to spur agricultural production of member countries and build higher tariff walls against outside products,[26] was under pressure from key farm groups to pull out of the negotiation if the EEC did not present realistic offers. Agriculture still loomed as a possible breaking point in

24. See Hermann Gross, "Kennedy-Runde und Ost-West Handel," *Der Donauraum*, 3. Heft, 1967, pp. 121–33.

25. Press release, U.S. Office of Special Representative for Trade Negotiations, Oct. 7, 1966.

26. *New York Herald Tribune*, international edition, Aug. 23, 1966.

the negotiations and the Americans made certain that others were aware of this danger.

The U.S. position on agriculture was outlined in speeches by Blumenthal in Rotterdam on September 28 and Brussels on October 28: [27] "We can only look at each offer from the viewpoint of our exports back home. . . . How much duty and levies were paid before the Kennedy Round when exporting to the Community? . . . How much *less* will have to be paid after the Kennedy Round? . . . We recognize that in certain cases it may not be sufficient to deal only with protection at the border. We are attempting, for example, to negotiate a more comprehensive arrangement for trade in cereals. Whatever the scope of such arrangements, however . . . the yardstick of increased export opportunity must still remain the basic criterion in judging the value of proposed offers." Summing up the unsatisfactory status of offers in agriculture, Blumenthal concluded: "A failure to take decisions necessary to rectify this situation could lead to a complete deadlock, if not a breakdown in the negotiations."

The EEC in return attempted to depict the American position as grossly exaggerated. Jean Rey expressed satisfaction with recent progress and found Herter's pessimism "incomprehensible." [28] Present at Blumenthal's Brussels speech, which covered not only agriculture but other outstanding issues as well, Rey was quoted as being in broad agreement with Blumenthal's analysis, "but with certain qualifications, and in a negotiation it is the refinements which count." He added in wry modesty, "I would not have been so apocalyptical." [29]

At the same time it was apparent that the EEC and especially the French were pursuing a more positive outward approach for bringing the Kennedy Round to a successful conclusion. Charles de Chambrun, French state secretary for foreign trade, stated that "for France, exporting is not just one option among others. It is a vital necessity." [30] Couve de Murville declared that "a success, or at least a partial success, must be hoped for in the Kennedy Round"; and picking up almost verbatim one of the points the Americans had been expounding for several months, he continued, "It is in the interest of the Common Market. If

27. Before the American Chamber of Commerce and the Association Belgo-Américaine, respectively.

28. Agence Europe Presse, Oct. 27, 1966.

29. *Ibid.*, Oct. 28, 1966.

30. *Le Monde* (Paris), Oct. 23, 1966.

the Geneva negotiations should result in a fiasco, a wave of protection-ism will be set in motion in the U.S." [31]

These favorable developments did not, however, affect a delicate tactical situation that was emerging over the November assessment. Any country for which the assessment resulted in a negative balance was expected to indicate modifications that might have to be made in its offers if improvements by others were not forthcoming.[32] The danger was that a preliminary withdrawal list might spark a competitive round of withdrawals and seriously damage the chances for a successful agreement.

One key factor was whether the EEC would submit some form of preliminary or conditional withdrawals. There was ample proof, based on almost any form of statistical measure, that the existing EEC offer was below the level of other major participants' offers and that improvements rather than withdrawals were in order. But with so many large sectors of the balance sheet still open, a tactical move by the Community to prepare a concrete threat of substantial withdrawals on whatever rationale might have put it less on the defensive. The final result of such a course would undoubtedly have been negative, leading to a "mini-Kennedy Round" (as in the current jargon), but there were lingering suspicions that this would have been a welcome outcome for at least one Community member.

The EEC, however, did not submit an assessment or a withdrawal list in November. The immediate reason was given as technical difficulties in reaching internal decision. Certainly the potentially endless exchange of withdrawals that might be demanded if such an operation got under way was apparent to all within the Community, especially the Commission. Some press reaction interpreted the absence of a Community assessment as another example of EEC procrastination. But the subsequent Community position that offers were roughly in balance—except for some necessary improvements by the EEC to the small EFTA countries—avoided the dangers of even a tentative list of withdrawals, and proved to be a critical point in resisting a competitive unraveling of the existing level of offers by the major Kennedy Round participants.

Once it became apparent that the EEC would not table a withdrawal

31. At a luncheon organized by *Réalités* in Paris, Oct. 18, 1966.
32. Participants were also expected to indicate improved offers where appropriate.

list, the burden of decision shifted to the other countries. A long list of potential withdrawals directed against the Community might induce, or force, the Common Market to respond in kind, this time on much stronger grounds. The United States held a long series of internal meetings, in both Washington and Geneva. Although there was agreement that improved offers were necessary by some other participants if the United States were to maintain its full existing offer, there was a divergence of views as to what was an appropriate single list of possible modifications. The composition of the list, especially the choice between economic withdrawals (the most sensitive domestically) and tactical withdrawals (the most apt to elicit additional concessions from particular trading partners), was the most exacting task. The final result was a reasonably modest list of possible withdrawals, plus some minor improvements, but emphatically conditioned on the outcome of the industrial sector groups and, especially, agriculture. The EFTA countries were also discreet, both in the length and in the composition of possible withdrawal lists. The Nordics presented a single consolidated list, their first formal presentation as a joint negotiating unit. Canada and Japan indicated significant improvements conditioned on favorable concessions in return.

The stage was thus set for the final phase of bargaining. The "year of decision" for the Kennedy Round drew to a close with only a modicum of decisions to its credit, but this did not greatly bother most people. The question was rather whether governments would now be willing to take the difficult decisions required to strike a bargain at a genuinely high level of overall achievement. The press tended to dramatize the approaching conflict. The *Economist* described the atmosphere in Washington: "Like weary infantry soldiers, officials here are deriving some solace from the fact that the final battle is close at hand." [33] The tension was well founded, for the big issues of contention had not yet been faced. Circumspection at the time of the November assessment was in one sense merely deferral of the real showdown to the first months of 1967.

Christian Herter was busily engaged marshaling the American administration for the final push. Despite his seventy-one years and poor health, he maintained a good grasp of the technical details of the negotiation. In mid-November he was briefed on the American selling price

33. Oct. 22, 1966.

problem by several of his advisors, including Ambassador Blumenthal who was in Washington on consultation. Prominent on the governor's well-ordered desk was the volume, *Building the Atlantic World*. He was in a good mood, and particularly sharp in probing the tables of statistics placed before him. He heartily disliked the American selling price problem which threatened so much over a secondary matter of trade importance, but was resigned to push it through to an equitable agreement. At the end of the briefing Herter spoke of a long awaited hunting trip in February with old friends, but unfortunately he was unable to make the reunion. On December 29, after an evening at home playing bridge, he retired to his room where he suffered a sudden heart attack and died two hours later. A deep sorrow was felt by all at Geneva who admired this man of dignity and purpose. He represented an earlier era of American diplomacy, but his influence will long be felt by the many younger people who had the privilege of working for and with him.

CHAPTER NINE

Agriculture

CONCESSIONS IN AGRICULTURE were the sine qua non for the United States in the Kennedy Round of negotiations under the General Agreement on Tariffs and Trade (GATT). The Americans repeatedly and unequivocally stated that no agreement would be signed unless adequate concessions on farm products were forthcoming. The central concern was the threat posed to U.S. exports by the emerging common agricultural policy of the European Economic Community (EEC). Virtually all countries, and certainly all European countries, are solicitous of their farmers and willing to pay the economic price of domestic support programs. The harmonization of agricultural policies of the six Common Market countries, however, appeared to be a new step toward still higher protection that might have serious adverse consequences for outside suppliers (see Chapter 2, pp. 32–36).

The need to maintain and expand U.S. agricultural markets in the EEC was a prominent theme of the campaign for the Trade Expansion Act. The reluctant support of the American Farm Bureau Federation was obtained only after the bill was amended to provide a firmer commitment on agriculture, and a Senate resolution sponsored by Senators Hubert Humphrey and Everett Dirksen, with the House concurring, expressed the sense of the Congress that U.S. negotiators obtain adequate assurance that access to EEC markets for American agricultural products would be maintained, so as to result in an expanding mutually beneficial system of world trade.[1] In order to secure this objective, U.S. negotiators at Geneva adopted a general strategy of linking progress in agriculture with progress elsewhere in the negotiation.

1. *Congressional Record*, Vol. 109, 88 Cong. 1 sess. (1963), p. 11570.

The steadfast American position in the Kennedy Round, in turn, became an important factor in the sequence of decisions within the EEC that established the common agricultural policy. Those within the Community who were anxious to reach early agreement on key elements of the internal farm policy, principally France and the Commission, used the Kennedy Round as a lever to secure these agreements. German acceptance of the Mansholt proposal for unified grain prices in December 1964 and the whole series of decisions on financial and marketing regulations following the Luxembourg compromise in January 1966 are cases in point. An official EEC bulletin goes as far as to say, "To the Community the main result of the Kennedy Round in the agricultural field has been that it greatly helped to define its own common policy." [2] But whereas internal agreement on farm policy became a necessary precondition for EEC agricultural offers in the Kennedy Round, the initial offers were by no means adequate from the American point of view, and the United States and the EEC disagreed over the level of agricultural offers until the last days of the negotiation.

Not only the U.S.-EEC confrontation made the agricultural sector of the Kennedy Round different from the industrial sector. The objectives of the industrial sector, for example, were far more specific. Linear tariff reduction, with special treatment for significant disparities, was a relatively straightforward commitment that lent itself to reasonable measurement and comparison among participants. In contrast, the section of the May 1963 ministerial resolutions dealing with agriculture stated only that the negotiation should "cover all classes of products . . . including agricultural products" and that "in view of the importance of agriculture in world trade, the trade negotiations shall provide for acceptable conditions of access to world markets for agricultural products . . . in furtherance of a significant development and expansion of world trade." The commitment by importers to provide "acceptable conditions of access" was important and should not be underestimated, but ways for achieving this objective were left completely open.

Another distinction between the industrial and agricultural sectors was the composition of export and import interests. For industrial products, each major participant was both an exporter and an importer, and therefore had a more or less balanced interest in a multilateral reduction of trade barriers. For agriculture, on the other hand, there was

2. *The Common Agricultural Policy* (European Community Information Service, July 1967), p. 29.

a large degree of polarization into exporting and importing countries. Japan and the countries in the European Free Trade Association (EFTA), with the exception of Denmark, were basically importers. The EEC had some specific export interests in farm products but was on balance an importer. Argentina, Australia, Canada, Denmark, New Zealand, and the United States were the major temperate zone exporters, while the developing countries were the exporters of tropical products. The only significant balanced negotiation in agriculture was between the United States and Canada, and this concerned largely products traded regionally across the border.

Initial Offers

The year between the GATT ministerial resolution of May 1963 and the formal opening of negotiations at Geneva in May 1964 served to clarify the difference in views as to what constituted "acceptable conditions of access" for agricultural products and "a significant development and expansion of world trade" in these products. It was a thoroughly discouraging period for exporters. The major development within the EEC was the Commission proposals—the Mansholt proposals—that came before the EEC Council in December 1963.[3] Mansholt I related to internal Community policy and was essentially a proposal to adopt unified grain prices in one step instead of in successive stages as had been planned. The level of unified prices was proposed at approximately halfway between the higher German prices and the lower French prices. Compensatory payments to member states with national prices above the unified price levels, principally Germany and Italy, would be phased out over a three-year period. The Germans, preferring higher unified prices, initially refused to accept the Commission's proposed price levels, and the issue was left open.

Mansholt II was a related proposal for EEC agricultural offers in the Kennedy Round. The Commission proposed, on the basis of reciprocity, that the current level of overall support for farm products be identified and bound for three years. For grains, the total level of support (*montant de soutien*) would of course include the unified prices of Mansholt I. In addition to binding the level of domestic support, the EEC proposed to establish a set of international reference prices for

3. See Chap. 4, pp. 72–73.

basic farm commodities, and the difference between the domestic and world prices would be used to determine the level of import levies and, where appropriate, export subsidies. The Council accepted these proposals as the basis for the EEC agricultural offer in the Kennedy Round.

The response of exporters at Geneva to these proposals was, as expected, extremely negative. The proposed unified grain prices, if adopted, would mean an increase in the return to French farmers, which could stimulate an expansion of French production at the expense of outside suppliers. No specific commitments were offered to assure access to the Community market nor to limit the effect of the variable levy system. Even the commitment to bind the level of domestic support for three years appeared to have loopholes. One important element of the EEC proposals not yet established was the level of internal grain prices, but it was highly unlikely it would be any lower than the level proposed by the Commission, and German opposition might even lead to a higher level of prices. Finally, a large number of agricultural products that were not subject to the variable levy but protected by a simple customs duty did not appear to be included in the offer in any way.

The United States response to the EEC proposals was stated in strong terms by Christian Herter in a speech before the Economic Club of Detroit on March 30, 1964. Calling the unified wheat and feed grain prices too high, he said, "A decision to unify grain prices at substantially lower levels would make an important contribution to the Kennedy Round." As for the proposal to bind the level of internal support, "there appear to be so many loopholes in this proposal that the commitments would not . . . be meaningful. . . . The Community's negotiating plan for agriculture seems to establish as the objective of the negotiations the binding of increased levels of protection rather than reductions in trade barriers and expansion of trade." Herter then went on to outline the "pragmatic rather than dogmatic" American approach to agriculture in the Kennedy Round. Products should be grouped by the nature of existing trade barriers. Where imports are bound duty free, such as cotton and soybeans in the Community, they should stay that way. Where fixed tariffs constitute the sole or major form of protection, they should be cut. Where a worldwide commodity arrangement is to be attempted, such as for grains, "the EEC proposals for measuring and freezing levels of protection may have application—

but only when combined with provisions for assuring continued access to the market . . . and opportunity to share in future growth . . . the primary objective of a commodity arrangement is . . . the creation of acceptable conditions of access to world markets."

By the summer of 1964 the argument over how to proceed for agriculture was deadlocked. Lengthy discussion of the intricacies of calculating the Community's internal support system or applying the variable levy did not uncover any positive basis for further discussion. Some critics of the common agricultural policy predicted no agreement as long as the EEC pursued the basic policy of high internal support prices to farmers with no restraint on production. Perhaps it would be preferable to avoid serious negotiation altogether at this time. Differences in approach for agriculture were so wide, and domestic interests so deep, that a confrontation over farm policy might provoke bitter consequences far in excess of any modest gains to trade or economic efficiency. John Coppock, evaluating agricultural policy in relation to other interests of the Atlantic community, warned, "We should at least take care that this particular self-produced red herring is not dragged across the path when truly important matters are up for discussion and negotiation." [4]

The United States nevertheless continued to insist that progress in the industrial sector be linked to parallel progress in agriculture. The immediate objective was to move from discussion of the abstract aspects of agricultural protection to the tabling of specific offers on individual products. In November 1964, however, in order not to postpone tabling exceptions lists for industrial products, and in the hope that the EEC would soon reach agreement on unified grain prices, thereby enabling specific Community offers in agriculture, the United States backed off somewhat and shifted to a lagged link which would lead to "substantive negotiations on both industrial and agricultural products . . . at an early date in 1965." [5]

This revised position appeared to pay off in mid-March 1965 when it was agreed that specific offers would be submitted for all agricultural products no later than September 16, 1965. Initial grains proposals were in fact submitted in May. But then the EEC internal crisis intervened in July 1965, creating for the other participants a dilemma

4. *Atlantic Agricultural Unity: Is It Possible?* (McGraw-Hill for Council on Foreign Relations, 1966), p. 222.
5. *New York Times*, Nov. 4, 1964. See Chap. 5, pp. 85–87.

over the September 16 date.[6] Again the decision was made to move ahead as scheduled, with the proviso that the EEC would catch up as soon as possible. The EEC crisis was resolved in January 1966, and after an additional few months of internal preparation, a completed set of specific agricultural offers was presented by the EEC in July 1966. The time had at last arrived to negotiate firm and specific commitments in agriculture.

Final Offers

In some respects the U.S. strategy of patience had borne results. The original American proposal that EEC offers be separated into three generic categories was adopted: items already bound free in GATT remained that way; items subject to fixed tariff protection were opened to negotiated tariff cuts; and markets in grains and other variable levy

Table 9–1. Imports of Agricultural Products from the United States, 1964

In millions of dollars [a]

Importer	Total imports	Imports bound free in GATT prior to Kennedy Round	Imports available for concession			
			Total	Wheat	Other grains	Nongrains
Linear countries	3,059	885	2,174	265	706	1,203
EEC	1,444	528	916	82	370	464
United Kingdom	489	112	377	26	126	225
Other EFTA	330	98	232	37	40	155
Japan	796	147	649	120	170	359
Canada	394	n.a.	209 [b]	33	n.a.	176 [b]

Source: U.S. Office of Special Representative for Trade Negotiations, *Report on United States Negotiations* (1967), Vol. 1, Pt. 1.
n.a. — not available.
a. Import values for linear countries are c.i.f., for Canada f.o.b.
b. Dutiable imports only.

items would be subject to a negotiated form of access, perhaps through a general commodity arrangement. A second result was that very substantial agricultural offers by other linear countries and Canada on imports from the United States were successfully brought into the negotiation. The figures for 1964 trade in these categories are given in Table 9–1. Out of $3.1 billion of farm imports from the United States in

6. See Chap. 7, pp. 114–16.

1964 by linear countries, about $0.9 billion was bound free in GATT prior to the Kennedy Round, $1.0 billion was in grains, and the remaining $1.2 billion was in other farm products "available for concession." Imports from the United States by countries other than the EEC listed in the table were more than double those of the EEC in nongrain products available for concession.

But the initial EEC offer, though its form was encouraging, was clearly inadequate. The negative reaction of the Americans was clearly stated, by both Herter and Blumenthal.[7] The intensive negotiations that began in September 1966 continued through the fall and winter. A long series of bilateral bargaining sessions between the United States and the EEC, literally over each point of reduction on each tariff position, continued into the spring of 1967. Some key concessions by the EEC on fixed tariff items became one element in the final compromise package settlement in May 1967. The priority given by the United States to agricultural concessions in the negotiations with the EEC and with other countries did eventually, however, result in a substantial degree of success. A résumé of the results for nongrain products is presented in Table 9–2. It shows that concessions were granted un-

Table 9–2. Imports of Nongrain Agricultural Products from the United States, 1964, Available for Concession in the Kennedy Round

In millions of dollars [a]

Importer	Nongrain imports available for concession	Kennedy Round action	
		Concessions	No concessions
Linear countries	1,203	656	547 [b]
EEC	464	238	226
United Kingdom	225	70	155 [b]
Other EFTA	155	103	52
Japan	359	245	114
Canada	176	89 [c]	87 [c]

Source: Same as Table 9–1.
a. Import values for linear countries are c.i.f., for Canada f.o.b.
b. Of this, $115 million was for manufactured tobacco on which the United Kingdom offered a 25 percent reduction in the Commonwealth preference under the separate American selling price agreement.
c. Dutiable imports only.

conditionally on $656 million of the $1,203 million of imports from the United States by linear countries; the United Kingdom offered another $115 million in concessions on tobacco imports, conditional on U.S. adoption of the separate agreement on the American selling price.

7. See Chap. 8, pp. 139–40.

The Grains Arrangement

Whereas in the nongrain sector of the agricultural negotiations the United States was the dominant *demandeur* of concessions, negotiation in the grains group was multilateral. Argentina, Australia, Canada, and the United States were exporters. Japan, the United Kingdom, and other EFTA countries were clearly importers. And the EEC had a foot in both camps. French exports of soft wheat created an export interest for the Community while very substantial imports of hard wheat and feed grain made the Community the largest commercial importer of total grains. The pattern of grain trade in 1965 is shown in Table 9–3.

The grains negotiations played a central role in the Kennedy Round for several reasons in addition to the large volume of trade involved. They were the major test of how the EEC variable levy approach might

Table 9–3. World Trade in Grains, by Principal Exporter, 1965

In thousands of metric tons

			Exporter		
Importer	Canada	United States	France	Australia [a]	Argentina [a]
Wheat and Wheat Flour					
All countries	12,497	19,097	4,573	6,469	4,252
EEC	1,720	1,197	768	1	1,347
EFTA	2,304	584	754	633	638
Japan	1,294	1,864	[b]	443	2
Developing countries	1,570	14,435	1,253	2,017	1,538
Sino-Soviet bloc	5,520	71	1,744	3,175	665
Other	89	946	54	200	62
Feed Grains					
All countries	755	20,875	2,377	750	5,184
EEC	150	8,803	1,217	327	4,014
EFTA	248	2,439	575	53	337
Japan	208	3,970	0	182	314
Developing countries	20	1,473	42	24	136
Sino-Soviet bloc	0	416	9	82	167
Other	129	3,774	534	82	216

Source: For Canada, the United States, and France, Organization for Economic Cooperation and Development, *OECD Commodity Trade: Exports, Series C, January–December 1965*; for Australia and Argentina, UN Food and Agriculture Organization, *World Grain Trade Statistics, 1964/1965* (1965). Feed grains are those included in Standard International Trade Classification categories 043, 044, and 045.

a. Figures are for July 1964–June 1965.
b. Negligible.

be accommodated to the world trading system. They were an attempt at a new form of commodity arrangement in temperate zone products that might, among other things, include a food aid commitment as an outlet for surplus production. And progress in grains more or less determined whether any significant action would be taken in the special groups for meat and dairy products. Participating countries had agreed to attempt to negotiate a global arrangement for grains aimed at promoting a balance in world production and consumption, assuring supply at equitable prices, encouraging consumption, and furthering orderly programming of food aid shipments, all in keeping with the 1963 ministerial meeting's objective of "acceptable conditions of access to world markets." To understand the events of the Kennedy Round, however, it is necessary to go back further in time.

An appropriate point of departure for events leading up to the Kennedy Round grains negotiations is the 1958 GATT study, the Haberler Report.[8] The agricultural section of the report focused on the high levels of protection, the accumulation of surpluses by low cost producers, and the inability of existing GATT rules and procedures to cope with the problem. A subsequent GATT working committee examined the policies of the individual countries and reported in detail on the generally autarkic policies that had evolved in member countries. Eric Wyndham White, on the basis of this report, stated in September 1961 that since GATT rules were not, in practice, applied to agricultural trade, it might be better to examine the prospects of negotiating terms of access to markets.[9]

A response to these suggestions was not long in coming. In statements by French Agricultural Minister Pisani at a United Nations Food and Agriculture Organization conference and Finance Minister Baumgartner at a GATT ministerial meeting, both in November 1961, France took the initiative to suggest a general approach to what might be called "market organization" for trade in basic agricultural commodities. While the Baumgartner-Pisani proposals covered all basic commodities, they suggested that in the initial phase, a single case—grains—be studied. If the approach proved successful, other commodities should be considered—coffee was mentioned specifically.

8. Gottfried Haberler, *Trends in International Trade* (General Agreement on Tariffs and Trade [GATT], 1958).
9. See Gerard Curzon, *Multilateral Commercial Diplomacy* (London: Michael Joseph Ltd., 1965), p. 197.

The proposals for grains were based on the assumptions that there was a large food deficiency in developing countries, protectionist policies in industrial countries had led to increased surplus stocks, and producing countries were engaged in a ruinous price war in subsidizing exports of foodstuffs. A policy should be developed to raise world prices to a "normal" level, which was not clearly defined, and in turn, to utilize the additional revenues gained thereby to finance shipments of surpluses to undernourished nations unable to afford imports.

The proposals were acknowledged for their boldness, but were generally not considered equitable or practical. The major importing countries, especially the United Kingdom and Japan, would pay higher prices for imports in order to finance food aid supplied by exporting countries. The assumptions of the proposals were themselves open to challenge: export subsidies for grains were not ruinous, but quite modest or nonexistent for low cost exporters; and the characterization of global supply and demand as balanced or even in deficit supply if only stocks in the rich countries could be transferred to the poor was not, at least in 1961, accepted as a long run situation. The prevailing outlook was that food aid was a temporary stopgap after which the specter of accumulating surpluses would reemerge. Under these circumstances a substantial increase in world prices, as suggested, would lead to oversupply on world markets and the need for market sharing by exporters, abhorrent to most traders and particularly to the United States. The proposals were also suspect as a rather transparent attempt of the French to finesse general acceptance of the EEC system of internal support prices and variable levies. In any event the French proposals were not considered a feasible basis for immediate negotiation, although the growing interest in establishing access to markets led to the formation of the special GATT group on grains in November 1961.

After the initial skirmishing in the Kennedy Round over general approach, participants of the grains group put forward proposals in May 1965. The subsequent discussions centered on three points:

International prices. The EEC, following the earlier French proposal, wanted to establish world reference prices substantially above existing prices for all grains. Importing countries were naturally opposed to paying higher prices for their imports. Exporters, on the other hand, had mixed feelings. Higher prices, or at least some safeguard against a decline in prices, would stabilize and perhaps increase export revenues, but a rigid and unrealistically high level of world prices might encourage additional production and require production restraints or a market sharing system for commercial markets. These apprehensions were reinforced during fruitless discussions among exporters seeking ways to restrain production when necessary to balance production and demand. Consequently, exporters, and the United States in particular, considered the preferred solution a form of agreed price ranges related to normal trading conditions.

The pressures on world prices for wheat were quite different from those on feed grains. Wheat markets were more likely to be influenced by competitive export subsidization, and were also directly affected by the large grants of wheat as food aid. The potential instability of wheat markets had led to the 1949 International Wheat Agreement establishing minimum world prices; the prices had been set below existing market prices and had never, in fact, been tested. World prices for feed grains, on the other hand, were principally affected by generally unsubsidized exports of the United States, and therefore did not present the same problems as wheat prices. Somewhat paradoxically, the EEC, the importer, advocated higher world feed grain prices in order to maintain the relative price structure among all grains, while the United States, the exporter, strongly resisted an arbitrary increase in feed grain prices that might weaken its strong price-competitive position in this growing market.

Food aid. There was general agreement that food aid should be connected in some way to a grains agreement, but views differed on how this should be done. The United States, for example, proposed a flat annual commitment independent of commercial market conditions while the EEC preferred food aid to be related to surplus production. The United Kingdom, Japan, and other importers were very reluctant to contribute to a food aid program that would benefit exporting countries.

Access. This was the most difficult issue. Exporters wanted firm assurances of access to commercial markets, especially the EEC market. Importers such as the EEC and the United Kingdom were not, however, prepared to make any firm commitment. Other importing countries, such as Japan and some EFTA countries, were willing to assure access at the present level of imports, a commitment with little substance because imports would certainly continue to rise in future years. The initial EEC offer to identify and bind the present level of support as a step toward adjusting imbalances of supply and demand was not accepted by other members of the grains group. The EEC binding for three years at the new unified grain prices was on balance a threat to rather than an assurance of access for outside suppliers. Moreover, no participant—not even the EEC—appeared willing to make a completely binding commitment on its domestic support policy.

Talks remained deadlocked, primarily over the question of access, but also in pace with the Community internal crisis, through the middle of 1966. By mid-1966, however, the approaching final day of reckoning for the Kennedy Round "concentrated the minds" somewhat. The EEC realized that without some form of access commitment exporters would not be willing to negotiate any form of agreement, and there were reasons why the Community was interested in a grains agreement. The French in particular wanted higher grain prices and some form of food aid undertaking to reduce the cost of export subsidies for wheat; and the Community as a whole hoped to gain its trading partners' acceptance of its farm policy. Exporters, on the other hand, sobered by the recent Community crisis, realized that the internally agreed common agricultural policy was now permanently established and that the Kennedy Round was probably the only forum for some time to come where a reasonable accommodation for outsiders might be secured.

Another significant factor was the recent trend of world grain production and trade. The food aid burden had increased substantially, particularly in India, depleting American wheat stocks to the point where the U.S. government in the summer of 1966 was forced to reactivate almost half of its idle croplands to meet anticipated needs. Under these circumstances a joint response to food aid had become far more urgent in 1966 than it had been a few years earlier. World food consumption had in fact been growing at a faster rate than production since the mid-1950s, and 1961 was significant (aside from being the year of the original French grain proposals) because the absolute level of total consumption passed world production in that year. From 1961 to 1966 reserve stocks were steadily drawn down at the rate of 14 million tons per year,[10] but this trend did not really cause alarm until India had successive droughts in 1965 and 1966 that coincided with poor Russian and mediocre American harvests.

World prices in commercial grain markets, moreover, had steadily strengthened so that a moderate increase, at least in the existing mini-

10. Orville Freeman, "Malthus, Marx and the North American Breadbasket," *Foreign Affairs*, Vol. 45 (July 1967), pp. 579–93.

mum world price for wheat, appeared not to be potentially disruptive. Finally, although EEC grain production was still expected to rise as a result of the unified grain prices, demand within the Common Market, especially for feed grains, was rising faster than expected. Revised grain projections prepared by the ECC Commission in June 1966 showed an anticipated net import deficit for grains in 1970 of over 10 million tons, or roughly the same as the existing import gap. Although other projections, including those of the U.S. Department of Agriculture, showed a smaller gap, there was obviously room for some firm commitment on EEC grain imports.

In June 1966, after considerable internal discussion, the Community put forward its completed grain proposals, including a form of access. The EEC offered to bind a maximum ratio of production to consumption, or "self-sufficiency ratio." The difference between total consumption and the self-sufficiency ratio would be reserved to net imports, and any excess domestic production would be withheld from commercial markets and either stocked, given as food aid, or disposed of in some other noncommercial way. This proposal was completely consistent, *in principle*, with the concept of access. The specific commitments, however, were very loose: the self-sufficiency ratio binding was offered at a level significantly higher than the existing level; [11] the duration of the binding would be in the order of three years with no guarantee after that time; the commitment was conditional on a global surplus of grain production; and the operation of the commitment was indirect and somewhat vague.

Exporters considered the commitments so weak as to make the proposals devoid of economic significance; negotiations from September 1966 until May 1967 worked toward a compromise that would provide reasonably certain access to markets protected by a self-sufficiency ratio commitment, particularly for the EEC and United Kingdom. These negotiations were unsuccessful, however, and the comprehensive approach to a grains arrangement, including access to markets, was finally abandoned. There was agreement, though, on a range of world prices for wheat and a joint food aid commitment of 4.5 million tons per year for three years. The agreed minimum wheat prices were higher than the existing International Wheat Agreement minimum but still

11. The EEC offered to bind a self-sufficiency level of 90 percent compared to the existing level of 85–87 percent and the Commission's own projection for 1970 of 86 percent (see Table 2–4, p. 35).

below prevailing world market prices. The food aid commitment constituted a major concession by importers, and the 1 million ton EEC share of the total amounted to about 10 percent of net grain imports.[12]

Reasons for Failure

It is impossible to pinpoint where or why the grains negotiators were unable to reach broader agreement. Some people felt that importers such as the EEC and the United Kingdom never intended to bind access for imports in such a way that domestic producers would be restrained. These countries are determined, in the longer run, to raise their self-sufficiency in food, partly for balance of payments reasons, and are prepared to pay the higher cost that this policy implies. A major limiting factor for all participants, however, was the considerable uncertainty about future production and trade. Production levels in Russia and Communist China have an important bearing on world trade, but these countries would be outside the purview of the agreement. Opinions on the prospects for agricultural programs in developing countries, especially India, varied widely. Production trends within the Common Market, which are subject to a number of uncertain variables, were also interpreted differently.

In any event the first attempt to build some general order and coordination into the trading practices for temperate agricultural products was not successful. Autarkic domestic farm policies and "beggar my neighbor" attitudes in world markets continue, and the question remains whether a comprehensive commodity arrangement could be negotiated that would improve the conditions of trade for some of these products. Is coordinated international price stability and buffer stocking a practical objective? Is the long run demand for food aid sufficient to warrant a system of international commitments related to commercial market conditions? Are governments prepared to accept some form of discipline on their domestic support policies that will maintain import levels and encourage a gradual shift toward a lower cost and more efficient distribution of world production and trade? The relative importance of these questions to the participants in the grains discussion varied substantially.

The attitudes of the participants on what was or should have been done for agricultural trade in the Kennedy Round were similar but

12. For further discussion of the grains arrangement, see Chap. 15, pp. 253–55.

their points of emphasis differed. While the overall results were "relatively disappointing" in the Community's view, "the EEC Commission hoped that the clarification of issues which occurred would lead to an improvement in world production and trade conditions for agricultural products. But it believed that further efforts needed to be made, especially with regard to commodity agreements." [13] Under Secretary of Agriculture John Schnittker summed up the American view before the Foreign Economic Policy Subcommittee of the Joint Economic Committee on July 11, 1967:

> American agriculture came to the Kennedy Round in a spirit of expectation. We sought a general lowering of agricultural trade barriers which would give efficient farmers, ours and in other countries, a greater opportunity to sell competitively in the world's expanding markets. . . . To some extent, our expectations were realized. Considering the problems encountered, we emerged with far better results than we thought possible during some of the darkest days when negotiations almost broke off. . . . But while the negotiation has given us modest trade liberalization, it also has made us aware of the problems we still face in bringing more order to world agricultural trade. To me, this is the really significant result at Geneva. . . . Even if countries were agreed, therefore, on the kind of order they wanted to put into the international trading system, the task of reshaping its numerous and complicated barriers to do this would be formidable. Even to catalog and understand them is difficult. To deal with them all in a comprehensive way is virtually impossible. This the Kennedy Round has made clear to us.[14]

13. *The Common Agricultural Policy*, p. 29.
14. *The Future of U.S. Foreign Trade Policy*, Hearings, 90 Cong. 1 sess. (1967), Vol. I, pp. 32–34.

CHAPTER TEN

Narrowing the Gaps

December 1966–March 1967

AN AIR OF GLOOMY resignation marked the opening of the final Kennedy Round countdown in January 1967. All governments were apparently determined not to let the negotiation fail, but the major issues still unresolved cast a pall on virtually every prediction of the outcome. A poignant editorial in *Die Welt* on January 18 stressed the approaching "crossroad of decision" and the firm deadline of June 30. But "even though the logic of political and economic interests of the participants would dictate success," the outcome remained uncertain. Tracing the history of the negotiations from John F. Kennedy's far-sighted ideas for a bold liberalization of trade to meet the political and economic challenge of European integration, the editorial observed that political aims were no longer important: "In Geneva, the large economic blocs wrestle strictly on the basis of pure material advantage.... In today's changed climate, events threaten to sink to the level of bargaining among indigent carpet peddlers." On the outcome, the editorial asserted: "Even a small success will help to fill the trade-political moat between the two European economic blocs and will give new buoyancy to trade with the U.S. If the negotiations fail, however, every force will venture stronger into daylight ... to speak of the disadvantages of world trade." A factual companion piece reported that experts at Geneva were forecasting a Kennedy Round tariff cut of 7–25 percent. A minimum settlement would be 7–9 percent, a realistic middle 15–18 percent, and 20–25 percent was considered very optimistic.

The range of problems caused a certain inertia among negotiators and necessary forward initiative appeared lacking as time slipped dangerously by. The *New York Times* viewed events "moving at a disappointing snail's pace"; Representative Thomas Curtis in mid-January admitted "that the 'careful optimism' I expressed just after my trip to Geneva in early December has faded. I am disturbed by the lack of forward momentum evident particularly since the middle of December"; Eric Wyndham White retained "sober optimism" but warned it was "foolish to underestimate the difficulties"; the *Gazette de Lausanne* foresaw the final phase of the Kennedy Round menaced by a deescalation of offers.[1]

Threats to Negotiations

U.S. officials were well justified in their caution. Trade policy, and particularly Kennedy Round policy, was under heavy attack at home. Criticism was especially severe in the powerful Senate Finance Committee. Senator Russell Long, Democratic whip and chairman of the committee, commented that "this nation in its trade and aid programs has played the part of an Andy Gump until it is on the verge of becoming an international Barney Google . . ." and the U.S. should insist on "a quid pro quo from those countries which are enjoying favors from Uncle Sam." Democratic Senator Vance Hartke predicted that the Trade Expansion Act would turn out to be a "colossal failure." [2] And Senate Minority Leader Everett Dirksen, describing present policy as in "great disarray," proclaimed "it is time the Congress restored some semblance of fairness and balance to our foreign trade policy." [3] These views were supported by such informed people as Stanley Metzger, one of the architects of the Trade Expansion Act, who scolded the administration for its "misappraisal" of European policies and promotion of "overblown expectations" in the Kennedy Round,[4] and *New York Times* correspondent Edwin Dale, who wrote in the *New Republic*: "Despite what the remaining diehards in the State Department, who believe that the European Common Market is God's greatest creation

---

1. *New York Times*, Jan. 20, 1967; Curtis, in *Congressional Record*, daily edition, Jan. 19, 1967, p. H410; Wyndham White, in press release, U.S. Information Agency, Information Service, Jan. 26, 1967; *Gazette de Lausanne*, Jan. 5, 1967.
2. Both senators were quoted in the *Journal of Commerce* (New York), Feb. 2, 1967.
3. *Washington Post*, Dec. 4, 1966.
4. *Foreign Policy Aspects of the Kennedy Round*, Hearings before the Subcommittee on Foreign Economic Policy of the House Committee on Foreign Affairs, 90 Cong. 1 sess. (1967). Metzger was nominated chairman of the Tariff Commission on Aug. 4, 1967.

since the Garden of Eden and can do no wrong, may say and argue, the US is going to get a fairly bad deal out of the Kennedy Round." [5]

The administration's response to these attacks was an unequivocal commitment that the United States would get full reciprocity in the Kennedy Round, or there would be no agreement. William Roth, who had been serving as acting special trade representative since Christian Herter's death in December, testified before the Senate Finance Committee on March 10: "Pronounced imbalances exist among the offers of major participants . . . several of our larger trading partners' offers fall short of matching ours . . . the decision of the United States to accept or reject the Kennedy Round will depend . . . on the United States being assured that overall reciprocity is achieved." Attitudes had also hardened within the administration because of the frustrations over Common Market intransigence in the Kennedy Round and General de Gaulle's disruptive policy toward the North Atlantic Treaty Organization, and partly because of the loss of influential Atlanticists such as George Ball and Herter. The fundamental, political motivation for the Kennedy Round had become obscured by economic self-interest. Though the surge of skepticism at home provided highly credible support to American firmness at Geneva, the uncertainty of its intensity and direction was hardly comforting.

The Kennedy Round was also threatened in early 1967 by several conflicting or competing issues that could divert the executive energy necessary to push through the difficult final Kennedy Round decisions. Most ominous was the renewed United Kingdom interest in membership in the European Economic Community (EEC). At Geneva, there was concern that a new U.K. move would dampen enthusiasm among Europeans for Kennedy Round tariff cuts. It might even raise demands for postponement of an agreement until the European situation was clarified. In any event, the appeal of a fresh alternative would shift attention from the Kennedy Round.

As it turned out, these fears were unjustified. Skepticism over British entry was sufficient to maintain immediate interest on the concrete negotiations underway at Geneva. It was also realized that a successful Kennedy Round would facilitate negotiations between the United Kingdom and the EEC. Lower tariff levels would reduce trade diversion, making British entry more palatable to the Americans in particular.

5. Feb. 11, 1967.

Moreover, the prolonged discussion within the British government of Britain's bid for entry softened the impact of Wilson's May 2 announcement and merely confirmed what everyone by this time expected: negotiations for British entry would not begin before autumn 1967 or safely beyond the Kennedy Round horizon.

A second issue, especially prominent in Europe in early 1967, was the U.S. investment–brain drain–technology gap problem.[6] The combination of direct investment in European industries by large American firms, loss of European scientists and engineers to attractive opportunities in the United States, and far higher expenditure for research and development in the United States than in Europe posed a threat to European industry. EEC Commissioner Robert Marjolin predicted that "if the six Common Market countries remain the main world importers of discoveries and exporters of brains, they will be condemning themselves to a cumulative underdevelopment which will soon render their decline irremediable." Prime Minister Harold Wilson warned of "an industrial helotry under which we in Europe produce only the conventional apparatus of a modern economy while becoming increasingly dependent on American business for the sophisticated apparatus which will call the industrial tune in the '70's and '80's."[7]

Though by early 1967 a number of constructive studies of the problem were underway, continued apprehension was apparent in the generally modest European tariff cuts in the electronics sector of the Kennedy Round. Electronics, and especially computers, were the symbol of American technological superiority, and the rationale for temporary retention of tariff protection was that European industry needed to develop or adjust to American style production.[8]

Still another related trade issue was the second United Nations Conference on Trade and Development (UNCTAD), scheduled for the summer of 1967 (it was subsequently postponed to February 1968). A spring agenda crowded with the completion of negotiations under the

6. Jean-Jacques Servan-Schreiber's *Le Défi Américain* (Paris: Editions Denoël, 1967) appeared several months after conclusion of the Kennedy Round.

7. Quoted in a survey of the problem of the technological gap by Bernard D. Nossiter, *New York Herald Tribune*, international edition, Feb. 8–12, 1967.

8. This infant (or adolescent) industry argument for maintaining protection is not without penalty. A tariff acts as a user tax, raising the cost throughout industry of these key inputs for technological advance and modernization. Computer time, for example, is far more expensive in Europe than in the United States, in part, at least, because of import restrictions.

General Agreement on Tariffs and Trade and preparation for UNCTAD would put a strain on officials responsible for adopting and defending liberal trade measures. Developing countries, whose problems were the motivating force in UNCTAD, could hardly let the quasi-rival GATT program endanger the schedule for UNCTAD. Moreover, their strong support for Kennedy Round measures might jeopardize enactment of similar UNCTAD measures presumably more beneficial to developing countries, such as tariff preferences. The most dangerous threat posed by UNCTAD was its convenience as an excuse to postpone Kennedy Round matters, but its approach also acted as a warning that unfulfilled expectations would be on the agenda of another trade forum.

Any split allegiance between GATT and UNCTAD was in fact of marginal significance to the final outcome of the Kennedy Round. Developing countries, while acknowledging benefits from tariff cuts in the Kennedy Round, did not enthusiastically press their interests during the negotiations. It is doubtful, though, whether a more dynamic response on their part would have made much difference.

The combination of negotiating stalemate, domestic disenchantment, and competing trade issues, all pitted against an inexorable terminal date, posed the fundamental predicament in the closing months of the Kennedy Round negotiations. "Serious" meetings, in which each side restated its "firm" position, simply wasted time. The EEC Commission's apparent lack of negotiating flexibility made activity at Geneva seem especially futile; yet a ministerial level meeting would clearly be premature. The essential job for the first weeks of 1967 was to negotiate the small issues and pare the large ones down to their key elements. Public statements of dismay continued, but meanwhile the first steps were being taken toward final agreement.

Hopeful Movements

Two important announcements appeared in the press on January 12, 1967. In Washington, President Johnson announced termination of the temporary "escape clause" tariff increases on watch movements and most sheet glass. Tariffs would be brought back (or in a few cases part way) to the rates prevailing in 1954 for watches and in 1962 for most sheet glass. These actions were taken after long technical investigation under the escape clause procedures of the Trade Expansion Act and its predecessors. The Office of Emergency Planning had reported that "horological-type defense items will continue to be available without regard to the level of imports of watches, movements and parts." [9] The Tariff Commission had reported the cuts would not imperil domestic industries, and Christian Herter, with the concurrence of other executive agencies, had forwarded a favorable recommendation to the President. In his economic message to the Congress on January 23, President Johnson reaffirmed the U.S. commitment to reducing trade barriers "as demonstrated by my recent action terminating the 1954 escape clause on watches, and rolling back the special tariff on imports of glass." He then went on to emphasize the need to resolve the remaining Kennedy Round issues: "Never before has there been such a splendid opportunity to increase world trade. It must not be lost."

At Geneva the relation of the President's announcement to Kennedy Round progress was even more obvious. Switzerland supplies 90 percent of U.S. imports of watch movements; watch movements had accounted for half of Swiss exports to the United States before 1954, then dropped to 30 percent after imposition of the escape clause tariff rates. Switzerland had made rollback of watch tariffs its primary objective vis-à-vis the United States during the Kennedy Round (although this matter was not part of the negotiations proper). In fact, there had been little direct negotiation between the two countries up to this point since their trade relations rested so heavily on the long pending watch investigation. Considering the role Switzerland might play in bringing pressure to bear on the Common Market, it would have been especially unfortunate had the United States been responsible for Switzerland's withdrawing a major share of its trade from the negotiation. The protracted escape clause and national security investigations during a period of improved economic circumstances for U.S. industry had elicited a long series of hostile press reactions in Switzerland. President Johnson, by taking what *La Suisse* called "a courageous step," arrested these protests and paved the way for a substantial agreement between the United States and Switzerland.[10]

Similarly, the rollback of sheet glass tariffs, of principal benefit to Belgium, consolidated Kennedy Round support within this Common

9. *New York Times*, Jan. 12, 1967. A watch industry official asserted that tariff reduction would lead to the elimination of an advanced horological technology in the United States.

10. *La Suisse* (Geneva), Jan. 23, 1967.

Market country.[11] In particular, it removed lingering resentment over the fact that the United States had instituted the tariff increases only shortly after the conclusion of the Dillon Round agreement.

The second important piece of news on January 12 was from the EEC. The Council of Ministers met on January 11 to set Kennedy Round strategy for the coming weeks and to provide the Commission with new instructions. Their official communiqué, in a rare display of unanimity, contained three basic points: (1) Although the potential withdrawal lists of the United States and the United Kingdom did not appear justified, and could become the point of departure for an "escalation of withdrawals," the EEC would not submit a withdrawal list of its own at this time, but try instead to convince the others to restore full offers. (2) The Commission should undertake bilateral negotiations with the Swiss and Nordics in order to attain a better balance of offers. (3) The Commission should actively pursue negotiations on other outstanding issues such as disparities and nontariff barriers, including the American selling price.

Press reports stressed the solidarity of the Common Market countries, both in their firmness "not to yield to the demands of the Anglo-Saxon negotiating partners" [12] and in the recognition that additional concessions were necessary for the small countries of the European Free Trade Association. The tone of the communiqué was firm, but it nevertheless contained indications that the substantial disagreement then existing over the balance of concessions might be compromised. Improved offers to the Swiss and Nordics, probably in such areas as paper, aluminum, and machinery, would not only assure a high level of offers by the EFTA countries, but would also have a favorable "fall-out" effect on the trade of other participants with secondary export interest in these products. The EEC position that offers were generally in equilibrium with the United States and the United Kingdom, moreover, did not exclude some later give in what was obviously a qualitative disagreement open to reasonable compromise.

The most interesting and least clear aspect of the Council decision, however, was the latitude given to the Commission for carrying out these directives. The lack of any real negotiating leeway by the Com-

11. Restoration of the lower U.S. tariff on glass led in turn to removal of EEC retaliatory tariff increases on certain chemical products imported from the United States.

12. *La Nation* (Paris), Jan. 14, 1967.

mission had, up to that time, made productive negotiation at Geneva almost impossible. The amount of flexibility now given the Commission was, of course, very uncertain, but it later became clear that the authority to negotiate ad referendum positions subject to Council approval, so necessary in the final days of the negotiation, originated at that Council meeting.

These early moves by the United States and the EEC were elements of hope rather than substance as far as the key negotiating issues were concerned. Agriculture was merely referred back to the 111 committee at the Council meeting; chemical talks remained completely deadlocked.

Antidumping Agreement

The first definitive accomplishment in the Kennedy Round came from a rather unexpected direction. Discussions in the special antidumping group had begun under what might have been considered favorable circumstances. National antidumping laws and practices are aimed at preventing imports from being dumped at less than fair value and causing injury to domestic producers, but they can also act as deterrents to trade beyond this function. Trading nations therefore shared an interest in developing procedures to avoid what could become an increasingly acrimonious problem. In particular, exporters to the United States wanted the U.S. regulations streamlined so as to minimize uncertainty and delay. The United States sought open and impartial procedures for its exporters instead of the confidential and discretionary methods generally in effect abroad. The Kennedy Round discussions were especially timely because the Common Market was in the process of implementing its own antidumping regulations and might be sympathetic to harmonization on a broader geographic basis. Finally, of particular trade importance to the United States was the prospect that Canada would give serious consideration to inclusion of an injury criterion. Until that time Canada was the only major trading nation that automatically applied antidumping duties when a differential between home market and export price in the exporting country occurred, whether or not it was likely to cause injury to Canadian industry, and this restrictive provision had become a long standing complaint of American exporters to Canada and a constant irritant to trade negotiations between the two countries.

But in spite of these propitious circumstances, the initial discussions at Geneva had made little progress. While other countries were outspoken in their criticism of U.S. regulations, they were reluctant to submit their own procedures to serious negotiation. The United States was also reluctant to discuss significant changes in its regulations, and was opposed to any agreement that would require legislative action. Congressional approval of such authority was unlikely and, in fact, several bills recently introduced in Congress would make the existing U.S. regulations decidedly protectionist.

Not until technical discussions had dragged on into 1966 were there signs that there was a middle ground for agreement. Between an ambitious international code that would require additional legislation by the United States and a paper agreement of lofty but empty phrases, the opportunity remained for improvement in American procedures of significant interest to foreign exporters. In return, others expressed willingness to consider action requested by the United States. In the fall of 1966 Ambassadors Blumenthal and Roth, in a series of meetings in Washington, including talks with Treasury Secretary Henry Fowler, won endorsement of their plan to proceed with serious negotiations within the framework of existing legislation. At that point, the negotiations went back to the experts who worked steadily but somewhat apart from the general Kennedy Round business. It therefore came to some as a surprise in early 1967 when the antidumping group reported being in agreement on the essentials and in the process of cleaning up the details. There was even some consternation that events had moved too swiftly, that the negotiators might appear to have been insufficiently obstinate. But this one measure of success gave impetus to the overall negotiation and a boost to flagging spirits.

The antidumping code was a balanced agreement, limited by practical considerations, but containing concessions on all sides. The United States had been criticized for its sometimes protracted investigations of alleged dumpings, and its frequent practice of withholding appraisement during the investigation.[13] The principal change in U.S. regulations agreed to was a maximum of ninety days for making appraisement. In addition, appraisement would not be withheld nor would investigations be initiated unless there were, in the judgment of the

---

13. Withholding of appraisement postpones the final determination of customs duties until an antidumping investigation is completed. Imports may be released under bond pending eventual appraisement, but the amount of duty to be paid remains uncertain.

administration, some evidence of injury. Other countries, in turn, adopted fair and open procedures for antidumping investigations along the lines of U.S. practice. Finally, and of perhaps greatest significance to the United States, Canada agreed to adopt an injury requirement similar to that of other countries.[14]

Industry Sector Progress

Industrial offers, meanwhile, depended heavily on negotiations in the special industry sector groups established almost two years earlier. Two of them, aluminum and pulp and paper, seemed headed for satisfactory though modest accomplishment. The EEC had finally put forward some offers in June 1966, and further improvements were anticipated in the final settlement with the Nordics. The cotton textile sector, of major interest to Japan and developing countries, was still uncertain, but the outlook was for an agreement of modest dimensions.

One sector that showed every indication of disintegrating was steel. During the negotiations, conditions in the industry had steadily worsened: there was overcapacity in EEC countries, a rapid rise of U.S. imports in 1965, and a sensitive political problem of possible industry nationalization in the United Kingdom. Though the temptation to abandon the whole sector was strong, it was realized that the repercussions of failure would be serious. Japan, for example, already faced with the prospect of minimum concessions for its textile exports, was almost certain to make large withdrawals if its other major export industry, steel, were to draw a complete blank. And the collapse of one important problem sector like steel would make it extremely difficult to reach agreement in other problem areas—the domino theory was clearly applicable to the Kennedy Round. It was at this point that the idea of matched rates for the United States and the EEC, which would form the basis of the final settlement, was introduced.[15] Agreement was still some way off, but the initial reactions were first tested on the reluctant participants during the early weeks of 1967.

Two big issues, however, remained in deadlock, and appeared equally likely to cause a breakdown in the entire negotiation: agricul-

14. For a more detailed discussion of the antidumping agreement, see John B. Rehm, "Developments in the Law and Institutions of International Economic Relations: The Kennedy Round of Trade Negotiations," *American Journal of International Law*, Vol. 62 (April 1968), pp. 427–34.

15. See Chap. 6, pp. 105–06.

ture and chemicals. In agriculture the grains group was engaged in discussions over an ambitious world commodity arrangement, but the critical points were unsettled; nongrain agricultural offers had barely begun. Chemical negotiations, in many respects, had not even reached the starting point.

Chemical Sector Problems

One of the most important issues in the final phase of the Kennedy Round negotiations was the American selling price system.[16] Established in 1922 to protect a segment of the infant American chemical industry against competition from established European producers, the system provides for duty assessment based on the value of a "like or similar" domestic product. This procedure can lead to an assessment substantially higher than that based on the value of the imported product and in some cases makes the ultimate figure uncertain. For example, if customs officials deem that no like or similar domestic product exists, other valuation procedures apply, resulting in most cases in a lower duty. About half of U.S. imports of chemical products potentially subject to the American selling price are admitted under this temporary status of noncompetitive products. If a like or similar product is deemed to exist, duty payment depends on the current domestic selling price of that product.

Only about one-tenth of U.S. chemical production consists of benzenoid chemicals, which the American selling price protects, and less than 5 percent of U.S. chemical imports are actually assessed on this basis (this latter figure, of course, is in part a result of the restrictive effect of the high tariff). While seventy separate categories of benzenoid chemicals were included in the U.S. tariff schedule,[17] three product groups—benzenoid intermediates, drugs, and dyes—accounted for roughly 80 percent of total benzenoid imports. The so-called basket category in each group was especially important. That category includes all products not specified elsewhere, and in an industry with constant

16. The importance of the system to the chemical sector discussions is covered in Chap. 6, pp. 109–10. Most of the following which relates to the U.S. chemical industry is taken from a statement by Ambassador Roth in *Elimination of the American Selling Price System*, Hearings before the House Committee on Ways and Means, 90 Cong. 2 sess. (1968).

17. In preparing a set of comparable rates converted to normal valuation procedures, the Tariff Commission subdivided some existing categories, thereby creating 38 new positions. The final American selling price agreement therefore lists 108 categories.

product innovation, trade potential lies predominantly in the basket categories. In 1964 the three principal baskets accounted for one-third of imports subject to the American selling price, but their qualitative importance was far greater. A brief description of the three groups follows.

Benzenoid intermediates. These basic chemical compounds provide the input for final products throughout the industry. Five integrated and diversified companies account for two-thirds of total production. Sales of domestic producers grew at a 9 percent annual rate from 1962 to 1966 and totaled $1,122 million in the latter year. U.S. exports in 1966 were estimated to be $164 million and U.S. imports $31 million (of which $22 million was competitive with domestic production). Pre-Kennedy Round American tariffs ranged from about 19 percent to 27 percent based on American selling price, or 19 percent to 115 percent when converted to a normal export value basis. The basket was 27 percent American selling price, 39 percent export value.

Drugs. This sophisticated sector of the chemical industry is typified by research and development and rapid product innovation. Sales of domestic producers grew at a 17 percent annual rate from 1962 to 1966 and totaled $446 million in the latter year. U.S. exports in 1966 were estimated to be $134 million and U.S imports $11 million (of which $4 million was competitive with domestic production). Pre-Kennedy Round American tariffs ranged from about 17 percent to 26 percent based on American selling price, or 17 percent to 106 percent when converted to a normal export value basis. The basket was about 26 percent under either method.

Dyes. Although four firms account for more than half of all domestic sales, and ten firms for three-quarters, there are also a number of small firms. Dye production has been asserted to be relatively labor intensive which may put domestic producers at a cost disadvantage relative to foreign suppliers. Sales of domestic producers grew at a 9 percent annual rate from 1962 to 1966 and totaled $332 million in the latter year. U.S. exports in 1966 were estimated to be $25 million and U.S. imports $26 million (of which $8 million was competitive with domestic production). Pre-Kennedy Round American tariffs ranged from 32 percent to 40 percent based on American selling price, or 34 percent to 172 percent when converted to a normal export value basis. The basket was 40 percent American selling price, 48 percent export value.

The Europeans, notably the EEC, the United Kingdom, and Switzerland, had put forward abolition of the American selling price system as a major Kennedy Round negotiating objective, related to the section of the ministerial resolution dealing with nontariff barriers. Although a 50 percent linear cut would bring most duties under the system down to a reasonable (if still relatively high) level, the long standing bitterness against its inequities made the system itself the overriding concern. Of course, the irregularity of the tariff incidence—and in particular the obscure and insignificant category, "Dyes, acid brown 19, acid red 133, etc.," which showed a record high converted rate of 172 percent and became known as "Mont Blanc"—added to the emotional fervor of the abolitionists.

The United States recognized the anomaly of the American selling price system, its conflict with GATT principles,[18] and its possible appropriateness as a nontariff barrier to be considered in the negotiation. But negotiation of the system raised three difficult questions. First was the matter of reciprocity. GATT negotiations were not predicated on morality but on compensatory concessions leading to expanded export opportunities for all participants, and so far others had offered only invective as an inducement to U.S. action on the American selling price system. Second, the President did not have authority to modify the system.[19] Any agreement, including concessions received in return, would have to be negotiated as a conditional package separate from the basic Kennedy Round agreement, and then submitted for later congressional approval. Finally, there were technical problems in converting American selling price valuations to normal valuations. The Tariff Commission had done its best to develop a set of converted rates that would afford equivalent tariff protection, but any method of calculation involved uncertainties, and the result was apt to be a scatter of unrelated rates for closely related products.[20]

18. The United States was permitted to continue to apply the system under GATT because of the "grandfather clause," which gives blanket tolerance to certain practices in effect before the formation of the GATT in 1947.

19. There was initially some belief that the President had authority under the Trade Expansion Act to modify the system, but after intensive examination it was concluded in early 1966 that he did not. See Rehm, "Developments in the Law and Institutions of International Economic Relations," pp. 417–18.

20. For example, the single dye category, 406.50, which carried a uniform American selling price rate of 40 percent, was split into ten categories in the Tariff Commission conversion, with rates ranging from 38 percent to 172 percent. It would be difficult at times to distinguish which category was applicable, especially if exporters altered the composition of their dyes slightly in order to receive a more favorable duty rate.

Although these problems had been clearly stated by the United States,[21] there had been little positive reaction to them. No reasonable response had been made to the working hypothesis put forward by the United States in June 1966 to convert from American selling price to normal valuations and cut by 50 percent; the EEC in fact had flatly rejected it. Nor were there specific offers on nontariff barriers, although action by the EEC on the discriminatory effect of road taxes "was not excluded." The only tangible indication of European intentions was an exhaustive list of exceptions, disparity claims, and offers conditional on elimination of the system. An estimate of the remaining chemical offer on the European side was at best a 10–15 percent average cut.

A token offer in chemicals by others would clearly elicit a scaling down of offers on the American side. In fact, part of the U.S. delegation set to work on this task. And a stalemate in this sector would be as foreboding for other areas of negotiation as failure in the steel talks. Moreover, since the United States is a large net exporter of chemicals, a minimum chemical settlement would adversely affect its overall balance of concessions. The United States exported $2.4 billion of dutiable chemicals in 1964 and imported only $0.7 billion. The consistently positive U.S. balance with each of the major Kennedy Round participants is illustrated by the following figures, in millions of dollars, for 1964: [22]

	U.S. imports from other countries	Other countries' imports from U.S.
EEC	175	465
United Kingdom	53	170
Japan	66	210
Switzerland	34	45
Total	328	890

Breakthrough in Chemicals

The frustration and mistrust generated by the chemicals issue posed a critical threat to the Kennedy Round negotiations. In January 1967 the disagreements seemed irreconcilable. A recent attempt by Wyndham White to suggest the broad lines of a comprehensive approach had

21. Blumenthal delivered a speech at Kronberg, Germany, on December 8, 1966, devoted entirely to this subject.
22. U.S. Office of Special Representative for Trade Negotiations, *Report on U.S. Negotiations* (1967), Vol. I, p. 176.

gone unheeded (although one element of his proposal later played an important role). Events came very close to a formal unraveling of offers that probably would have been irretrievable.

The breakthrough in the sector talks—and the word is fully appropriate—came, in fact, at an unexpected moment. During a routine meeting of the chemical sector group,[23] the EEC representative departed from the agenda and wondered aloud whether a new and ambitious approach might not be contemplated for some difficult areas of the sector. He suggested that virtually no exceptions be made to the 50 percent cut, and a general ceiling be adopted for rates that were still high after the cut; a ceiling of 20 percent was mentioned for the United States and of 12½ percent for the EEC and the United Kingdom (Swiss rates were only about 5 percent at the outset); because of the ceiling, the EEC would refrain from invoking any disparities; and while the United States would convert its American selling price system to normal valuation, the ceiling would obviate negotiation of individual conversions for the many tariff headings.

The immediate reaction was to adjourn the meeting for lunch. The suggestions, while completely noncommittal, were apparently serious and might develop into a balanced and far-reaching solution, beneficial both to the chemical talks and to the Kennedy Round as a whole. But it was not clear whether the EEC Commission had the authority—wholly unprecedented—to discuss even on an ad referendum basis a new approach of this nature. Perhaps they were only probing how far the United States would go. There were also many vague points in the initial presentation that could develop into important loopholes to a major commitment. Finally, any premature public disclosure of an ambitious hypothesis of this kind—especially a form of tariff ceiling for the United States—could force a harried rejection, considering the prevailing negative atmosphere in capitals. It would be necessary, before frightening people with sweeping general proposals, to clarify all essential details. In particular, the precise scope of the European offer and the availability of safeguards had to be established.

It was therefore decided to investigate this "big package," as it was called, without obligation by any party before attempting to pursue it formally. The task was undertaken by a group consisting of Michael Blumenthal for the United States, the soft-spoken Luxembourger

23. At this point, participation was limited to the United States, the United Kingdom, the EEC, and Switzerland. Japan joined the group at a later point.

Fernand Braun for the Community, British representative Roy Denman, whose experience in the chemical industry provided him with a rare and Cambridge-intoned mastery of the polysyllabic chemicals involved, and Swiss Ambassador Albert Weitnauer. In a series of informal and highly confidential meetings they probed the significant elements of the package for chemicals. It was established that the "no exceptions–no disparities" rule would apply to the entire chemical sector and not just items related to the American selling price. This was a major benefit to the United States which had important export interests throughout the sector. The U.K. tariff on a number of important basket categories was 33⅓ percent, and its rate for plastics was low but unbound; it was accepted that the 33⅓ percent rates would be cut by over 60 percent to the 12½ percent ceiling, and that the duties on plastics, which the United Kingdom had up to this point excepted from any commitment, would be cut slightly and bound at about 9 percent.[24] Finally, it was agreed that each country would make some nontariff or comparable contribution to the package.

Little headway was made on one central issue during these initial talks: how would the unconditional Kennedy Round concessions be separated from those that were conditional on subsequent congressional approval for abolition of the American selling price system? The nontariff concessions by others would obviously be tied to the system, but how were tariff cuts to be divided? The informal group accepted the practice of calling this problem "*découpage.*" [25]

By mid-February the broad outline of the chemical package had been prepared for submission to capitals. It followed the maximum objectives contained in the original hypothesis, but the possibility of some exceptions to these objectives was deferred for later negotiation— it was suspected, for example, that the United States would insist on

24. In effect, the U.K. and the EEC rates would be matched for plastics.
25. An interesting development in the Kennedy Round was that French terms like "*écrêtement,*" "*double écart,*" "*montant de soutien,*" "*taux d'arrivé*" (final rates for the big chemical package), and "*découpage*" were widely adopted for general use. A notable exception was the French phrase for the rate of self-sufficiency for grains, "*le taux d'autoapprovisionment,*" which had a compelling soporific effect, especially during the long summer meetings of July 1966. English, however, was generally the spoken language for informal meetings, and U.S. dollars were used throughout for comparable trade values.

special treatment for its dye-making industry. The proposals would still require careful consideration and hard negotiation, especially on the open issue of *découpage*, but the foundation had been laid for a reasonable solution for this sector, fully in keeping with the ministerial resolution for substantial trade liberalization.

An important byproduct of these chemical meetings was the indirect settlement of the major area of the disparity controversy. The most concentrated and complicated disparity claims had always been in the chemicals sector. It was the only important industry where the United States and the United Kingdom had high tariffs and a large export surplus. EEC acceptance of the ceiling approach for chemicals in lieu of disparity claims therefore greatly reduced the scope of the disparity controversy. The problem was further diminished by the matched rate approach for the steel sector, eliminating the question in that area. Rollback of U.S. watch tariffs put this potential disparity problem more appropriately in the context of an EEC-Swiss bilateral negotiation. Textile offers were uninspired on all sides. And the EEC—in keeping with its "European clause"—dropped a number of possible disparities in deference to the export interests of small EFTA countries. Thus, only a modest list of residual disparity claims was actually invoked by the EEC in early 1967. A handful of these were dropped in the final phase of bargaining and the rest were absorbed, with relatively minor trade impact, in the overall balance.

The first wind of change in the press appeared in *Le Monde* and *Les Echos* on February 16 and 17. They reported a press conference by Pierre Millet, formerly of the EEC Commission, and at that point a representative of the French Union des Industries Chimiques. His keynote was, "We are desirous of making the maximum concessions on the Common External Tariff in order to obtain concessions on the American tariff." For those aware of Millet's influence, especially with the possibly reluctant French industry, it was clear that his appeal "le maximum pour le maximum" represented a radically new approach by the Common Market for chemicals. On February 21 an Associated Press wire story announced that the major countries "have reached a landmark by agreeing on lowering tariffs" and that "concessions for trading chemicals had been a major contribution to the agreement." This was a gross exaggeration of the tentative steps taken up to that point, and it drew a quick denial by the U.S. spokesman at Geneva: "Although intensive negotiations have been going on in many areas of the Kennedy Round, no agreements of any kind have been reached. . . ." Only the denial appeared in the next day's press.[26]

The Negotiating Deadline

The outlook in mid-February was moderately encouraging. Issues were at least being discussed constructively. In a number of areas the adamance of only two months earlier had given way to a search for acceptable compromise solutions. There was a limit, however, to how far the Geneva based delegates, in day to day bargaining, could go in making substantive decisions. At some point the senior representatives from capitals would have to assume their proper responsibility in negotiating the final overall settlement. William Roth, who was nominated by President Johnson on January 26 to move up to the position of special representative for trade negotiations, commented that "it is in the nature of a major negotiation such as this that the toughest decisions cannot be taken until the final bargaining phase begins." [27]

An essential part of preparing for the final bargaining phase of a negotiation is establishing a firm time schedule for decision.[28] For the Kennedy Round the United States had an incontrovertible termination date of June 30, which had been accepted as the final date for signing an agreement. The effective date for settling the substantive points of the negotiation therefore had to be well before that time. Roth outlined the U.S. negotiating deadline in his testimony before the House Foreign Economic Policy Subcommittee on February 15: "Between now and the end of March the outcome of this long effort will be determined. . . . We believe that three months is the minimum time required, first to translate the results of the bargaining into legal documentation; second,

---

26. *New York Herald Tribune*, international edition, Feb. 21, 1967.
27. *Foreign Policy Aspects of the Kennedy Round*, Hearings.
28. Harold Nicolson cites the following: "Thus the Macedonian ambassadors who came to Rome in 197 B.C. were informed on arrival that, unless the negotiations resulted in agreement within sixty days, they would be regarded, not as a diplomatic mission enjoying immunity, but as spies or 'speculatores', and as such, conducted under armed guard to the coast. This form of ultimatum, (however enticing may be its appeal to future negotiators) is not one which today could be employed with equal directness: more silky methods have now to be devised to forestall or prevent deliberate procrastination." (*The Evolution of Diplomatic Method* [Macmillan, 1954], p. 21.)

to permit thorough analysis of this documentation by all interested government agencies; and, third, to secure Presidential approval of the results. Other governments must follow similar procedures." [29]

There was a wide and varied press response to Roth's "Easter deadline." "Ultimatum" was used frequently. The *New York Times*, however, provided a somber note of warning: [30]

> So the next few weeks are critical. There is no time left for leisurely discussions or for deliberate stalling if the objective is to arrive at a realistic deal. The Europeans know that the American delegation is eager to come home with some concrete results. But the Europeans will be making a serious mistake if they think that they can use the timetable either to force United States acceptance of an unfavorable settlement or to win an extension of the deadline.

29. *Foreign Policy Aspects of the Kennedy Round*, Hearings.
30. Feb. 20, 1967.

CHAPTER ELEVEN

Package Deal

March 1967–May 15, 1967

WILLIAM MATSON ROTH remained in the background until the final six months of the Kennedy Round negotiation. As Christian Herter's Washington deputy, he had worked primarily on coordination of policy within the executive branch and on relations with Congress. When he arrived in Geneva for the final bargaining, Europeans were impressed with his business-oriented and relatively nonpolitical approach to the negotiation, which Roth himself had depicted before a congressional committee: "We are traders, not diplomats." [1] *Le Courrier de Genève* expressed its approval: "The new head of the American delegation ... has quickly impressed others as a fine diplomat, admirably knowledge-able of his own dossier ... and those of his [negotiating] partners. While his predecessor was a man of political stature, towering over a negotiation which, at its origin, followed the vast political design of unifying the Atlantic world ... Mr. Roth is the man of the new situa-tion. The objective of the negotiation is no longer a question of political design but of economic interests." [2]

Deadline Postponed

Roth did not win acceptance of his proposed Easter deadline for ending negotiations. That date, considered unrealistic by many foreign delegates and the secretariat of the General Agreement on Tariffs and Trade, was revised at a meeting of the Trade Negotiations Com-mittee on March 9. There would be a high level Geneva meeting at the

1. See *New York Times*, May 16, 1967.
2. Feb. 9, 1967.

end of March, but the date for a final negotiating package was pushed up to early April, allowing time for one additional meeting of the European Economic Community's Council of Ministers. Acceptance by governments of this final package would require two or three weeks; the termination date of the negotiations was therefore firmly set for April 30. While Roth "would have preferred an earlier conclusion," he acceded to the later date in view of the amount of work outstanding, and in particular the cumbersome process of decision making within the EEC.

The high level meetings at Geneva beginning March 29—the "*petit sommet*"—were the opening phase of the final confrontation. This was the first official negotiation in which Roth and Jean Rey headed the two largest delegations. It was the first attempt to seek high level, multilateral agreement among all major countries on the thorny sector problems. The simultaneous negotiation in various arenas proved an exhausting schedule for key delegates. It was a sobering experience, and little of substance was accomplished.

One issue that received a thorough airing was *découpage*. The Americans wanted European cuts on all but a small share of chemicals to be made unconditionally in the Kennedy Round while the Europeans were thinking of token cuts with most items tied to the separate agreement on American selling price. Rey, lacking authority to negotiate the matter, merely agreed to report the U.S. position back to Brussels. Disagreement could hardly have been more complete, although a measure of negotiating maneuver was generally read into these initial positions.

The procedure to be used for cutting the chemical sector's big package into two parts also became an important issue. Two basic approaches were discussed.[3] The first approach would distinguish European tariff items as related or not related to the American selling price. Presumably, small cuts or no cuts would be made in the Kennedy Round on the former group. This approach, though logical, was fraught with problems. European tariff schedules do not distinguish benzenoid chemicals (those affected by the American selling price), and about two-thirds of all European chemical imports are in tariff categories that include benzenoids. Deleting such categories would disrupt the relative rate structure if the conditional cuts were not eventually made. More-

3. Although it may have added to rather than detracted from the confusion, the first was called "vertical" and the second "horizontal" *découpage*.

over, implementation of reductions on benzenoid chemicals would have to be suspended from the start, pending U.S. action on the American selling price system. Another problem was that the Kennedy Round package did not take account of disparities in rates on nonbenzenoids, and the high U.K. rates were predominantly in that area. Finally, Switzerland, whose export interest was concentrated in benzenoids, particularly dyes and drugs, would suffer most if the American selling price package were not implemented.

The second approach was to treat all chemicals alike but—after a designated number of steps in the normal Kennedy Round phasing— to suspend implementation of tariff cuts if the American selling price system had not been abandoned. Larger unconditional cuts could be made selectively in order to benefit Switzerland or for very high rates. For example, on the basis of an overall cut of 50 percent (in the big package), the following criteria could apply to tariff cuts by the EEC and the United Kingdom: [4] (1) The first 20 percent cut would be made for all chemicals whether or not any action were taken on the American selling price. (2) The last 30 percent cut would only be made if the system were abolished. (3) If the existing rate were high (25 percent or more), however, 30 percent instead of 20 percent would be cut unconditionally. (4) If Switzerland had the main export interest, 30 percent or even more would be cut unconditionally.

In late 1966 Eric Wyndham White, in an appraisal of the chemical sector, had suggested this latter approach, in a general way, including the 20 percent basic cut for the EEC and the United Kingdom. Although no one accepted this initial attempt at mediation, the alternative became a focal point of discussion.

The essential problem in the chemicals sector, however, was the Europeans' commitment to obtaining U.S. conversion to normal valuation procedures. They were willing to make a general 50 percent cut for all chemicals—and even more for high U.K. rates—and a contribution in the nontariff area. But in return they wanted reasonable assurance that the American selling price system would be abolished, and their apprehensions, heightened by U.S. press accounts of industry's and Congress's views, led them to the conclusion that they should hold virtually all of their concessions conditional until the United States had acted on the system.

4. This example follows the general lines of the final agreement on *découpage*.

The Americans, on the other hand, made it clear that presenting Congress with a completely unbalanced deal, in which there was no reasonable choice, would be unacceptable both to the executive and to the Congress. The only way to obtain a favorable response from Congress was to negotiate a package that was clearly in the U.S. trade interest, but that was independent of the basic Kennedy Round settlement, and that Congress could consider, free and unencumbered, on its own merits. Moreover, the Americans were legally bound to obtain unconditional reciprocity in the Kennedy Round, and could not tie concessions to any subsequent agreement. Therefore, if the Europeans withheld all chemical concessions for the separate package, the United States would have to limit its offer also. And this, in turn, would greatly aggravate the problem of achieving overall balance within the Kennedy Round,[5] increase the difficulty of reaching firm decisions in other problem areas of the negotiation, and perhaps most important, decrease chances of congressional approval of the American selling price agreement.

Offers Specified

After four days of talks through Saturday, April 1, the *petit sommet* meetings recessed until the following Wednesday. Attention centered on the EEC Council meeting scheduled for April 10–12. Two key issues were *découpage* and the continuing problems in the agricultural sector. The grains discussions were at an impasse, partially over the American demand for an independent commitment on food aid. The unlikely prospects for a comprehensive grains agreement of benefit to exporters had increased American insistence that at least an unequivocal commitment be made on food aid.

A third major issue for the Council was a last minute submission by the Nordics of a withdrawal list keyed to their outstanding requests to the Community. Bilateral talks on the problems between the two trading blocs had up to that point resulted in only small progress as far

---

5. The situation becomes more complicated as additional countries are considered. Swiss chemical duties are inconsequentially low, and if others had made their entire chemical offer conditional—which would have covered a major Swiss export interest—Switzerland might have had to make offers outside the chemical sector conditional in return. If Japan had taken chemicals out of the unconditional Kennedy Round agreement, the U.S.-Japanese balance would have been upset in view of the large U.S. export surplus with Japan in chemicals.

as the Nordics were concerned. The EEC reacted strongly to the sudden appearance of proposed withdrawals. Peter Dreyer commented in the *Journal of Commerce:* "It has provoked unprecedented outcries of indignant fury in Commission circles," but it is not clear whether "the shock is merely a matter of tactics." [6]

The *petit sommet* resumed in Geneva on April 5 for three more days of uneventful sessions on such matters as steel and textiles, and then adjourned until after the Council meeting. The Council met, as planned, on April 10–12, but remained unmoved on all issues save one—it agreed to participate in a multilateral food aid program. This was a major concession by Germany, which had been in the throes of a budgetary crisis and had strongly resisted any commitment on public expenditures. On all other issues, however, the Council took a completely unyielding view. As for *découpage*, the Six rejected the need for any separation of EEC chemical offers from abolition of the American selling price system.

Another Council meeting was scheduled for the end of April but it was difficult to see how any real progress could be made in the interim. A series of unresolved issues—industry sectors, grains, other agriculture, exceptions, especially in the machinery sector, and the residual list of disparities—all awaited some unforeseen impulse. Aside from food aid, in fact, little had been accomplished in March or the first half of April. Speculation about an extension of the April 30 deadline prompted a quick trip to Brussels by Roth and Blumenthal on April 17 to stress the importance of the deadline. There was considerable uncertainty as to how the participants would go about the final confrontation over the outstanding issues.

At this point Wyndham White suggested that the time had come for participants to specify their positive offer lists in light of the current situation. In some areas this simply meant withdrawals; in areas such as steel and textiles it called for a belated documentation of the existing vague state of offer positions.

The submission of positive offer lists by the United States, the United Kingdom, and the Swiss (the Nordics had already submitted theirs) provided a target for the final accounting and bargaining. The U.S. list included careful explanations of the circumstances that would require

6. *Journal of Commerce* (New York), April 7, 1967.

revisions in its offer and those under which no withdrawals would be necessary. Though the risk of retaliatory responses to the lists was great, the consequences of a continuing stalemate were more menacing. The EEC Council meeting, finally scheduled for May 2, would be the last opportunity for deliberation before a final attempt at Geneva to reach agreement, and other participants would have to make their intentions clear before that time.

There were faint signs during the last days of April of a willingness on all sides to move toward compromise solutions. Some minor issues were tentatively agreed and the EEC appeared disposed, though reluctant, to negotiate *découpage* and go significantly further in nongrain agriculture. There was even a fleeting, euphoric hope that a "reverse sequence" would develop: the Community and the United States would settle their bilateral differences first and then each would concentrate on the increasingly difficult bargaining with third countries. But this optimistic speculation was overshadowed by the large gaps remaining between positions on the key issues and the small amount of time left to bridge them.

At the end of April the Geneva negotiators returned home for final consultation with their superiors: Rey to his Council of Ministers, Roth to President Johnson. During his short stay in Washington, Roth, in addition to meeting with the President, held a working dinner in his Georgetown home that ran long into the night. The subcabinet Washington officials responsible for the negotiation, coordinated by White House Assistant Francis Bator, went over the many intricacies of substance and tactics with Roth and Blumenthal. The recurring question was whether Rey would return to Geneva with sufficient flexibility to negotiate a settlement on the remaining issues. If he did not, there might be no alternative to a ministerial level confrontation at Geneva. There was general opposition by other countries to a ministerial meeting, especially because of the uncertainty as to how unified the Six might be in such a situation, and the danger of an irreconcilable blow-up. The EEC Commission was also reluctant to have control of the final negotiations shifted from Rey to the member state ministers. But although one State Department veteran referred to a ministerial meeting as a "possible kiss of death," the senior American officials concluded that, in view of the little time remaining, such a meeting would have to be called if the Community did not return with negotiating flexibility in the key outstanding issues.

When Rey arrived at Geneva on May 4, he told reporters: "I came back [from Brussels] with a certain flexibility." [7]

Bilateral Settlements

As all outstanding matters converged during the long and almost continuous meetings in April, the burden on heads of delegations multiplied. The multilateral negotiation had always depended on carefully developed bilateral accounts, and they became the focal point of discussion when the bargaining reached the stage of specific requests for improved offers or threats of withdrawal. A voluminous dossier had been developed for each account containing interminable lists of requests, possible withdrawals, and esoteric arguments on the condition of reciprocity as currently disagreed. The series of meetings between heads of delegations required continually putting out of mind the minutiae of one meeting and absorbing those of the next.

The style of the negotiations changed also, principally in that meetings involved fewer people and were more informal. This was most obvious in multilateral matters, such as the industry sector problems, where participation at meetings became limited to a few key people from the major countries. Ad hoc subgroups were often established to thrash out technical problems. In addition, there was more frequent personal contact between delegation heads and with Wyndham White. It became difficult for any other than a few chief negotiators to keep abreast of events. Some larger delegations held daily staff meetings and press conferences, but these forums seldom revealed the more intimate areas of negotiation.

The U.S. negotiations were the most complicated because its trade interests were the most diversified. The major emphasis of this study has been on multilateral issues, often polarizing around U.S.-EEC problems, because a great deal more was involved than straightforward bargaining of tariff cuts. But this concentration in the discussion understates the relative trade importance of other countries, and the effort which was devoted to negotiations with them. The two countries that are the largest trading partners of the United States are Canada and

7. "D'une certaine souplesse." See New York Herald Tribune, international edition, May 5, 1967, and Le Monde (Paris), May 6, 1967.

Japan; U.S. trade with EFTA countries is almost two-thirds that with the EEC; and negotiations with developing countries and other participants involved important trade interests. The United States had prepared for this diversity of negotiating objectives by dividing into teams and during the final weeks of the negotiations responsibility in each area was assigned to one of Roth's senior advisers.

The bases for the bilateral negotiations varied considerably. Negotiations with EFTA countries came closest to a straightforward linear tariff reduction; trade is fairly balanced in industrial goods, though not in farm products, where the United States has a substantial export surplus except with Denmark. Particular problems existed, of course, such as the special wine-gallon assessment on American imports of Scotch whiskey, the preferential United Kingdom revenue tariff on tobacco, the United Kingdom embargo on coal imports, and free bindings. There was no overwhelming conceptual disagreement, however, on the value of trade concessions. Hard-nosed haggling continued up to the last minute—the U.K. delegation broke out a bottle of Scotch labeled "Stand-Fast" at one critical meeting—but final agreement was reached with offers at a high, basically across-the-board level. Although precise bilateral balancing was not intended, it is interesting that the United States reduced tariffs on $831 million of industrial imports from the United Kingdom while the United Kingdom cut on $832 million of U.S. trade.[8]

The bilateral negotiation between the United States and Japan was also based on linear reductions, but there were many tempering factors on each side. The threat posed by Japanese imports has long been a serious concern for a large part of U.S. industry. Japan, for its part, has moved cautiously toward liberal trade.[9] The bargaining situation was aggravated by a lopsided, almost two-to-one, ratio of dutiable industrial trade favoring Japan. Linear cuts, therefore, would tend to be more stimulating for Japanese than for U.S. exports. An overall trade

8. All trade figures are for 1964. For a full account, including principal products involved, see U.S. Office of Special Representative for Trade Negotiations, *Report on United States Negotiations* (1967), Vol. 1.

9. A relatively cautious policy of tariff reduction was in part related to the uncertain effect of liberalization elsewhere. During 1963–64, Japan shifted from its transitional status within the International Monetary Fund to full membership, thus assuming broad obligations of liberality and nondiscrimination; the United Kingdom and the EEC finally renounced discrimination against Japan under Article 35 of GATT; and Japan became a full member of the Organization for Economic Cooperation and Development.

surplus by the United States resulted from large volumes of generally unprocessed goods that entered Japan duty free and U.S. agricultural exports. Finally, on both sides the trade significance of tariff cuts was marred by nontariff restraints.

The issue of reciprocity was raised when Japan initially tabled a comparatively long exceptions list, although it later improved its offer. Once negotiation moved away from a straight linear cut, the qualitative appraisal was bound to be contentious. In the last months of the negotiation, the United States significantly reduced its offers, particularly in steel and textiles, although a substantial agreement involving average tariff cuts of 30–35 percent in each direction was ultimately achieved. Reductions were made on a wide range of Japanese exports and on U.S. exports of chemicals, machinery, and farm products in particular. But the final negotiations were strained on almost every issue—tariff cuts, quotas, grains agreement, free bindings—and round-the-clock meetings appeared to generate little but hard feelings.

Although the substance of the U.S.-Japanese negotiation lent itself to such contention, other factors were also at work. The Japanese, who identify in many ways with advanced Western industrial states, are often so fully accepted by these countries that they are assumed to have all the aggressive give and take that Western countries accord to each other. The Japanese, however, are still feeling their way into the international diplomatic arena and hesitate to overextend themselves. In the Kennedy Round they accepted the linear approach to tariff cutting hesitantly and then diluted its simplicity with a lengthy initial exceptions list. If Japan had, like the EFTA countries, made no initial exceptions, she might not only have improved her own tactical situation but contributed a major impetus to the entire negotiation as well. A good part of Japan's caution undoubtedly was attributable to economic concern for Japanese industry and a perennial sensitivity about her trade balance; but another factor is the lag between Japan's emergence as an industrial power and her assumption of a strong role in world affairs. The Kennedy Round, in fact, was the first major postwar diplomatic effort in which Japan played a leading role. Her importance was particularly apparent in the informal but fairly frequent "big four" meetings (the United States, the EEC, the United Kingdom, and Japan) held by Wyndham White to assess the course of the negotiations.

U.S.-Canadian negotiations were an undertaking of major importance to the two North American countries. Canada is America's largest national trading partner, accounting for roughly one-fifth of total U.S. trade. In 1964, 69 percent of Canada's imports and 54 percent of its exports were from and to the United States.[10] Many products, industrial and agricultural, are traded almost exclusively across the border, often within a unified corporate production or marketing system.

Unique characteristics of U.S.-Canadian trade bore heavily on the negotiations. The United States maintained a substantial export surplus with Canada, normally offset by the northward flow of capital. Moreover, Canadian exports to the United States were concentrated in primary or partially processed goods, while U.S. exports were largely finished manufactures.[11] This trade structure reinforced the imbalance in duty payments from the generally higher level of Canadian tariffs because tariffs are normally highest on manufactures and low or nil on raw materials and lightly processed goods. Whereas Canadian duties on American exports were largely in the 17–25 percent range, the average duty paid on U.S. imports from Canada was only 3.4 percent.[12]

Because of this special trade structure, Canada was unwilling to accept linear tariff reduction as a basis for negotiation. Linear cuts by Canada would lead to relatively large reductions on price-sensitive imports of manufactures, while Canadian exports, basically price insensitive, would receive very modest duty cuts in absolute terms. The net effect would be strongly negative to the Canadian trade balance. Other Kennedy Round participants accepted Canada's special status, but did not specify criteria that would provide "a balance of advantages based on trade concessions . . . of equivalent value." The two limits of a possible reciprocal Canadian offer were an *average*, although not linear, cut of 50 percent, and a balanced cut based on loss of duties collectible,[13] requiring an average Canadian cut of only about 10 percent. Between these two extremes was the wide range of potential negotiation. Both the United States and Canada recognized that neither extreme would be a satisfactory outcome, but the dialogue moved slowly

10. Since 1964 the share has risen further largely because of the two-way trade generated by the U.S.-Canadian automotive agreement.

11. Half of total Canadian exports to the United States in 1964 consisted of iron ore, unfinished lumber, wood pulp, petroleum, natural gas, newsprint and basic papers, primary aluminum, nickel, and copper. Three-quarters of U.S. exports to Canada were chemicals, textiles, iron and steel, machinery, transport equipment, precision instruments, and miscellaneous manufactures. A comparison limited to nonagricultural products would be even more striking.

12. See Table 13–13.

13. See Chap. 8, pp. 132–33.

beyond that point. In fact, since the qualitative value of a tariff cut varied so greatly from product to product, negotiations centered on a series of specific request and offer lists.

A further complication was Canada's proposal to revise its tariff structure on machinery, affecting almost $400 million of U.S. exports. The existing system levied 22½ percent duties on machinery of "a class or kind made in Canada," and 7½ percent on machinery not made in Canada. The new proposal reduced the 22½ percent rate to 15 percent and changed the 7½ percent to either "free" or 15 percent depending on certain economic criteria. The final agreement provided for a maximum 9 percent overall tariff incidence (that is, duties paid as a share of imports) for machinery to insure that a sufficient share of the former 7½ percent trade would henceforth enter in the free category.

Up until the final weeks of the negotiation the Canadian talks were among the most difficult for the United States, mainly because of differing interpretations of reciprocity. A number of factors, however, worked to narrow the differences. The 9 percent incidence binding on machinery strengthened the Canadian offer in this sector; the anti-dumping agreement, while multilateral, was especially important to U.S. exporters to Canada; agricultural talks developed a fairly balanced package, often with matched rates on two-way trade; and the residual balance, helped by last minute concessions on both sides, including elimination of duty on $580 million of trade, resulted in a very substantial final agreement. Canadian tariffs were cut on $1.4 billion of imports from the United States, almost half of them by more than 25 percent; the United States, in turn, cut tariffs on $1.25 billion of imports from Canada.

Bilateral negotiations between the United States and developing countries were of limited significance. The United States, like other industrial participants, had given priority to tariff cuts on items of special interest to developing countries from the start, and there was little more to negotiate in the final months. Developing countries were pressed to make some offer in return, but the value of their offers was often symbolic rather than substantive. In negotiations with the so-called borderline countries,[14] which were not accorded the developing-country right to withhold reciprocity, only limited numbers of products were involved. Outstanding requests by developing countries—

14. In particular Spain, Portugal, Israel, and Yugoslavia.

advanced implementation of tariff cuts, compensation for loss of preferences, liberalization of the cotton textile arrangement, action on tropical products—were usually handled multilaterally, or discussed separately with commodity specialists flown in for the occasion. The pace of bilateral talks with developing countries was also irregular, and final agreements with some were not reached until well into June.

The various U.S. bilateral negotiations also involved many recurring minor issues that were both time-consuming and irritating. And U.S. negotiations, though more diversified geographically, were no more problem-laden than those between other countries. The broad objective of the Kennedy Round was a multilateral balance, but differences in view were often first approached bilaterally. In late April all of the issues began to loosen up. But change, or possible change, in the balance sheet with one country or in one industry sector inevitably affected others. The final bargaining moved ahead like a complicated Bach fugue, although with far less balance or harmony. And the Geneva negotiators were fortunate in having on the podium the experienced GATT director general, Eric Wyndham White.

U.S.-EEC Marathon

The task of an international secretariat in a negotiation, like that of any honest broker, is to maintain a delicate balance between objective restraint and well timed initiative. The GATT secretariat during the Kennedy Round was a model of effective conduct. Technical support was objective, and the coordination of meetings was carried out so as to instill an impulse of progress but without becoming overbearing. As in past negotiations, the secretariat's role was dominated by the expertise of its director general.

The supreme test for Wyndham White, and for everyone concerned with the Kennedy Round negotiation, began on Thursday, May 4, when delegates reconvened at Geneva after final consultations in their capitals. Chemicals, steel, grain, other EEC agricultural offers, exceptions, and residual disparities were all to be settled in the next six days. Jean Rey likened the negotiation to the European bicycle marathon. Rey's general optimism at this point, however, was not matched by the Americans. Roth, instead, stressed the critical element of time: "It is the U.S. position that, if we are to meet the deadline, we must have completed substantial agreement early next week." If agreement cannot be reached, he warned, "we would be glad to participate in a ministerial meeting." [15]

Hopes were quickly dampened on Friday by the chemical sector group. The two major items on its agenda were *découpage* and the U.S. exception of dyestuffs from the 20 percent ceiling.[16] The EEC was believed to be ready to negotiate seriously on *découpage* but the meeting never got that far. The collective European condemnation of the U.S. exception on dyes was so vehement and uncompromising that Roth declared the problem insoluble and left the meeting. That was the last meeting of the full sector group.

Over the weekend, activity continued on many fronts. The steel group deadlocked over British refusal to make any offer in response to the U.S.-EEC offer to match their rates. Bilateral negotiations, particularly the U.S.-Canadian talks, on the other hand, made substantial headway. The grains group remained in continuous day and evening session, but with no indication of a settlement. Center stage, however, was held by the "big four"—the United States, the EEC, the United Kingdom, and Japan—meeting in lengthy sessions in Wyndham White's office. The main topic was again chemicals and this time there was significant forward movement. Rey finally accepted *découpage*, in principle, although he initially spoke in terms of small—little more than token—cuts in the Kennedy Round. Roth offered a slight improvement on dyestuffs to a final offer of 30 percent.[17]

The two catchwords at this point were "package deal" and "marathon." It was believed that the outstanding differences in the negotiation could only be bridged with an overall package settlement. Wyndham White's role in proposing such a "package deal" was much discussed, but the GATT director general realized that it was premature at this point, both in time and substance, for him to try to bridge the differences.

The "marathon" negotiation, perfected during recent years at Brussels, had developed its own mystique for bringing complicated negotia-

15. Press release, U.S. Information Agency, Information Service, May 3, 1967.
16. "Exception" here refers to the 20 percent ceiling for the chemical agreement rather than to the 50 percent linear cut.
17. The final U.S. offer on items subject to American selling price consisted of cuts greater than 50 percent on very high rates and cuts of less than 50 percent on a few key items, particularly the dyestuff and drug baskets. Weighted by 1964 imports, the average cut amounted to 53 percent for benzenoid intermediates, about 35 percent for dyestuffs, and about 30 percent for drugs.

tions to a conclusion, and Monday, May 8, was established as the date for the final U.S.-EEC marathon to settle the Kennedy Round. This would permit a meeting of the steering group [18] on Tuesday morning and Rey's departure in the afternoon for a scheduled Council meeting on Wednesday. The American delegation, though somewhat amused by the melodramatic forward billing of the marathon, was concerned about the length and complexity of the agenda, and the questionable efficiency of personnel during an all-night negotiation. They also realized that if this critical session failed, a second chance might not be possible. Roth had clearly stated his intention of returning to Washington at the end of this negotiating period if agreement could not be reached. And even if a follow-up ministerial meeting were proffered, it was highly unlikely that the six EEC ministers could reach unanimous agreement on the specifics of a settlement that Rey had failed to achieve.

As the participants gathered a little after nine in the evening at the picturesque nineteenth century Villa Le Bocage that serves as GATT headquarters, a small group of press people had already begun the long night vigil. A tightening of security to insure the confidentiality of the proceedings in Wyndham White's spacious office was represented by "a bearded GATT 'gorilla,' helped by a posse of enthusiastic minions, to keep prowling reporters back in the shrubbery." [19]

The agenda for the meeting was to begin with industry and then move to agricultural problems. The program immediately bogged down, however, over chemicals, and the subtleties of *découpage* in particular. It was really the first serious attempt to reach a settlement on this question. About two in the morning Rey announced that he could, as a final position, accept the general lines of the chemical sector suggestion put forward several months earlier by Wyndham White: the EEC would cut 20 percent unconditionally in the Kennedy Round and an additional 30 percent after abolition of the American selling price system. The Americans, while pointing out other, though relatively minor, aspects of the Wyndham White proposal, replied that they could not maintain their full offer in chemicals in response to a simple 20/30 contribution by the Europeans. A long silence followed, and then, as delegates avoided each other's glances across the table, Wyndham White

18. An ad hoc group consisting of chief delegates from the United States, the EEC, the United Kingdom, the Nordics, Switzerland, Canada, Japan, and Australia.
19. *Times* (London), May 8, 1967.

closed the discussion with the dry observation that the participants were unable to reach agreement in the chemical sector.

The remainder of the heralded marathon was almost pro forma. A significant move in grains was the American proposal to drop demands for a commitment on access to the EEC market and limit talks to a flat commitment on food aid and a new set of minimum world prices for wheat. But there was no mood to negotiate further. The marathon had failed to solve the key issues. Rey would return to Brussels without a settlement, and the EEC Council could, in reasonably good conscience, refuse any further flexibility to its negotiator. Roth had reached his negotiating deadline without the agreement he sought. The first rays of dawn were on the horizon as the tired delegates emerged from the meeting into a swarm of waiting reporters. The next day's gloomy headline was written plainly on their faces.

Proposals Accepted

Fortunately, four years of effort were not permitted to depend on one night's tribulation.[20] By Tuesday morning there were already rumors of a conciliation. Appropriately, Swedish Ambassador Montan acted as neutral host to Roth and Rey at a luncheon that resulted in agreement on one more consultation for Rey at Brussels and one more absolutely final deadline of midnight, Sunday, May 14. A meeting of the steering group later in the day officially adopted their schedule, and Wyndham White summed it up in a press release:

> The major trading nations participating in the Kennedy Round negotia-
> tions have engaged in intensive bilateral and multilateral talks over the last
> four days with a view to reaching by today an agreement in principle on
> the major outstanding issues in the negotiations. While some progress
> has been made, it has not proved possible to reach such an overall agree-

20. Bernard Béguin of the *Journal de Genève* wrote a fitting evaluation on May 11 entitled, "The Exasperating Marathon": "After four years of discussion on a familiar theme, one wonders how qualified officials can reach a point where the success or failure of their work depends on one night's seance, or a week-end of the last chance. . . . It is a fact, however—regrettable but incontestable fact—that the history of reciprocally advantageous negotiations is marked by these absurd suspenses which allow delegations to claim later before restive opinion that they did not concede except to save the essential. . . . However, it would be unjust to the Kennedy Round negotiators . . . to imagine that they had purposely put off to the last minute the key solutions of the negotiation in order to dramatize the results. . . . The situation is that the negotiation has become more and more difficult through the years . . . and that it is really necessary to have a last minute strenuous effort to pull it through."

ment. . . . It has therefore been agreed that discussions will continue throughout this week with a final concluding date of Sunday, May 14. All are agreed that it would not be possible to prolong the negotiating schedule any further and that failure to come to a general agreement by May 14 would necessarily lead to the joint conclusion that the Kennedy Round cannot be successfully concluded at all.

While there are serious obstacles to be overcome, all have expressed the view that . . . the possibility remains that a major Kennedy Round agreement can be concluded by May 14 and they have pledged their best efforts towards this end.

The reprieve restored hope to the strained Geneva atmosphere. Rey's optimism that the negotiation would not fail over the few differences outstanding was sustained by the EEC Council meeting in Brussels on Wednesday and Thursday. The Council approved virtually all of the Commission's action thus far with the notable exception of ingot aluminum, on which no reduction in the 9 percent rate was permitted. The official communiqué announced that the Council "renewed its full confidence in the Commission" and gave it a "certain number of directives" to bring the negotiations to a conclusion.[21] The "full confidence" dispelled for the last time any doubt that the French might undermine final agreement and the new directives indicated that Rey was prepared to negotiate further, at least on some issues. The unexpected U.S. proposal to limit the grains arrangement to food aid and minimum wheat prices was accepted by the Council with mixed feelings. Commissioner Mansholt commented: "Ours was a long-term political solution. The Americans have a hard short-term commercial solution. If it is settled on this basis, our farmers will be very glad."[22]

Roth did not return to Washington, but the U.S. mission's communications unit worked overtime along with everyone else. White House Press Secretary George Christian announced on Wednesday that President Johnson "has kept up on the discussions there [Geneva]. He of course welcomes the announcement by the Director-General that all the parties are prepared to conclude the negotiation on or before May 14." He went on to say that Roth had "full authority" to reach agreement for the United States, and although the United States had indicated willingness to send Cabinet-level officials to Geneva, "this now appears unnecessary."[23] The latter point was clear recognition that

21. *Le Monde* (Paris), May 13, 1967.
22. *New York Herald Tribune*, international edition, May 10, 1967.
23. Press release, U.S. Information Agency, Information Service, May 11, 1967.

Rey had received, during these final days, a sufficiently flexible mandate to negotiate effectively for the six member Community.

The meetings resumed at Geneva on Friday. They went on for three days, mostly informally and on a bilateral basis.[24] The smaller issues were resolved, but not the big ones. Everyone was now talking about "package deal" and "Wyndham White compromise." There was also a good deal of serious if subtle discussion between delegates and with the secretariat about what might be in such a package. But Wyndham White bided his time as the Sunday night deadline approached. If he did act, it would have to be on a final take-it-or-leave-it basis, and he wanted delegates to get as close to agreement as they could on their own. He let them have the Sunday night deadline all to themselves.

The clock was stopped Sunday at midnight and talks went on into Monday. At midday Wyndham White finally circulated a set of compromise proposals on each of the three key issues: (1) *Chemicals*. There were some further concessions to the United States. The Americans would cut only 20 percent on low duties in the Kennedy Round,[25] the Europeans (primarily, as it worked out, the British) would cut 30 percent instead of 20 percent on high duties; Switzerland and Japan would maintain their full chemical offers (in other words, they would not reserve part of their offers for the American selling price agreement). Under these circumstances, the United States was to accept the basic 20/30 *découpage* formula for chemical offers of the EEC and the United Kingdom. (2) *Agriculture*. The EEC would make additional tariff cut offers on certain priority requests of the United States. (3) *Steel*. The British would make a general 20 percent cut in steel rates in conjunction with the matched rate offers of the United States and the EEC.

24. There was a certain amount of confusion. For example, in a display of modern management technique, one U.S.-EEC meeting was arranged in "two tiers." Rey met with Roth and Blumenthal in one room while the technicians convened next door. The principals intended to discuss the larger aspects of an issue and then pass on the details to the second tier. The technicians waited patiently for their first batch of details. Finally, one of them poked his head into the ambassadorial office to see what progress was being made. The room was empty. The principals had been called off hurriedly and had forgotten to inform the second tier.

25. The other 30 percent cut would be made in the American selling price package. Cuts which would have to be greater than 50 percent to reach the average 20 percent level (almost all in the American selling price sector) were also, of course, part of the package.

There was a flurry of activity to calculate the precise meaning of the proposals. A late afternoon meeting at Wyndham White's office confirmed general agreement on the package but firm commitments were withheld. Another meeting was scheduled for ten o'clock that night.

At 9:25, Ambassador Roth, napping in his room at the Hotel Richemond, was awakened by a telephone call from Jean Rey. Rey requested an informal meeting which Roth gladly accepted and, with Michael Blumenthal, they met in the hotel room. Within ten minutes the package was agreed essentially as proposed by Wyndham White. The Kennedy Round, after four long and harrowing years, was at last clearly bound for a successful conclusion.

By ten o'clock all major participants had accepted the final compromise proposals. Le Bocage was adorned with the familiar crowd of press stalwarts but the gathering was otherwise very different. Instead of the few official cars, furtively delivering a handful of serious, statistic-laden delegates, a line of vehicles backed up bumper to bumper, and delegates by the dozen poured into the villa. Flashbulbs, handshakes, light-hearted banter—it was all over, and the spontaneous relief as the delegates gathered was in perfect harmony with Wyndham White's opening words: "The essential elements of the Kennedy Round have now been successfully negotiated." [26]

26. Press release no. 990, General Agreement on Tariffs and Trade (GATT), May 17, 1967.

CHAPTER TWELVE

Finishing Touches

May 16, 1967–June 30, 1967

THE MAJOR ISSUES had been resolved, but the Kennedy Round was still not quite over. When Ambassador Roth and his colleagues arrived at the U.S. mission for a midnight press conference on May 15, one conference room was closed off: a U.S.-Japanese session was in full swing, with little apparent sign of agreement, and because of the pace of events, unaware that the "essential elements of the Kennedy Round" had been agreed. In fact, a great deal of business was still outstanding, and the race with the clock continued over the ensuing six weeks right up to the day before the official signing on June 30.

World Reaction

But there was no question that May 15 marked the climax, the decisive agreement, and that the remaining unresolved points would not be permitted to undo the accord announced that evening. The conclusion was hailed enthusiastically. Congratulations arrived from heads of state, legislators, and business leaders. U Thant praised the successful outcome as a "major step towards improved world trade relations." [1] Average tariff cuts of 35 percent for all industrial products, covering $40 billion of world trade, and a government food aid commitment of 4.5 million tons per year were the featured economic achievements. The strengthening of ties between members of the Atlantic community and the unity displayed by the European Economic Community (EEC)

1. Press release, United Nations, May 16, 1967.

received the major political emphasis.[2] The individual negotiators received high praise, especially Eric Wyndham White whose "timely interventions" were "crucial" to the outcome. Frequent tribute was paid to the late President Kennedy.

Erwin Canham wrote in the *Christian Science Monitor*: [3]

> I was present in Secretary of State Cordell Hull's office in the old museum-piece State, War, and Navy Building in 1933 when he first announced officially his proposals for a reciprocal trade agreements program. And I was also at the London Economic Conference in July 1933, when he urged his program on the nations. The Conference was a fiasco, but the Hull idea lived on. . . .
>
> And now, following the "Kennedy Round" agreements, tariffs affecting four-fifths of the world's trade will be cut by over one-third. This is an almost incredible achievement. It is a triumph for broad-based enlightened self-interest.

There were, of course, voices of dissent. Parts of the American chemical industry reacted in an outspokenly negative way to the two-package chemical agreement. James D. Mahoney, president of the Synthetic Organic Chemical Manufacturers Association—the traditional defender of the American selling price system—called the agreement "one of the most blatantly one-sided bargains in the history of American trade negotiations." [4] The president of a dye firm lamented, "Disastrous is the only way I can describe the [chemical] agreement." [5] And the most articulate spokesman for protectionism in the United States, Oscar Strackbein, commented that "enough is known to greet it as a time bomb loosed against the American economy." [6] But amidst the nearly unanimous enthusiasm, dissent was barely heard.

More significant than small pockets of outright opposition was the qualified approval given by developing countries. It had been evident

2. *Le Figaro* (Paris) described the agreement "a proof of the growing maturity of the Europe of the Six which has shown itself capable of conducting difficult negotiations in perfect unity. It has been able to give great confidence to the European Commission." *Le Monde* (Paris) commented, "One of the most striking results . . . was uncontestably to forge the personality of the EEC, which has had in recent months to conduct very difficult discussions with the United Kingdom and the other countries of Western Europe. The Six have thus been able to measure in the action the strength they acquired from their unity of representation and initiative." (Quoted in press release, U.S. Information Agency, Information Service, May 22, 1967.)

3. Boston, May 17, 1967.

4. *Newsweek*, May 29, 1967.

5. *Wall Street Journal* (New York), May 17, 1967.

6. *Journal of Commerce* (New York), May 18, 1967.

for some time that important exports of these countries would not fare well in the final accounting. The problem was that the exports of developing countries were concentrated in the most difficult sectors for substantial trade liberalization.[7] Even in manufactures, the area where greatest tariff cuts were achieved, the largest category of interest to developing countries—cotton textiles—received only modest cuts. Reductions were on the order of 20 percent despite a three-year extension of the Long-Term Arrangement Regarding International Trade in Cotton Textiles, as requested by importers, and in the last minute these cuts were made conditional on possible future extensions of the arrangement. In other areas of special interest to developing countries, such as processed agricultural products in general or tropical products in particular, the prospects from the start had been dim and the results were in keeping with expectations.

Wyndham White, in his brief statement on May 15 announcing "essential elements . . . successfully negotiated," added that "tariff cuts have been agreed on many other products of principal, or potential, export interest to the developing countries." He spoke of possible further improvements in offers to these countries, and raised the question of advanced implementation of tariff cuts for developing countries which "will be a major determining factor in their overall appraisal of the concessions received." Regarding the disappointing results for tropical products, he bluntly stated that "it was not possible to reach agreement at this stage on the elimination or reduction of tariffs because of the existence of preferential arrangements."[8]

At a Trade Negotiations Committee meeting the next day to establish a procedural schedule for the remaining weeks, the developing countries pressed these points, especially the demand for implementing tariff cuts for their exports more rapidly than the normal five annual steps. It was agreed that some positive plans should be made for advanced implementation, and industrial countries agreed to submit, by October 15, 1967, lists of products on which such action would be taken, but no definite commitments were made. The United States would require additional congressional authority to modify implementation of tariff cuts in this way and was unwilling to make a commit-

7. See Chap. 13, pp. 227–31.
8. These were primarily EEC preferences to associated overseas countries. For one product group, tropical hardwoods, the industrial countries did agree to duty elimination in the Kennedy Round.

ment to seek such authority. In fact, the only significant development in the final days concerning the developing countries was unfavorable to them. In the absence of a global arrangement for meat, negotiation had reverted to individual bilateral concessions, including an EEC offer to Argentina on beef. In the last weeks, however, the EEC withdrew its earlier proposal and instead offered a less attractive one that elicited a sharp public rebuttal by the Argentine government.[9]

Preparations for June 30

The remaining weeks were taken up with loose ends of negotiation and with preparing and checking the final legal documents. Draft schedules of offers were to be circulated by May 31, checked by recipients, and submitted in final form to the GATT secretariat by June 19, in order that the final protocols would be ready for signature at the end of June. The separate chemical agreement concerning the American selling price system developed into a complicated exercise in legal drafting, and the commitment on food aid required further specification.

These basically procedural matters became tangled with a large number of unsettled substantive issues. Bilateral negotiations continued into June, in some cases over one or two key items of concession. The package agreement on "essentials" of May 15 required some additional negotiation, including a quick trip back to Geneva by William Roth in early June to settle outstanding U.S.-EEC differences with Jean Rey. The most important issue during this period concerned Japanese participation in the joint food aid program. After hectic high level consultation, especially between Washington and Tokyo, it was agreed that Japan would have the option to substitute other aid for grains.

The question of phasing tariff cuts presented administrative problems. All agreed that tariff cuts would be spread over five annual stages, as specified in the Trade Expansion Act. The United States and some others were prepared to make the first two cuts on January 1, 1968 and 1969. The EEC, however, had adopted July 1, 1968, as the date for final alignment of member state tariffs to the common external tariff, and instead of revising customs duties three times between January 1,

9. See *Le Monde* (Paris), July 1, 1967.

1968, and January 1, 1969, proposed to implement the first two Kennedy Round cuts on July 1, 1968—in other words, the first cut six months later than the United States and the second cut six months earlier. The final three stages of Kennedy Round cuts would be made simultaneously by all countries on January 1, 1970, 1971, and 1972.

Approval of the final agreement by governments also had to be obtained during the weeks before June 30. It was highly unlikely that a head of government would reject the settlement negotiated by his representative, especially in view of the close consultation between Geneva and capitals during the days prior to May 15. Official approval, however, usually required a thorough statement and analysis of the elements of the agreement, which added to the work load of delegations. Another time consuming matter was answering inquiries about the final offers on particular products. Final offer lists remained confidential until June 30, partly because minor changes were still being made, partly because no concession was official until authorized signatures were recorded; inquiries, therefore, had to be handled carefully. One inadvertent breach was the Japanese Ministry of Trade and Industry's announcement in the first week of June of a long list of U.S. concessions of primary benefit to Japanese exporters.[10]

The final weeks were filled also with farewells as delegates who had worked closely together for three or four years celebrated their mission accomplished and prepared to move on to new assignments.

On the afternoon of June 29, a lengthy meeting in Michael Blumenthal's office was interrupted by a phone call from the ambassador of another major country. A technical problem in his capital, it seemed, would prevent signature the following day on one of the basic documents. Blumenthal explained that he couldn't sign unless the others did, and that U.S. authority to sign expired definitively at midnight June 30. During the next hour and a half a series of telephone calls went back and forth between the two missions, senior officials in the two capitals, and the GATT secretariat. The meeting in Blumenthal's office continued, except for these occasional phone interruptions, and at the end of ninety minutes the matter was settled satisfactorily. It was the last of the minor crises that had plagued the weeks leading up to June 30. It was also a good example of the importance of a modern communication system in the operation of foreign affairs.

10. *New York Herald Tribune*, international edition, June 7, 1967.

Signing the Agreement

The June 30 signing ceremony was bound to be anticlimactic after the suspense and drama of the May 15 breakthrough, even though the physical presence was more imposing. Delegates, press, wives, tourists, all assembled in the majestic main conference room of the Palais des Nations for the ceremony. The meeting opened on a humorous note, with Wyndham White introducing the presiding officer, Swiss Minister Hans Schaffner, in French, which, though fluent, fell somewhat short of Parisian in intonation. Schaffner, however, then proceeded to speak in his nearly perfect English.[11]

The laudatory phrases of the speakers were punctuated with impressive figures on the results of the negotiations. There was no question that a major reduction in barriers to world trade had been accomplished. Measured against predictions, the Kennedy Round emerged amazingly well. The closing day, however, was appropriate also for comment on the problems that remained. Wyndham White spoke with special concern for the trade prospects of developing countries: [12]

> The results of the Kennedy Round for developing countries are less impressive. . . . It is clear that the less-developed countries will derive substantial advantages from the Kennedy Round, and equally clear that all their legitimate desires and aspirations are not fully achieved. Those— and there are many—which are heavily dependent upon exports of agricultural products suffer from the general modesty of the results in the agricultural field. . . . It is also significant—and regrettable—that in a major area of manufactures where some less-developed countries have a clear competitive advantage—and despite their concurrence in the extension of the Cotton Textiles Arrangement—tariff reductions fell far short of the 50 percent target and in some important cases are only granted conditionally.
>
> On looking ahead, however, a large place will have to be found in the future programme of GATT—in partnership with other international organizations—for a determined and concerted attack on the formidable obstacles which lie in the path of the less-developed countries in their struggle for the economic advancement of their peoples. This is not their problem alone, it is a clear responsibility for the international community as a whole.

11. The *Journal de Genève* (July 1, 1967) good naturedly commented that Schaffner, "to keep all the Swiss satisfied, spoke in English."
12. See Appendix D.

If there was any doubt about the reactions of developing countries to the final outcome, it was quickly dissipated by the curt statement of the Peruvian delegate, José Encinas, who spoke on their behalf: "Today when the Kennedy Round of negotiations has come to an end, the developing countries participating in these negotiations wish to state that the most important problems of most of them in the field of trade taken up within the framework of these negotiations, still remain unresolved. These developing countries deeply regret that they are not in a position to share, to the same extent, the satisfaction of the developed countries at the conclusion and the achievements of the Kennedy Round." [13]

The signing ceremony proceeded alphabetically, the photographers blocking the delegates from view for the most part. Representatives of forty-six nations signed the Final Act.[14] Blumenthal signed for the United States and his picture duly accompanied the next day's front page story: "Biggest Trade Deal Ever." [15] The Kennedy Round was officially concluded. One last round of champagne after the signing, and delegates were on their way. Many, in fact, had departed well before June 30. There was a crowded agenda of trade policy matters to attend to: melding the grains agreement into the broader-based International Wheat Council activities; drawing up legislation for the American selling price agreement; reopening dossiers for possible U.K.-EEC negotiations; developing an agenda for the second United Nations Conference on Trade and Development; negotiating a cocoa agreement; preparing a balanced and forward-looking commercial policy for the years ahead. Eric Wyndham White stressed the need for continued effort in his final note of warning as the curtain lowered on the sixth round of GATT negotiations: [16]

---

13. Press release no. 994, General Agreement on Tariffs and Trade (GATT), June 30, 1967.

14. There were nine separate agreements to be signed: the Final Act, which summarized the substantive agreements; the general GATT protocol embodying tariff reductions and bindings; the American selling price agreement; the grains agreement; the antidumping agreement; and agreements for GATT accession by Argentina, Iceland, Ireland, and Poland. For further discussion of the legal aspects of the agreements, see John B. Rehm, "Developments in the Law and Institutions of International Economic Relations: The Kennedy Round of Trade Negotiations," *American Journal of International Law*, April 1968, pp. 427–34.

15. *New York Herald Tribune*, international edition, July 1, 1967.

16. See Appendix D.

The General Agreement of 1967 extends and consolidates the impressive achievements of twenty years of international trade and cooperation. It points the way ahead to further achievement. At the same time the structure is fragile and constantly subject to attack. So far it has not been tested by periods of economic stress and recession. We cannot confidently say whether it would take the strain. If national economic policies are managed without sufficient awareness of the economic interdependence of nations, there is always the risk that governments may feel impelled to revert to policies of external restriction. . . . The price of economic liberalization—as of liberty—is eternal vigilance.

CHAPTER THIRTEEN

Tariff Levels
on Nonagricultural Products

THE MAJOR ACCOMPLISHMENT of the Kennedy Round of the General Agreement on Tariffs and Trade was the reduction of tariff levels. And the greatest reductions were made on nonagricultural products; those achievements are summarized in this chapter, and their effect on trade patterns is discussed in the next. In Chapter 15 the less spectacular results of the negotiations on agricultural products are examined. The analysis is based primarily on tariff rates and import data, in most cases for 1964, available during the negotiations.

The analysis of average tariff levels for nonagricultural products (excluding mineral fuels) includes cuts in the chemical sector that are conditional on acceptance of the separate agreement related to American selling price, although the difference in reductions in the event the agreement, which must be approved by Congress, is not implemented is generally explained in footnotes. Following is a listing, by country, of tariff reductions on chemicals as they are affected by the American selling price agreement:

United States. If the American selling price agreement is adopted, the average reduction of duties on chemicals will increase only slightly. The reduction will vary, however, by product group. Benzenoid chemicals—the only ones subject to American selling price, and comprising about 10 percent of domestic production—will receive a flat 50 percent cut if the agreement is *not* enacted, and a variable reduction if the agreement is adopted, based on post-Kennedy Round levels of 30 percent for dyestuffs and approximately 20 percent for most other benzenoids.[1] An average reduction if the agreement is adopted is difficult to calculate because of the very high rates involved, but if weighted by 1964 imports, the average is a little less than 50 percent. Products throughout the chemical sector with duties of 8 percent or less will be reduced by only 20 percent if the agreement is *not* enacted, and by 50 percent if it is. All other U.S. imports of chemicals are unaffected by the American selling price agreement.

European Economic Community. With few exceptions, chemical duties will be cut 20 percent unconditionally and 50 percent if the agreement is enacted.

United Kingdom. Chemical duties will be reduced by an *average* of about 20 percent unconditionally and 50 percent if the agreement is enacted.[2]

Japan and Switzerland. All tariff reductions will be made whether or not the agreement is enacted.

Nordic countries and Austria. Reductions in the chemical sector will follow a pattern similar to that of the EEC but with numerous exceptions to the rule.

The American selling price agreement also contains a number of nontariff contributions—the conversion of the basis of valuation for U.S. imports of benzenoid chemicals from American selling price to normal valuation procedures, the elimination of the discriminatory elements in European road taxes, a 25 percent reduction in the United Kingdom tobacco tariff preference, and the removal of Swiss limitations on imports of canned fruit preserved with corn syrup. In the following analysis of tariff levels the effects of these nontariff factors are ignored.[3]

---

1. Most benzenoids other than dyes are subject to a compound duty—for example, 1 cent per pound plus 18 percent. In these cases the specific component equals the difference between 20 percent and the ad valorem component, *on the average* (in the example, an average of 2 percent). For individual chemicals, however, the tariff incidence varies depending on the value per pound; in some cases it will be less, in others more than the average. See *Elimination of the American Selling Price System*, Hearings before the House Committee on Ways and Means, 90 Cong. 2 sess. (1968), pp. 45–47 and especially Table 8.

2. See Chap. 10, p. 174.

3. For American selling price, the nontariff effect is the uncertainty and variability of the system compared with normal valuation procedures. The change in tariff levels for benzenoid chemicals is taken into account by converting all tariff rates, before and after Kennedy Round cuts, to a comparable c.i.f. basis.

Average Tariff Levels

If a constant rate of duty were levied on all imports, there would be no problem in assessing the level of tariff protection for all products. Once tariff rates become dispersed, however, two basic questions arise: How is an average tariff level calculated for groups of individual products? How is the tariff rate on a particular product related to the rates on other products that are components, or inputs, for that product?

The averaging problem has troubled economists for years. The aggravating fact is that since high duties tend to restrict imports and very high duties to prohibit imports, the *average* duty paid understates the level of protection. In the extreme case, where a tariff schedule consists of duty free categories and completely prohibitive rates, the average duty paid on imports is zero. But in the ordinary case, how close an approximation of average tariff level is the average duty paid, and how can the discrepancies be minimized? Analysis of various forms of tariff averaging (see Appendix A) reveals that: (1) There is no completely satisfactory method for computing an average tariff level, although differences in results between the various measures, at least for dutiable nonagricultural imports, are not very large. (2) The average tariff for dutiable nonagricultural imports weighted by a country's own imports is biased downward. The degree of bias is probably only 10–15 percent for the United States before Kennedy Round cuts and less than 10 percent after; for European countries it is considerably smaller; and for Japan the bias is uncertain but possibly larger than that for the United States. (3) For computing the level of tariff protection for dutiable nonagricultural trade, an average tariff weighted by own imports is generally a better alternative to an ideal average weighted by the level of imports possible under free trade than an average weighted by world imports or by consumption, or the simple arithmetic mean of individual tariff rates.

The averaging method used here (described in detail in Appendix A) was chosen for its appropriateness to the principal areas of negotiation in the Kennedy Round and because it provides reasonable comparability between countries. The computations are based on the roughly nine hundred categories of dutiable nonagricultural imports in the four-digit breakdown of the Brussels Tariff Nomenclature—the finest universally applicable breakdown available. Where more than one national rate falls within a single Brussels category, an arithmetic average of these rates is generally used. When several categories are combined in larger industry groups, they are weighted by the country's own imports from all most-favored-nation sources.

Tables 13–1 through 13–4 summarize tariff levels before and after Kennedy Round cuts for the United States, the EEC, the United Kingdom, and Japan. The overall tariff reduction, whether for total dutiable imports or only for manufactures, falls in the range of 36–39 percent for each country. Because of the margin of error in the averaging procedure, no further distinction can be made than to say that each of the four largest participants in the Kennedy Round made an average reduction of slightly more than 35 percent in its nonagricultural tariff levels.

A few industry categories dominate the overall average for each country. Chemicals and machinery account for 46–47 percent of dutiable imports for Japan and the United Kingdom, and 42 percent of the total for the EEC. The United States shows an import concentration in textiles, steel, machinery, and transportation equipment. While the average cuts vary considerably by industry, the performance by country for major industries is more nearly uniform.

For chemicals, reductions were 46–50 percent for each country. The relative share of total imports in the chemical sector varies substantially, however, from 5.7 percent for the United States, which is a large net exporter, to 13.1–18.2 percent for the other three participants.

Tariff cuts on nonelectrical and electrical machinery were 48–50 percent for the United States and 36–42 percent for the others. Again the United States is a strong net exporter, and the share of U.S. dutiable imports in the machinery sector is only 12.9 percent compared with 28.7–30.2 percent for the EEC, the United Kingdom, and Japan.

The situation is reversed somewhat for transportation equipment, where imports are relatively more important to the United States than to other countries. The deep U.S. cut of 51 percent is dominated by the duty on passenger automobiles, which was reduced, under the U.S. authority to round off tariffs to the nearest whole percent, from 6.5 percent to 3 percent. The smaller percentage cuts in this sector by the EEC and Japan result primarily from the exception of trucks from tariff reduction by the EEC and of aircraft by Japan. The absolute reductions for transportation equipment, however, reflect the relatively low level of U.S. tariffs. The U.S. absolute reduction was 3.6 points versus a 4.5–9.0 point reduction by others.

Table 13–1. United States Tariff Levels for Nonagricultural Products (Other than Mineral Fuels), before and after Kennedy Round Cuts [a]

| Category | Dutiable imports, before cuts | | Average tariff on dutiable imports, as percentage of c.i.f. value | | Percent cut in Kennedy Round |
| | As percentage of total imports [b] | As percentage of total dutiable imports | Before cuts | After cuts | |
	(1)	(2)	(3)	(4)	(5)
Mineral products	18(17)	1.9	9.9	7.5	24
Chemical products	59(58)	5.7	17.8	9.3	48 [c]
Rubber products	25	1.0	11.3	6.0	47
Hides, furs, leather products	47	2.0	16.2	10.4	36
Raw hides, skins, fur	8(7)	0.2	4.1	3.6	54
Articles of leather, fur	100	1.8	17.5	11.2	36
Wood and cork products	86(36)	7.7	6.8	7.1	49
Wood, natural cork	58(30)	0.7	0.9	0.3	89
Articles of wood, cork	90(37)	7.0	7.4	7.9	49
Pulp and paper	6	1.0	10.9	5.5	50
Pulp	0	—	free	free	—
Paper	9	1.0	10.9	5.5	50
Textiles	85(72)	15.8	21.4	20.1	20
Natural fiber and waste	52(50)	2.3	18.3	15.9	16
Yarn and basic fabrics	100(68)	7.2	19.1	21.8	24
Special fabrics, apparel, other	90	6.3	25.0	20.6	18
Footwear and headwear	100	2.2	16.1	12.1	25
Stone, ceramic, and glass products	100(99)	3.2	21.0	15.0	29
Base metals and metal products	93(83)	23.4	8.5	6.3	34
Unwrought, pig iron, scrap	84(58)	8.1	5.2	5.0	35
Basic shapes and forms	100(99)	11.0	8.5	6.4	25
Steel	100	9.4	6.5	5.7	12
Other	100(95)	1.6	19.6	10.4	47
Articles of base metal, misc.	97(95)	4.3	14.7	7.7	48
Nonelectrical machinery	75(74)	7.9	11.9	6.0	50
Electrical machinery	100	5.0	13.6	7.1	48
Transportation equipment	96	11.4	7.1	3.5	51
Precision instruments	100	4.9	21.1	13.1	38
Miscellaneous	52	6.9	19.5	11.5	41
Total	68(61)	100.0	13.5	9.6	36
Manufactures [d]	—	86.8	14.3	9.9	36

Source: See Appendix A.

a. Based on c.i.f. value (converted from f.o.b. or American selling price value), 1964 imports.

b. Figures in parentheses are post-Kennedy Round percentages of total imports that are the result of duty eliminations. It should be noted that where the share of imports dutiable has declined as a result of duty elimination, the post-Kennedy Round tariff level is higher than the pre-Kennedy Round level reduced by the percent cut in column 5.

c. Includes cuts conditional on acceptance of the separate agreement on American selling price; the reduction would otherwise be about 45 percent.

d. Includes all categories except mineral products; raw hides, skins, fur; wood, natural cork; pulp; natural fiber and waste; unwrought, pig iron, scrap.

Table 13–2. European Economic Community Tariff Levels for Nonagricultural Products (Other than Mineral Fuels), before and after Kennedy Round Cuts [a]

Category	Dutiable imports, before cuts		Average tariff on dutiable imports, as percentage of c.i.f. value		Percent cut in Kennedy Round
	As percentage of total imports [b] (1)	As percentage of total dutiable imports (2)	Before cuts (3)	After cuts (4)	(5)
Mineral products	2	0.2	9.4	5.5	42
Chemical products	91	13.1	14.3	7.6	47 [c]
Rubber products	26	1.2	15.0	7.8	48
Hides, furs, leather products	22	1.1	9.2	5.7	38
Raw hides, skins, fur	0	—	free	free	—
Articles of leather, fur	22	1.1	9.2	5.7	38
Wood and cork products	17(12)	1.8	10.9	8.8	41
Wood, natural cork	9(3)	0.7	6.5	4.0	75
Articles of wood, cork	100(99)	1.1	13.8	9.5	31
Pulp and paper	92	10.9	10.7	7.5	30
Pulp	83	4.8	6.0	3.0	50
Paper	100	6.1	14.4	11.1	23
Textiles	37	9.9	16.0	12.6	21
Natural fiber and waste	5	0.6	3.0	3.0	0
Yarn and basic fabrics	97	4.7	13.0	11.4	12
Special fabrics, apparel, other	93	4.6	20.7	14.9	28
Footwear and headwear	100	0.6	17.8	12.4	30
Stone, ceramic and glass products	100	2.1	14.1	8.0	43
Base metals and metal products	60	13.6	9.9	7.0	29
Unwrought, pig iron, scrap	30	3.8	7.4	6.8	8
Basic shapes and forms	100	6.1	9.7	7.0	28
Steel	100	5.2	9.4	6.7	29
Other	99	0.9	11.4	8.8	23
Articles of base metal, misc.	98	3.7	12.8	7.2	44
Nonelectrical machinery	100	21.7	11.1	6.4	42
Electrical machinery	100	7.0	14.2	9.1	36
Transportation equipment	94	8.3	15.4	9.9	36
Precision instruments	100	6.1	13.3	8.4	37
Miscellaneous	24	2.4	16.5	9.8	41
Total	60	100.0	12.8	8.1	37
Manufactures [d]	—	89.9	13.5	8.6	36

Source: See Appendix A.

a. Based on c.i.f. value, 1964 imports; excludes trade within EEC and imports from associated countries.

b. Figures in parentheses are post-Kennedy Round percentages of total imports that are the result of duty eliminations. It should be noted that where the share of imports dutiable has declined as a result of duty elimination, the post-Kennedy Round tariff level is higher than the pre-Kennedy Round level reduced by the percent cut in column 5.

c. Includes cuts conditional on acceptance of the separate agreement on American selling price; the reduction would otherwise be about 20 percent.

d. Includes all categories except mineral products; raw hides, skins, fur; wood, natural cork; pulp; natural fiber and waste; unwrought, pig iron, scrap.

Table 13–3. United Kingdom Tariff Levels for Nonagricultural Products (Other than Mineral Fuels), before and after Kennedy Round Cuts [a]

Category	Dutiable imports, before cuts — As percentage of total imports [b] (1)	Dutiable imports, before cuts — As percentage of total dutiable imports (2)	Average tariff on dutiable imports, as percentage of c.i.f. value — Before cuts (3)	Average tariff on dutiable imports, as percentage of c.i.f. value — After cuts (4)	Percent cut in Kennedy Round (5)
Mineral products	6(5)	0.5	9.3	4.8	48
Chemical products	86	15.8	18.8	9.4	50 [c]
Rubber products	95	1.3	13.6	7.8	43
Hides, furs, leather products	37(35)	1.4	17.7	13.1	30
Raw hides, skins, fur	3(0)	0.1	9.4	free	100
Articles of leather, fur	100	1.3	18.2	13.1	28
Wood and cork products	88(31)	9.2	5.2	7.3	50
Wood, natural cork	87(10)	6.5	1.5	4.8	60
Articles of wood, cork	91(85)	2.7	13.6	8.0	46
Pulp and paper	59	2.5	16.6	13.2	21
Pulp	1	neg.	10.0	5.3	47
Paper	99	2.5	16.6	13.2	21
Textiles	54	11.4	20.6	16.9	18
Natural fiber and waste	1(neg.)	0.1	8.4	6.2	60
Yarn and basic fabrics	100	6.6	19.1	15.0	22
Special fabrics, apparel, other	97	4.7	22.9	19.6	14
Footwear and headwear	100	1.3	22.8	14.7	36
Stone, ceramic and glass products	99	2.0	16.4	10.3	37
Base metals and metal products	59(58)	9.2	12.8	9.0	30
Unwrought, pig iron, scrap	20(18)	1.5	6.9	6.1	30
Basic shapes and forms	97	5.0	11.8	9.2	22
Steel	100	4.2	11.3	9.2	19
Other	82	0.8	14.6	9.1	38
Articles of base metal, misc.	92	2.7	17.9	10.9	39
Nonelectrical machinery	100	23.3	14.2	8.6	39
Electrical machinery	100	6.9	20.1	12.4	38
Transportation equipment	89	6.1	20.0	11.0	45
Precision instruments	100	5.4	26.4	13.5	49
Miscellaneous	41(40)	3.7	20.1	10.5	48
Total	72(68)	100.0	16.6	10.6	39
Manufactures [d]	—	91.3	17.8	10.8	39

Source: See Appendix A.

a. Based on c.i.f. value, 1964 imports; excludes imports from the EFTA and the Commonwealth.

b. Figures in parentheses are post-Kennedy Round percentages of total imports that are the result of duty eliminations. It should be noted that where the share of imports dutiable has declined as a result of duty elimination, the post-Kennedy Round tariff level is higher than the pre-Kennedy Round level reduced by the percent cut in column 5.

c. Includes cuts conditional on acceptance of the separate agreement on American selling price; the reduction would otherwise be about 20 percent.

d. Includes all categories except mineral products; raw hides, skins, fur; wood, natural cork; pulp; natural fiber and waste; unwrought, pig iron, scrap.

Table 13–4. Japanese Tariff Levels for Nonagricultural Products (Other than Mineral Fuels), before and after Kennedy Round Cuts [a]

Category	Dutiable imports, before cuts		Average tariff on dutiable imports, as percentage of c.i.f. value		Percent cut in Kennedy Round
	As percentage of total imports [b] (1)	As percentage of total dutiable imports (2)	Before cuts (3)	After cuts (4)	(5)
Mineral products	9	3.3	12.0	6.2	48
Chemical products	85	18.2	19.7	10.7	46
Rubber products	25	1.7	15.1	7.5	50
Hides, furs, leather products	19	0.6	19.9	12.7	36
Raw hides, skins, fur	3	0.1	16.0	15.0	6
Articles of leather, fur	100	0.5	20.6	12.3	40
Wood and cork products	2	0.4	15.6	10.1	35
Wood, natural cork	1	0.2	10.9	6.7	39
Articles of wood, cork	89	0.2	20.4	13.6	33
Pulp and paper	92	4.6	6.7	6.4	5
Pulp	91	3.6	5.0	5.0	0
Paper	100	1.0	13.2	11.4	14
Textiles	7	2.8	23.5	13.6	42
Natural fiber and waste	neg.	0.1	15.1	7.7	49
Yarn and basic fabrics	100	1.7	23.2	12.8	45
Special fabrics, apparel, other	89	1.0	24.8	15.5	38
Footwear and headwear	100	0.1	26.3	22.7	14
Stone, ceramic and glass products	99	0.8	16.9	9.5	44
Base metals and metal products	66	22.3	11.0	7.1	36
Unwrought, pig iron, scrap	64	19.7	10.2	6.6	35
Basic shapes and forms	100	1.1	19.2	13.1	32
Steel	100	0.6	15.6	10.3	34
Other	100	0.5	23.4	16.3	30
Articles of base metal, misc.	100	1.5	15.5	9.3	40
Nonelectrical machinery	100	24.3	15.6	10.0	36
Electrical machinery	100	4.0	17.8	10.8	39
Transportation equipment	100	7.7	18.4	13.9	25
Precision instruments	100	4.2	19.1	10.0	48
Miscellaneous	84	5.0	14.7	8.5	42
Total	47	100.0	15.5	9.5	39
Manufactures [c]	—	73.0	17.6	10.7	39

Source: See Appendix A.

a. Based on c.i.f. value, 1964 imports.

b. There were no significant decreases in percent of total imports dutiable as a result of duty eliminations in the Kennedy Round.

c. Includes all categories except mineral products; raw hides, skins, fur; wood, natural cork; pulp; natural fiber and waste; unwrought, pig iron, scrap.

The results for basic steel products were far more modest and also more difficult to interpret. Japan cut the most—34 percent—but imports were insignificantly small. The United Kingdom made a basically uniform cut averaging 19 percent. The EEC cut, listed in Table 13–2 as 29 percent, was calculated from the level of tariffs in effect since February 1964 (the "9 percent level"); based on the lower rates applied in the European Coal and Steel Community prior to February 1964 (the "7 percent level"), the average cut drops to about 10 percent. The U.S. average cut for steel of 12 percent, which is subject to statistical shortcomings, should be regarded as an approximation.[4] For steel, in sum, modest cuts were for the most part applied to moderate rates on all sides.

Finally, the textile sector received average cuts of only 18–21 percent by all countries except Japan, whose 42 percent cut is a reflection of a strong net export position.

Another disclosure of Tables 13–1 through 13–4 is the relative level of tariffs within industries. Product categories are subdivided into groups composed of the raw material or unprocessed inputs, the processed goods, and finished products.[5] Presumably, industrial countries admit raw materials at low or nil duties and scale the level of tariff protection upward as the processing continues. This relation is important to the concept of effective tariff protection discussed later in this chapter. Three factors in Tables 13–1 through 13–4 are relevant to this relation: the share of imports dutiable, the level of tariffs, and the percent reduction in tariffs. In the industry groups hides, furs, leather products; lumber and wood products; and pulp and paper, for all four participants the share of dutiable imports is lower—usually much lower—in the raw materials subgroup, and the average tariff for the remaining dutiable imports is also lower. Moreover, in almost every case, the percent cut in the Kennedy Round was also larger in the raw material

4. The harmonization aspect of the U.S. offer on steel resulted in consistently deeper cuts in higher rates. Weighting imports by percent cut (as in U.S. Office of Special Representative for Trade Negotiations, *Report on United States Negotiations* [1967], Vol. 2, which gives an average cut of 7.5 percent) does not reflect this distinction nor the possible concentration of imports in low duty items because the duties are low. The unweighted averages used here, on the other hand, may tend to overstate the cut. Perhaps a figure of 10 percent as the average cut is a good compromise for what was in any event a small reduction of less than one point in absolute terms.

5. For some industry categories, such as rubber products, the raw material (crude rubber) is duty free or almost so in the four countries shown; subdivision was therefore unnecessary for tariff averages based on dutiable imports.

subgroup, thus reinforcing the existing relative disparity in rate levels. The only exception is Japan which made no reduction in the duty on pulp and a smaller reduction on raw materials than on finished products in hides, furs, leather products (although duty suspensions are prevalent in the former case and 97 percent of imports in the latter case already enter duty free).

The two most important industries for which subdivisions are shown are textiles and metals. For textiles the share dutiable and rate pyramiding are again generally apparent in the progression from natural fiber to yarn and fabrics and on to apparel. The differential is less marked for the United States because of the substantial duty levied on raw wool imports. The Kennedy Round cuts, while modest in all cases, are not as closely gauged to the level of production as in the other industries cited. The EEC, in fact, made deeper cuts on special fabrics and apparel than on yarn and basic fabrics. The metals group, while following the scaled pattern for share dutiable and average tariff levels, differs markedly in Kennedy Round reductions. For each participant the percent cut on finished articles is significantly deeper than the cuts on either unwrought metal or basic shapes and forms. The range of tariff cuts by the four participants on unwrought metals is 8–35 percent, on basic steel shapes and forms 12–34 percent, and on finished metal articles 39–48 percent.

Finally, the tariff level tables reveal the extent of change in the share of imports that are subject to duty (column 1). The principal duty elimination in the Kennedy Round—in the wood, natural cork subgroup—resulted from action on tropical hardwoods taken to benefit developing countries. This was the major United Kingdom duty elimination and the only significant EEC elimination. The United States also eliminated low duties on substantial imports of lumber (in articles of wood, cork), jute fabric (in yarn and basic fabrics), and pig iron and nickel (in unwrought, pig iron, scrap).

Distribution of Tariff Rates

The two basic dimensions of a tariff structure are the average level and the frequency distribution of individual rates. Average levels by country do not vary greatly among the major industrial countries, although variation by industry can be substantial. The relative dispersion of rates, however, is considerably different from one country to another, and this was the underlying reason for the tariff disparity issue. The sharpest contrast at the outset of the Kennedy Round was between the widely dispersed U.S. tariff, which included several hundred rates above 30 percent, and the largely uniform Common Market tariff.

Tariff dispersions of the principal Kennedy Round participants are presented in Tables 13–5 through 13–9. The product coverage is the same as for the tariff level tables. As before, rates within Brussels categories are generally averaged arithmetically to provide comparability between countries. The principal disadvantage of this simple extension of the analysis used for average tariff levels is that a degree of dispersion is lost within categories, but this dispersion is normally very small except for the United States, and is probably not very significant even in this case. The distributions of rates after Kennedy Round

Table 13–5. Distribution of Dutiable Nonagricultural Products (Other than Mineral Fuels) by Tariff Level, before and after Kennedy Round Cuts [a]

	Percentage of product categories									
	Before cuts				After cuts					
Tariff level [b]	U.S.	EEC	U.K.	Japan	U.S.	EEC	U.K.	Japan	Sweden	Switzerland
0.1– 2.5	1.3	0.5	0.1	0.1	3.7	3.0	1.6	1.6	7.5	41.1
2.6– 5.0	3.2	2.9	0.2	1.7	21.3	18.3	13.1	7.5	46.9	22.3
5.1– 7.5	6.8	6.7	1.2	0.8	25.3	35.2	14.1	29.2	16.3	16.2
7.6–10.0	14.7	18.2	16.2	7.7	17.7	26.8	34.3	27.8	18.9	8.3
10.1–12.5	15.8	17.4	4.4	3.7	9.5	8.3	14.2	12.7	3.5	5.6
12.6–15.0	11.8	25.8	15.6	32.4	7.7	5.0	7.4	10.1	6.0	2.9
15.1–17.5	11.8	13.6	13.7	10.7	5.5	2.4	7.1	4.0	0.9	1.7
17.6–20.0	7.3	10.6	19.7	21.0	2.8	0.8	6.1	4.3	—	0.7
20.1–25.0	11.0	4.0	15.2	12.3	4.2	0.1	2.1	2.4	—	0.7
25.1–30.0	8.8	0.1	6.7	5.9	1.5	—	—	0.4	—	0.5
30.1–40.0	4.7	0.1	6.7	3.3	0.5	—	—	—	—	—
Over 40.0	2.8	0.1	0.3	0.4	0.3	0.1	—	—	—	—
Cumulative										
0.1– 5.0	4.5	3.4	0.3	1.8	25.0	21.3	14.7	9.1	54.4	63.4
0.1–10.0	26.0	28.3	17.7	10.3	68.0	83.3	63.1	66.1	89.6	87.9
0.1–15.0	53.6	71.5	37.7	46.4	85.2	96.6	84.7	88.9	99.1	96.4
0.1–20.0	72.7	95.7	71.1	78.1	93.5	99.8	97.9	97.2	100.0	98.8
0.1–30.0	92.5	99.8	93.0	96.3	99.2	99.9	100.0	100.0	100.0	100.0

Source: See Appendix A.
a. Based on four-digit Brussels Tariff Nomenclature categories.
b. Percentage rate based on c.i.f. value, 1964 imports; U.S. rates are converted from f.o.b. or American selling price.

cuts include Sweden and Switzerland as examples of low duty, small EFTA countries.[6]

Table 13–5, on all products, confirms the difference in patterns of dispersion. Before Kennedy Round cuts, 85.6 percent of EEC rates fell in the tariff range of 7.6 percent–20 percent compared with 61.4 percent for the United States. Only 0.2 percent of EEC rates were above

Table 13–6. Distribution of Dutiable Chemical Products by Tariff Level, before and after Kennedy Round Cuts [a]

Tariff level [b]	Percentage of product categories									
	Before cuts				After cuts					
	U.S.	EEC	U.K.	Japan	U.S.[c]	EEC[c]	U.K.[c]	Japan	Swe-den[c]	Swit-zer-land
0.1– 2.5	0.6	—	—	—	4.4	2.7	1.6	1.7	7.5	69.1
2.6– 5.0	4.4	3.2	—	1.7	34.4	26.3	25.5	10.7	36.8	16.9
5.1– 7.5	11.9	7.0	—	0.6	21.8	37.2	23.4	19.7	10.4	7.6
7.6–10.0	21.8	20.4	26.7	12.9	15.0	28.0	24.5	41.0	43.4	4.3
10.1–12.5	13.8	17.2	6.0	2.8	6.9	4.8	24.5	17.4	1.9	0.5
12.6–15.0	8.1	25.8	16.8	20.2	10.6	0.5	0.5	5.6	—	1.1
15.1–17.5	7.5	18.3	7.1	14.6	1.9	—	—	1.1	—	0.5
17.6–20.0	6.9	5.4	11.4	30.4	0.6	—	—	1.7	—	—
20.1–25.0	10.0	2.7	10.3	11.2	2.5	0.5	—	1.1	—	—
25.1–30.0	7.5	—	1.6	3.4	1.9	—	—	—	—	—
30.1–40.0	4.4	—	20.1	2.2	—	—	—	—	—	—
Over 40.0	3.1	—	—	—	—	—	—	—	—	—
Cumulative										
0.1– 5.0	5.0	3.2	0.0	1.7	38.8	29.0	27.1	12.4	44.3	86.0
0.1–10.0	38.7	30.6	26.7	15.2	75.6	94.2	75.0	73.1	98.1	97.9
0.1–15.0	60.6	73.6	49.5	38.2	93.1	99.5	100.0	96.1	100.0	99.5
0.1–20.0	76.2	97.3	68.0	83.2	95.6	99.5	100.0	98.9	100.0	100.0
0.1–30.0	92.5	100.0	79.9	97.8	100.0	100.0	100.0	100.0	100.0	100.0

Source: See Appendix A.
a. Based on four-digit Brussels Tariff Nomenclature categories.
b. Percentage rate based on c.i.f. value, 1964 imports; U.S. rates are converted from American selling price.
c. Includes cuts conditional on acceptance of the separate agreement on American selling price.

30 percent versus 7.5 percent of the American rates. The United Kingdom also had a significant share of its rates—7.0 percent—above the 30 percent level, but these were almost all at the 33⅓ percent uniform level and very few were extremely high. There is a dramatic shift downward in the distribution of tariffs after Kennedy Round cuts. From 63.1

6. Canada is excluded throughout because comparable tariff and trade statistics are not available.

percent to 89.6 percent of rates for each country are at a level of 10 percent or less, and well over 90 percent of rates are 20 percent or less. U.S. rates above 30 percent have dropped to less than 1 percent of the total, and only 2.3 percent are above the 25 percent level. The lowest concentration of rates is found in Sweden and Switzerland where close to 90 percent of all rates are at levels of 10 percent or less.

The industry sector tables are self-explanatory. In the chemical sector, virtually all European tariffs after Kennedy Round cuts are at a level of 12.5 percent or less, while the higher U.S. rates are mostly the converted American selling price items which are about 20 percent generally and 30 percent for dyes (or on a c.i.f. basis, as presented in the table, roughly 18 percent and 27 percent respectively). The change in the distribution resulting from the Kennedy Round cuts in textiles and metals is less striking although there has been a widespread elimi-

Table 13–7. Distribution of Dutiable Textile Products by Tariff Level, before and after Kennedy Round Cuts [a]

					Percentage of product categories					
	Before cuts				After cuts					
Tariff level [b]	U.S.	EEC	U.K.	Japan	U.S.	EEC	U.K.	Japan	Swe-den	Swit-zer-land
0.1– 2.5	1.0	1.0	—	—	2.9	4.0	1.9	—	—	20.0
2.6– 5.0	2.9	4.0	—	1.0	7.6	7.1	9.3	10.1	7.5	16.4
5.1– 7.5	4.8	5.0	1.8	4.0	8.6	16.2	1.9	17.1	12.9	23.6
7.6–10.0	3.8	9.1	4.5	7.1	19.0	23.2	12.0	19.2	24.7	17.3
10.1–12.5	2.9	12.1	5.5	2.0	10.5	17.2	3.7	22.2	15.1	9.1
12.6–15.0	6.7	14.1	11.8	25.3	10.5	17.2	14.8	13.1	33.3	6.4
15.1–17.5	14.2	19.3	4.5	5.1	15.1	10.1	23.1	5.1	6.5	3.6
17.6–20.0	14.2	20.3	19.1	18.2	8.6	5.0	22.2	6.1	—	0.9
20.1–25.0	19.0	14.1	32.8	24.2	12.4	—	11.1	5.1	—	1.8
25.1–30.0	20.0	—	19.1	9.1	3.8	—	—	2.0	—	0.9
30.1–40.0	8.6	1.0	0.9	4.0	—	—	—	—	—	—
Over 40.0	1.9	—	—	—	1.0	—	—	—	—	—
Cumulative										
0.1– 5.0	3.9	5.0	0.0	1.0	10.5	11.1	11.2	10.1	7.5	36.4
0.1–10.0	12.5	19.1	6.3	12.1	38.1	50.5	25.1	46.4	45.1	77.3
0.1–15.0	22.1	45.3	23.6	39.4	59.1	84.9	43.6	81.7	93.5	92.8
0.1–20.0	50.5	84.9	47.2	62.7	82.8	100.0	88.9	92.9	100.0	97.3
0.1–30.0	89.5	99.0	99.1	96.0	99.0	100.0	100.0	100.0	100.0	100.0

Source: See Appendix A.
a. Based on four-digit Brussels Tariff Nomenclature categories.
b. Percentage rate based on c.i.f. value, 1964 imports; U.S. rates are converted from f.o.b.

nation of very high rates. The machinery and transportation sector has the most uniform level of moderate and low tariffs after cuts, with the bulk below 10 percent and almost all below 15 percent.

An analysis of tariff rate distribution and the Kennedy Round would not be complete without some discussion of the famous "800 peaks" in the U.S. tariff. Table 13–10 presents a comparison of U.S. nonagricultural rates, before and after cuts, that were 30 percent or more (f.o.b.) at the outset of the negotiation. Initially there were 789 nonagricultural rates (f.o.b.) of 30 percent or higher. Of this total 31 percent was textiles, 16 percent chemicals, and 8 percent watches. After Kennedy Round cuts only 190 of the rates were still at 30 percent or higher, and 108 of those were in the 30.1–40.0 percent range. Textiles comprised 46 percent of the 190 rates that remained over 30 percent, and watches

Table 13–8. Distribution of Dutiable Metal Products by Tariff Level, before and after Kennedy Round Cuts [a]

	Percentage of product categories									
	Before cuts				After cuts					
Tariff level [b]	U.S.	EEC	U.K.	Japan	U.S.	EEC	U.K.	Japan	Swe-den	Swit-zer-land
0.1– 2.5	3.1	—		—	4.8	—	1.5	—	6.4	29.2
2.6– 5.0	3.9	0.8	—	—	9.7	9.1	2.2	5.2	61.8	22.6
5.1– 7.5	5.5	11.4	0.7	0.7	38.8	46.9	5.9	31.1	29.1	23.4
7.6–10.0	15.8	21.2	18.5	5.9	27.4	36.3	65.3	33.2	2.7	9.5
10.1–12.5	18.1	10.6	4.4	5.9	4.8	6.1	9.6	3.0	—	8.0
12.6–15.0	12.6	34.8	11.9	29.7	7.3	0.8	3.7	11.9	—	3.6
15.1–17.5	18.1	12.9	21.5	7.4	4.0	0.8	7.4	11.9	—	1.5
17.6–20.0	4.7	8.3	31.2	27.5	0.8	—	3.7	3.0	—	1.5
20.1–25.0	6.3	—	8.1	9.6	0.8	—	0.7	0.7	—	0.7
25.1–30.0	7.1	—	2.2	8.1	0.8	—	—	—	—	—
30.1–40.0	2.4	—	1.5	5.2	0.8	—	—	—	—	—
Over 40.0	2.4	—	—	—	—	—	—	—	—	—
Cumulative										
0.1– 5.0	7.0	0.8	0.0	0.0	14.5	9.1	3.7	5.2	68.2	51.8
0.1–10.0	28.3	33.4	19.2	6.6	80.7	92.3	74.9	69.5	100.0	84.7
0.1–15.0	59.0	78.8	35.5	42.2	92.8	99.2	88.2	84.4	100.0	96.3
0.1–20.0	81.8	100.0	88.2	77.1	97.6	100.0	99.3	99.3	100.0	99.3
0.1–30.0	95.2	100.0	98.5	94.8	99.2	100.0	100.0	100.0	100.0	100.0

Source: See Appendix A.
a. Based on four-digit Brussels Tariff Nomenclature categories.
b. Percentage rate based on c.i.f. value, 1964 imports; U.S. rates are converted from f.o.b.

13 percent. The mean of the 789 rates dropped from 42.7 percent to 24.7 percent as a result of Kennedy Round cuts, or by 42 percent.[7]

A separate distribution is given in Table 13–10 for the 789 rates converted to a c.i.f. basis of valuation, to produce a set of figures comparable to those in the other tables in this chapter. The effect of this adjustment is to lower the level of U.S. tariffs; consequently the number of rates at 30 percent or above is reduced to 613 before and 124 after Kennedy Round cuts.

Table 13–9. Distribution of Dutiable Machinery and Transportation Equipment by Tariff Level, before and after Kennedy Round Cuts [a]

	Percentage of product categories									
	Before cuts				After cuts					
Tariff level [b]	U.S.	EEC	U.K.	Japan	U.S.	EEC	U.K.	Japan	Swe-den	Swit-zerland
0.1– 2.5	—	—	—	0.8	—	—	—	0.8	1.7	47.2
2.6– 5.0	—	—	—	—	45.2	22.4	2.4	1.6	76.5	32.8
5.1– 7.5	6.8	2.4	—	—	34.2	54.4	33.3	51.9	9.2	12.0
7.6–10.0	28.2	23.2	3.1	1.6	10.3	14.4	41.3	13.4	8.4	2.4
10.1–12.5	29.9	39.2	2.4	0.8	5.1	4.0	13.5	13.4	2.5	2.4
12.6–15.0	16.2	20.0	31.5	68.4	2.6	1.6	6.3	11.8	1.7	1.6
15.1–17.5	10.3	8.0	32.3	5.5	1.7	2.4	—	0.8	—	0.8
17.6–20.0	2.6	4.0	11.8	13.4	—	0.8	3.2	4.7	—	—
20.1–25.0	4.3	3.2	16.5	7.9	0.9	—	—	1.6	—	—
25.1–30.0	1.7	—	2.4	0.8	—	—	—	—	—	0.8
30.1–40.0	—	—	—	0.8	—	—	—	—	—	—
Over 40.0	—	—	—	—	—	—	—	—	—	—
Cumulative										
0.1– 5.0	0.0	0.0	0.0	0.8	45.2	22.4	2.4	2.4	78.2	80.0
0.1–10.0	35.0	25.6	3.1	2.4	89.7	91.2	77.0	67.7	95.8	94.4
0.1–15.0	81.1	84.8	37.0	71.6	97.4	96.8	96.8	92.9	100.0	98.4
0.1–20.0	94.0	96.8	81.1	90.5	99.1	100.0	100.0	98.4	100.0	99.2
0.1–30.0	100.0	100.0	100.0	99.2	100.0	100.0	100.0	100.0	100.0	100.0

Source: See Appendix A.
a. Based on four-digit Brussels Tariff Nomenclature categories.
b. Percentage rate based on c.i.f. value, 1964 imports; U.S. rates are converted from f.o.b.

Major reductions were made in the peaks in the U.S. tariff schedule, and the bulk of these rates was reduced below the 30 percent level in the Kennedy Round. The remaining high rates are concentrated in textiles and watches. There are also a number of specific duties on ob-

7. The average cut for all nonagricultural products, calculated in Table 13–1 to be 36 percent, is not comparable with the 42 percent given here because the weighting systems differ and because watches and glass are treated differently.

scure products that were converted to high rates, according to a small and possibly nonrepresentative sampling of 1964 imports. Ironically, one of the highest post-Kennedy Round rates is for unmounted gold leaf, which faces a 117 percent tariff barrier to entry into the United States.[8]

Tables 13–5 and 13–10 show appreciable differences in the distributions of U.S. rates. Table 13–5 indicates that 25 percent of the tariffs on all nonagricultural products were above 30 percent, although presumably some dispersion is lost in averaging within categories of the Brussels Tariff Nomenclature. Table 13–10 shows 609 U.S. rates above

Table 13–10. Number of U.S. Tariff Rates on Nonagricultural Products at Various Levels, before and after Kennedy Round Cuts [a]

	Number of rates at f.o.b. value		Number of rates at c.i.f. value	
Tariff level [b]	Before cuts	After cuts	Before cuts	After cuts
0.1– 15.0	—	54	—	125
15.1– 20.0	—	296	—	288
20.1– 25.0	—	184	—	165
25.1– 29.9	—	65	176	87
30.0	70	29	4	1
30.1– 40.0	365	108	352	85
40.1– 50.0	224	30	177	24
50.1– 60.0	69	14	35	9
60.1– 70.0	26	4	22	—
70.1– 80.0	17	—	6	1
80.1– 90.0	4	1	7	1
90.1–100.0	4	1	4	1
Over 100.0	10	3	6	2
Total 30 percent or more	789	190	613	124

Source: See Appendix A.
a. Based on Tariff Schedule of the United States.
b. Rates for benzenoid chemicals are converted from American selling price; the seventy rates in use during the 1963–64 disparity discussions are used (see p. 169). Rates for watches and glass before cuts are those that were in force under escape clause action; rates after cuts are those resulting from the 1967 modification of these actions, which, although not part of the Kennedy Round agreement proper, were an important factor in the disparity debate.

30 percent (of c.i.f. value), or about 13 percent of all nonagricultural rates. As discussed in Appendix A, however, this figure probably overstates the significance of high rates, since the U.S. Tariff Schedule

8. The item, 644.48, is actually limited to unmounted gold leaf "over 1140 square inches in area." The duty was reduced from 82.5 cents per 1140 square inches to 41 cents per 1140 square inches in the Kennedy Round. The value of imports was $1,000 in 1964 and less than $500 in 1965.

breakdown used in Table 13–10 is very fine for sensitive high tariff industries. In consequence, the share of U.S. tariffs above 30 percent at the outset of the Kennedy Round falls within the limits of 7.5 percent and 13 percent of the total, each limit biased toward the other. About 10 percent is a reasonable supposition for the figure, and similarly about 2 percent of U.S. nonagricultural tariffs after cuts are above 30 percent.

Trade Diversion from European Integration

A major objective of the Kennedy Round was to reduce trade diversion resulting from the formation of the EEC and the EFTA. The elimination of duties on trade within these groups established a margin of preference among the members equal to the most-favored-nation tariff level. Tariff cuts of slightly more than 35 percent in the Kennedy Round reduced the preference by that amount. If the Kennedy and Dillon rounds are taken together, European tariffs are almost down to half the level existing at the inception of the trade blocs. Perhaps some trade that was diverted earlier will not be restored, but it is reasonable to estimate that the GATT negotiations have prevented a third to a half of the anticipated trade diversion resulting from European integration.

The averaging of national tariffs within the EEC to form the common external tariff also resulted in tariff increases by some member countries, especially Germany and the Benelux countries. This, like the tariff preferences, adds to the burden on traditional outside suppliers to these markets. Moreover, the use of unweighted averages of national tariffs to determine the common external tariff was criticized as being, on balance, disadvantageous to the United States since American exports were often concentrated in the lower duty markets.[9] The degree by which the Kennedy Round (and Dillon Round) tariff cuts

9. Of course, U.S. exports may have been concentrated in the lower duty markets because the duties were low. A more complex analysis to demonstrate the increased protection of the common external tariff through unweighted averaging of national rates is made by Walter S. Salant and others, *The United States Balance of Payments in 1968* (Brookings Institution, 1963). They argue that the large low-cost producers determine the competitive position of the Common Market as a whole, and the national tariff in these dominant supplier countries is the measure of adequate protection to maintain the existing competitive situation. Since the low-tariff countries, usually Germany and Benelux, turn out to be the dominant suppliers in most cases, the tariff is judged to have resulted in an increased level of protection (*ibid.*, pp. 99–104).

were able to offset tariff increases by EEC member states can be estimated by comparing the EEC tariff levels after Kennedy Round cuts with tariff levels of member states before formation of the EEC. Thirty-three instances where the member state rate was below the original common external tariff and imports from the United States in 1958 were at least $5 million are listed in Table 13–11 together with the tariff level after Kennedy Round cuts and 1966 imports from the United States. The reduction in the tariff differential is shown in column 6 as the ratio of the differences between the original tariff and the level after the cuts, on the one hand, and between the original tariff and the EEC member state level, on the other. For example, if the original tariff was 10 percent, that after cuts 6 percent, and the member state rate 5 percent, the reduction of the original differential (10 percent–5 percent) is 80 percent (10 percent–6 percent). The averages for all thirty-three entries combined are weighted by 1958 imports.

The overall reduction in the differential is 112 percent. In other words, the average common external tariff after Kennedy Round cuts for these commodities of special export interest to the United States is *lower* than the level existing in the member states before the formation of the EEC. In nineteen individual cases, reductions are over 100 percent of the original differential, and in only five are reductions less than 80 percent. One of the largest trade categories is aircraft and parts, for which duties are largely suspended. If this category is excluded from the average, the 112 percent figure rises to 120 percent.

The member state tariff levels were those in effect in March 1958 when the Rome Treaty was signed. Germany, however, temporarily reduced most of its tariffs by 25 percent in July 1958 to offset adverse effects of cyclical business conditions. If all German tariffs in Table 13–11 are reduced by 25 percent, the average decrease in the differential changes from 112 percent to 96 percent.

These figures indicate that the common external tariff has been reduced at least to, and perhaps a little lower than, the levels in Germany and the Benelux countries at the time of the Rome Treaty for items of principal export interest to the United States. The continued expansion of U.S. exports in these areas is shown by the level of trade in 1966. Imports by Germany and the Benelux countries in these categories increased from $451 million in 1958 to $1,208 million in 1966, or by 168 percent, compared to an increase of 165 percent for all EEC imports of manufactures from the United States in the same period.

Table 13–11. Effect of Kennedy and Dillon Round Cuts on Principal U.S. Exports Adversely Affected by Common External Tariff

Product [a] and EEC importer	Average national tariff, 1958 [b] (1)	Common external tariff [b] Original level (2)	After Kennedy Round cuts (3)	Percent reduction in differential [c] (4)	U.S. exports (in millions of dollars) 1958 (5)	1966 (6)
Inorganic chemicals						
Benelux	1.0	11.0	5.9 [d]	51	6.5	11.3
Germany	6.0	11.0	5.9 [d]	102	6.3	36.3
Organic chemicals						
Benelux	9.0	15.0	8.5 [d]	108	8.8	48.1
Germany	8.0	15.0	8.5 [d]	93	33.6	64.8
Medicinal and pharmaceutical products						
Benelux	9.0	15.0	7.1 [d]	132	14.1	13.6
Germany	12.0	15.0	7.1 [d]	263	6.1	8.1
Synthetic plastic materials						
Benelux	9.0	16.0	7.7 [d]	119	11.7	35.8
Germany	8.0	16.0	7.7 [d]	104	16.2	27.3
Miscellaneous chemicals						
Benelux	7.0	13.0	7.5 [d]	92	5.8	21.6
Germany	11.0	13.0	7.5 [d]	275	16.5	29.0
Yarn and thread of man-made fiber						
Germany	11.0	17.0	9.7	122	6.2	13.5
Manufactures of metal, not elsewhere specified						
Benelux	11.0	16.0	8.0	160	6.1	21.6
Power generating machinery (except electric)						
Benelux	8.0	14.0	6.0	133	18.0	27.8
Germany	5.0	14.0	6.0	89	7.8	25.9
Office machinery						
Benelux	9.0	14.0	6.8	144	7.8	21.8
Germany	6.0	14.0	6.8	90	10.2	52.9
Machine tools for working metals						
Germany	3.0	8.0	5.6	48	7.6	18.0
Excavating, construction, etc., machinery						
Benelux	7.0	13.0	7.0	100	7.1	22.0
Germany	4.0	13.0	7.0	67	8.4	30.1
Textile machinery						
Germany	5.0	13.0	5.3	96	5.2	9.9

Table 13–11. Continued

Product[a] and EEC importer	Average national tariff, 1958[b] (1)	Common external tariff[b] Original level (2)	Common external tariff[b] After Kennedy Round cuts (3)	Percent reduction in differential[c] (4)	U.S. exports (in millions of dollars) 1958 (5)	U.S. exports (in millions of dollars) 1966 (6)
Other industrial machinery						
Benelux	7.0	13.0	6.0	117	24.4	111.7
Germany	6.0	13.0	6.0	100	26.1	128.4
Electrical generators, etc.						
Benelux	10.0	15.0	6.4	172	33.7	18.6
Germany	5.0	15.0	6.4	86	7.7	25.7
Other electrical machinery						
Benelux	11.0	16.0	8.1	158	15.2	43.4
Germany	7.0	16.0	8.1	88	16.3	84.3
Passenger autos						
Germany	22.0	29.0	11.0	257	18.6	7.7
Road motor vehicles other than autos, buses, and trucks						
Germany	17.0	26.0	12.3	152	5.3	6.0
Aircraft and parts						
Benelux	7.0	13.5	7.9	86	40.0	87.6
Germany	5.0	13.5	7.9	66	32.5	90.2
Ships and boats						
Germany	1.0	4.0	2.2	60	9.2	1.8
Precision instruments						
Benelux	13.0	17.0	9.3	193	6.6	28.4
Germany	8.0	17.0	9.3	86	5.6	35.2
Total	8.2	14.7	7.4	112	451.2	1,208.4

Sources: *Atlantic Tariffs and Trade* (London: Political and Economic Planning, 1963); *Tableaux Analytiques 1966* (Office Statistique des Communautés Européennes); and Appendix A.

a. Based on the Standard International Trade Classification. The earlier version of this classification used in *Atlantic Tariffs and Trade* has been converted to the revised nomenclature.

b. Percentage rate based on c.i.f. value of imports. Average national tariff and original common external tariff are from *Atlantic Tariffs and Trade*; the common external tariff after cuts, from Appendix A, has been adjusted, where possible, to correspond to the others. The former averages were calculated from the midpoint of the range of individual rates within four-digit Brussels categories, the latter from an arithmetic average. The variance within a Brussels category of the common external tariff, however, is usually very small and this difference is unlikely to have a significant effect. Free items were included in the averages of tariffs after cuts to make them comparable with the other averages; the adjustment was significant in only one case, ships and boats.

c. Column 2 minus column 3 divided by column 2 minus column 1.

d. Includes Kennedy Round cuts conditional on acceptance of the separate agreement on American selling price; these averages would otherwise be about 60 percent higher.

Intra-European Tariff Levels

Relative tariffs on individual products, and particularly those peaks in the U.S. schedule, were a prominent topic in the Kennedy Round because of the disparity issue. But matching rates or reducing tariff differentials between trading partners has always been a minor objective of GATT negotiations; in the Kennedy Round it was an important aspect of the U.S.-Canadian negotiations. Of even broader significance, however, was the leveling of European tariffs, especially differences between the United Kingdom and the EEC. Tariff harmony between these two participants would facilitate any future reduction in trade barriers among European countries. It would also reduce the amount of dislocation and adjustment should the United Kingdom join the Common Market and adopt the common external tariff. Even in day-to-day trade relations, matched tariff rates can mitigate industry complaints of unfair disadvantages caused by tariff differentials.

Linear tariff cuts will narrow existing tariff differentials by the same degree. To illustrate the effect of the modified linear reductions in the Kennedy Round on differences within Europe, Table 13–12 gives the percentage distribution of the point spread between the U.K. and EEC tariff levels. It clearly shows that, as indicated in Tables 13–2 and 13–3, the United Kingdom tariff is significantly higher than the common external tariff. For total nonagricultural trade, 79.9 percent of the categories before Kennedy Round cuts show a U.K. level at least one point higher than the EEC level, versus only 9.7 percent of those where the EEC is higher. Partly as a result of a slightly deeper overall cut by the United Kingdom, and partly from a larger share of categories moving into the range from 0 to ±0.9, the difference in shares after cuts narrowed: 73.9 percent higher U.K. level versus 12.0 percent higher EEC level. The average point spread between the U.K. and the EEC was lowered from 6.7 to 3.9, or by 42 percent. This indicates a somewhat larger reduction than that in absolute tariff levels (36–39 percent).[10]

The above average reduction in tariff differences is mainly attributed to the chemical sector where the average difference was reduced by two-thirds, from 7.6 points to 2.6 points. Since differences were greatest in

10. The differences in tariff levels are calculated from unweighted averages of Brussels categories, the absolute levels from averages weighted by imports; thus the figures are not precisely comparable.

Table 13–12. Point Spread between United Kingdom and EEC Tariff Levels for Dutiable Nonagricultural Products (Other than Mineral Fuels), before and after Kennedy Round Cuts [a]

Point spread [b]		All products		Chemicals		Textiles		Metals		Machinery and transportation equipment		Other	
From	To	Before cuts	After cuts	Before cuts	After cuts	Before cuts	After cuts	Before cuts	After cuts	Before cuts	After cuts	Before cuts	After cuts
						Percentage Distribution							
+20	>+20.0	3.3		2.7		3.5		2.2				5.3	
+14	+19.9	7.5	0.5	18.8		1.8	1.8	1.5	0.7	2.4		7.5	0.3
+12	+13.9	4.0	0.5	3.8		9.7		0.7	0.7	3.2		3.8	0.9
+10	+11.9	6.4	4.0	2.7	1.1	9.7	11.5	9.6	0.7	3.2	1.6	7.2	5.3
+8	+9.9	5.7	6.1	3.2	0.5	9.7	15.9	3.0	6.7	7.9	4.0	6.0	6.6
+6	+7.9	13.2	7.7	7.5	2.7	19.4	17.7	14.9	7.4	13.5	1.6	13.6	9.8
+5	+5.9	6.6	7.1	3.2	4.8	8.0	10.6	8.9	8.9	4.8	6.3	7.9	6.6
+4	+4.9	8.2	8.5	7.5	12.4	8.0	3.5	13.4	9.6	7.9	8.7	6.6	7.6
+3	+3.9	10.7	11.5	11.3	10.2	5.3	13.3	10.4	17.1	24.6	11.9	6.9	9.1
+2	+2.9	8.5	13.0	7.5	7.5	1.8	5.3	9.6	14.9	12.7	27.8	9.5	12.3
+1	+1.9	5.8	15.0	5.4	18.9	1.4	8.0	5.9	12.6	6.3	19.0	6.3	14.9
0	±0.9	10.4	14.1	12.3	24.8	10.6	6.2	11.1	8.9	12.7	13.5	7.9	13.2
−1	−1.9	2.2	3.9	1.6	7.0	1.8	4.4	3.0	2.2			3.1	4.1
−2	−2.9	1.5	3.1	1.1	4.8	2.7		2.2	4.4		1.6	1.6	3.1
−3	−3.9	1.7	1.9	2.2	3.2	0.9		1.5	3.0	0.8	0.8	2.2	1.9
−4	−4.9	1.0	1.3	2.7	0.5			0.7	2.2			0.9	2.2
−5	−5.9	0.6	0.6	1.6			0.9	0.7			0.8	0.3	0.9
−6	−19.9	2.6	1.1	4.9		1.6	2.7	0.9	0.7		2.4	3.1	0.9
−20	<−20.0	0.1	0.1									0.3	0.3
+1	>+20.0	79.9	73.9	73.6	58.1	81.3	87.6	80.1	79.3	86.5	80.9	80.6	73.4
0	±0.9	10.4	14.1	12.3	24.8	10.6	6.2	11.1	8.9	12.7	13.5	7.9	13.2
−1	<−20.0	9.7	12.0	14.1	17.1	8.1	6.2	8.8	11.8	0.8	5.6	11.5	13.4
						Dispersion of Rates							
Mean difference from zero [c]		6.7	3.9	7.6	2.6	7.3	5.9	5.4	3.8	4.8	3.2	7.4	4.1
Percent reduction in mean difference			42		66		19		30		33		45
Root-square deviation from zero [c]		8.9	5.0	10.0	3.6	9.1	7.0	7.1	4.7	6.0	4.2	9.7	5.4
Percent reduction in root-square deviation			44		64		23		34		30		44

Source: See Appendix A.

a. Based on four-digit Brussels Tariff Nomenclature categories.

b. Plus means U.K. rates are higher than EEC rates. The degree of overall dispersion in rates is reduced somewhat because calculations are based on average levels within Brussels categories, but dispersion within such categories is usually small for the EEC and the U.K.; moreover, substantial revision and harmonization of the U.K. rate structure during the Kennedy Round greatly reduced dispersion within Brussels categories.

c. This measure of dispersion differs from the standard deviation in that it calculates the root-square difference from zero rather than from the mean.

this sector, the large degree of harmonization achieved in the Kennedy Round will be especially helpful for any future move toward tariff alignment. The chemical sector harmonization is the result of the American selling price agreement under which the high U.K. tariffs are cut by more than 60 percent while the low U.K. tariffs on plastics are reduced by only a small amount in order to match the EEC rates. Even if the agreement were not enacted, differences in chemical rates would be reduced by a larger degree than the reduction in absolute levels. The reduction of about 20 percent in absolute levels under these circumstances would lead to an approximate 33 percent reduction in the average spread between the EEC and the U.K. rates.[11]

The reduction of tariff differences in textiles and metals follows roughly the degree of tariff cuts. For machinery and transportation equipment the relative reduction of tariff differences is slightly less than the absolute cuts although the point spread was the smallest in the major industry groups.

The harmonization of tariffs within Europe resulting from the Kennedy Round, in sum, appears to be somewhat greater than the reduction in tariff levels. Certain key products will remain a problem in any further attempt to align tariffs. Rates on unwrought aluminum, for example, did not change (free in the United Kingdom, 9 percent most-favored-nation with a 5 percent quota in the EEC) in the Kennedy Round. But in general, and especially for chemicals, rate disparities between the United Kingdom and the EEC have been greatly reduced.

Products of Export Interest to Developing Countries

The rules and procedures of the Kennedy Round included two innovations that substantially improved the position of developing countries. The linear approach to tariff reductions covered all products regardless of which participants were the major exporters. And the adoption of the nonreciprocity principle for developing countries ex-

---

11. United Kingdom imports (before cuts) are roughly divided into three equal categories: high 33⅓ percent rates, low plastic rates, and all others. If the American selling price agreement were not enacted, the United Kingdom would cut the first category by 30 percent, the second by zero, and the third by 20 percent. The EEC would cut virtually all of its rates by 20 percent. The resulting narrowing of differences would be about 40 percent, 40 percent, and 20 percent, respectively, or 33 percent overall.

plicitly excepted their export interests from the threat of last minute withdrawals to achieve balance. Within the context of the general procedures, products of interest to these countries were given high priority for maximum concession by the industrial nations.

Nevertheless, because most of the accomplishments of the Kennedy Round were in areas where developing countries have relatively smaller export interests, the benefits they derived were smaller. The dominant achievement of the negotiations was a substantial reduction of tariffs on manufactured products, and within this area the largest reductions were in such technologically advanced industries as chemicals and machinery. The exports of developing countries, however, are concentrated in primary materials and basic agricultural products, which generally are imported duty free by the industrial countries, and to a lesser extent in processed agricultural products and textiles, which received only modest tariff reductions in the Kennedy Round.

The concentration of exports of developing countries in low duty or duty free categories was illustrated in the evaluation of the Kennedy Round results by the secretary general of the United Nations Conference on Trade and Development (UNCTAD).[12] The report lists combined imports of the United States, the EEC, the United Kingdom, and Japan from developing countries in 1964 at $19.7 billion. Of this total, $9.9 billion entered in duty free categories, and another $2.4 billion entered under preferential arrangements, largely free of duty. The remaining $7.5 billion of dutiable most-favored-nation imports included $3.3 billion of crude petroleum alone, which is subject to nontariff barriers of greater importance than the customs duty.

The contrast in the relative importance of tariffs can also be seen in the average incidence of duty payments on U.S. imports from various groups of countries, shown in Table 13–13. Duties paid on imports from Europe and Japan are three to four times higher (11.5–15.6 percent) than duties paid on imports from the developing countries of Asia, Africa, and Latin America (1.6–4.2 percent). For EEC imports the contrast is not as great because nonassociated developing countries face substantial tariffs on some basic agricultural products. For nonagricultural products, however, the average tariff incidence for nonassociated

---

12. *The Kennedy Round: Preliminary Evaluation of Results, with Special Reference to Developing Countries* (Sept. 4, 1967).

Table 13–13. Average Tariff Incidence of U.S. Imports by Geographic Region, 1965

Duty collected as percentage of total net imports

Region	Average tariff incidence [a]
Hong Kong	23.2
Japan	15.6
EFTA	11.6
Other European countries	11.6
EEC	11.5
Australia, New Zealand, South Africa	9.1
Middle East	6.2
Latin America	4.2
Canada	3.4
Asia (except Japan and Hong Kong)	3.4
Africa	1.6

Source: U.S. Bureau of the Census, unpublished machine tabulations.
a. Based on f.o.b. value.

developing countries as a group is less than 2 percent, based on 1964 EEC imports.[13]

This low overall level of tariff incidence obscures the importance of tariffs to some developing countries. For one thing, export gains for these countries must be evaluated in terms of future potential, and the advantages of tariff reductions would thus not show up in calculations based on current trade. In some cases, export potential is dependent on the development of new industries. In other cases, as discussed in the following section, the effective protection on lightly processed products is prohibitively high, thereby confining exports to the duty-free primary product categories.

Moreover, there is great diversity in the ability of individual developing countries to compete on world markets. A number of borderline countries are already exporting substantial amounts of manufactured products and they are most apt to realize gains in these exports, while other least developed countries, especially the African nations, are still a long way from being competitive exporters even if tariffs were reduced to zero.

The growing importance of tariff barriers to the exports of the more advanced developing nations is illustrated in Table 13–14. The data suggest that the level of duty paid on a country's exports may be a

13. Derived from Office Statistique des Communautés Européennes, *Statistiques Tarifaires*, Import 1964, Tab. 2–3.

Table 13–14. Average Duty Paid and Commodity Diversification for U.S. Imports from Seven Selected Countries, 1961 and 1965

Country	Average duty paid [a]		Percentage change in average duty paid	Ten largest commodities as percentage share of total imports		Percentage change in share of imports
	1961	1965		1961	1965	
Brazil	2.1	2.6	+24	88.7	83.1	−6
Argentina	5.8	8.0	+38	79.7	67.2	−16
Mexico	7.1	8.2	+15	59.3	54.2	−9
Israel	8.9	9.5	+7	85.4	82.9	−3
Yugoslavia	11.2	11.3	+1	59.7	61.5	+3
Spain	12.2	12.1	−1	47.7	40.5	−15
Greece	12.8	12.4	−3	92.4	84.5	−9

Source: U.S. Bureau of the Census, unpublished machine tabulations.
a. Percentage rates are based on f.o.b. value of imports.

helpful criterion for defining the level of economic development: as development progresses, products are efficiently produced that are competitive with production abroad and therefore tend to be subject to higher levels of tariffs. Three of the selected countries—Yugoslavia, Spain, and Greece—already appear to have reached the stage of mature exporting nations. Their exports were subject to average duties of 11–12 percent in the U.S. market, and this level remained roughly stationary between 1961 and 1965. The other four countries—Brazil, Argentina, Mexico, and Israel—still pay significantly lower duties, but the average level increased markedly in each case from 1961 to 1965. All but Brazil are now reaching a respectable level of duty payment not far below that paid on trade among industrial countries.

Another aspect of the changing pattern of exports in the more advanced developing countries is the greater product diversification. Table 13–14 also shows what share the ten largest commodities comprise of total U.S. imports from each of the countries. In all except Yugoslavia the share held by the ten largest commodities declined between 1961 and 1965.

Another question of basic importance to developing countries is the extent to which tariffs were reduced in the Kennedy Round on products of special interest to them as compared with all products. Table 13–15 is based on a selected list of such products, broken down between textiles and nontextiles. In order to maintain comparability with Tables

Table 13–15. Kennedy Round Tariff Reductions on Products of Export Interest to Developing Countries

Products	Weighted by most-favored-nation imports, all sources				Weighted by developing countries imports
	EEC	U.K.	Japan	U.S.	U.S.
All products					
Dutiable imports as percentage of total imports, before cuts	48.0	63.0	36.0	63.0	32.0
Average tariff on dutiable imports, before cuts [a]	12.3	15.2	13.5	14.7	10.0
Percent reduction in tariff	33.0	32.0	37.0	32.0	35.0
Textiles					
Dutiable imports as percentage of total imports, before cuts	33.0	48.0	5.0	85.0	72.0
Average tariff on dutiable imports, before cuts [a]	16.7	20.4	24.8	22.9	9.6
Percent reduction in tariff	22.0	18.0	41.0	18.0	35.0
Nontextiles					
Dutiable imports as percentage of total imports, before cuts	52.0	68.0	47.0	59.0	21.0
Average tariff on dutiable imports, before cuts [a]	11.5	14.1	13.1	12.3	10.3
Percent reduction in tariff	36.0	37.0	36.0	39.0	36.0

Source: *Products Notified as Being of Export Interest to Less Developed Countries* (General Agreement on Tariffs and Trade, June 27, 1966); and Appendix A. Items selected were listed by at least two developing countries; where the bulk of a category was of doubtful export interest to developing countries, the items were excluded. The resulting list contained slightly over 200 Brussels categories, or a little less than one-quarter of all categories in the nonagricultural sector.

a. Percentage rate based on c.i.f. value, 1964 imports.

13–1 through 13–4, and to take account of developing countries' potential export interest, the individual categories are weighted by total most-favored-nation imports. For the United States, however, a second calculation is given for categories weighted by imports from developing countries.

The results of Table 13–15 indicate a somewhat lower average cut for items of special interest to developing countries. The average cut by the major industrial participants came to 32–37 percent on these selected items compared with cuts of 36–39 percent for all nonagricultural products. The difference is almost entirely due to the poor showing of textiles; on nontextile items, average cuts are in the range of 36–39 percent.[14] The U.S. figure for textiles weighted by imports from developing countries shows a much lower tariff level (9.6 percent) and a deeper tariff cut (35 percent) than that weighted by most-favored-nation imports mainly because the low duty on jute fabric covering a large volume of imports from developing countries was reduced to zero.

Table 13–15 also indicates that the share of dutiable imports for items of interest to developing countries is consistently lower than that for all imports shown in Tables 13–1 through 13–4. Although this is true of the most-favored-nation imports from all sources, it is far more striking in the case of the United States when limited to imports from developing countries.

In sum, nonagricultural products of special interest to developing countries received substantial cuts of over 30 percent on the average in the Kennedy Round, but nevertheless smaller cuts than for all products. This conclusion is supported in studies both by UNCTAD [15] and by the GATT secretariat.[16]

Developing countries were also disappointed by the lack of progress in the nontariff barrier field. Quota restrictions and fiscal charges are imposed on a number of their export products, particularly in the agricultural sector.[17] The single most important quota restriction, however, is the Long-Term Arrangement Regarding International Trade in Cotton Textiles. This agreement was extended for three years in the Kennedy Round, and the two largest importing areas, the EEC and the United States, made their tariff cuts of about 20 percent on these products conditional on the continuation of the arrangement. Finally, the

14. Since cuts for all nontextiles would be higher as well, this 36–39 percent is still slightly below average.

15. *The Kennedy Round: Preliminary Evaluation of Results.* The report, based on a sample of 500 tariff items, separates items of interest to developing countries from "all *other* items," producing a wider difference than a comparison with "all items," as given above. It finds the reduction on items of interest to developing countries ranges from 30 percent to 36 percent; on all other items from 39 percent to 46 percent.

16. *GATT Trade Negotiations, Brief Summary of Results* (June 30, 1967); it states that for "dutiable manufactured products of actual interest to developing countries, 24 percent by value of imports into the main industrialized participants will not be the subject of tariff reductions, 29 percent will be the subject of reductions of less than 50 percent and 47 percent will be the subject of reductions of 50 percent or more. Comparable figures for all manufactured products are: no reduction, 16 percent; less than 50 percent reductions, 29 percent; reductions of 50 percent or more, 55 percent."

17. See UNCTAD, *The Kennedy Round: Evaluation of Results*, Pt. 3.

developing countries pressed for advanced implementation of tariff cuts on their exports instead of the five-year staging generally required. Some accelerated cuts were made by European countries in January 1968 and a handful were implemented by the United States under the low duty authority which does not require staging.

Nominal versus Effective Tariffs

Nominal tariff rates are those that appear in national tariff schedules. A 10 percent nominal tariff means that the duty levied amounts to 10 percent of the total value of the imported product. Nominal tariffs directly influence the relative prices of final products and thereby consumption patterns. They are the basis for all forms of further analysis, including the level of effective tariff protection. They are the legal and only precise set of rates on individual products, and therefore inevitably become a focal point of policy matters, including trade negotiations.

The limited economic significance of the level of nominal tariffs has been recognized for some time, however, and many of its weaknesses as a standard of evaluation have been exposed in recent discussion of effective tariff protection.[18] Effective protection is basically the rate of protection on the value added in processing goods; it is derived from the relation between the nominal tariffs (and other import restrictions) on the early stages of production, or inputs, and the nominal tariff on the product in question. For example, assume that paper sells on the domestic market at $150 per ton, $100 of which covers the cost of pulp and $50 the value added during the manufacture of pulp into paper. Assume further that the nominal duty on paper is 10 percent and that pulp enters duty free. Under these circumstances, a foreign exporter, with equal access to pulp, will be required to manufacture paper with a value added of no more than $36.36 per ton in order to compete at the protected domestic price of $150 ($100 for pulp, $36.36 for value added, plus the nominal duty of 10 percent on $136.36, or $13.64, which brings the duty paid import price to $150.00). Because pulp enters duty free, the 10 percent duty on paper falls entirely on the value added during

---

18. For both a discussion and a bibliography of earlier work, see Herbert G. Grubel and Harry G. Johnson, "Nominal Tariffs, Indirect Taxes and Effective Rates of Protection: The Common Market Countries 1959," *Economic Journal*, Vol. 77 (December 1967), pp. 761–76.

the manufacture of pulp into paper. If the duty payment, $13.64, is taken as a percent of the foreign value added, $36.36, the effective level of protection for the domestic processing of pulp into paper is about 38 percent.

In view of the progressively higher levels of nominal tariffs from raw materials to semiprocessed goods to finished products, the effective rates of tariff protection on finished products are generally higher than the nominal rates. When tariffs are reduced, in some cases, trade may shift to imports of a higher level of production—from pulp to paper or from cotton cloth to shirts—and the overall level of imports will increase only by an amount equal to the value added in producing the finished goods.

The levels of effective tariff protection have been tested empirically using two separate approaches. The general approach utilizes multi-sector input-output coefficients and thus takes account of all interrelations of inputs throughout the economy. The principal shortcoming of this approach is its limitation to the aggregate industries of the input-output table, which can obscure the situation for individual commodities. Balassa and Basevi, pioneers of this method, estimate that effective tariff protection on manufactures is one and a half to two times higher than the average level of nominal tariffs.[19] Balassa concludes incidentally that the relative degree of dispersion in tariffs between the United States and the EEC is considerably less for effective tariffs than for nominal tariffs (1.4 versus 1.9).[20] The reason for this is that while U.S nominal tariffs on manufactures are much more widely dispersed than the EEC's, both have a wide disparity between the low level of tariffs on raw materials and the higher level on manufactures.

The second, or partial, approach for measuring effective tariff protection is to deal with individual products. It is especially appropriate for many items of interest to developing countries, where the prospect is to move from the export of raw materials to the first stages of processed goods. Examples of very high effective tariff levels include the

19. Bela Balassa, "Tariff Protection in Industrial Countries: An Evaluation," *Journal of Political Economy*, Vol. 73 (December 1965), pp. 573–94 (reprinted in Richard E. Caves and Harry G. Johnson [eds.], *Readings in International Economics* [Irwin, 1968], pp. 579–604); Giorgio Basevi, "The United States Tariff Structure: Estimates of Effective Rates of Protection of United States Industries and Industrial Labor," *Review of Economics and Statistics*, Vol. 48 (May 1966), pp. 147–60.

20. In Caves and Johnson, *Readings*, p. 597.

European tariff on processed soy bean oil which is estimated to rise from a nominal rate of 10 percent to an effective rate of 160 percent and the U.S. tariff on refined coconut oil which rises from a nominal rate of 5.7 percent to an effective rate of 57.5 percent.[21] The difficulties of this partial approach are that it requires detailed and often unavailable information on production costs and that it ignores the effects of tariffs on related products.

Initial investigations of effective tariffs have also uncovered some problems in the application of the theory to actual conditions of trade. Other price-distorting influences such as import quotas or domestic excise taxes and subsidies must, as equivalents of tariffs, be included in the analysis. Grubel and Johnson have demonstrated that the combination of excise taxes and nominal tariffs can produce a very different set of effective tariffs than that based on nominal tariffs alone. Although based on somewhat crude data, their results show much lower effective tariffs in Common Market countries in 1959 when excise taxes are included.[22]

Market imperfections also must be considered. The theory of effective tariff protection is based on the assumption of a competitive market, and a reduction in tariff is consequently assumed to lead to a corresponding reduction in the level of domestic prices. But this assumption often is not realistic, especially in a large economy with small average import penetration like the United States. A further analytical problem concerns products that are not imported and would not be imported even under circumstances of free trade. There may be advantages to vertical integration, or the product might be perishable or transportation costs prohibitive. The domestic prices of products that are competitively exported are also unlikely to be significantly affected by a reduction in tariffs.

Finally, interpretation of the trade significance of computed rates of effective protection is complicated because in most instances they are not related to empirical estimates of price behavior. Estimates of the price elasticity of demand for imports, for example, are usually based on the relative prices of the final products rather than the values added at individual stages of production. Basevi, for instance, calculated effec-

21. Harry G. Johnson, *Economic Policies Toward Less Developed Countries* (Brookings Institution, 1967), p. 91.
22. "Nominal Tariffs, Indirect Taxes and Effective Rates of Protection," p. 766.

tive protection on labor content alone, and derived levels of protection of 200 percent and 300 percent.[23] But what does it mean to say that protection on one stage of production for labor content in isolation is 200 percent? It might as easily be demonstrated that India can face a 500 percent or 1000 percent effective tariff and still compete. It is interesting that some products with the highest levels of effective protection— leather gloves, cutlery, carpets and rugs—show a high degree of import penetration despite the level of protection.

Effective tariff levels, in sum, are an essential part of the analysis of tariff protection but a great deal of uncertainty exists at this point as to the magnitude or the meaning of these levels. The effective level of protection is generally higher than the nominal protection for manufactured products. Much higher protection is apparent in a number of individual cases, usually involving one additional level of processing. It is hazardous, however, to attempt to determine precise levels of effective protection or make quantitative estimates of the trade significance of these levels.

Some general observations from the levels of nominal tariffs presented in this chapter, however, are relevant to effective tariff levels.[24] The overall cut of about 35 percent in nominal tariffs will, if applied uniformly, result in a reduction in effective protection of about 35 percent. If the analysis is limited to tariffs (as in the Balassa and Basevi studies), this means 35 percent of the way to zero. If other factors such as excise taxes are included (as in Grubel and Johnson), it means about 35 percent of the way to the level of protection in the absence of tariffs. In fact, there is some indication that a 35 percent cut in nominal tariffs will result in a slightly larger cut in the level of effective protection.[25]

A more qualified appraisal, based on the differentiated cuts in nomi-

23. "The United States Tariff Structure," p. 153.
24. For estimates of effective tariff protection in the United States and the United Kingdom before and after Kennedy Round cuts, see Robert E. Baldwin, *Nontariff Distortions of International Trade* (Brookings Institution, in preparation).
25. Grubel and Johnson show that the change in effective protection with a change in nominal tariffs is not linear. The change depends on the relative levels of nominal tariffs on inputs and final product and, where relevant, excise taxes. When nominal tariffs were uniformly cut in half, disregarding excise taxes, effective protection was reduced to 45.5–47.9 percent of its former level in each of five Common Market countries. If excise taxes are also taken into account the same comparison is not possible, but the effect of doubling nominal tariffs in this case suggests a similar and perhaps stronger geometric progression. ("Nominal Tariffs, Indirect Taxes and Effective Rates of Protection," p. 772.)

nal tariffs, is possible for some major industries. The moderate differences between nominal and effective tariff levels for machinery [26] and the quite low nominal rates after Kennedy Round cuts indicate that the importance of the distinction in any event is not great, although effective protection would generally be slightly higher. For chemicals and metals, effective protection should be reduced by significantly more than the average reduction for nominal tariffs. The American selling price agreement involved a measure of harmonization, with larger cuts on very high rates, and the tariff reductions on finished metal products were consistently deeper than cuts on basic shapes and forms. The situation in textiles is not clear, but the EEC, at least, cut more on finished goods and apparel, thereby tending to make a greater relative cut in the effective protection on these products. For some smaller industries, greater cuts were made in the unprocessed goods, which would lead to a smaller reduction in effective protection on the finished products, although in most cases this effect is dampened by the large share of unprocessed goods already entering free of duty.

26. See Caves and Johnson, *Readings*, p. 589.

CHAPTER FOURTEEN

Trade in Nonagricultural Products

VARIOUS ASPECTS OF tariff levels for nonagricultural products and changes in these levels resulting from the Kennedy Round agreement were discussed in Chapter 13. This chapter provides a summary of the corresponding volumes of trade involved and an estimate of the changes in trade flows that are likely to result from the tariff reductions.

Volume of Trade Subject to Concessions

Concessions made by the main industrial participants in the Kennedy Round—the European Economic Community (EEC), Japan, Sweden, Switzerland, the United Kingdom, and the United States—accounted for about four-fifths of all concessions made in the negotiation. A summary of the figures for these countries for the nonagricultural sector is presented in Table 14–1 (the industry groups are not exactly comparable with those given for tariff levels in Chapter 13). Out of total non-agricultural imports, excluding mineral fuels, of $39.5 billion, $13.8 billion already entered duty free. Much of this free trade had previously been bound in the General Agreement on Tariffs and Trade, and $2.8 billion was bound in the Kennedy Round. Duty reductions were made on 84 percent of the $25.7 billion of dutiable imports, and two-thirds of these reductions were for 50 percent or more. The variation of this pattern by industry follows that for average tariff cuts given in Chapter 13: greater cuts for chemicals and machinery and transportation equipment; lesser cuts for metals and textiles.

A summary of the bilateral breakdown of U.S. concessions with each major participant is presented in Table 14–2. The scope of nonagricul-

Table 14–1. Effect of Kennedy Round on Combined Nonagricultural Imports (Other than Mineral Fuels) of the Major Industrial Countries [a]

In billions of dollars and, in parentheses, percentage of total

Imports	Raw materials	Metals and metal products	Chemicals	Machinery and transportation equipment	Textiles and clothing	Other	Total
Total	10.2	5.7	3.6	10.2	2.7	7.1	39.5
Already duty-free	8.5	1.2	0.8	0.4	0.1	2.8	13.8
Bound in Kennedy Round	1.8	0.1	0.3	0.1	—	0.5	2.8
Dutiable	1.7(100)	4.5(100)	2.8(100)	9.8(100)	2.6(100)	4.3(100)	25.7(100)
No cut in Kennedy Round	0.3(18)	1.2(27)	0.2(7)	0.9(9)	0.9(35)	0.7(16)	4.2(16)
Kennedy Round cuts	1.4(82 b)	3.3(73 b)	2.6(93 b)	8.9(91 b)	1.7(65 b)	3.6(84 b)	21.5(84 b)
20 percent and less	0.05(4)	0.96(30)	0.13(5)	0.67(7)	0.75(44)	0.39(11)	2.95(14)
Over 20 percent to less than 50 percent	0.04(3)	0.75(23)	0.25(10)	1.78(20)	0.46(27)	0.84(23)	4.12(19)
50 percent	0.48(34)	1.35(41)	1.94(75)	6.32(71)	0.33(19)	2.03(57)	12.45(58)
Over 50 percent to less than 100 percent	0.03(2)	—	0.27(10)	0.14(2)	—	0.01	0.45(2)
100 percent	0.80(57)	0.20(6)	0.01	—	0.16(10)	0.31(9)	1.48(7)

Source: Press release no. 992, GATT, June 30, 1967.
a. Based on 1964 value of imports from most-favored-nation sources by the EEC, Japan, Sweden, Switzerland, the United Kingdom, and the United States.
b. This figure would equal 100 percent for total Kennedy Round cuts.

tural trade is slightly different in this case, mainly because fuels are included. However, few concessions were made on imports of fuels, so that the figures on concessions shown in Table 14–2 are roughly comparable with those on tariff levels. This table also differs in that it excludes concessions that are conditional on the American selling price agreement. The principal effect of this exclusion is to shift slightly over $600 million of EEC, United Kingdom, and other European Free Trade Association (EFTA) concessions to the United States from cuts of 50 percent or more in Table 13–1 to lesser cuts of 20–30 percent (in Table 14–2).

The United States made concessions on $4.9 billion of imports from the countries that participated in the linear tariff cutting and another $1.5 billion on imports from Canada. In return, concessions were made by linear countries on $5.4 billion of U.S. trade, and by Canada on $1.4 billion. Limited to duty reductions, U.S. concessions were $4.9 billion and $1.3 billion, respectively, and concessions in return were $4.6 bil-

Table 14-2. Kennedy Round Concessions on Nonagricultural Trade between the United States and Other Industrial Countries [a]

In millions of dollars

Item	U.S. imports from industrial countries						Industrial countries' imports from U.S.					
	Linear countries						Linear countries					
	EEC	Japan	United Kingdom	Other EFTA	Total	Canada	EEC	Japan	United Kingdom	Other EFTA	Total	Canada
Total imports	2728.4	1882.4	1176.4	797.8	6585.0	4203.4	3623.6	1827.5	1225.0	920.0	7596.1	4821.3
Duty-free	253.6	73.1	254.9	155.9	737.5	2535.2	916.6	854.7	262.4	235.6	2269.3	2434.6
Bound	242.7	67.9	231.7	153.6	695.9	2298.6	623.5	352.9	91.9	69.6	1137.9	n.a.
Unbound	10.9	5.2	23.2	2.3	41.6	236.6	293.1	501.8	170.5	166.0	1131.4	n.a.
Dutiable	2474.8	1809.3	921.5	641.9	5847.5	1695.2	2707.0	972.8	962.6	684.4	5326.8	2386.7
Available for concession [b]	2485.7	1814.5	944.7	644.2	5889.1	1931.8	3000.1	1474.6	1133.1	850.4	6458.2	n.a.
Total duty reductions	2076.3	1435.8	830.9	541.5	4884.5	1310.5	2503.9	666.9	832.3	593.3	4596.4	1447.5
1–24 percent	217.3	414.2	58.9	91.7	782.1	154.6	888.0	27.3	187.1	71.4	1173.8	784.7
25–49 percent	73.2	78.8	25.3	11.9	189.2	74.1	321.4	55.1	350.7	162.6	889.8	456.9
50 percent	1763.3	931.2	738.2	391.4	3824.1	585.1	1280.7	584.5	261.2	322.3	2443.7	84.5
More than 50 percent	22.5	11.6	8.5	46.5	89.1	496.7	13.8	0.3	33.3	37.0	84.1	121.4
Duty bindings	6.6	—	—	0.1	6.7	0.1	0.3	0.3	22.1	42.7	65.4	n.a.
Free bindings	11.0	5.2	23.2	2.6	42.0	196.0	286.8	264.7	56.5	136.0	744.0	n.a.
Total tariff concessions [c]	2093.9	1441.0	854.1	544.2	4933.2	1508.6	2791.0	931.9	910.9	772.0	5405.8	n.a.

Source: U.S. Office of Special Representative for Trade Negotiations, *Report on United States Negotiations* (1967), Vol. 1.

n.a. = not available.

a. Based on c.i.f. value (converted, where appropriate, from f.o.b. or American selling price value), 1964 imports.

b. Unbound duty-free plus dutiable imports.

c. Total duty reductions plus duty bindings plus free bindings.

lion and $1.4 billion. The larger share of U.S. reductions in the categories of 50 percent or more is mainly attributable to exclusion of concessions based on the American selling price agreement and the pattern of Canadian concessions, which generally consisted of cuts less than 50 percent.

Trade Impact of Tariff Reductions

The ultimate question is how much imports will increase as a result of the Kennedy Round tariff reductions. There are in fact two related questions: By what degree will the overall level of trade increase? And how balanced will this increase be between exports and imports for individual participants? Unfortunately, there are no easy answers to these questions. Trade projections are no more reliable than their underlying assumptions and these assumptions are always crude and often conjectural. The most sensible approach is to make a series of projections, varying assumptions widely so as to test the difference in the results. A thorough analysis also requires taking into account the effect of nontariff restrictions to trade and the relevant characteristics of pricing and marketing in the major industry sectors. The analysis here is limited to a brief discussion of the problems involved in the principal assumptions, and to the calculation of one simplified projection to give a rough idea of the expected increase in world trade resulting from the Kennedy Round.

A logical procedure is to discuss the increase of imports generated by a tariff reduction in three steps: (1) the change in the rate of tariff protection, (2) the change in the level of import price, relative to the level of domestic price, caused by the tariff change, and (3) the change in the volume of imports caused by the change in import price.

Change in the rate of tariff protection. The average level of nominal tariffs on dutiable nonagricultural products for the four largest industrial participants, calculated at 12.8–16.6 percent prior to the Kennedy Round (see Tables 13–1 through 13–4), was reduced by 36–39 percent, or by a little more than 5 percentage points. There are shortcomings to any measurement of average nominal tariff levels, but the degree of error, as discussed in Appendix A, is probably not large. A more serious problem involves the level of effective protection on individual products or on various stages of production for a particular product. Because raw material imports are normally subject to lower duties than manufactured goods, the effective protection is generally higher than nominal protection for manufactures. Extremely high effective tariffs can be found for individual cases. The overall degree of reduction in effective tariffs is similar to that for nominal tariffs, but the absolute change or the change in effective protection for particular products is not known.

Change in import price relative to domestic price. Under the assumptions of an infinite elasticity of supply for foreign exporters and perfect competition, the tariff reduction would be fully reflected in a corresponding drop in the level of import price. The change in import price can be less than the tariff change, however, if either of these assumptions does not hold. Infinite elasticity of supply means that exporters will expand output as much as required at the existing price. Two factors are prominent in reaching a judgment on the degree to which this assumption holds. First, a larger share of exports of total production requires a greater percentage increase in production for a given percentage expansion in exports and will therefore be more likely to lead to increased production costs.[1] Second, a higher level of utilization of the factors of production throughout the economy is more apt to result in higher costs from a given expansion of the export sector. In a balanced reduction of trade barriers, in which both exports and imports increase, the expansion in exporting industries can be offset by the relative contraction of import competing industries to the extent that the factors of production are able to make the shift. This shift is facilitated by the fact that much of the impact of trade liberalization apparently takes the form of greater product specialization within industries rather than overall expansion in some industries and decline in others.[2]

The second assumption, perfect competition, is certainly not fully applicable. Trade in manufactures and semimanufactures is typified by imperfectly competing products in which quality, performance, taste, and market convenience distinguish the domestic from the imported product. A number of prices and price differentials exist for a particular product, and a lower import price will widen or narrow the differential and increase the share of the market held by imports. An exporter's estimate of the magnitude of this substitution effect will influence his decision whether to raise the export price to absorb the tariff reduction

1. It is also possible, especially for smaller countries, that the expansion of exports will provide economies of large-scale production and thereby lower costs.
2. See Bela Balassa, "Tariff Reductions and Trade in Manufactures among the Industrial Countries," *American Economic Review*, Vol. 56 (June 1966), pp. 466–73.

as increased profits or to allow the after-duty price in the foreign market to fall. In addition to product differentiation, large firms that hold a significant share of the total market may adopt oligopolistic pricing policies that could lead to partial or full absorption of tariff reduction as increased profits.

Finally, since the determining factor is the change in *relative* prices, it must be assumed that domestic price remains unchanged in order for the tariff reduction to be fully reflected in the reduction of import price relative to domestic price. To the extent that domestic producers reduce prices to offset the advantage accruing to importers from the tariff cut, however, the reduction in import price relative to domestic price will be less than the absolute reduction in the import price.

In sum, the tariff reduction equals the maximum possible reduction of relative import price, but several factors tend to limit the actual reduction. Many studies have assumed a 100 percent incidence of tariff change on relative import price, although one researcher, at least, has concluded, "It appears plausible that close to half of the benefit from tariff concessions granted by the United States accrued to foreign exporters in the form of increased export prices." [3] Perhaps, as a result of the Kennedy Round, more can be learned about the relation of tariff cuts to changes in relative import price. For some products, like Volkswagens, Scotch whiskey, ingot aluminum, or even basic steel goods, observation might be relatively simple. For intrafirm shipments or highly differentiated consumer goods, on the other hand, the relationship is more difficult to determine.

Change in demand caused by change in import price. Even if the reduction in the effective protection and the corresponding change in relative import price are known, the response of buyers—the price elasticity of demand—remains elusive. A number of studies in recent years have concluded that volume of imports is highly responsive to the level of import price relative to domestic price for manufactures and semimanufactures. A 1 percent change in the relative level of import prices, for major industrial countries, has been estimated to cause a change (in the opposite direction) of 2–4 percent in the level of imports.[4] This general conclusion is important (even though the numbers

3. Mordechai E. Kreinin, "Effect of Tariff Changes in the Prices and Volume of Imports," *American Economic Review*, Vol. 51 (June 1961), pp. 310–24.

4. For a brief evaluation of some of these estimates, see Bela Balassa, *Trade Liberalization Among Industrial Countries* (McGraw-Hill for Council on Foreign Relations, 1967), pp. 186–90.

are rough estimates) because it means that changes in relative prices can be an effective and stabilizing mechanism in the international payments system.

But beyond the general statement of high price sensitivity for manufactures as a group, the evaluation of demand elasticity is inconclusive. The price elasticity for individual products is virtually impossible to estimate reliably, but even for broad generic groups of products, differences in demand elasticities are not clearly distinguishable. Semimanufactures, for example, might be considered particularly price elastic because the products are more homogeneous, thus increasing the ease of substitution between imports and domestic production, but empirical studies show conflicting results.[5] The largest single group of traded products, machinery, is characterized by quality differentials that make a pure price comparison extremely difficult. It is widely felt that consumer goods are relatively more price sensitive than other products, although again there is no reliable empirical support for this belief. Kreinin, in a rough estimate of the relative price sensitivity for imports of machinery, transportation equipment, and chemicals on the one hand, and imports of all other manufactures on the other hand, shows a much higher price elasticity in the latter category.[6] Although a good deal of follow-up work and refinement is necessary before a definitive appraisal can be made,[7] Kreinin's hypothesis is of major importance to the U.S. trade balance because U.S. exports are concentrated in the former groups of products while U.S. imports are relatively larger in the latter. Finally, the issue of effective versus nominal protection and the possible

5. A lower price elasticity for semimanufactures than for manufactures is estimated by R. J. Ball and K. Marwah, "The U.S. Demand for Imports, 1948–1958," *Review of Economics and Statistics*, Vol. 44 (November 1962), pp. 395, 401, and by M. E. Kreinin, "Price Elasticities in International Trade," *Review of Economics and Statistics*, Vol. 49 (November 1967), p. 514. A higher price elasticity for semimanufactures than for manufactures is suggested by Maurice FitzGerald Scott, *A Study of United Kingdom Imports* (Cambridge University Press, 1963), p. 182.

6. "Price Elasticities in International Trade," pp. 510–16.

7. The calculations are based on highly aggregated data and the correlation is quite low, especially for the heterogeneous "all other" category. The period observed, 1954–58, may no longer be representative for U.S. imports in that category, since steel, now a large import, was not so earlier, and cotton textiles now are largely under quota restrictions. Although Kreinin attempts to fill the empirical gap in support of the presumption that the elasticity of demand for consumer goods is greater than for capital goods, more than half of the "all other" category is not consumer goods (at least for U.S. imports in recent years), and in fact the largest groups of products are semimanufactures, such as basic metals and textile yarn and fabric, which are shown elsewhere in the article to have below-average price elasticity.

shift of imports to a higher or lower stage of production complicate attempts to separate statistically the impact of price change on imports of various classes of goods.

Lack of empirical verification also prevents any clear answer to the question of whether the general level of price elasticity is higher in one country than in another. It can be demonstrated analytically that a higher ratio of imports to consumption will reduce the price elasticity of demand for imports, other things being equal, by reducing the degree by which further imports can substitute for domestic products. But many Europeans, in particular, feel that other things are not equal. They claim that there is a formidable fixed cost in establishing and maintaining an effective distribution and sales organization in the American market, and that this cost outweighs the possible advantage of holding a very small share of the market. Many American firms, in contrast, control a sufficiently large share of the European market to warrant a highly efficient distribution system, often in conjunction with local production facilities.

Another factor that might distinguish the price elasticity of demand between countries is the level of per capita income. Does the high level of income in the United States induce a relatively larger elasticity of demand for imported goods, or is the marginal dollar more apt to be spent on services and other nontradeable commodities? Again there is no clear answer.

Clearly, many problems prevent accurate forecasting of the trade impact from a reduction in trade barriers. They are all relevant to the following calculations, which are meant only to give a rough approximation of the expansion of trade resulting from Kennedy Round reductions. Two basic assumptions made here are that the tariff cut is fully reflected in a reduction of relative import price, and the price elasticity of demand for dutiable nonagricultural imports (except fuels) is -2 in each country.

These assumptions are completely neutral between products and countries. While this neutrality was adopted for simplicity, it conveniently includes two offsetting qualifications to neutrality. Although the first assumption probably overstates the change in relative import price, the second might well understate the average elasticity. Regarding the impact on the U.S. trade balance, the incidence of tariff change on import price is probably higher for U.S. exports than for U.S. imports, while the overall price elasticity may well work in the opposite way.

On this basis the tariff reductions from Tables 13–1 through 13–4 have been combined with estimates for Sweden and Switzerland to correspond with the volume of total dutiable imports shown in Table 14–1 ($25.7 billion).[8] Applying the two assumptions to this basic data, the projected increase of imports for the six participants, based on 1964 imports, amounts to $2.2 billion, or 8.6 percent of dutiable imports in the base year.

A similar calculation was made for the U.S. bilateral balance with the other major industrialized countries as shown in Table 14–2. The tariff reductions for Sweden and Switzerland are used as an approximation for "other EFTA," and an estimate is used for Canada.[9] Accuracy is further sacrificed in the use of average tariffs weighted by imports from all sources rather than on a bilateral basis, but there is no reason to expect that the difference would consistently result in larger or smaller tariff reductions. This calculation, based on 1964 imports (c.i.f. value of nonagricultural products, excluding fuels), produces an increase in U.S. imports of $537 million and an increase in U.S. exports of $541 million.

A number of additional factors are relevant to the impact on the U.S. trade balance with other industrial countries. The above projection does not take account of the reduction of trade diversion from European integration. The expected loss in U.S. exports of manufactures from European integration was $239 million in terms of 1958 trade,[10] a figure that would be roughly doubled for 1964 levels of trade.[11] Probably part of this loss is nonretrievable, but even if the 36–39 percent reduc-

---

8. The six countries have been combined using most-favored-nation dutiable nonagricultural imports (except fuels) as weights. For Sweden and Switzerland, the mean of the frequency distribution of Brussels Tariff Nomenclature categories (Table 13–5) has been used as the level after Kennedy Round cuts, and an average cut of 37 percent applied. The latter figure is based on U.S. Office of Special Representative for Trade Negotiations, *Report on United States Negotiations* (1967), Vol. 1, which gives the average cut by Switzerland on imports from the United States as 37.5 percent, and the average cut by Sweden, excluding chemical concessions conditional on the American selling price agreement, as 34 percent.

9. The average reduction for tariff concessions made by Canada was estimated at 5 points from a level of 20 percent before cuts.

10. Lawrence B. Krause, *European Economic Integration and the United States* (Brookings Institution, 1968), Chap. 2.

11. Since movement to free trade within the European groupings proceeded by stages over the period 1958–68, an estimate adjusted step by step would fall somewhere between the two limits.

tion in European tariffs in the Kennedy Round reduced trade diversion by only a fourth, it would still mean a net gain for U.S. exports of roughly $100 million.[12] Another factor is the inclusion of tariff reductions conditional on the separate American selling price agreement. Excluding the agreement, the increase in U.S. imports would remain about the same (under the mechanical procedure used here which does not take account of possible qualitative differences in the basis for assessing duty), but the increase in U.S. exports would be reduced by $54 million [13] (from $541 million to $487 million).

Still another factor in the projections is the level of imports in the base year. During the negotiation the most recent year for which detailed import statistics were available for all major participants was 1964.[14] The implementation of tariff cuts, however, is spread over the period 1968–71. The growth of trade between the base year for calculations and the period of implementation will result in a correspondingly higher level of estimated trade expansion, although in percentage terms the estimate would remain about the same except for changes in the commodity composition of trade. Moreover, a change in the balance of trade between these periods would affect the estimated impact of the Kennedy Round on a particular country's trade balance. The United States, in fact, has experienced a decline in its trade balance that would produce a negative effect on the projection of the Kennedy Round impact on the U.S. trade balance. It is unlikely, however, that this effect would be as great as the relative change in the trade balance because the largest advances in imports have been in such categories as basic steel shapes and forms, for which little or no tariff cuts were made, automobiles, for which the U.S. tariff is very low, and automotive products from Canada, which relate to the U.S.-Canadian automotive agreement and not to the Kennedy Round.

In sum, U.S. trade with other industrial countries in the nonagricultural sector, based on 1964 levels of trade, could be expected to increase by about $500–$600 million for imports and for exports as a result of

12. The comparability of this figure depends on consistency in the underlying assumptions. An import demand elasticity of −2 applied to the Krause projections would yield close to the $239 million cited here. See Krause, *ibid.*, pp. 250–52.

13. Based on a 20 percent cut in the chemical sector by the EEC, the United Kingdom, and Sweden.

14. Statistics for later years—U.S. imports through 1966, for example—were available and used in some instances during the Kennedy Round, but an overall balance required comparable data for all major countries.

tariff reductions in the Kennedy Round. This comes to roughly 10 percent of dutiable trade. The net effect on the trade balance would be approximately neutral, and the swing factor not more than about $100 million one way or the other. In the longer run, however, the realization of new opportunities for trade expansion, both for exports and for imports, depends largely on the underlying balance of trade, which in turn depends on continued price competitiveness and the active promotion of export markets.

Almost all of the trade not included in the previous discussion is accounted for by exports of the developing countries. A basic assumption underlying the nonreciprocity rule for developing countries is that their development programs entail a chronic deficit in foreign exchange requirements. Any additional export revenues resulting from a lowering of trade barriers by the industrial countries will be fed back in a higher level of imports by developing countries. This effect varies somewhat in its geographic composition. Latin American countries tend to spend a higher share of new export earnings on imports from the United States, for example, while African nations tend to spend a larger share on imports from Europe. But the overall balance of exports and imports between the developing and the industrial countries is assumed to remain unchanged.

This leads to the question of how much the exports of developing countries will increase as a result of the Kennedy Round.[15] What is a reasonable price elasticity of demand for imports from developing countries? There is no reasonable estimate. The ability of these countries to increase exports, particularly of manufactured products, depends primarily on the establishment of new production facilities and the adoption of modern production techniques. There will be no exports until the first factory is in operation. Consequently it is not possible to estimate the impact of a change in the tariff level of industrial countries on the existing volume of exports by developing countries.

Mineral Fuels

This sector has been separated from the rest of nonagricultural trade for two reasons: no significant reduction of trade barriers was accom-

15. In addition to increasing the volume of exports, a tariff reduction can improve the terms of trade for developing countries to the extent that export prices are increased. This effect might be particularly important for cotton textile exports subject to quota restriction.

plished, and nontariff restrictions severely distort the meaning of tariff levels. The principal traded commodities in this sector are coal, crude petroleum, and petroleum products. The GATT summary of the Kennedy Round results records total imports of these products by the major industrial countries at $9.1 billion in 1964, of which $5.3 billion entered duty free. Only 16 percent of the remaining $3.8 billion of dutiable products was subject to duty reduction in the Kennedy Round, and over half of this consisted of EEC reductions in statutory rates on petroleum products that were above the rates actually applied. There was no appreciable reduction in the applied rates on these products.

The form of protection varies greatly for crude petroleum. The United States applies a low duty in conjunction with strict quota restrictions. The EEC permits free entry (which was bound in the Kennedy Round) but also applies some nontariff controls, notably quota restrictions in France. Most countries apply high consumption taxes. For the United Kingdom this tax takes the form of an explicit revenue duty. For Switzerland, a similar duty is applied but it is not specified "revenue" (in fact a large number of Swiss duties are levied principally for revenue purposes). Japan maintains a moderate duty on petroleum.

Exports of coal, primarily by the United States, also face a wide range of nontariff restrictions. The United Kingdom has a total embargo on coal imports. Licensing restrictions are common. Germany permits an annual quota to enter duty free and maintains a prohibitive tariff on additional imports; the tariff was reduced by 50 percent in the Kennedy Round, but it will probably still be prohibitive after the reduction.

CHAPTER FIFTEEN

Agreements on Agricultural Trade

IN THE KENNEDY ROUND agricultural negotiations, two separate working procedures were used. Special groups for grains, meat, and dairy products attempted to negotiate general arrangements for improving the conditions of trade. Only the grains group was able to reach a measure of concrete agreement. Negotiations on the wide range of other farm products, on the other hand, were conducted primarily on a bilateral basis, with varying degrees of success.

As discussed in Chapter 9, the agricultural talks were also distinguished from those in the industrial sector by a sharper cleavage between exporters and importers. The special groups were on many issues divided into exporting and importing factions (although there was by no means consistent harmony on objectives within the subgroups). In the bilateral negotiations on the broader range of farm products the United States was the *demandeur* in talks with the European countries (with the notable exception of Denmark) and Japan, while the developing countries were the principal beneficiaries in the tropical products sector. The only significant two-way negotiation in agriculture was between the United States and Canada.

The results in the agricultural sector cannot be evaluated by the analytical procedures applied to the nonagricultural sector. In some cases the entire domestic support program is relevant to the level of protection and trade. The proliferation of quotas, licensing requirements, variable levies, and other nontariff barriers in a number of countries makes choosing a basis for analysis extremely difficult and complex. Even the qualitative distinction among tariff concessions on farm products was more important than in the nonagricultural sector since offers were made largely in response to particular requests rather than on an across-the-board basis. Consequently, the discussion that follows is limited to the general trade coverage of concessions, and little attempt is made to predict the impact of these actions on the level of protection or the volume of trade.[1]

Agricultural Concessions

Table 15–1 presents summary figures on the agricultural sector, excluding trade in the three special groups, although some bilateral concessions were made in the meat and dairy groups after the attempt for

Table 15–1. Effect of Kennedy Round on Combined Agricultural Imports (Other than Cereals, Meat, and Dairy Products) of the Major Industrial Countries [a]

In billions of dollars and, in parentheses, percentage of total

Imports	Tropical products	Nontropical products	Total
Total	4.8	6.3	11.1
Already duty-free	2.2	1.4	3.6
Bound in Kennedy Round	0.2	0.2	0.4
Dutiable	2.6(100)	4.9(100)	7.5(100)
No cut in Kennedy Round	1.5(58)	2.4(49)	3.9(52)
Kennedy Round cuts	1.1(42 [b])	2.5(51 [b])	3.6(48 [b])
20 percent and less	0.54(49)	0.67(27)	1.21(34)
Over 20 percent to less than 50 percent	0.19(17)	0.26(10)	0.45(12)
50 percent	0.13(12)	1.27(50)	1.40(38)
Over 50 percent to less than 100 percent	0.09(8)	0.05(2)	0.14(4)
100 percent	0.16(14)	0.27(11)	0.43(12)

Source: Press release no. 992, GATT, June 30, 1967.
a. Based on 1964 value of imports from most-favored-nation sources by the EEC, Japan, Sweden, Switzerland, the United Kingdom, and the United States.
b. This figure would equal 100 percent for total Kennedy Round cuts.

a comprehensive arrangement had been abandoned. The table shows total agricultural imports by the main industrial countries in 1964 of $11.1 billion, broken down into $4.8 billion of tropical products and

1. A detailed description of individual concessions in the agricultural sector is available in United Nations Conference on Trade and Development, *The Kennedy Round: Preliminary Evaluation of Results, with Special Reference to Developing Countries* (Sept. 4, 1967), Supplement 3, pp. 11–36, and U.S. Department of Agriculture, *Report on the Agricultural Trade Negotiations of the Kennedy Round*, FAS-M-193 (September 1967).

$6.3 billion of nontropical. Of the tropical products, $2.6 billion was dutiable, and of this $1.1 billion was subject to duty reduction. About two-thirds of these reductions were for cuts of less than 50 percent. In the nontropical category, $3.6 billion out of $7.5 billion of dutiable imports was subject to duty reduction, and over half of the reductions were for 50 percent or more. The overall picture indicates substantial tariff reductions, although much smaller than those for nonagricultural products. If the import values in Table 15–1 of all dutiable products are weighted by tariff cut (using the midpoint where a range of cuts is given), the average tariff reduction on dutiable imports is 16 percent for tropical products, 22 percent for nontropical, and 20 percent for all products.

Table 15–2 presents figures on the U.S. balance of agricultural concessions comparable to those for nonagricultural concessions in Table 14–2. In this case meat and dairy products are included and only grains are excluded.[2] The linear total columns [3] clearly show the large export surplus which the United States maintained with other industrial countries. U.S. imports totaled $338 million from the linear countries as a group, compared with $2,088 million of linear country imports from the United States. Limited to dutiable trade, the corresponding figures are $308 million and $1,022 million.

The volume of linear country trade subject to duty reduction also shows an almost four-to-one U.S. trade surplus: $141 million of U.S. imports versus $553 million of imports by others from the United States. In addition, other linear countries bound free $100 million of U.S. imports while the U.S. bound the present level of duty on $77 million. The U.S. duty binding was on the low—approximately 4 percent—rate for canned hams, a particularly valuable concession to foreign suppliers. The average cut for dutiable imports, calculated in the same way as for import values in Table 15–1, was 27 percent for linear country imports from the United States. The U.S. reduction depends on how the duty binding on canned hams is averaged. If it is treated as no reduction—in other words, the same as items that were excepted entirely from the agreement—the U.S. cut is only 17 percent. If hams

2. As in Table 14–2, the scope of trade is not the same as the Brussels breakdown, but for trade among industrial countries in particular, the two are highly comparable.

3. The term "linear countries" is carried over into this chapter for convenience even though the linear tariff cut commitment did not apply to agriculture.

Table 15–2. Kennedy Round Concessions on Agricultural Trade (Other than Grains) between the United States and Other Industrial Countries [a]

In millions of dollars

Item	U.S. imports from industrial countries						Industrial countries' imports from U.S.					
	Linear countries [b]						Linear countries [b]					
	EEC	Japan	United Kingdom	Other EFTA	Total	Canada	EEC	Japan	United Kingdom	Other EFTA	Total	Canada
Total imports	219.6	24.2	16.7	77.5	338.0	161.7	992.2	506.3	336.9	252.5	2087.9	397.1
Duty-free	17.3	1.0	9.4	1.9	29.6	36.0	549.7	214.5	138.4	163.1	1065.7	203.2
Bound	16.4	1.0	9.4	1.9	28.7	34.9	527.7	147.3	111.6	97.4	884.0	n.a.
Unbound	0.9	—	—	—	0.9	1.1	22.0	67.2	26.8	65.7	181.7	n.a.
Dutiable	202.3	23.2	7.3	75.6	308.4	125.7	442.5	291.8	198.5	89.4	1022.2	193.9
Available for concession [c]	203.2	23.2	7.3	75.6	309.3	126.8	464.5	359.0	225.3	155.1	1203.9	n.a.
Total duty reductions	93.7	21.9	4.9	20.2	140.7	72.2	220.4	219.3	56.4	56.9	553.0	96.0
1–24 percent	30.0	0.1	—	—	30.1	0.7	117.4	1.4	—	3.0	121.8	15.8
25–49 percent	45.5	0.8	0.1	0.5	46.9	—	51.3	32.1	9.9	10.7	104.0	29.4
50 percent	16.6	21.0	4.8	19.4	61.8	40.6	19.9	25.4	20.1	28.3	93.7	27.4
More than 50 percent	1.6	—	—	0.3	1.9	30.9	31.8	160.4	26.4	14.9	233.5	23.4
Duty bindings	28.1	—	—	49.1	77.2	4.8	0.3	—	—	2.6	2.9	n.a.
Free bindings	0.1	—	—	0.1	0.1	1.1	17.6	25.4	13.7	43.3	100.0	1.3
Total tariff concessions [d]	121.9	21.9	4.9	69.3	218.0	78.1	238.3	244.7	70.1	102.8	655.9	n.a.

Source: U.S. Office of Special Representative for Trade Negotiations, *Report on United States Negotiations* (1967), Vol. 1.

n.a. = not available

a. Based on c.i.f. value (converted, where appropriate, from f.o.b. value), 1964 imports.
b. Linear cuts were made only on nonagricultural trade; the term "linear countries" denotes the major industrial participants in the Kennedy Round.
c. Unbound duty-free plus dutiable imports.
d. Total duty reductions plus duty bindings plus free bindings.

are simply excluded from the dutiable base, the average cut rises to 23 percent, and if the binding on hams is considered as having virtually the same value as a 50 percent reduction, the overall U.S. cut is 30 percent.

The U.S. and Canadian concessions are about equal. Canadian concessions covered a larger volume of imports but generally consisted of shallower cuts.

The Grains Arrangement [4]

The grains arrangement agreed to at Geneva consisted of price ranges for international wheat trade and a joint food aid commitment. Wheat trade among the signatories to the accord was about 13 million tons in 1966, while their exports to all destinations amounted to about 58 million tons, or 90–95 percent of world wheat trade. The initial accord was adapted to the administrative and institutional structure of the eighteen-year-old International Wheat Agreement during follow-up negotiations, with broader geographic participation, in the summer of 1967. The final result, the International Grains Arrangement of 1967, replaced the existing agreement, applying for a three-year period beginning July 1, 1968.

The minimum world prices for wheat in the new arrangement are about 20 cents a bushel higher than those under the older agreement, whose prices were never tested in world trade since market prices remained above the minimum. A significant departure is the establishment of price differentials based on differences in quality and location. Where the earlier agreement provided only one minimum wheat price—based on little-traded Canadian Manitoba Wheat No. 1—the International Grains Arrangement establishes minimum prices for fourteen major wheats, the prices differing according to agreed premiums and discounts that apply at a common location. The minimum prices range from $1.50 to $1.95½ per bushel, with U.S. No. 2 Hard Winter Wheat at $1.73. Maximum world prices have been set 40 cents above the minimums.

Another innovation is the provision for a prices review committee that has the power to adjust minimum prices in response to changes in

4. See U.S. Special Representative for Trade Negotiations, *Report on United States Negotiations*, Vol. 1, pp. 169–71, and U.S. Department of Agriculture, *International Grains Arrangement of 1967* (November 1967).

competitive conditions. Although the committee is expected to obtain agreement on required adjustments, an exporting country can offer its wheat at competitive prices below the minimums if the committee's action is not successful.

The food aid commitment was undertaken in order to distribute the burden of furnishing food aid to developing countries. The program provides for total aid of 4.5 million tons annually of wheat or its equivalent, of which 4.2 million tons was subscribed during the negotiations. The contributions are expected to be primarily wheat, but other grains fit for human consumption or even cash may be contributed. Japan maintains the option to give other aid in substitution for grains. The minimum country contributions are as follows: [5]

	Percent of total	Thousands of metric tons
United States	42.0	1,890
Canada	11.0	495
Australia	5.0	225
Argentina	0.5	23
EEC	23.0	1,035
United Kingdom	5.0	225
Switzerland	0.7	32
Sweden	1.2	54
Denmark	0.6	27
Norway	0.3	14
Finland	0.3	14
Japan	5.0	225

The effectiveness of the grains arrangement depends in good part on the trends of world supply and demand and on close cooperation among the major exporting countries. The international price ranges for wheat can provide short term stability in world markets but a sustained imbalance between supply and demand would require adjustments that are not specified. The existence of the arrangement, however, provides a ready forum for attempting appropriate adjustments.

The food aid commitment will almost certainly lead to an increase of grain sales on world commercial markets corresponding to the amount of new aid committed. If, for example, the EEC's share were not contributed as aid, it would either be (1) consumed domestically as wheat, thereby displacing wheat imports; (2) denatured and consumed as feed grain, thereby displacing feed grain imports; (3) exported to

5. *Report on United States Negotiations*, Vol. 1, p. 171.

commercial markets (under subsidy), thereby displacing sales by some other exporter to that market; (4) stocked; or (5) suppressed through domestic disincentives to production. Food aid as an alternative to any of the first three possibilities will lead to a direct gain for other commercial exporters. The fourth possibility would lead to a direct or indirect gain depending on whether the stocking were an immediate need to maintain minimum levels or a temporary withholding of grain that would later be released on commercial markets. And the fifth possibility seems highly unlikely.

The distribution of these gains among exporters depends on whether the alternative would have been a displacement of wheat or of feed grain. The United States supplies only about 15 percent of world commercial wheat exports, but almost half of total feed grain exports. If the United States were to gain on the average one-quarter of the benefits from the food aid program, this would mean 250,000 tons from the EEC commitment, a little more than 100,000 tons from the United Kingdom and Japan, and smaller amounts elsewhere. Based on the $1.73 per bushel price, which is the level specified in the arrangement for calculating wheat equivalent, the corresponding net gain to the U.S. trade balance would be approximately $25 million per year.

Beyond its effect on total grain exports, the food aid commitment may alter the level of world prices in commercial markets. So long as world food aid requirements and total world grain supplies are at fixed levels for a given period, and the United States commits itself as donor of last resort, the joint food aid commitment will be merely a transfer of markets with no effect on prices in commercial markets. If food aid is supplied out of additional supplies, such as a drawing down of U.S. grain reserves, however, an aid contribution by other countries will tend to strengthen prices in commercial markets.

CHAPTER SIXTEEN

An Evaluation: Present and Future

IN THE KENNEDY ROUND of negotiations on the General Agreement on Tariffs and Trade the major trading nations continued their efforts to reduce tariff and other encumbrances to world trade. An attempt has been made in this study to sort out and explain the many interrelated issues. This concluding chapter presents a brief evaluation of the major achievements and shortcomings of the negotiation. How successful it was can be judged in relation to the initial agreed goals and to the situation that probably would have resulted in the absence of an agreement. It is not reasonable, however, to expect the outcome to measure up to the maximum objectives of any one party at the outset. Nor can a comprehensive agreement like the Kennedy Round be judged by individual segments in isolation: a "balanced" agreement implies a balancing out of plus and minus components.

The first two sections of the chapter contain a discussion of the economic and political significance of the agreement. The final section relates the Kennedy Round to the probable course of future trade policy.

The Economic Consequences

The GATT ministerial meeting in November 1961 called for a major effort to reduce industrial tariffs, suggesting linear cuts as a possible new technique for accomplishing this objective. The United States subsequently obtained congressional authority to reduce almost all tariffs by a maximum of 50 percent. The May 1963 GATT ministerial meeting adopted the objective of substantial linear reductions with a

bare minimum of exceptions, and added, at the insistence of the
European Economic Community (EEC), that special rules should apply
where there were significant disparities in tariff levels for individual
products.

Thus the average Kennedy Round reduction of 36–39 percent by all
major industrial countries was fully in keeping with the ambitious initial objectives. About two-thirds of tariff cuts were for 50 percent or
more, while a degree of tariff harmonization greater than that inherent
in linear cuts was achieved in the steel and chemical sectors as well as in
scattered cases elsewhere. There was not, however, a high degree of
tariff reduction in all industries. Only modest reductions were accomplished in the textile sector, leaving it more prominent than ever as a
major industry enjoying a high level of protection against imports.
Tariff reductions were also small for iron and steel although the level
of tariffs, which is generally low, is not of great significance to trade in
this sector. The largest reductions were achieved in industries typified
by advanced technology, product innovation, and large, often international, firms. Prominent among these were the machinery, transportation equipment, and chemical sectors; a notable exception was the
electronics industry.

The distinction between industries might be described in terms of
homogeneous products produced under relatively static technology
and quality-differentiated ones characterized by a dynamic technology.
A reduction of trade barriers is easily accepted by the latter group
because conditions and products are constantly changing in any event.
Rapid overall market growth and diversity in the firm's product mix
also make the adjustment process easier for this group. Somewhat
paradoxically, many industries that show the clearest gains from trade
in the classical comparative advantage sense, such as textiles and steel,
are in the homogeneous product category where reductions in trade
barriers are less easily accommodated and smaller reductions were accomplished in the Kennedy Round. Transmission of new developments
in technology and establishment of effective international competition
within industries that are dominated by national oligopolies, however,
are valid trade gains, although they cannot be measured in simple terms
of land and labor, wine and cloth.

The Kennedy Round agricultural negotiations, in keeping with expectations, achieved mixed results. Substantial tariff reductions were
made on a wide range of individual products, but negotiations in the

special groups on grains, meats, and dairy products were not generally successful. Only the grains group was able to reach a measure of agreement, including the important precedent of a joint food aid commitment. The broader question of conditions of access to commercial markets remained unresolved. In particular, a full accommodation of the Common Market farm policy to the GATT trading system, despite the laborious preliminary discussion, did not materialize. A confrontation on this issue, however, would almost certainly have ended in bitter disagreement. The Common Market was willing to negotiate seriously, though unsuccessfully, on the limitation of the common agricultural policy for grains by means of some form of self-sufficiency ratio. This attitude, in sharp contrast with the Common Market's dogmatic stand at the outset of the negotiations on access to its markets, may suggest a possible means of adjustment for problems emerging from the Community farm policy.

The prospects for trade in farm products, however, will continue to depend largely on national commitments to the domestic farm sector. They will also depend on attitudes concerning the ability of market forces to adjust levels of supply to demand on world markets. The large and at times ruinous domestic swings in prices for basic farm commodities have led governments to establish parity levels of return to producers and to insure them with various forms of market intervention. Subsidies for production and export can lead to excessive price competition in world markets, where it is often governments rather than private producers who compete. A further complicating factor in international trade in temperate zone products is the relation between food aid contributions and access to commercial markets. These fundamental facts of trade in basic agricultural products were acknowledged but not fully confronted in the Kennedy Round.

The Kennedy Round made a significant start in the field of nontariff barriers. The agreement on an international antidumping code brought national policies into closer harmony and eliminated some of the trade-inhibiting features of national antidumping regulations. The American selling price agreement included action on several long-standing nontariff irritants to trade, notably the U.S. valuation procedure for benzenoid chemicals and the European road taxes that discriminate against American-style automobiles.

The consistent dissatisfaction of the developing countries with progress in the Kennedy Round was due to the relatively lower level of concessions on products of interest to them, somewhat exaggerated expectations, and economic ideology. The scope of tariff reductions on products of particular export interest to these countries was substantial—over 30 percent on the average, for example, on all nonagricultural products other than petroleum. But the degree of cuts was significantly less than that on trade among industrialized countries almost wholly because of the below average results for textiles and processed agricultural products. Particularly embittering was the stipulation that even the modest tariff reductions by the EEC and the United States on cotton textiles were conditional on the continued operation of the GATT long-term quota arrangement. Expectations for a major immediate gain in export earnings for most developing countries were unfounded in any event, however, because 80–90 percent of their exports are in bulk, unprocessed commodities that face low or nil tariffs and stood to gain little from the Kennedy Round. Finally, mistrust of the basic GATT principles as a means for encouraging exports of the developing countries was another reason for these countries' wariness of the negotiation. Reciprocity was waived for developing countries in the Kennedy Round, and concessions were made by the developed countries on an across-the-board basis to all participants, but the malaise was, nevertheless, widespread.

The large differences in the present production capabilities of developing countries, however, make their export interests in the GATT approach to world trade largely dissimilar. For the more advanced of these countries, such as Taiwan, South Korea, and some Latin American countries, unlimited and stable access to the major world markets, with only low or moderate tariff restrictions on the bulk of industrial products, offers an unprecedented opportunity for the development of new export industries. A number of products are still subject to high effective tariff protection, but the carefully constructed postwar system of world trade is based on quota-free, nondiscriminatory access to markets. It provides a scope of market opportunity that should not be disparaged lightly. The alternative of quota and discriminatory restrictions on trade, on the other hand, is a real threat, and the ability of the present system to withstand pressures to move in this direction depends, in good part, on the consistent support of all its beneficiaries.

What do the Kennedy Round reductions in trade barriers mean for the expansion of world trade? Based on very crude projections, the dutiable nonagricultural imports of the major industrialized countries, after the final rates are in effect, might be expected to increase by about 10 percent above the level that would have been reached without the Kennedy Round reductions, or by about $2–$3 billion per year based on 1964 levels of trade. Increases in agricultural trade are even more hazardous to predict, although the joint food aid commitment should distribute the burden of aid more widely and strengthen commercial sales for the present donors, particularly the United States.

Was the Kennedy Round agreement a balanced one in strictly economic terms? Again no precise answer is possible. It is, in fact, impossible to make comparisons between such elements in the final agreement as tariff reductions, bindings on tariffs and on duty-free entry, food aid, and nontariff barriers. The average tariff cut of 36–39 percent on industrial products by major participants is prima facie evidence of approximate balance. The trade impact of these cuts, at least for the United States based on trade figures available at the time of the agreement, also indicates a roughly neutral effect. The other factors cannot be quantified in the same way as tariff cuts on industrial products, but the balances for tariff bindings, food aid, and agricultural concessions in general were all heavily weighted in favor of the United States vis-à-vis Europe and Japan.

Finally, what would have been the consequences of failure to reach agreement? Without question, the opportunity to reduce the margin of tariff preference between members of the European blocs and outside trading partners before these preferences produced irrevocable dislocations in trade would have been lost. Improved access for the exports of developing countries would also have suffered from even a temporary delay. But aside from the timing of particular actions, failure at Geneva would in all likelihood have seriously altered the present course of commercial relations. The inability to reach agreement and the ensuing mutual recriminations would have encouraged opposition to a liberal trade policy and increased pressure for rounds of higher tariffs and other restrictive measures. The appeal of exclusive regional blocs or selective commodity arrangements would have been strengthened, challenging the basis of the present multilateral system.

The Political Significance

The Kennedy Round, although an economic negotiation in substance, was politically significant as well, particularly for the members of the

Atlantic community. President Kennedy's principal interest in the Trade Expansion Act lay in its political objectives. His message to Congress on January 25, 1962, listed "the growth of the European Common Market" as the first of several "new and sweeping developments [which] have made obsolete our traditional trade policy," and warned then "the two great Atlantic markets will either grow together or they will grow apart." [1] The Kennedy Round negotiation, held during a period of strain within the Atlantic community, was for much of this time the only active undertaking to strengthen ties among these nations. The failure of the United Kingdom to gain entry to the Common Market in January 1963, only a few months before the ministerial meeting setting the Kennedy Round objectives, was followed by crisis within the North Atlantic Treaty Organization (NATO), problems in international finance and nuclear nonproliferation, and finally, the tension caused by the steadily expanding conflict in Vietnam. Successful negotiation in the trade sector, though only one of the ties among members of the Atlantic community, played a vital role in relieving the general tension and misgivings of that period.

A major focus of political analysis and speculation during the Kennedy Round was the attitude of General de Gaulle. His options were basically to accept a genuinely successful outcome, to attempt a watering down of the final agreement to the level of an inconsequential commercial accord, or to undermine the negotiation completely through a French veto on essential issues. In much of the negotiation the French attitude was a critical factor. The May 1963 ministerial confrontation over *écrêtement* and disparities, the tabling of nonagricultural exceptions to the linear rule in November 1964, the decision of the EEC not to submit a withdrawal list in November 1966, and the acceptance of the final bargaining package were the most important points of decision. And the French, despite a consistently tough negotiating posture, usually couched in terms of painful reluctance, nevertheless acquiesced at each critical point.

Why did President de Gaulle agree to a successful Kennedy Round? An important and perhaps decisive factor was the "package deal" reached within the Community, and in particular the linking of a French commitment to go along with the Kennedy Round to German acceptance of the internal Community decisions on farm policy. This

1. See Appendix B.

was evident in the exceptions list and unified grain price decisions in the fall of 1964, and was central to the decisions emanating from the Luxembourg compromise in January 1966. A second factor in the French attitude toward the Kennedy Round was economic self-interest. An international grains agreement promised an outlet for French surplus wheat production, and mutual reductions in barriers to industrial trade received support from many segments of the French business community—witness Millet's call in February 1967, on behalf of the French chemical industry, for a maximum reduction of trade barriers in this sector.[2] Still another possible factor in the choice between a modest, undistinguished outcome and the very substantial agreement that did result was a miscalculation about the course of events and the possibility of paring down the agreement in the final bargaining. Until the early months of 1967 a highly successful agreement seemed remote. But once the impasse was broken in the chemical sector, a high level of offers had been firmly committed through the linear approach that only a large pullback could significantly change. And the strategy of Eric Wyndham White in the final weeks, supported by the major participants including the EEC Commission, of seeking upward adjustments to a highest possible level of balanced offers, would have been extremely difficult for the French to reverse without bearing fully the onus of responsibility.

One mitigating aspect of the negotiation for General de Gaulle was the equal power status of the United States and the Common Market. There was no equivalent of the nuclear deterrent which tends to perpetuate American hegemony in NATO or of the special reserve status of the dollar which so heavily influences international monetary affairs. The balance of concessions in the final agreement reflected a corresponding balance of bargaining power. The Kennedy Round was in fact the first major negotiation of a common interest across the Atlantic in which neither side was more equal than the other.

The Kennedy Round contributed also to political development within the Common Market. It was the most important multilateral negotiation in which the members participated under the unified command of the Commission, and the outcome was bound to affect attitudes as to the ability of the Community to cope with such situations. Spanning

2. See Chap. 10, p. 175.

the difficult period from the aftermath of the French veto of United Kingdom membership in January 1963 through the major Community crisis of July 1965–January 1966 and up to the final group of internal decisions during 1966, the successful negotiation at Geneva provided an antidote to lagging spirits at Brussels. The Kennedy Round was also astutely used by the Commission to accelerate the schedule of economic integration, especially in reaching decisions on the internal farm policy.

Moreover, the discretionary power assumed by the Commission during the closing phase of the Geneva negotiations, and the Commission's skill and judgment in exercising this authority, may have established a precedent for future external relations of the Community. The praise received by the Commission from all member states after agreement had been reached was especially noteworthy in view of General de Gaulle's sharp rebuke less than two years earlier.

It was recognized from the outset that the Kennedy Round would affect political relations between the industrial and the developing countries, but the results turned out to be rather inconclusive. The final agreement received a highly qualified voice of approval by the developing countries. But a breakdown of the negotiation, for whatever reason, would have alienated the developing countries from GATT and cast grave doubt on the desire of Western industrial countries to encourage exports of the less developed countries. Wyndham White's emphasis, at the close of the negotiation, on the need for expanding the exports of developing countries indicated that the Kennedy Round had increased the relative importance of trade relations between the rich nations and the poor.

The political importance of the Kennedy Round to the remaining participants was less direct and varied considerably. For the members of the European Free Trade Association (EFTA) it lowered the wall between the two halves of Western Europe and improved the prospects for closer association with the Common Market, including membership for the United Kingdom and some others, though the negotiation can hardly be considered a decisive factor on this count. Japan participated as one of the four major powers but remained wary of assuming a primary position in the active leadership of the negotiation. Canada, by refusing to accept the obligations of other industrial countries, and in particular the linear approach to tariff reduction, restricted its role principally to commercial interests with the United States and a few major commodities. Finally, participation of Eastern European countries—Czechoslovakia, Yugoslavia, and Poland—was politically note-worthy in that politics never entered the discussion.

Observations for Future Trade Policy

There is no guarantee that what was accomplished in the Kennedy Round will endure or encourage further actions toward the expansion of world commerce. Events since the conclusion of the negotiation have confirmed Walt Whitman's dictum that "from any fruition of success, no matter what, shall come forth something to make a greater struggle necessary." [3] The experience of the Kennedy Round should in any event be helpful in determining the direction of future trade policy and in dealing with the new mix of trade problems.

The Kennedy Round clearly demonstrated that the major elements of a successful agreement are shaped by prevailing circumstances and attitudes. Fifty percent linear cuts for industrial products, an antidumping agreement, and a joint food aid commitment were all attainable in the Kennedy Round because of the dispositions and expectations of the major trading nations at the time. In the post-Kennedy Round situation, such factors as new developments in Europe, the ability of developing countries to stimulate domestic food production, and greater understanding of the relation between trade and presumed technological gaps [4] may demand quite different initiatives. Formulation of future policy, in short, is as apt to be influenced by new circumstances as by old successes.

Despite this general caveat, however, the results of the Kennedy Round will limit or perhaps to some extent delineate the scope for future negotiations in a number of specific areas.

Tariffs on Industrial Products

Although a linear reduction of tariffs for all industrial products was the major innovation and an important ingredient in the high degree of achievement in the Kennedy Round, its application in future negotiations to all countries and all products is very unlikely. This is in part

3. Quoted in Arnold J. Toynbee, *A Study of History*, abridgment by D. C. Somervell (Oxford University Press, 1946), Vol. 1, p. 189.
4. See, for example, John Diebold, "Is the Gap Technological?" *Foreign Affairs*, Vol. 46 (January 1968), pp. 276–91.

a result of its success in the Kennedy Round in reducing tariff levels in many sectors to modest if not inconsequential levels, and in part a result of its lack of success in a few particular cases. For industries where the new level of tariffs is quite low, a concerted move to complete elimination of tariffs has strong appeal. In sectors such as textiles, on the other hand, where Kennedy Round reductions were small and tariffs remain relatively high, reluctance to make substantial reductions is likely to continue in the near future. It is far more difficult today than it was in 1961 to visualize a general rule for tariff reduction.

Consequently, free trade within selected industry sectors is a possible future means of tariff reductions.[5] In addition to the possible economic gains from increased trade, complete tariff elimination would do away with the administrative inconveniences of duty assessment (the nuisance effect of low tariffs) and put all nations on an equal basis in regard to import duties. Sectoral free trade would also diminish the uncertainty of future trading conditions and thereby facilitate planning both for traders and international firms. The most likely candidates for future sector discussion might not be among the five problem sectors of the Kennedy Round but those industries in which a minimum of potential problems exists. Tariffs on investment goods, for example, were almost all lowered to 10 percent or less in the Kennedy Round. Considering the importance of these products to technological advance and the large and dynamic firms involved, complete elimination of tariffs in this sector could provide important economic gains with relatively little adverse impact on individual producers or nations.

Sectoral free trade, of course, would present special problems of negotiation. The most obvious is the traditional—though not necessarily essential—objective of a balance of benefits among participating countries, and hence the problem of finding that difficult combination of industries to balance new export opportunity against import competition. The investment goods sector is one of the few where an extensive multilateral trade exists among industrial countries, the large net export position of the United States having been substantially reduced since 1964. Other problems might involve nontariff barriers to trade and the dislocation of domestic firms and workers. The Kennedy Round demonstrated that nontariff matters can be discussed effectively within sector groups, and problems of domestic adjustment can be

5. Among suggestions of this possibility is Eric Wyndham White's, included in Appendix D, pp. 299–300.

eased by use of adjustment assistance, perhaps under more liberal criteria than those of the Trade Expansion Act.

Any new move for tariff reduction on industrial products is closely linked, however, to the possible further extension of regional free trade. A successful United Kingdom bid for Common Market membership is the most obvious possibility, but other arrangements, including some form of broader free trade area, are receiving significant attention. The Kennedy Round was motivated largely by the success and the challenge of the Common Market, and the urgency of its successful outcome increased markedly after General de Gaulle's rejection of the first United Kingdom attempt for EEC membership in January 1963. Similarly, the timing and impetus for future tariff negotiations will be strongly influenced by the more politically oriented efforts toward regional economic integration.

Finally, and of particular relevance to the United States, the Kennedy Round illustrated the difficulties that insufficient leeway in negotiating authority can impose on participants. Linear tariff cuts were generally accepted as a basis for negotiations at the GATT ministerial meeting in November 1961 and did, in fact, constitute the bulk of the final agreement. But the precise conditions of a negotiated settlement cannot be known in advance or anticipated fully, and such serious problems as developed in the disparity controversy and the dispute over the method of assessing duty on benzenoid chemicals were made more difficult by the limitations on American negotiating authority—limitations that are the result of the Congress' intent to keep clearly defined limits on the negotiating authority of the President. Fortunately the importance of tariffs on industrial products was greatly diminished in the Kennedy Round, and negotiating flexibility—at least in this respect—should thus be less of a problem in the future. In a new multilateral effort to reduce tariffs, for example, U.S. authority to eliminate duties of $7\frac{1}{2}$ percent or lower would affect about half of all industrial categories, and should duties up to 10 percent be included, this share would rise to two-thirds.[6] Sector tariff negotiations, on the other hand, might be negotiated flexibly under a geographically broadened form of the authority that permitted complete tariff elimination on goods in which U.S.-EEC trade amounted to at least 80 percent of world trade.[7]

6. The Trade Expansion Act authorized elimination of duties of 5 percent or lower. These shares are derived from data in Table 13–5.

7. The unsuccessful Reuss-Douglas amendment to the Trade Expansion Act would have extended coverage to the EFTA. See p. 52.

Trade in Agricultural Products

The task of reshaping the barriers to world agricultural trade is formidable. As U.S. Agriculture Under Secretary John Schnittker commented, "Even to catalog and understand them is difficult. To deal with them all in a comprehensive way is virtually impossible. This the Kennedy Round has made clear to us." [8] It is not clear, however, whether this realization will encourage bolder moves or inhibit policy makers in the future. Some tariffs and quotas, especially on processed farm products, can still be discussed more or less individually, and this is a subject of continuing concern to many developing countries. But the broader question of domestic support programs for basic temperate zone crops and products, and the degree to which these programs are related to conditions in world markets, will remain the central issue of trade in agricultural products. Perhaps action will depend on current crises, as did the International Grains Arrangement of 1967—and especially the food aid commitment—on the serious food shortages in India during 1965 and 1966. Prospective candidates for new problems are numerous. Poultry trade continues under the cloud of potentially unmanageable surplus production. The return to producers for butter is 70–80 cents per pound in some major producing countries while world market prices in early 1968 were as low as 10–15 cents per pound. The present system of trade for many agricultural products, in short, is highly inefficient and the question is whether major trading countries are in a position and disposed to do something about it.

Nontariff Barriers

Nontariff barriers to trade are receiving the greatest attention today. As tariffs are progressively lowered and bound in GATT, the efforts of those seeking protection from import competition, and therefore the trade problems that occupy the time of commercial policy officials, are shifting more heavily to nontariff barriers.

The diversity of problems—from antidumping regulations to government procurement to border taxes—precludes any logical progression from one area to another. The Kennedy Round demonstrated that such trade problems as antidumping and the American selling price system could be negotiated, but it also underlined the complexity and

8. See p. 158.

difficulty of dealing with nontariff issues. Of special importance to the United States is the lack of executive authority in many areas to make commitments that involve domestic laws, and the opposition within Congress to the general procedure of ad referendum agreements undertaken by the President for subsequent congressional approval. Perhaps in the future some form of declaration of intent by the Congress can give the executive general support in certain areas or within broadly defined limits for serious negotiation leading to detailed ad referendum agreements.

East-West Trade

The Kennedy Round, though too early for a dramatic move forward in East-West trade relations, did demonstrate GATT's usefulness as a neutral forum for discussing and negotiating some of these trade interests. Sudden changes in East-West trade relations are unlikely, in any event; on the contrary, relations will probably develop gradually— somewhat distinctly for each Eastern European country—through a continuing series of bilateral arrangements with Western countries. Under these circumstances, GATT, which already includes Czechoslovakia, Poland, and Yugoslavia as full members, could serve as coordinator of bilateral relations and might in the process develop a form of common law of trade practices between East and West.

The application by the United States of high, Smoot-Hawley tariffs (rather than the most-favored-nation tariffs) to all Eastern European countries except Poland and Yugoslavia severely limits its trade contacts with these countries and prevented, for example, any bilateral contact with Czechoslovakia during the Kennedy Round. The greater interest and willingness of Western European countries in increasing trade with Eastern Europe could lead to exclusion of American commercial interests in this area unless existing tariff and nontariff restrictions are eased.

Exports of the Developing Countries

Most of the export opportunities discussed above apply to developing countries. Realization that something extra must be done for them steadily grew during the Kennedy Round, partially influenced by developments within the United Nations Conference on Trade and Development (UNCTAD). Eric Wyndham White's statement at the close of the Kennedy Round clearly stresses the future goal of an expansion of exports of developing countries.[9] Under the present GATT program, more advanced developing countries already benefit substantially from the general lowering of tariffs, and these benefits can be expected to increase in future years. Relaxation of quotas and further reduction or elimination of duties on products dominantly supplied by developing countries would accelerate the expansion of their export opportunities. And, of course, the implementation of the Long-Term Arrangement Regarding International Trade in Cotton Textiles—and in particular the degree to which orderly expansion of access to world markets can be provided in this one area where developing countries have established an efficient and competitive industry—will continue to be a vital concern of many of these countries.

Other aspects of trade policy toward developing countries will largely fall outside the purview of GATT or will be shared with other organizations. GATT has recently merged its trade promotion organization with that of UNCTAD, while such central commercial policy issues as tariff preferences for developing countries or commodity arrangements for tropical products—still the principal export sector for many developing countries—are being handled mainly in UNCTAD or in separate commodity organizations. Finally, a program for improving the trade position of developing countries, whether in regard to specific measures like compensatory financing of shortfalls in export earnings or the broader relations between trade and economic development, inevitably spills over into other policy areas. Trade performance, international financial stability, and domestic programs of economic growth and employment are particularly sensitive and interrelated in these countries. GATT has proven to be a highly effective organ for international negotiation of trade issues, although limitations in its scope of action and, to a decreasing extent, its geographic membership will require a continual sharing of responsibility in trade matters, especially with UNCTAD, and a general responsiveness to efforts outside the trade field to promote economic development.

The interrelation of trade and other policies is by no means restricted to developing countries, however. Its importance in all countries has been growing steadily in recent years, largely as a result of the reduction of barriers to the international movement of goods and capital. The increasing economic interdependence between nations and the concomitant problems of maintaining a reasonable equilibrium in inter-

9. See Appendix D.

national accounts are putting a severe strain on all available policy instruments—or, according to Richard Cooper, "The 'loads' are outrunning the 'capabilities.'"[10] Thus any discussion of new steps to lower trade barriers might well appear optimistic. Indeed, during most of 1968, in order to cope with disequilibrium, attention was focused on measures that would inhibit the freedom of exchange between nations: import quotas, export subsidies, investment controls, travel restrictions.

But there are alternatives to these restrictive measures that can be utilized to maintain a balanced international economy. Adjustments within domestic economies, adequate international reserves to finance temporary imbalance, actions by surplus countries to lower trade barriers and encourage the export of capital, especially to capital-deficit developing countries, or, in some instances, adjustment of the exchange rate can all serve to minimize the need for restrictive action.

The choice of alternatives rests with governments. Much attention in future trade matters will undoubtedly be given to the effect of changes in the level of trade barriers on financial equilibrium; hopefully, coordinated actions to maintain and improve trade opportunities will prevail over uncoordinated actions to curtail them. The Kennedy Round did not establish a helpful precedent, for by maintaining a strict rule of reciprocity of trade benefits, it, like previous GATT negotiations, ignored the possibility of combining a reduction of trade barriers with an improvement in the international payments situation. The efforts during 1968 to accelerate Kennedy Round cuts by Europeans and others to help ease the U.S. balance-of-payments deficit (or more precisely to forestall action by the United States to impose import restrictions) was only a limited step in the direction of such a combination.

It is difficult to anticipate optimistically the future course of trade policies. As Eric Wyndham White has said, the structure of the present trading system "is fragile and constantly subject to attack." But trade is the most intimate and pervasive area of contact between sovereign states. It is vitally important to the economic well-being of certain sectors in each country, and especially in some smaller nations it is the principal determinant of economic activity. Today, more than ever, development of harmony and prosperity in world commerce depends on the interests of all trading partners. Whether a mutual reduction

10. *The Economics of Interdependence* (McGraw-Hill for Council on Foreign Relations, 1968), p. 278.

of trade barriers be attempted, or unilateral action to erect new barriers be threatened, there is no more fitting warning than that of Robert Frost: [11]

> *Before I built a wall I'd ask to know*
> *What I was walling in or walling out,*
> *And to whom I was like to give offense.*

11. From "Mending Wall" from *Complete Poems of Robert Frost*, Copyright 1930, 1939 by Holt, Rinehart and Winston, Inc. Copyright © 1958 by Robert Frost. Copyright © 1967 by Lesley Frost Ballantine. Reprinted by permission of Holt, Rinehart and Winston, Inc.

APPENDIX A

Alternative Methods of Averaging Tariffs

THERE IS NO completely satisfactory way to summarize a dispersed tariff schedule with a single average figure. For most purposes related to this study, the average should ideally be weighted by the level of imports that would enter under conditions of free trade. But these weights are not available, and using the level of imports under protection may seriously distort the result. Cases can be cited in which a country following a protectionist policy, admitting unprocessed goods free of duty and maintaining highly restrictive duties on manufactures, has an average tariff, weighted by actual imports, lower than that of more liberal trading countries.[1]

The purpose of this appendix is to determine whether the particular tariff levels for industrial countries before and after the Kennedy Round lend themselves to a "reasonable" averaging procedure, and if so, what method of averaging is likely to give the best results. This task is simplified greatly by two limitations. First, the calculations exclude agriculture and mineral fuels, and pertain only to the industrial sector where tariffs are principally responsible for restricting imports. Second, the average is limited to dutiable imports since they were the subject of Kennedy Round tariff talks. They are also an advantageous measure because they exclude the large volume of duty-free raw materials that can dominate an overall average figure. The more limited question, therefore, is what degree of distortion can be expected in calculating the average level of tariffs for dutiable nonagricultural imports.

Four approaches have been suggested or used for computing an average from individual tariff rates: (1) an average weighted by a country's own imports; (2) an average weighted by world imports; (3) an average weighted by consumption; and (4) an unweighted average of individual rates. Each of these procedures has its shortcomings. Weighting by own imports, however, is the only one linked to the ideal weighting situation of a counry's imports under conditions of free trade. As tariffs are progressively lowered, the im-

---

1. "As judged by these methods, England in 1925 (on account of her high revenue duties) had a higher tariff than Italy or Germany! Again, to take another example, the average duty-burden upon American imports averages, according to this method, 13.70 per cent from 1926 to 1930 as against 23 per cent from 1906 to 1910. . . . In order to avoid these ridiculous results, other methods have been adopted." Gottfried Haberler, *The Theory of International Trade with Its Applications to Commercial Policy* (London: William Hodge & Co., 1936, p. 356).

port weights in this case approach the norm. One question, therefore, is whether an estimate can be made of the differential. The problem with own imports, on the other hand, is that it has an obvious downward bias—with a given elasticity of demand, high duties tend to reduce import weights by a greater degree than low duties—and this effect has led to its general disrepute as a satisfactory averaging technique. There is, however, an advantage to at least knowing the direction of the bias, which further supports the possibility of empirical testing.

Weighting tariffs by the world imports for each product is a widely used, second-best technique for averaging tariffs. It is recognized that if all countries maintain relatively high duties on particular products—for example, textiles—insufficient weight will still be given to these products. The broader range of countries, however, and the large volume of preferential, duty-free trade within the European Economic Community (EEC), the European Free Trade Association (EFTA), and the British Commonwealth, plus the generally moderate levels of tariffs in many European countries, would tend to mitigate substantially the resulting downward bias. What has not been fully realized, though, when world imports are used, is that the distinction between a country's dominantly export- and import-competing industries is blurred. Japan would receive the same relative weight for steel sheets or cotton cloth as the United States in its tariff average even though the Japanese tariff has little or no significance for the level of imports of these export-oriented products. Similarly, the U.S. tariff on computers or jet aircraft would receive far greater weight in the average than the import prospects would justify. This basic distortion, moreover, would not disappear as tariffs are lowered.

Weighting tariffs in proportion to a nation's (or worldwide) consumption presupposes that the ratio of imports to consumption would be more or less uniform under conditions of free trade. But this is not necessarily a reasonable a priori assumption. Some products, because of transportation costs, perishability, or other marketing conveniences, are not generally tradeable. Other products are exported rather than imported. Weighting by consumption is usually ruled out in any event because comparable statistics on a sufficiently narrow commodity basis for tariff nomenclature and consumption are not available. A simple test of the relationship, however, was made in this analysis based on data from a study of 183 U.S. manufacturing industries.[2] First, to show the wide dispersion in the existing ratio of imports to consumption, the industries were grouped by the import/consumption ratio:

Import/consumption ratio	Number of industries
0– 0.9	52
1.0– 3.9	65
4.0– 9.9	33
10.0–19.9	18
20.0–50.0	12
Over 50	3
Total	183

2. Trade Relations Council, *Employment, Output, and Foreign Trade of U.S. Manufacturing Industries, 1958–64/65* (1966).

Out of the 183 observations, 117 have an import ratio of less than 4 percent while 15 industries have ratios of 20 percent or more. A tariff weighted by consumption would obviously give far less weight to the 15 heavy import industries and dominant weight to the 117 that show only a small actual level of imports.

It is doubtful whether this wide dispersion of import/consumption ratios would change greatly with the elimination of tariffs, but in order to determine the direction of change, the correlation between the import/consumption ratio and the level of tariff incidence for the 183 industries was tested. The correlation was positive at the 90 percent confidence level for all 183 industries, and the confidence level was over 99.5 percent if two unprocessed goods, wood pulp and sawmill products, were excluded. This correlation of high tariff levels with high existing ratios of imports to consumption suggests that dispersion of import ratios would become greater rather than less under free trade.

Finally, unweighted averages of tariff items have occasionally been used under the assumption that the "law of large numbers" will achieve a reasonable approximation. Because of the wide variance in the trade importance of individual tariff items, however, this procedure gives inordinate weight to many obscure products. Moreover, there is probably a strong upward bias in an unweighted average of individual tariff items because the product breakdown is usually more detailed for highly protected, import sensitive industries. This tendency is especially obvious in the U.S. tariff. Out of approximately 7,000 individual U.S. tariff items, no less than 1,058 cover one product, cotton cloth.[3] Passenger automobiles, on the other hand, are covered by a single tariff rate even though imports are several times larger than for cotton cloth. The EEC, incidentally, has only six rates for cotton cloth, thereby making an international comparison based on unweighted averages highly suspect as well. A similar if not quite as drastic splintering of the U.S. tariff is evident for other high tariff industries such as watches, gloves, and benzenoid chemicals.

The problems with unweighted averages can be reduced somewhat if a common code, such as the Brussels Tariff Nomenclature, is used to define the basic unit. This will at least achieve comparability between countries. There is still probably an upward bias in the unweighted average of Brussels categories, though, because the breakdown for normally higher duty, finished manufactures is generally finer than for semimanufactures. This distinction is particularly apparent in the metals and metal products sector.

The difference in results from these alternative methods of averaging tariffs can only be evaluated by actual calculation. Table A–1 presents various averages of U.S. tariffs on dutiable nonagricultural imports before Kennedy Round cuts. The first column is the average tariff weighted entirely by own

3. The official distinction between legal tariff categories in the U.S. tariff is the five-digit level of the Tariff Schedule of the United States. The 1,058 categories of cotton cloth refer to this five-digit level, but since the physical size of such a list is formidable, the items are usually grouped in tens even in detailed publications of U.S. imports. Even so, over 100 entries appear for cotton cloth (out of an adjusted total of some 6,000 items). This latter grouping is used, where relevant, throughout the analysis in Chap. 13.

imports, including the inherent downward bias. In the second column the import weights are adjusted to approximate the free trade situation. The adjustment was designed to estimate the maximum degree of the downward bias, and was calculated on the assumptions that the entire tariff reduction is reflected in a reduction of import price, and the price elasticity of demand for imports is -4. In addition (and partly to simplify the calculations), the adjustment was made on the unweighted averages of the nine hundred Brussels categories, which generally give still greater weight to the extremely high and restrictive individual rates. The percentage increase in the adjusted incidence over the actual incidence average appears in the third column. Column 4 presents the averages modified by own imports, from Table 13–1. Column 5 is an approximation of an average weighted by world imports. Finally, column 6 is an unweighted average of the Brussels categories (actually a two-tier unweighted average since rates within categories have already been averaged arithmetically).

Perhaps the most interesting result is that the estimate of the maximum downward bias in the actual incidence average is only 14 percent overall, and varies from 1 percent to 24 percent for individual industries. Once Kennedy Round reductions come into effect, moreover, this bias should be reduced by roughly a third, or probably to less than 10 percent. It would be especially reduced in the important chemicals and metals sectors where rates were harmonized substantially in the Kennedy Round. Another interesting result is that the modified-own-import average used in Chapter 13 and the average based on world imports are both very close to the adjusted estimate of 14 percent in column 2. The unweighted average in column 6, as anticipated, is higher, especially for metals and transport equipment (in the latter case because it gives little weight to the low U.S. tariff on automobiles). The difference between the two extremes—the downward-biased actual incidence and the upward-biased unweighted average—is only 30 percent,[4] which might be considered comparatively modest.

Although the differences between the averages based on modified own imports and world imports are generally small, the preferable measure is, for several reasons, a form of own imports. The variance by industry around the adjusted incidence in column 2 is greater for world imports. The margin of error after Kennedy Round reductions are in effect should be reduced for modified own imports but not necessarily for world imports. And the application of other forms of analysis is more apt to be distorted with the use of world imports. For example, the average Kennedy Round reduction for the United States, as measured and presented in Chapter 13, is 36 percent. Using world imports, however, the reduction is significantly greater—39–40 percent. The reason for this difference is that world imports give less relative weight for the United States in textiles and steel, where actual import penetration is high and Kennedy Round cuts small, and greater relative weight to such sectors as machinery and aircraft, where the United States has smaller

---

4. The absolute difference is 4.2 points. If the adjusted incidence of column 2 is used as a base, the difference is 30 percent.

Table A–1 U.S. Tariff Averages for Dutiable Nonagricultural Products (Other than Mineral Fuels) before Kennedy Round Cuts, under Various Weighting Schemes [a]

| Category | Tariff weighted by own imports | | | Tariff weighted by modified own imports [b] | Tariff weighted by world imports [c] | Un-weighted tariff |
	Actual incidence (1)	Adjusted incidence (2)	Percentage change in incidence (3)	(4)	(5)	(6)
Mineral products	10.9	11.1	+2	9.9	9.4	9.0
Chemical products	16.0	17.6	+10	17.8	18.6	15.9
Rubber products	9.0	9.1	+1	11.3	11.5	13.8
Hides, furs, leather products	15.4	18.6	+21	16.2	13.8	12.4
Wood and cork products	5.2	6.4	+24	6.8	6.8	11.1
Pulp and paper	8.3	8.4	+1	10.9	10.2	11.7
Textiles	20.9	22.8	+9	21.4	24.9	21.0
Footwear and headwear	15.9	16.2	+2	16.1	16.5	19.6
Stone, ceramic and glass products	22.4	24.0	+7	21.0	19.1	18.4
Base metals and metal products	6.7	7.6	+13	8.5	9.4	15.2
Nonelectrical machinery	10.9	11.7	+7	11.9	12.3	12.3
Electrical machinery	12.3	12.4	+1	13.6	14.0	13.8
Transportation equipment	6.9	7.1	+3	7.1	7.9	11.5
Precision instruments	18.8	19.7	+5	21.1	23.1	23.9
Miscellaneous	17.7	19.5	+10	19.5	20.8	21.4
Total	12.3	14.0	+14	13.5	14.5	16.5

a. Based on four-digit Brussels Tariff Nomenclature categories, c.i.f. value (converted from f.o.b. or American selling price), 1964 imports.

b. Tariffs are normally unweighted within single Brussels categories; when categories are combined in larger industry groups, tariffs are weighted by own imports. These are the averages from Table 13–1.

c. Tariffs are weighted by most-favored-nation dutiable imports of the United States, the EEC, the EFTA, and Japan.

imports but larger cuts. In this case, the use of world import weights clearly distorts the results.

A comparison for the other major participants, presented in Table A–2, is limited to the last three columns of the table for the United States. The EEC and the United Kingdom show relatively small differences, in keeping with the greater degree of harmonization within their tariff structures, although some minor effects, such as the upward bias of the unweighted average in

Table A-2. Tariff Averages of the EEC, United Kingdom, and Japan for Dutiable Nonagricultural Products (Other than Mineral Fuels) before Kennedy Round Cuts, under Various Weighting Schemes [a]

Category	EEC tariff			U.K. tariff			Japanese tariff		
	Weighted by modified own imports [b] (1)	Weighted by world imports [c] (2)	Unweighted (3)	Weighted by modified own imports [b] (4)	Weighted by world imports [c] (5)	Unweighted (6)	Weighted by modified own imports [b] (7)	Weighted by world imports [c] (8)	Unweighted (9)
Mineral products	9.4	6.4	9.4	9.3	9.9	10.4	12.0	12.9	11.7
Chemical products	14.3	14.6	12.6	19.9	18.6	18.5	19.7	20.2	17.4
Rubber products	15.0	14.2	12.6	13.6	18.1	15.3	15.1	18.5	15.2
Hides, furs, leather products	9.2	10.7	11.8	17.7	16.7	15.8	19.9	23.5	21.9
Wood and cork products	10.9	11.1	11.1	5.2	8.3	12.1	15.6	14.3	15.9
Pulp and paper	10.7	12.3	16.2	16.6	14.7	17.2	6.7	11.5	14.4
Textiles	16.0	16.4	15.0	20.6	20.2	19.9	23.5	21.0	19.1
Footwear and headwear	17.8	18.3	15.8	22.8	23.0	23.0	26.3	25.4	24.1
Stone, ceramic and glass products	14.1	15.3	13.3	16.4	16.2	16.9	16.9	15.3	15.0
Base metals and metal products	9.9	10.2	12.6	12.8	13.3	16.8	11.0	16.2	18.9
Nonelectrical machinery	11.1	10.9	10.9	14.2	14.5	15.0	15.6	15.8	15.6
Electrical machinery	14.2	14.4	13.9	20.1	19.6	19.1	17.8	18.5	16.8
Transportation equipment	15.4	18.5	14.1	20.0	20.0	18.5	18.4	29.5	17.4
Precision instruments	13.3	13.7	14.2	26.4	26.2	27.8	19.1	20.6	20.0
Miscellaneous	16.5	14.5	13.7	20.1	19.9	19.8	14.7	20.8	21.6
Total	12.8	13.4	13.1	16.7	17.0	18.2	15.5	19.0	18.0

a. Based on four-digit Brussels Tariff Nomenclature categories, c.i.f. value, 1964 imports.
b. Tariffs are normally unweighted within single Brussels categories; when categories are combined in larger industry groups, tariffs are weighted by own imports. These are the averages used in Tables 13–2, 13–3, and 13–4.
c. Tariffs are weighted by most-favored-nation dutiable imports of the United States, the EEC, the EFTA, and Japan.

the metals sector, is evident. Kennedy Round cuts should reduce differences further, especially for the United Kingdom which included a large measure of tariff revision and harmonization in its final offer. Japan is more difficult to assess. Imports are presently concentrated heavily in raw materials, semi-processed goods, and investment goods, but this pattern may gradually change as tariffs are lowered and internal costs rise. The Japanese tariff is fairly uniform within industries or at least subsectors of industries, but the averaging into larger industry groups may entail a substantial downward bias from higher tariffs on finished goods, as shown in the difference between the overall tariff weighted by own and world imports—15.5 percent versus 19.0 percent.

The conclusion from these various forms of tariff averaging is that a margin of error exists in each case, but that the degree of error for dutiable industrial products is relatively moderate. A weighting system based on a country's own imports seems most favorable because of the direct relation to the ideal free trade situation, although there is some downward bias in the results. Adjustment for this bias is possible through the application of assumed import price elasticities or some other means of giving greater weight to the higher tariff rates. The results presented in this appendix, however, indicate a fairly small bias for the United States, and even smaller biases for European countries. Tariff reductions as a result of the Kennedy Round should, of course, reduce this bias further.

Procedure and Sources for the Calculations Presented in Chapter 13

The calculations presented in Chapter 13 were based on commodity categories as defined at the four-digit level of the Brussels Tariff Nomenclature. There are approximately nine hundred such categories in the nonagricultural sector (excluding mineral fuels). The EEC, the EFTA countries, and Japan apply this nomenclature uniformly at the four-digit level. For the United States, a preliminary concordance between the Tariff Schedule of the United States and the Brussels schedule, prepared by the U.S. Tariff Commission, was used. The industry groups and subgroups are defined in terms of the Brussels nomenclature in Table A–3.

Where a Brussels category includes more than one national tariff rate (national tariffs contain 3,000–6,000 rates), the alternatives were to use an averaged weighted by imports, an unweighted average, or some measure of the range of rates. An average weighted by imports presents at least three problems. It virtually excludes from the average some very high individual rates that greatly restrict trade. Import data are not readily available where, as a result of the Kennedy Round, a single rate was split into two or more new rates. And the overall quantity of calculations increases enormously. A measure of the range of rates, the midpoint for example, is probably subject to upward bias because the distribution of rates is skewed toward the upper range and one extremely high rate is frequently associated with several low

Table A-3. Brussels Tariff Nomenclature Categories Included in Industry Groups

Industry group	Brussels identification [a]
Mineral products	25–26
Chemical products	28–39
Rubber products	40
Hides, furs, leather products	41–43
Raw hides, skins, fur	4101, 4301
Articles of leather, fur	other
Wood and cork products	44–46
Wood, natural cork	4401–05, 4501–02
Articles of wood, cork	other
Pulp and paper	47–48
Pulp	47
Paper	48
Textiles	50–63
Natural fiber and waste	5001–03, 5301–05, 5401–02, 5501–04, 5701–04
Yarn and basic fabrics	other
Special fabrics, apparel, other	58–63
Footwear and headwear	64–65
Stone, ceramic and glass products	68–70
Base metals and metal products	73–83
Unwrought, pig iron, scrap	7301–03, 7401, 7501, 7601, 7701, 7801, 7901, 8001
Basic shapes and forms	those in following subgroups
Steel	7304–20
Other	7402–12, 7502–04, 7602–07, 7702, 7802–05, 7902–04, 8002–05
Articles of base metal, miscellaneous	other
Nonelectrical machinery	84
Electrical machinery	85
Transportation equipment	86–89
Precision instruments	90–92
Miscellaneous	49, 66, 67, 71, 72, 93–99

a. A two-digit figure indicates the entire Brussels chapter and includes all four-digit categories within that chapter.

or moderate rates (to take the extreme case of the U.S. tariff schedule as a whole, the highest rate before Kennedy Round cuts was over 200 percent, which would make the midpoint of the range of the U.S. tariff over 100 percent). The basic procedure in this analysis was to take an unweighted average of the individual rates within a Brussels category. However, in exceptional cases where an unweighted average within a category would significantly distort a reasonable appraisal of the tariff level, the individual rates were weighted by imports. These exceptions were made for about 2 percent of the Brussels categories although they constituted a larger proportion of imports.

Adjustments were made to convert U.S. tariffs based on f.o.b. or American selling price valuation to a comparable c.i.f. base. American selling price rates were converted on the basis of information in *Tariff Commission Report 181* (1966). F.o.b.-c.i.f. conversion factors for industry groupings were derived from the U.S. Tariff Commission study, *C.i.f. Value of U.S. Imports* (February 7, 1967), but in presenting individual Brussels categories (such as the tariff dispersion tables, 13–5 through 13–10), a flat 10 percent adjustment was used. Specific and compound rates were converted to an ad valorem equivalent based on import value and duties collected during a recent year; in a few cases, where lack of data prevented a reasonable estimate, the items were excluded.

Revenue duties clearly identified as an offset to a domestic excise tax were excluded, although there were very few significant cases in the nonagricultural sector excluding mineral fuels.

The calculations are based on the permanent most-favored-nation rate and do not take account of temporary duty suspensions or tariff quotas below the most-favored-nation rate. Such duty suspensions are relatively minor and are normally for unprocessed goods in the industry subgroups rather than for manufactured products.

Unless specified otherwise, tariff and trade data are from official national and EEC sources. A complete listing of tariff concessions made in the Kennedy Round is contained in the GATT publication, *General Agreement on Tariffs and Trade: Legal Instruments Embodying the Results of the 1964–67 Trade Conference* (5 vols.; 1967). A convenient and much cheaper listing of U.S. concessions, including the level of 1964 and 1965 imports, is contained in U.S. Office of the Special Representative for Trade Negotiations, *Report on United States Negotiations* (1967), Vol. 2.

APPENDIX B

President Kennedy's Call
for the Trade Expansion Act

Following is the text of John F. Kennedy's Special Message to the Congress on Foreign Trade Policy, January 25, 1962. Public Papers of the Presidents, 1962, pp. 68–77.

To the Congress of the United States:

Twenty-eight years ago our nation embarked upon a new experiment in international relationships—the Reciprocal Trade Agreements Program. Faced with the chaos in world trade that had resulted from the Great Depression, disillusioned by the failure of the promises that high protective tariffs would generate recovery, and impelled by a desperate need to restore our economy, President Roosevelt asked for authority to negotiate reciprocal tariff reductions with other nations of the world in order to spur our exports and aid our economic recovery and growth.

That landmark measure, guided through Congress by Cordell Hull, has been extended eleven times. It has served our country and the free world well over two decades. The application of this program brought growth and order to the free world trading system. Our total exports, averaging less than $2 billion a year in the three years preceding enactment of the law, have now increased to over $20 billion.

On June 30, 1962, the negotiating authority under the last extension of the Trade Agreements Act expires. It must be replaced by a wholly new instrument. A new American trade initiative is needed to meet the challenges and opportunities of a rapidly changing world economy.

In the brief period since this Act was last extended, five fundamentally new and sweeping developments have made obsolete our traditional trade policy:

The growth of the European Common Market—an economy which may soon nearly equal our own, protected by a single external tariff similar to our own—has progressed with such success and momentum that it has surpassed its original timetable, convinced those initially skeptical that there is now no turning back and laid the groundwork for a radical alteration of the economics of the Atlantic Alliance. Almost 90 percent of the free world's industrial production (if the United Kingdom and others successfully complete their negotiations for membership) may soon be concentrated in two great markets—the United States of America and the expanded European Economic Community. A trade policy adequate to negotiate item by item tariff reductions with a large number of small independent states will no longer be adequate to assure ready access for ourselves—and for our traditional trading partners in Canada, Japan, Latin America and elsewhere—to a market nearly as large as our own, whose negotiators can speak with one voice but whose internal differences make it impossible for them to negotiate item by item.

The growing pressures on our balance of payments position have, in the past few years, turned a new spotlight on the importance of increasing American exports to strengthen the international position of the dollar and prevent a steady drain of our gold reserves. To maintain our defense, assistance and other commitments abroad, while expanding the free flow of goods and capital, we must achieve a reasonable equilibrium in our international accounts by offsetting these dollar outlays with dollar sales.

The need to accelerate our own economic growth, following a lagging period of seven years characterized by three recessions, is more urgent than it has been in years—underlined by the millions of new job opportunities which will have to be found in this decade to provide employment for those already unemployed as well as an increasing flood of younger workers, farm workers seeking new opportunities, and city workers displaced by technological change.

The communist aid and trade offensive has also become more apparent in recent years. Soviet bloc trade with 41 non-communist countries in the less-developed areas of the globe has more than tripled in recent years; and bloc trade missions are busy in nearly every continent attempting to penetrate, encircle and divide the free world.

The need for new markets for Japan and the developing nations has also been accentuated as never before—both by the prospective impact of the EEC's external tariff and by their own need to acquire new outlets for their raw materials and light manufactures.

To meet these new challenges and opportunities, I am today transmitting to the Congress a new and modern instrument of trade negotiation—the Trade Expansion Act of 1962. As I said in my State of the Union Address, its enactment "could well affect the unity of the West, the course of the Cold War and the growth of our nation for a generation or more to come."

The Benefits of Increased Trade

Specifically, enactment of this measure will benefit substantially every state of the union, every segment of the American economy, and every basic objective of our domestic and foreign policy.

Our efforts to expand our economy will be importantly affected by our ability to expand our exports—and particularly upon the ability of our farmers and businessmen to sell to the Common Market. There is arising across the Atlantic a single economic community which may soon have a population half again as big as our own, working and competing together with no more barriers to commerce and investment than exist among our 50 states—in an economy which has been growing roughly twice as fast as ours—representing a purchasing power which will someday equal our own and a living standard growing faster than our own. As its consumer incomes grow, its consumer demands are also growing, particularly for the type of goods that we produce best, which are only now beginning to be widely sold or known in the markets of Europe or in the homes of its middle-income families.

Some 30 percent of our exports—more than $4 billion in industrial goods and materials and nearly $2 billion in agricultural products—already goes to the members and prospective members of the EEC. European manufacturers, however, have increased their share of this rapidly expanding market at a far greater rate than American manufacturers. Unless our industry can maintain and increase its share of this attractive market, there will be further temptation to locate additional American-financed plants in Europe in order to get behind the external tariff wall of the EEC. This would enable the American manufacturer to contend for that vast consumer potential on more competitive terms with his European counterparts; but it will also mean a failure on our part to take advantage of this growing market to increase jobs and investment in this country.

A more liberal trade policy will in general benefit our most efficient and expanding industries—industries which have demonstrated their advantage over other world producers by exporting on the average twice as much of their products as we import—industries which have done this while paying highest wages in our country. Increasing investment and employment in these growth industries will make for a more healthy, efficient and expanding economy and a still higher American standard of living. Indeed, freer movement of trade between America and the Common Market would bolster the economy of the entire free world, stimulating each nation to do most what it does best and helping to achieve the OECD target of a 50 percent combined Atlantic Community increase in Gross National Product by 1970.

Our efforts to prevent inflation will be reinforced by expanded trade. Once given a fair and equal opportunity to compete in overseas markets, and once subject to healthy competition from overseas manufacturers for our own markets, American management and labor will have additional reason to maintain competitive costs and prices, modernize their plants and increase their productivity. The discipline of the world market place is an excellent measure of efficiency and a force to stability. To try to shield American industry from the discipline of foreign competition would isolate our domestic price level from world prices, encourage domestic inflation, reduce our exports still further and invite less desirable Government solutions.

Our efforts to correct our adverse balance of payments have in recent years roughly paralleled our ability to increase our export surplus. It is necessary if we are to maintain our security programs abroad—our own military forces overseas plus our contributions to the security and growth of other free countries—to make substantial dollar outlays abroad. These outlays are being held to the minimum necessary, and we are seeking increased sharing from our allies. But they will continue at substantial rates—and this requires us to enlarge the $5 billion export surplus which we presently enjoy from our favorable balance of trade. If that surplus can be enlarged, as exports under our new program rise faster than imports, we can achieve the equilibrium in our balance of payments which is essential to our economic stability and flexibility. If, on the other hand, our surplus should fail to grow, if our exports should be denied ready access to the EEC and other markets—our overseas position would be endangered. Moreover, if we can lower the external tariff wall of the Common Market through negotiation our manufacturers will be under less pressure to locate their plants behind that wall in order to sell in the European market, thus reducing the export of capital funds to Europe.

Our efforts to promote the strength and unity of the West are thus directly related to the strength and unity of Atlantic trade policies. An expanded export program is necessary to give this Nation both the balance of payments equilibrium and the economic growth we need to sustain our share of Western military security and economic advance. Equally important, a freer flow of trade across the Atlantic will enable the two giant markets on either side of the ocean to impart strength and vigor to each other, and to combine their resources and momentum to undertake the many enterprises which the security of free peoples demands. For the first time, as the world's greatest trading nation, we can welcome a single partner whose trade is even larger than our own—a partner no longer divided and dependent, but strong enough to share with us the responsibilities and initiatives of the free world.

The communist bloc, largely self-contained and isolated, represents an economic power already by some standards larger than that of Western Europe and hoping someday to overtake the United States. But the combined output and purchasing power of the United States and Western Europe— nearly a trillion dollars a year—is more than twice as great as that of the entire Sino-Soviet world. Though we have only half the population, and far less than half the territory, we can pool our resources and resourcefulness in an open trade partnership strong enough to outstrip any challenge, and strong enough to undertake all the many enterprises around the world which the maintenance and progress of freedom require. If we can take this step, Marxist predictions of "capitalist" empires warring over markets and stifling competition would be shattered for all time—Communist hopes for a trade war between these two great economic giants would be frustrated—and Communist efforts to split the West would be doomed to failure.

As members of the Atlantic Community we have concerted our military objectives through the North Atlantic Treaty Organization. We are concerting our monetary and economic policies through the Organization for Economic Cooperation and Development. It is time now to write a new chapter in the evolution of the Atlantic Community. The success of our foreign policy depends in large measure upon the success of our foreign trade, and our maintenance of Western political unity depends in equally large measure upon the degree of Western economic unity. An integrated Western Europe, joined in trading partnership with the United States, will further shift the world balance of power to the side of freedom.

Our efforts to prove the superiority of free choice will thus be advanced immeasurably. We will prove to the world that we believe in peacefully "tearing down walls" instead of arbitrarily building them. We will be opening new vistas of choice and opportunity to the producers and consumers of the free world. In answer to those who say to the world's poorer countries that economic progress and freedom are no longer compatible, we—who have long boasted about the virtues of the market place and of free competitive enterprise, about our ability to compete and sell in any market, and about our willingness to keep abreast of the times—will have our greatest opportunity since the Marshall Plan to demonstrate the vitality of free choice.

Communist bloc nations have negotiated more than 200 trade agreements in recent years. Inevitably the recipient nation finds its economy increasingly dependent upon Soviet goods, services and technicians. But many of these nations have also observed that the economics of free choice provide far greater benefits than the economics of coercion—and the wider we can make the area of economic freedom, the easier we make it for all free peoples to receive the benefits of our innovations and put them into practice.

Our efforts to aid the developing nations of the world and other friends, however, depend upon more than a demonstration of freedom's vitality and benefits. If their economies are to expand, if their new industries are to be successful, if they are to acquire the foreign exchange funds they will need to replace our aid efforts, these nations must find new outlets for their raw materials and new manufactures. We must make certain that any arrangements which we make with the European Economic Community are worked out in such a fashion as to insure nondiscriminatory application to all third countries. Even more important, however, the United States and Europe together have a joint responsibility to all of the less developed countries of the world—and in this sense we must work together to insure that their legitimate aspirations and requirements are fulfilled. The "open partnership" which this Bill proposes will enable all free nations to share together the reward of a wider economic choice for all.

Our efforts to maintain the leadership of the free world thus rest, in the final analysis, on our success in this undertaking. Economic isolation and political leadership are wholly incompatible. In the next few years, the nations of Western Europe will be fixing basic economic and trading patterns vitally affecting the future of our economy and the hopes of our less-developed friends. Basic political and military decisions of vital interest to our security will be made. Unless we have this authority to negotiate and have it this year—if we are separated from the Common Market by high tariff barriers on either side of the Atlantic—then we cannot hope to play an effective part in those basic decisions.

If we are to retain our leadership, the initiative is up to us. The revolutionary changes which are occurring will not wait for us to make up our minds. The United States has encouraged sweeping changes in Free World economic patterns in order to strengthen the forces of freedom. But we cannot ourselves stand still. If we are to lead, we must act. We must adapt our own economy to the imperatives of a changing world, and once more assert our leadership.

The American businessman, once the authority granted by this bill is exercised, will have a unique opportunity to compete on a more equal basis in a rich and rapidly expanding market abroad which possesses potentially a purchasing power as large and as varied as our own. He knows that, once artificial restraints are removed, a vast array of American goods, produced by American know-how with American efficiency, can compete with any goods in any spot in the world. And almost all members of the business community, in every state, now participate or could participate in the production, processing, transporting, or distribution of either exports or imports.

Already we sell to Western Europe alone more machinery, transportation equipment, chemicals and coal than our total imports of these commodities from all regions of the world combined. Western Europe is our best customer today—and should be an even better one tomorrow. But as the new external tariff surrounding the Common Market replaces the internal tariff structure, a German producer—who once competed in the markets of France on the same terms with our own producers—will achieve free access to French markets while our own producers face a tariff. In short, in the absence of authority to bargain down that external tariff, as the economy of the Common Market expands, our exports will not expand with it. They may even decline.

The American farmer has a tremendous stake in expanded trade. One out of every seven farm workers produces for export. The average farmer depends on foreign markets to sell the crops grown on one out of every six acres he plants. Sixty percent of our rice, 49 percent of our cotton, 45 percent of our wheat and 42 percent of our soybean production are exported. Agriculture is one of our best sources of foreign exchange.

Our farmers are particularly dependent upon the markets of Western Europe. Our agricultural trade with that area is four to one in our favor. The agreements recently reached at Brussels both exhausted our existing authority to obtain further European concessions, and laid the groundwork for future negotiations on American farm exports to be conducted once new authority is granted. But new and flexible authority is required if we are to keep the door of the Common Market open to American agriculture, and open it still wider. If the output of our astounding productivity is not to pile up increasingly in our warehouses, our negotiators will need both the special EEC authority and the general 50 percent authority requested in the bill described later in this message.

The American worker will benefit from the expansion of our exports. One out of every three workers engaged in manufacturing is employed in establishments that export. Several hundred times as many workers owe their jobs directly or indirectly to exports as are in the small group—estimated to be less than one half of one percent of all workers—who might be adversely affected by a sharp increase in imports. As the number of job seekers in our labor force expands in the years ahead, increasing our job opportunities will require expanding our markets and economy, and making certain that new United States plants built to serve Common Market consumers are built here, to employ American workers, and not there.

The American consumer benefits most of all from an increase in foreign trade. Imports give him a wider choice of products at competitive prices. They introduce new ideas and new tastes, which often lead to new demands for American production.

Increased imports stimulate our own efforts to increase efficiency, and supplement anti-trust and other efforts to assure competition. Many industries of importance to the American consumer and economy are dependent upon imports for raw materials and other supplies. Thus American-made goods can also be made much less expensively for the American consumers if we lower the tariff on the materials that are necessary to their production.

American imports, in short, have generally strengthened rather than weakened our economy. Their competitive benefits have already been mentioned. But about 60 percent of the goods we import do not compete with the goods we produce—either because they are not produced in this country, or are not produced in any significant quantity. They provide us with products we need but cannot efficiently make or grow (such as bananas or coffee), supplement our own steadily depleting natural resources with items not available here in quantity (such as manganese or chrome ore, 90 percent or more of which must be imported if our steel mills are to operate), and contribute to our industrial efficiency, our economic growth and our high level of consumption. Those imports that do compete are equal to only one or one and one-half percent of our total national production; and even these imports create jobs directly for those engaged in their processing, distribution, or transportation, and indirectly for those employed in both export industries and in those industries dependent upon reasonably priced imported supplies for their own ability to compete.

Moreover, we must reduce our own tariffs if we hope to reduce tariffs abroad and thereby increase our exports and export surplus. There are many more American jobs dependent upon exports than could possibly be adversely affected by increased imports. And those export industries are our strongest, most efficient, highest paying growth industries.

It is obvious, therefore, that the warnings against increased imports based upon the lower level of wages paid in other countries are not telling the whole story. For this fear is refuted by the fact that American industry in general—and America's highest paid industries in particular—export more goods to other markets than any other nation; sell far more abroad to other countries than they sell to us; and command the vast preponderance of our own market here in the United States. There are three reasons for this:

(a) The skill and efficiency of American workers, with the help of our machinery and technology, can produce more units per man hour than any other workers in the world—thus making the competitive cost of our labor for many products far less than it is in countries with lower wages. For example, while a United States coal miner is paid eight times as much per hour as the Japanese miner, he produces fourteen times as much coal—our real cost per ton of coal is thus far smaller—and we sell the Japanese tens of millions of dollars worth of coal each year.

(b) Our best industries also possess other advantages—the adequacy of low cost raw materials or electrical power, for example. Neither wages nor total labor costs is an adequate standard of comparison if used alone.

(c) American products can frequently compete successfully even where foreign prices are somewhat lower—by virtue of their superior quality, style, packaging, servicing or assurance of delivery.

Given this strength, accompanied by increasing productivity and wages in the rest of the world, there is less need to be concerned over the level of wages in the low wage countries. These levels, moreover, are already on the rise, and, we would hope, will continue to narrow the current wage gap, encouraged by appropriate consultations on an international basis.

This philosophy of the free market—the wider economic choice for men and nations—is as old as freedom itself. It is not a partisan philosophy. For many years our trade legislation has enjoyed bi-partisan backing from those members of both parties who recognized how essential trade is to our basic security abroad and our economic health at home. This is even more true today. The Trade Expansion Act of 1962 is designed as the expression of a nation, not of any single faction, not of any single faction or section. It is in that spirit that I recommend it to the Congress for prompt and favorable action.

[*The section of the message dealing with the provisions of the bill is omitted.*]

The purpose of this message has been to describe the challenge we face and the tools we need. The decision rests with the Congress. That decision will either mark the beginning of a new chapter in the alliance of free nations—or a threat to the growth of Western unity. The two great Atlantic markets will either grow together or they will grow apart. The meaning and range of free economic choice will either be widened for the benefit of free men everywhere—or confused and constricted by new barriers and delays.

Last year, in enacting a long-term foreign aid program, the Congress made possible a fundamental change in our relations with the developing nations. This bill will make possible a fundamental, far-reaching and unique change in our relations with the other industrialized nations—particularly with the other members of the Atlantic Community. As NATO was unprecedented in military history, this measure is unprecedented in economic history. But its passage will be long-remembered and its benefits widely distributed among those who work for freedom.

At rare moments in the life of this nation an opportunity comes along to fashion out of the confusion of current events a clear and bold action to show the world what it is we stand for. Such an opportunity is before us now. This bill, by enabling us to strike a bargain with the Common Market, will "strike a blow" for freedom.

Kennedy Round Objectives Established in May 1963

Following is the text of the conclusions and resolutions adopted at the ministerial meeting of the General Agreement on Tariffs and Trade on May 21, 1963. Press release number 794, GATT, May 29, 1963.

At the close of the ministerial meeting held at Geneva from 16 to 21 May the Ministers adopted the following Conclusions and Resolutions relating to the three items of their agenda:

Measures for the Expansion of Trade of Developing Countries as a Means of Furthering Their Economic Development

Conclusions Adopted on 21 May 1963 on Item 1 of the Agenda

1. The Ministers during their meeting from 16 to 21 May 1963, discussed the question of measures for the expansion of trade of developing countries as a means of furthering their economic development. The Ministers had before them the reports of Committee III and of the Special Group on Trade in Tropical Products, and considered the following *Programme of Action* [1] which had previously been examined in Committee III;

(i) STANDSTILL PROVISION

No new tariff or non-tariff barriers should be erected by industrialized countries against the export trade of any less-developed country in the products identified as of particular interest to the less-developed countries. In this connexion the less-developed countries would particularly mention barriers of a discriminatory nature.

---

1. The Action Programme was sponsored by the following GATT countries: Argentina, Brazil, Burma, Cambodia, Ceylon, Chile, Cuba, Ghana, Haiti, India, Indonesia, Israel, Federation of Malaya, Federation of Nigeria, Pakistan, Peru, Tanganyika, Tunisia, United Arab Republic, Uruguay and Yugoslavia.

(ii) ELIMINATION OF QUANTITATIVE RESTRICTIONS

Quantitative restrictions on imports from less-developed countries which are inconsistent with the provisions of the GATT shall be eliminated within a period of one year. Where, on consultation between the industrialized and the less-developed countries concerned, it is established that there are special problems which prevent action being taken within this period, the restriction on such items would be progressively reduced and eliminated by 31 December 1965.

(iii) DUTY-FREE ENTRY FOR TROPICAL PRODUCTS

Duty-free entry into the industrialized countries shall be granted to tropical products by 31 December 1963.

(iv) ELIMINATION OF TARIFFS ON PRIMARY PRODUCTS

Industrialized countries shall agree to the elimination of customs tariffs on the primary products important in the trade of less-developed countries.

(v) REDUCTION AND ELIMINATION OF TARIFF BARRIERS TO EXPORTS OF SEMI-PROCESSED AND PROCESSED PRODUCTS FROM LESS-DEVELOPED COUNTRIES

Industrialized countries should also prepare urgently a schedule for the reduction and elimination of tariff barriers to exports of semi-processed and processed products from less-developed countries, providing for a reduction of at least 50 per cent of the present duties over the next three years.

(vi) PROGRESSIVE REDUCTION OF INTERNAL FISCAL CHARGES AND REVENUE DUTIES

Industrialized countries shall progressively reduce internal charges and revenue duties on products wholly or mainly produced in less-developed countries with a view to their elimination by 31 December 1965.

(vii) REPORTING PROCEDURES

Industrialized countries maintaining the above-mentioned barriers shall report to the GATT secretariat in July of each year on the steps taken by them during the preceding year to implement these decisions and on the measures which they propose to take over the next twelve months to provide larger access for the products of less-developed countries.

(viii) OTHER MEASURES

Contracting parties should also give urgent consideration to the adoption of other appropriate measures which would facilitate the efforts of less-developed countries to diversify their economies, strengthen their export capacity, and increase their earnings from overseas sales.

2. The Ministers of all industrialized countries, with the exception of the Ministers of the member States of the European Economic Community, agreed to the above Programme of Action [2] subject to the understandings

2. The additional conclusions of Ministers on the points of the Action Programme relating to the removal of barriers to trade in tropical products (point iii and also point vi) are set out in paragraphs 10 to 23 while the conclusions on point viii, relating to other action for assisting the less-developed countries, are taken up in paragraphs 24 to 31.

set out in paragraphs 3 and 4. The Ministers of the member States of the European Economic Community endorsed, in principle, the general objectives of the Programme of Action and declared themselves ready to contribute, for their part, to the fullest extent possible, towards the development of the developing countries. With respect to the most appropriate methods of achieving the objectives mentioned above, the position of the Ministers of the member States of the European Economic Community is contained in paragraph 6.

3. It was agreed by the Ministers of the industrialized countries, other than those of the EEC, that, in the first instance, the above Programme of Action relates to the products identified by Committee III, it being understood that the Programme of Action might subsequently be extended to an enlarged list of products to be agreed upon. It was also recognized that acceptance of the Programme was without prejudice to the rights and obligations of contracting parties under the provisions of the General Agreement, under arrangements negotiated within the framework of the GATT or covered by international commodity arrangements. Further, it should be understood that, where action under the Programme would affect the interest of third countries, as under preferential arrangements, countries granting such preferences would need to take into account the interests of the trade partners concerned. As regards tariffs on primary products, these Ministers indicated that their governments would work towards the elimination or, where this was not possible, at least towards the substantial reduction of tariffs on these products. In respect of tariffs on semi-processed and processed products of substantial interest to the developing countries, these Ministers indicated that their governments would work towards a substantial reduction of the tariffs on these products. Action in connexion with the reduction of tariffs on primary, semi-processed and processed products from less-developed countries would be taken within the framework of the GATT trade negotiations, and while not precluding action in advance of the trade negotiations, these Ministers proposed to ensure, as far as possible, that these products would be included in their offer lists in the negotiations and not be excepted therefrom in accordance with the principles agreed on for the negotiations.

4. Ministers of industrialized countries, other than those of the EEC, stated that they would conform to the standstill provision except where special and compelling circumstances rendered departure from it unavoidable, in which case adequate opportunity for consultation would be afforded to the developing countries mainly interested in the products concerned. Such consultation would occur prior to the introduction of measures constituting a departure from the standstill unless this were impossible or impracticable. The Austrian and Japanese Ministers indicated that, while it was their intention to remove quantitative restrictions maintained inconsistently with the GATT as soon as possible, they regretted that they might not be able to meet the target date of 31 December 1965 in respect of a few products. With respect to tariff

reductions, the United States Minister pointed out that United States legislation required such reductions to be staged over a period of five years.

5. The Ministers of a small number of countries, mainly dependent for their export earnings on a narrow range of primary products, welcomed the Action Programme and undertook to give effect to it to the best of their ability. However, since they, like many less-developed countries, were in the process of diversifying their economies through industrial development, they would have difficulty in accepting inflexible tariff commitments for certain products.

6. Addressing themselves to the Action Programme, the Ministers of the European Economic Community and the States associated with the EEC stated that, while they recognized that some of the points contained in the Programme could be regarded as objectives to which, to the fullest extent possible, concrete policies should be adapted, the first seven points of the Programme referred only to measures for the elimination of barriers to trade, whereas, in their view, more positive measures were required to achieve the marked and rapid increase in the export earnings of the developing countries as a whole, which was the fundamental objective. Accordingly, these Ministers urged:

(a) that international action should, in particular, be directed to a deliberate effort to organize international trade in products of interest to the less-developed countries. Such an effort would have to take into account economic inequalities between the less-developed countries themselves and the fact that certain less-developed countries cannot at present, without a transitional phase, face competition from the countries which have already achieved a certain degree of development or from the long-industrialized countries without suffering damage;

(b) that an effort should therefore be made to ensure increasing exports at remunerative, equitable and stable prices for the less-developed countries producing primary products. In this respect any desirable arrangement made at the world level could be inspired by arrangements already tried out on a regional, bilateral or even national level. As regards processed and semi-processed products, a study should be made to determine the selective measures, specially conceived to meet the needs of developing countries, which could assure these countries the necessary markets for the products in question. In this connexion various relaxations of present rules regarding non-discrimination might be considered (in particular the suggestions made at the ministerial meeting by Mr. Brasseur, Minister for Foreign Trade and Technical Assistance of Belgium). A rapid study of them by a special group should enable decisions to be taken without delay.

In the view of the Ministers of the EEC, the decisions which would be taken following the report by such a group could eliminate many of the reasons which have prevented or still prevent the effective implementation, in a manner beneficial to all, of the Programme of Action set forth in paragraph 1.

7. In the opinion of certain Ministers, the same special group could, as a matter of urgency, analyze the possibility and conditions for establishing within the framework of GATT a centre for trade information and market research with a view to the expansion of exports of the less-developed countries.

8. The Ministers finally emphasized that further measures and more ambitious goals should not stand in the way of, or serve as an excuse for not implementing as quickly and as fully as possible, the present Programme of Action which would represent a positive contribution which the industrialized countries could make to the development of the trade of the less-developed countries within the field in which GATT was specially competent.

9. The Ministers of the less-developed countries sponsoring and supporting the Programme of Action, expressed disappointment with the understandings and positions as set out by some industrialized countries and found them to be unhelpful. They emphasized that the eight point Programme of Action fell far short of the minimum conditions necessary to enable the less-developed countries to make their full contribution to the expansion of international commerce and represented a practical compromise between the difficulties stated by some industrialized countries and their responsibilities under the GATT. In particular, attention was drawn to the fact that all contracting parties are committed to carry out their obligations in respect of quantitative restrictions, without any qualifications. The Ministers of these less-developed countries therefore urged that the Programme of Action should be implemented in full, within the time-table proposed therein, in the interest of the accelerated economic development of their countries. They trusted that industrialized countries would be able to make substantial tariff concessions on primary, semi-processed and processed products, exported by less-developed countries in advance of the forthcoming trade negotiations. They also expressed the hope that products of interest to the less-developed countries should not be excluded from offer lists during negotiations.

Trade in Tropical Products—Free Access to Markets of Industrialized Countries for Tropical Products

GENERAL CONCLUSIONS

10. The Ministers other than those of the EEC and the States associated with the Community:

(a) endorsed the general objective of free access to markets for tropical products, in view of the great importance of these products to the foreign exchange earnings and economic development of many less-developed countries;

(b) agreed that the instability of prices and inadequacy of earnings are the principal problems affecting producers of tropical products;

(c) agreed that governments should not erect any new tariff or non-tariff barriers against trade in tropical products. If, in practice, a government for compelling reasons felt that it had to take any measures which would have such effects, it should afford adequate opportunity for prior consultations with the exporting countries mainly interested in the products affected;

(d) regretted the difficulties which had delayed the implementation of the relevant part of the Ministerial Declaration of November 1961 relating to the removal of revenue duties and internal charges and urged governments to take the necessary steps to secure such implementation as soon as practicable, but in any event not later than 31 December 1965;

(e) decided that, where prior action had not already been taken on barriers to trade and restraints on consumption of tropical products, these should be dealt with in the context of the forthcoming GATT trade negotiations.

11. The Ministers of the EEC and the States associated with the Community were unable to support the above general conclusions. They emphasized their belief that the general and primary objective was to organize markets and to increase the export earnings of the less-developed countries. With that end in view they referred to their Declaration concerning the Programme of Action as set forth in paragraph 6.

12. The Minister for Austria indicated that his Government agreed to the programme relating to tropical products under present conditions and without prejudice to its rights and obligations under the General Agreement. He added that his Government could feel compelled to reconsider certain aspects of its acceptance if circumstances would require this.

The remainder of the less-developed country section of the text is omitted. It contains a discussion of individual tropical products and other measures to further the trade and development of these countries, and a general resolution to carry out the program.

Arrangements for the Reduction or Elimination of Tariffs and Other Barriers to Trade, and Related Matters
and
Measures for Access to Markets for Agricultural and Other Primary Products

Resolution Adopted on 21 May 1963 on Items II and III of the Agenda

A. PRINCIPLES

1. That a significant liberalization of world trade is desirable, and that, for this purpose, comprehensive trade negotiations, to be conducted on a most-favoured-nation basis and on the principle of reciprocity, shall begin at Geneva on 4 May 1964, with the widest possible participation.

2. That the trade negotiations shall cover all classes of products, industrial and non-industrial, including agricultural and primary products.

3. That the trade negotiations shall deal not only with tariffs but also with non-tariff barriers.

4. That, in view of the limited results obtained in recent years from item-by-item negotiations, the tariff negotiations, subject to the provisions of paragraph B3, shall be based upon a plan of substantial linear tariff reductions with a bare minimum of exceptions which shall be subject to confrontation and justification. The linear reductions shall be equal. In those cases where there are significant disparities in tariff levels, the tariff reductions will be based upon special rules of general and automatic application.

Note: The Chairman offered paragraphs A4 and B3(b) as amendments to paragraphs A4 and B3(b), respectively, in the U.S. proposal. In presenting this amendment, the Chairman established the following two interpretations for the record:
"In paragraphs A4 and B3(b) 'significant' means 'meaningful in trade terms' and this is accepted by the Conference."
"The purpose of the special rules mentioned in paragraphs A4 and B3(b) is, among other things, to reduce such disparities, and this is accepted by the Conference." U.S. Department of State, Bulletin, June 24, 1963.

5. That in the trade negotiations it shall be open to each country to request additional trade concessions or to modify its own offers where this is necessary to obtain a balance of advantages between it and the other participating countries. It shall be a matter of joint endeavour by all participating countries to negotiate for a sufficient basis of reciprocity to maintain the fullest measure of trade concessions.

6. That during the trade negotiations a problem of reciprocity could arise in the case of countries the general incidence of whose tariffs is unquestionably lower than that of other participating countries.

7. That, in view of the importance of agriculture in world trade, the trade negotiations shall provide for acceptable conditions of access to world markets for agricultural products.

8. That in the trade negotiations every effort shall be made to reduce barriers to exports of the less-developed countries, but that the developed countries cannot expect to receive reciprocity from the less-developed countries.

B. PROCEDURES

1. That a Trade Negotiations Committee, composed of representatives of all participating countries, shall be set up, and that it shall be the function of the Trade Negotiations Committee, directly or through committees (including the Special Groups referred to in paragraph 3(d) below):

(a) To elaborate a trade negotiating plan in the light of the principles in paragraphs A1–8 above, with a view to reaching agreement on the details of the plan of tariff reductions referred to in paragraph A4 above by 1 August 1963, and to completing the remainder of the task by the date of the beginning of the twenty-first session of the Contracting Parties.

(b) To supervise the conduct of the trade negotiations.

2. That the trade negotiating plan will have to take into account the issues raised by the Ministers, and that the acceptability of the trade negotiating plan, from the point of view of individual countries, will depend upon the degree to which it succeeds in dealing with such issues.

3. That the Trade Negotiations Committee in elaborating the trade negotiating plan, shall deal *inter alia* with the following issues and special situations:

(a) The depth of the tariff reductions, and the rules for exceptions.

(b) The criteria for determining significant disparities in tariff levels and the special rules applicable for tariff reductions in these cases.

(c) The problem for certain countries with a very low average level of tariffs or with a special economic or trade structure such that equal linear tariff reductions may not provide an adequate balance of advantages.

Note: The Chairman offered paragraph B3(c) as an amendment to paragraph B3(c) in the U.S. proposal. In presenting this amendment, the Chairman established the following interpretation for the record:

"Under this language, the Trade Negotiations Committee will consider the case of certain countries where it is established that their very low average level of tariffs or their economic or trade structure is such that the general application of equal linear tariff reductions would not be appropriate to achieve an adequate balance of advantages. For such countries the objective shall be the negotiation of a balance of advantages based on trade concessions by them of equivalent value, not excluding equal linear reductions where appropriate."

In response to a question by the Australian Delegation, the Chairman established the following additional interpretation for the record:

"The reference to 'special trade structure' includes countries whose exports consist predominantly of agricultural or other primary products, and this is accepted by the Conference." U.S. Department of State, Bulletin, June 24, 1963.

(d) The rules to govern, and the methods to be employed in, the creation of acceptable conditions of access to world markets for agricultural products in furtherance of a significant development and expansion of world trade in such products. Since cereals and meats are amongst the commodities for which general arrangements may be required, the Special Groups on Cereals and Meats shall convene at early dates to negotiate appropriate arrangements. For similar reasons a special group on dairy products shall also be established.

(e) The rules to govern and the methods to be employed in the treatment of non-tariff barriers, including *inter-alia* discriminatory treatment applied to products of certain countries and the means of assuring that the value of tariff reductions will not be impaired or nullified by non-tariff barriers. Consideration shall be given to the possible need to review the application of certain provisions of the General Agreement, in particular Articles XIX and XXVIII, or the procedures thereunder, with a view to maintaining, to the largest extent possible, trade liberalization and the stability of tariff concessions.

APPENDIX D

Wyndham White's Closing
of the Kennedy Round

Following is the text of the statement by Eric Wyndham White, director general of the General Agreement on Tariffs and Trade, at the meeting of the Trade Negotiations Committee at Geneva on June 30, 1967. Press release number 993, GATT, June 30, 1967.

It is now nearly twenty years ago that here in this same Assembly Hall the original contracting parties set their signature to the General Agreement on Tariffs and Trade. The event did not attract much attention. It was nevertheless momentous. It set in motion—and on a scale hitherto unseen—the process of tariff disarmament which has reached its apogee in the negotiations which we are today formally concluding. The tariff reductions agreed upon in the 1947 negotiations were substantial and far-reaching, but perhaps their greatest significance and importance were the extensive reduction in the tariffs of the United States. All the more so in that whilst almost all other markets were severly restricted by import controls, there were, except for a few limited number of agricultural products, no restrictions in the United States market other than the customs tariff. Thus when productive facilities in Europe were restored after a period of reconstruction, European industries were able rapidly to increase their exports to the rich North American market and overcome the dollar gap which many had considered an almost ineradicable problem. This manifestation of what it was then fashionable to call—although it is now less so—a good creditor policy also proved a good investment for the United States.

Looking beyond these specific aspects of the 1947 negotiations their general and long-term significance was that they marked the determination of the principal trading nations to work together to restore—or rather to create—a multilateral, non-discriminatory world trading system. Despite the sceptics this effort was to succeed beyond, perhaps, even the expectations at that time of its promoters. The provisional and makeshift arrangement—the GATT—which was to have been absorbed by the International Trade Organization—was to become the central framework for international trade cooperation. It provides the legal framework for world trade in the form of a code of rights and obligations, as well as the specific tariff commitments agreed upon in a series of tariff conferences. It provides a mechanism for consultation and for settlement of differences, as well as the basis for progressively broadening the scope of international co-operation in commercial policy. It provides the essential institutional framework for the complex international relationships of trade.

We are gathered here today to set our signature to the results of the most far-reaching international trade negotiation of all times. May I briefly summarize the results.

The industrialized countries participating in the Kennedy Round made duty reductions on 70 per cent of their dutiable imports, excluding cereals, meat and dairy products. Moreover, two thirds of these cuts were of 50 per cent or more. Around another fifth were between 25 and 50 per cent. Of the total dutiable imports on which no tariff cuts have been negotiated (31 per cent of the total), one third are subject to duties of 5 per cent ad valorem or less. All this can be stated in another way. Of the imports by the participating industrialized countries (other than cereals, meat and dairy products) 66 per cent are either duty-free or are to be subject to cuts of 50 per cent or more; on another 15 per cent there are to be cuts of less than 50 per cent and 19 per cent remain unaffected. As for cereals, meat and dairy products, the aim, as you know, was the negotiation of general arrangements. In the case of cereals, agreement relating to prices and food aid has been reached. Some bilateral agreements have been concluded on meat. Very little has been obtained in the negotiations on dairy products. On scores of other agricultural products, significant duty reductions were made.

The duty reductions affected various sectors differently, being most extensive in the field of chemicals, pulp and paper, machinery, transport equipment and precision instruments, raw materials other than fuels and agricultural raw materials, base metals and miscellaneous manufactures. Both the depth of cuts and the range of items affected were below the average in the case of agricultural products, textiles and clothing, iron and steel, tropical products and fuels.

In addition to these tariff cuts, agreements were also reached on chemical products and on anti-dumping policies which will contribute in an important way to the reduction of non-tariff barriers to trade.

The results of the Kennedy Round for the developing countries are less impressive. If the appraisal is made on the basis of those products which were designated by the developing countries as of interest to them, a list which, quite properly, included both goods presently exported and those of potential export interest, the results are, in general, as favourable as the overall results just cited. This should be no cause for surprise, because the developing countries regard as of potential interest to them a range and variety of goods very similar to the range and variety of goods traded among the developed countries. If, however, one bases an appraisal on the goods for which the developing countries presently have significant exports, the results show that of their manufactured exports subjected to duties, some 51 per cent will benefit from tariff cuts by the industrialized countries of 50 per cent or more, and some

25 per cent by tariff cuts of less than 50 per cent. We have not yet been able to complete our calculation of the results for the developing countries with respect to their agricultural exports but it is known that, as for farm products generally, the results were not impressive.

Despite their limitations—and we must recognize that there were failures in some cases—these results are impressive and will, I hope, especially if shortly followed by improvements in the international monetary framework, provide the basis for continued steady expansion of international trade.

But the success of the negotiations may also, I hope, be construed as a reaffirmation of support by governments for the world-wide multilateral trading system of which GATT is the symbol and the expression. Some observers have recently seen a threat to this system from the appearance of powerful regional, economic groupings. In fact, however, and our meeting here today is eloquent proof of this, never has the momentum of world-wide trade liberalization been so marked, and it is reasonable to say that the formation of large economic groupings has provided stimulus to the movement toward this liberalization.

It is for this reason that it is appropriate today that, whilst recording with satisfaction what we have achieved in these last few years, we should also be looking ahead. In the course of the Kennedy Round we have learned a great deal. To some problems we have only been able to bring partial solution. But the discussion and analysis of these questions in detailed negotiations has more clearly revealed their basic characteristics, and suggested the lines along which more radical solutions should be sought. Much has been said and more will be said of the limitations of the results in the field of agriculture. These results should not be underestimated and are certainly greater than anything that has gone before. But perhaps more importantly this difficult sector of economic activity is clearly now within the field of international negotiation and it can no longer be doubted that these negotiations go beyond tariffs and other commercial devices and embrace all aspects of national policies, production, prices, and supports. This is an area in which the GATT has great possibilities and opportunities in the future. In the negotiations we also made a valuable beginning in limiting the restrictive effects of non-tariff barriers to trade. Again this is only a beginning and the question increases in importance with the reduction of tariff barriers. In passing, I would note that differences in tariff nomenclatures gave rise to difficulties in the negotiations and clearly demonstrate the desirability of those who have not done so adopting the Brussels Nomenclature. While there was some progress in the negotiations on problems connected with valuation for customs purposes, other difficulties remain in this area and we should consider setting up machinery within the GATT to deal more effectively with them. Finally, in certain major sectors of modern industry we have now achieved such modest rates of tariff protection that the question arises whether, by working together on new and broader measures of international negotiation and co-operation, including the new elements resulting from technological advances, we cannot remove the various structural obstacles that may still obstruct the path to free trade.

We have made a significant advance in dealing with trade relationships between countries with different economic systems, through the agreement on the terms of accession of Poland to the General Agreement.

I now come to the trade problems of the less-developed countries. This is an area in which GATT has been a pioneer, and I am particularly glad that the importance of this problem has now been universally recognized internationally through the establishment of UNCTAD with which we in the GATT are developing an increasingly close partnership. The GATT secretariat will certainly regard as one of its most important tasks in the next few months to contribute what it can to assisting in the preparation of the second UNCTAD Conference in New Delhi.

In the meantime, it will be our urgent task in the competent organs of GATT to analize in depth the contribution which the Kennedy Round has made to alleviating the trade problems of the less-developed countries, to assess what remains to be done, to complete unfinished tasks, and to initiate as soon as possible early positive action within the scope and possibilities of the organization.

From the data we have at hand it is clear that the less-developed countries will derive substantial advantages from the Kennedy Round, and equally clear that all their legitimate desires and aspirations are not fully achieved. Those—and there are many—which are heavily dependent upon exports of agricultural products suffer from the general modicity of the results in the agricultural field. We failed to achieve free trade for tropical products, though here the major, if not the only, problem is the difficult one of reconciling the desire of some for larger markets in all developed countries with the reluctance of beneficiaries of existing preferences to surrender these in exchange for free and open competition on open markets. It is also significant—and regrettable—that in a major area of manufactures where some less-developed countries have a clear competitive advantage—and despite their concurrence in the extension of the Cotton Textiles Agreement—tariff reductions fell far short of the 50 per cent target and in some important cases are only granted conditionally.

On looking ahead, however, a large place will have to be found in the future programme of GATT—in partnership with the other international organizations—for a determined and concerted attack on the formidable obstacles which lie in the path of the less-developed countries in their struggle for the economic advancement of their peoples. This is not their problem alone, it is a clear responsibility for the international community as a whole.

I will conclude on a mixed tone of optimism and caution. The General Agreement of 1967 extends and consolidates the impressive achievements of twenty years of international trade co-operation. It points the way ahead to further achievement. At the same time the structure is fragile and constantly subject to attack. So far it has not been tested by periods of economic stress and recession. We cannot confidently say whether it would take the strain.

If national economic policies are managed without sufficient awareness of the economic interdependence of nations, there is always the risk that governments may feel impelled to revert to policies of external restriction. The happily brief episode of the United Kingdom surcharge is warning of what could happen. In recent days too, we have seen carefully negotiated agreements—of vital interest to the parties concerned—frustrated by powerful sectoral pressures. In the course of the negotiations we have also seen a great economic power withhold from negotiations a whole sector of production—alas again in the field of agriculture—even though this action frustrated any hope of co-operative action by other participants to develop more liberal policies. The price of economic liberalization—as of liberty—is eternal vigilance.

Kennedy Round Chronology

	1957
March	Rome Treaty signed
	1959
November	EFTA agreement signed
	1960
September	Dillon Round begins
	1961
January	John F. Kennedy inaugurated EEC Council of Ministers adopts basic farm policy
July	United Kingdom applies for membership in EEC
November	GATT ministerial meeting, including consideration of linear tariff reductions
	1962
January	Trade Expansion Act submitted to Congress
March	U.S. negotiations in Dillon Round concluded
October	Trade Expansion Act signed by President Kennedy
	1963
January	General de Gaulle vetoes U.K. membership in EEC
January–March	GATT working party on rules for Kennedy Round; EEC raises "peaks and lows" issue
April	EEC adopts *écrêtement* proposals
May 16–21	GATT ministerial meeting establishes objectives for Kennedy Round, including special rule for disparities
November	Trade Negotiations Committee reports on disparities
December	EEC Council adopts *double écart* formula for disparities and Mansholt proposal for EEC agricultural offers in Kennedy Round

1964

March 5–6	U.S.-EEC high level meeting at Washington on disparities
May 4–6	GATT ministerial meeting officially opens Kennedy Round 50 percent cuts adopted as working hypothesis
November 3	U.S. and EEC agree to proceed on schedule and table exceptions lists on November 16
November 16	Sixteen countries present exceptions to linear tariff cuts
December	EEC Council agrees on unified grain prices

1965

March	Kennedy Round participants agree to schedule for agricultural offers
May	Proposals for grains agreement exchanged
July 1	EEC internal crisis begins
September 16	Major Kennedy Round participants, except EEC, present agricultural offers

1966

January	Luxembourg compromise; EEC crisis ends
June	U.S. Senate adopts resolution that American selling price system should not be negotiated in Kennedy Round; EEC Council rejects U.S. working hypothesis on system
July 8	Trade Negotiations Committee adopts Wyndham White's timetable, including assessment of balance by November
July 27	EEC Council agrees on outstanding Kennedy Round offers
September	Intensive negotiations on agriculture begin
November	Assessments and potential withdrawals submitted; EEC does not submit an assessment

1967

January 11	President Johnson announces termination of escape clause on watches and glass EEC Council declares rough balances of offers except with Swiss and Nordics, instructs Commission to pursue negotiations on American selling price
February 15	Roth calls for final agreement by end of March
March 29–April 7	*Petit sommet;* senior officials confront outstanding issues
April 12	EEC Council accepts food aid commitment
April (last week)	Positive offer lists submitted by United States, United Kingdom, and Switzerland (Nordics had done so earlier) Delegates return to capitals for final consultations
May 4	Final negotiating period begins

May 5   Chemical sector group meets with no success

May 8   U.S.-EEC marathon meeting; deadlock principally over *découpage*

May 9   Wyndham White announces May 14 as agreed final negotiating deadline

May 14   Clock stopped at midnight

May 15   Wyndham White circulates compromise proposals, which major participants accept

June 30   Final Kennedy Round agreement signed at Geneva

Glossary

Ad valorem duty A duty levied as a percentage of the assessed value of a commodity.

American selling price The basis in the United States for duty assessment on certain benzenoid chemicals and a few other products; assessment is based on the selling price of a competitive American product rather than the value of the traded commodity.

Binding A commitment that the rate of duty on a product will not be increased or that no duty will be imposed on a duty-free product.

C.i.f. (cost, insurance, and freight) The basis for duty assessment in the EEC, the EFTA, Japan, and some other countries; duty is assessed on the value of the traded commodity plus certain in-transit costs, or roughly the import price.

Common agricultural policy The agricultural policy of the EEC. For basic commodities such as grains and dairy products, guaranteed internal support prices have been established, and imports are prevented from underselling domestic products through a variable import levy which is roughly the difference between the support price and the import price.

Common external tariff The uniform tariff applied by all EEC member states to imports from nonmembers. It was derived principally by averaging the rates of individual member states.

Découpage The Kennedy Round formula for splitting tariff reductions on chemicals into two parts, one conditional on elimination of American selling price, the other unconditional.

Disparity A significant difference in tariff rates between countries for a particular product.

Double écart The disparity formula proposed by the EEC in the Kennedy Round. A significant disparity would exist if the rate in one country were at least twice that in another and the difference in rates were at least ten points. For semimanufactures the minimum ten point spread was not applicable.

Ecrêtement The harmonization formula proposed by the EEC as an alternative to linear tariff cuts in the Kennedy Round. Tariffs would be cut half way to specified target levels.

Escape clause A provision in U.S. trade legislation that permits the President to increase duties if domestic industry suffers injury.

Exception A nonagricultural product for which the Kennedy Round linear tariff cut of 50 percent was *not* offered.

F.o.b. (free on board) The general basis for duty assessment in the United States, Canada, and some other countries; duty is assessed on the value of the traded commodity at the point of export, or roughly the export price.

Linear country A Kennedy Round participant which accepted the 50 percent linear reduction as the basis for negotiating on nonagricultural products. The United States, the EEC, seven EFTA countries (including Finland but excluding Portugal), Japan, and Czechoslovakia were the linear countries.

Linear tariff cut Reduction of all tariffs by the same percent. In the Kennedy Round the general linear cut for nonagricultural tariffs was 50 percent.

Most-favored-nation treatment The application of duties on the same, most-favorable basis to all countries afforded such treatment.

Specific duty A duty levied as a fixed money charge per physical unit, such as 10 cents per pound.

Index